FUR, FASHION AND TRANSATLANTIC TRADE DURING THE SEVENTEENTH CENTURY

FUR, FASHION AND TRANSATLANTIC TRADE DURING THE SEVENTEENTH CENTURY

CHESAPEAKE BAY NATIVE HUNTERS, COLONIAL RIVALRIES AND LONDON MERCHANTS

John C. Appleby

THE BOYDELL PRESS

First published 2021
The Boydell Press, Woodbridge

ISBN 978 1 78327 579 3

The Boydell Press is an imprint of Boydell & Brewer Ltd
PO Box 9, Woodbridge, Suffolk IP12 3DF, UK
and of Boydell & Brewer Inc.
668 Mt Hope Avenue, Rochester, NY 14620–2731, USA
website: www.boydellandbrewer.com

A catalogue record for this book is available
from the British Library

CONTENTS

ACKNOWLEDGEMENTS

I began work on this study many years ago, when I was able to benefit from the advice and encouragement of Kenneth R. Andrews and David B. Quinn, two scholars who towered over the field of early English expansion but who, sadly, are no longer alive. I am particularly grateful for their support and critical reading of early chapters, which have since been revised in the light of recent publications and research. Though diverted by other work and commitments, I presented papers on various aspects of the subject at the Institute of Historical Research, London, the Posthumus Institute, the University of Utrecht, and at Lock Haven University, Pennsylvania. I am grateful to the organizers of these events, and to the participants, for their helpful comments and questions. I was delighted to be able to speak on the Susquehannocks and the fur trade, almost by the banks of the Susquehanna River, at Lock Haven, and I am deeply grateful to Sandy Barney and her colleagues for the warm welcome, and their kindness and hospitality. Scholarship is a shared activity and, in using a wide and varied range of studies and sources, I have drawn on the work of many scholars to whom I am indebted. I am very grateful to the late Howard Todd for organizing a tour of Kent Island while I was a Taft Fellow at the University of Cincinnati. I have benefited from the anonymous reader's report on an outline of this study, which gave me the opportunity to refine and reconsider key aspects of it, and for subsequent comments on a draft of the work itself. I have accumulated other debts to friends and colleagues who have listened and commented on work in progress, passed on references, and provided support at crucial moments. They include Stephen Behrendt, Paul Dalton, Simon Hill, Janet Hollinshead, Fiona Pogson and Sonja Tiernan, as well as the late Robert J. Hunter. In addition, I am indebted to Carol Devine and her colleagues in the inter-library loan service at Liverpool Hope University for their sterling work in procuring books and other material for me, and to Sandra Mather for preparing the maps with such skill. It has been a great pleasure to work with Boydell and Brewer, and I am very grateful to Peter Sowden for his support, advice and patience.

A NOTE ON CONVENTIONS

I follow the common convention of using old-style English dates which were slightly out of step with the new style adopted by many other European countries after 1582. The start of the year is taken as 1 January. Quotations are given in the original spelling, with some minor modifications, including the expansion of abbreviations and contractions. To avoid unnecessary and potentially tiresome repetition, throughout this study I have usually employed the Bay as shorthand for the Chesapeake Bay. English currency is in pounds, shillings and pence (£ s d), according to which 12 pence made up one shilling, while 20 shillings were equivalent to one pound. Providing modern values for money during the sixteenth and seventeenth centuries is difficult. There are helpful guides to conversion rates at www.nationalarchives.gov.uk/currency-converter and at www.bankofengland.co.uk/monetary-policy/inflation/inflation-calculator. According to the latter, goods or services valued at £2 (the cost of certain types of beaver hats) in 1600 would be worth £614 in 2019.

ABBREVIATIONS

APC	*Acts of the Privy Council*
BL	British Library, London
C	Chancery
CO	Colonial Office
CSPD	*Calendar of State Papers Domestic*
CSPC	*Calendar of State Papers Colonial*
Documents of New York	*Documents Relative to the Colonial History of the State of New York*
E	Exchequer
HCA	High Court of Admiralty
HMC	*Historical Manuscripts Commission*
Force	Peter Force (ed.), *Tracts and Other Papers, Relating Principally to the Origin, Settlement, and Progress of the Colonies in North America, from the Discovery of the Country to the Year 1776*, 4 vols. (Washington, 1836–47)
MHM	*Maryland Historical Magazine*
PC	Privy Council
RVC	*Records of the Virginia Company of London*
Smith, *Works*	*The Complete Works of Captain John Smith (1580–1631)*
SP	State Papers
TNA	The National Archives, Kew, London
VMHB	*Virginia Magazine of History and Biography*
WMQ	*William and Mary Quarterly*

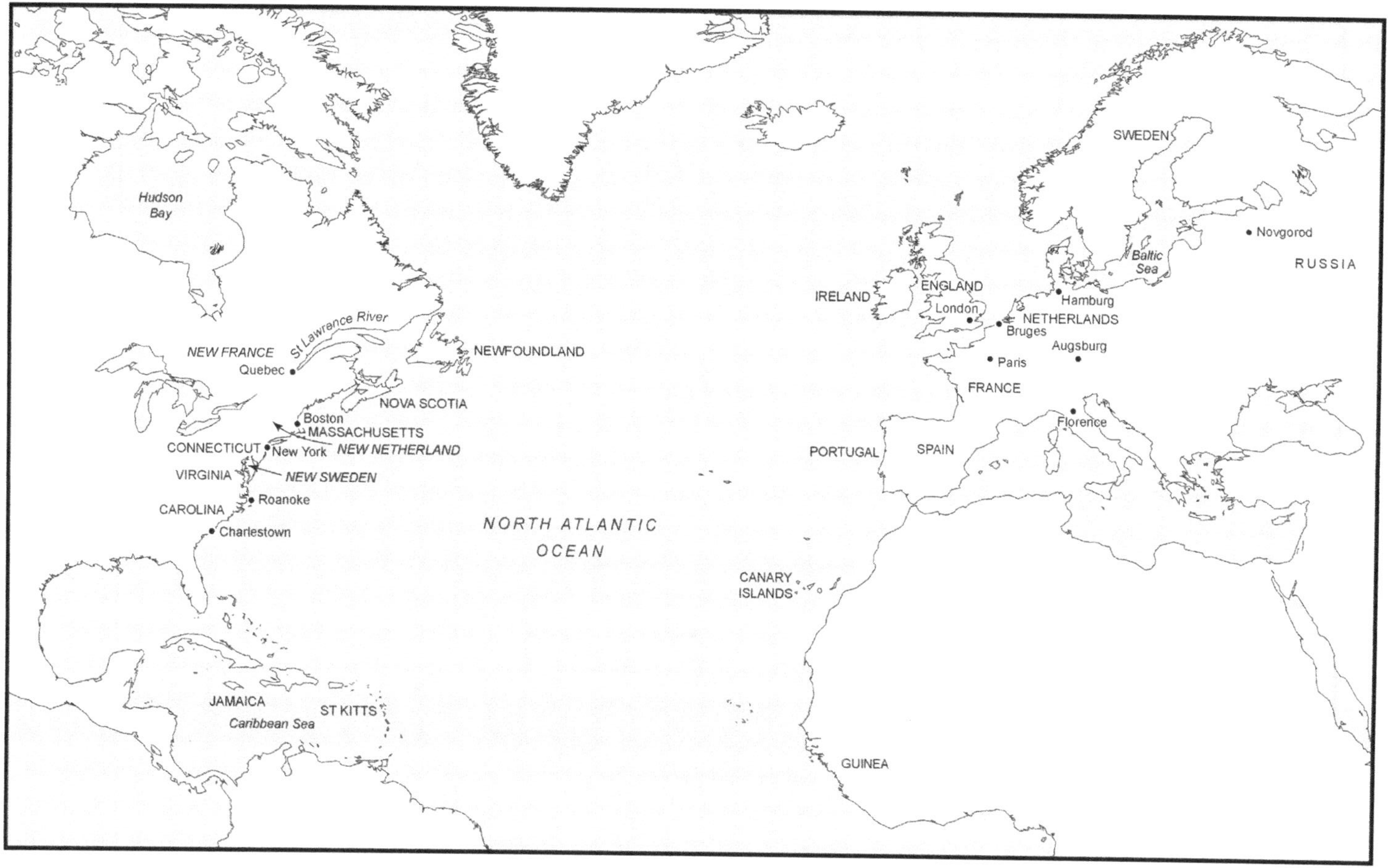

Map 1. The North Atlantic

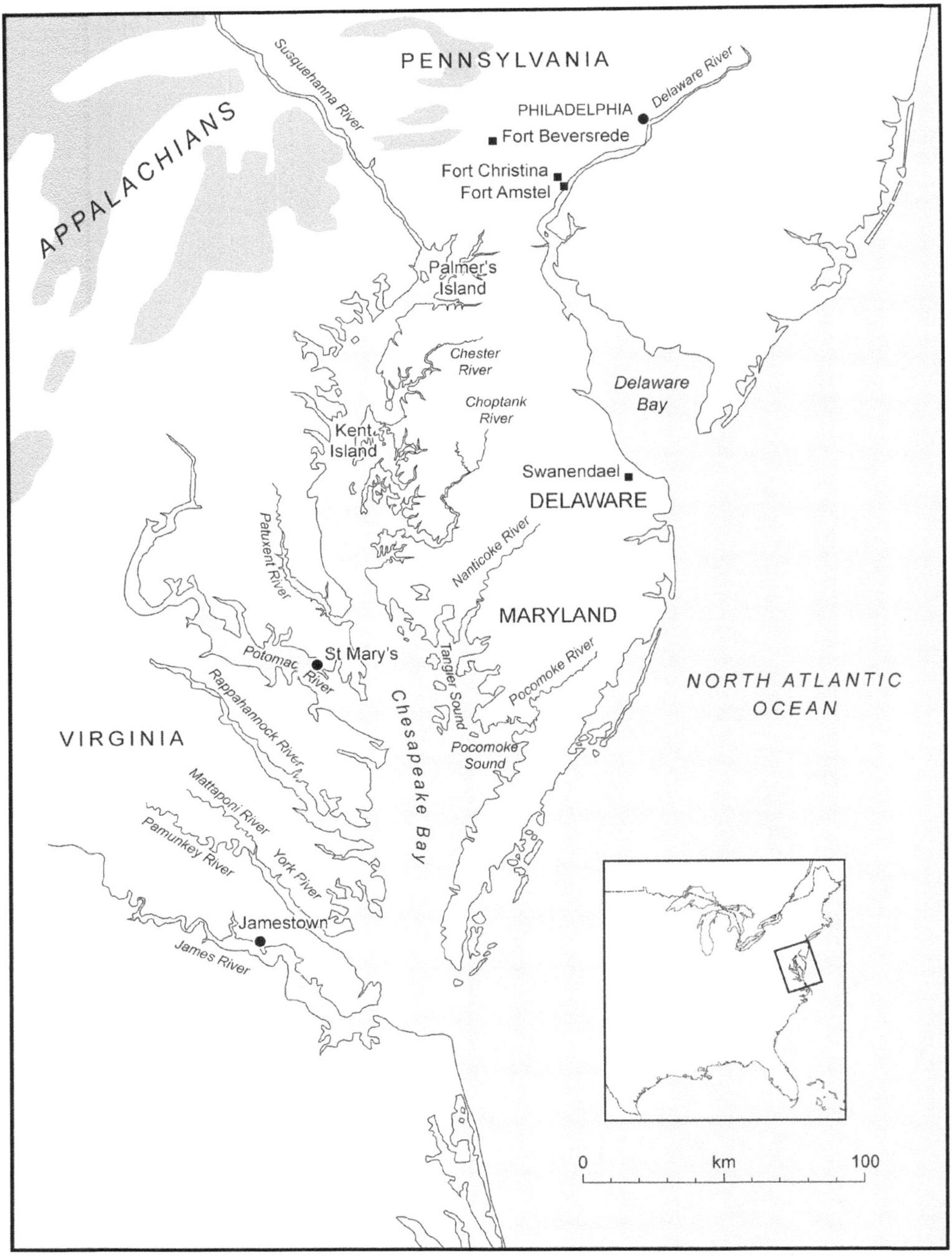

Map 2. Chesapeake Bay

Introduction

By a peculiar combination of opportunistic probing and visionary imagining, Chesapeake Bay became the location for the first successful English colony in North America. Following a period of successive failures, which included Sir Walter Raleigh's attempted settlement of Roanoke during the 1580s, the tiny outpost of Jamestown, established in 1607, paved the way for the emergence of colonial Virginia. It experienced a harrowing beginning. Lacking a successful model for colonization and left in the hands of private enterprise – the Virginia Company of London – Jamestown nearly succumbed to a deadly combination of disease and demoralization. Indian hostility, which culminated in a devastating attack on the small colony in 1622, also took a toll. It is, in the words of one recent study, 'the creation story from hell'.[1] Yet the settlement survived, outliving the collapse of its parent company in 1624. Indeed, its persistence and emerging profitability created an encouraging environment for the establishment of another colony, a decade later. But the new settlement of Maryland, under the authority of a Catholic lord proprietor, was an unwelcome intrusion, threatening the projection of a 'greater Virginia'.[2] Relations between these neighbouring, but rival, colonies dramatically re-shaped the Chesapeake, injecting intense competition for trade and territory into an emergent colonial world.

Economically, both colonies became wedded to the cultivation of tobacco. Its rapid spread during the 1620s and beyond secured the future of the newcomers, providing a profitable cash crop dependent on expanding consumption across the Atlantic. Over the course of the seventeenth century, exports from the Bay increased at a staggering rate, to the financial benefit of colonial planters, London merchants and the monarchy. Despite some diversification, it was the mainstay of economic development. The emergence and elaboration of a distinctive tobacco culture left an indelible imprint on the evolution of the

1 Karen Ordahl Kupperman, *The Jamestown Project* (Cambridge, Mass., 2007), pp. 1, 8, 192–209; Bernard Bailyn, *The Peopling of North America: The Barbarous Years, the Conflict of Civilizations, 1600–1675* (New York, 2012), pp. 42–80; Daniel K. Richter, *Before the Revolution: America's Ancient Pasts* (Cambridge, Mass., 2011), pp. 101–17.

2 D.W. Meinig, *The Shaping of America: Volume 1 Atlantic America, 1492–1800* (New Haven, 1986), pp. 144–60.

Chesapeake colonies. Within a few decades the demands of a labour-intensive and exploitative agricultural system focused the attention of settlers on land, encouraging early expansion along the rivers. According to Robert Beverley, author of the earliest colonial history of Virginia, published in London in 1705, it provided an incentive for the newcomers with alarming consequences for the natives. Glossing over the means by which land was acquired, he claimed that the colonists 'now knew their own Property, and having the Encouragement of Working for their own Advantage, many became very industrious, and began to vie one with another, in Planting, Building, and other Improvements'.[3] It was an idealistic and nostalgic view which overlooked the forceful conduct of settlers, particularly their self-made elites who strove to direct the development of both colonies.

The establishment of this tidewater tobacco economy is one of the staples of historical study of the Chesapeake. A substantial body of work demonstrates its profound and wide-ranging impact, marked by local and regional variation. The transatlantic trade, on which it depended, encouraged expansion, tied to market prices in England. Profit was offset by indebtedness, sharpening the socio-economic distinctions between a small group of wealthy planters and a much larger number of poor farmers and freedmen. Tobacco culture led to a specific labour system, initially based on bound or indentured servants from various parts of the British Isles. It was overlaid by the growing use of African slaves in Virginia during the 1640s and 1650s, as well as Indian captives thereafter. Bound and servile labourers, working at the direction of masters, and in association with a growing number of livestock, manipulated and re-designed the land, leading to the transformation of the Bay.[4]

[3] Robert Beverley, *The History and Present State of Virginia*, ed. Louis B. Wright (Chapel Hill, 1947), p. 48. On tobacco and land, see Lorena S. Walsh, *Motives of Honor, Pleasure and Profit: Plantation Management in the Colonial Chesapeake, 1607–1763* (Chapel Hill, 2010), pp. 34–8, 181–7; Allan Kulikoff, *Tobacco and Slaves: The Development of Southern Cultures in the Chesapeake, 1680–1800* (Chapel Hill, 1986), pp. 31–48; for trade, Ralph Davis, 'English Foreign Trade, 1660–1700' in W.E. Minchinton (ed.), *The Growth of English Overseas Trade in the Seventeenth and Eighteenth Centuries* (London, 1969), pp. 80–1 and Nuala Zahedieh, *The Capital and the Colonies: London and the Atlantic Economy, 1600–1700* (Cambridge, 2010), pp. 197–210.

[4] Walsh, *Motives of Honor*, pp. 20–1, 115–19, 155–8; Edmund S. Morgan, *American Slavery, American Freedom: The Ordeal of Colonial Virginia* (New York, 1975), pp. 108–30; Thad W. Tate and David L. Ammerman (eds.), *The Chesapeake in the Seventeenth Century: Essays in Anglo-American Society* (Chapel Hill, 1979) for contributions on social aspects; Jack P. Greene, *Pursuits of Happiness: The Social Development of Early Modern British Colonies and the Formation of American Culture* (Chapel Hill, 1988), pp. 9–15; Jean B. Russo and J. Elliott Russo, *Planting an Empire: The Early Chesapeake in British North America* (Baltimore, 2012), pp. 11–12,

Yet the focus on tobacco has tended to neglect the fur trade, a shadowy but distinctive form of enterprise with far-reaching consequences for colonial development. This study examines the emergence of the trade during the seventeenth century, a fluid and formative period of socio-economic and institutional change. Ranging from the 1580s, when the propagandists and promoters of transatlantic settlement drew attention to the value of North American fur, to the 1690s, by which time the trade within the Bay was in terminal decline, it seeks to chart the vicissitudes and varied fortunes of a new and challenging business. Though determined by profit, fur trading enterprise was associated with wider colonial aims, while its characteristics were rarely just economic in scope. Arguably, its non-economic aspects were of greater significance for the colonization of the Chesapeake. Building on a substantial body of work, this study explores the interconnections between cross-cultural commerce and diplomacy, colonial rivalries, conflict and competition, to survey the rise and fall of an important component of early colonial enterprise.[5]

From the outset, the prospect of trade attracted English adventurers into a region where geography and environment invited commercial penetration. It gained greater shape and specificity by a transatlantic dynamic that was driven by consumption and fashion. As such, the Bay was one of the earliest of several discrete trading zones which included New England and Canada. Across these regions, the supply of fur depended on Indian hunters and traders. Trade gave native groups unexpected agency, influencing the character and direction of intercultural commercial and diplomatic relations. Under varied conditions these encounters facilitated a profound re-ordering of native worlds. Despite sharing broad characteristics, however, North American fur trades bore subtle differences related to environmental and human contexts, intermixed with distinct colonial objectives and Atlantic influences.[6] Within the Chesapeake,

---

49–70; April Lee Hatfield, *Atlantic Virginia: Intercolonial Relations in the Seventeenth Century* (Philadelphia, 2004), pp. 137–54, 167–8; Stephen J. Hornsby, *British Atlantic, American Frontier: Spaces of Power in Early Modern British America* (Hanover, 2005), pp. 88–102; Virginia DeJohn Anderson, *Creatures of Empire: How Domestic Animals Transformed Early America* (New York, 2004), pp. 9–11, 32–3, 80–3, 114–30. A number of African slaves were present in Virginia before the 1640s, alongside a small number of free Africans on the Eastern Shore. For recent discussion see John C. Coombs, 'Beyond the "Origins Debate": Rethinking the Rise of Virginia Slavery', in Douglas Bradburn and John C. Coombs (ed.), *Early Modern Virginia: Reconsidering the Old Dominion* (Charlottesville, 2011). There is a broad consensus that Maryland followed at a slower rate.

[5] See Hatfield, *Atlantic Virginia*; Cynthia J. Van Zandt, *Brothers among Nations: The Pursuit of Intercultural Alliances in Early America 1580–1660* (Oxford, 2008); and contributions by F. J. Fausz noted below.

[6] Hornsby, *British Atlantic, American Frontier*, pp. 26–125 for a broader examination of Atlantic and continental economic systems.

the focus of an unruly settler colonialism, trade failed to shield Indian groups from the advance of agricultural development. Their marginalization and removal reflected an aggressive, unregulated, and competitive colonial project which ultimately threatened the resource base on which the trade rested.

The response of the native inhabitants to the arrival of the newcomers, and their reaction to colonial settlement, exposed difficult questions regarding intercultural relations, which have attracted considerable scholarly attention over the past four decades. Despite limited evidence, heavily based on English accounts and reports with self-evident difficulties in its interpretation, Indian groups were of fundamental importance to the creation of the colonial Chesapeake. Recent work challenges assumptions that the Indians were passive victims of English colonization. Instead, native groups responded creatively, demonstrating adaptability and innovation in their response to a growing number of immigrants.[7] Inadvertently, nonetheless, interethnic commercial relations and associations enabled colonial settlement and expansion. Over the course of the seventeenth century, decline and dependency or resistance and relocation became an all-too-common experience for the indigenous people of the Bay.

Beverley drew attention to the plight of the Indians of Virginia during the late seventeenth and early eighteenth centuries. In most cases he seemed to be describing people who were on the verge of cultural annilihation. The survivors of the colonial encounter lived poorly, and in fear of hostile groups beyond the confines of the colony. Unable to raise 500 warriors, they paid an annual tribute of three arrows and 20 beaver skins to the governor for their land and protection. With a drastically reduced population, some small groups resorted to amalgamation as a survival strategy. Others remained isolated and insecurely located. In Northumberland County, established during the 1640s, the Wicomicos had 'but three men living, which yet keep up their Kingdom, and retain their Fashion; they live by themselves, separate from all other *Indians*, and from the *English*'.[8]

[7] Daniel K. Richter, *Facing East from Indian Country: A Native History of Early America* (Cambridge, Mass., 2001), pp. 69–78; James Horn, *A Land as God Made It: Jamestown and the Birth of America* (New York, 2005), pp. 59–71; James D. Rice, 'Escape from Tsenacommacah: Chesapeake Algonquians and the Powhatan Menace' in Peter C. Mancall (ed.), *The Atlantic World and Virginia, 1550–1624* (Chapel Hill, 2007), pp. 97–140 and works cited therein. On the wider problem of trying to recover native voices see Toby Morantz, 'Plunder or Harmony? On Merging European and Native Views of Early Contact', in Germaine Warkentin and Carolyn Podruchy (eds.), *Decentring the Renaissance: Canada and Europe in Multidisciplinary Perspective, 1500–1700* (Toronto, 2001), pp. 48–67.

[8] Beverley, *History of Virginia*, pp. 232–3. In July 1666 Thomas Ludwell reported that Indians held no land in Virginia, but what 'is granted them', *CSPC 1661–68*, pp. 400–1. For the wide impact of English settlement see James Axtell, *The Invasion Within: The Contest of Cultures in Colonial North America* (New York, 1985),

Reflecting on the early years of the colony, Beverley regretted the failure of accommodation between settlers and natives. Among the latter, the first to encounter the English were groups of Powhatans, who formed a complex association of tribes under the leadership of a paramount chief. Beverley blamed the newcomers for missing an opportunity to create a mixed society, by failing to respond to an Indian proposal for intermarriage. However, despite the marriage between Pocahontas, a daughter of the leader of the Powhatans, and John Rolfe, in 1613, there is little evidence that the prospect aroused much interest among either group. Nor was the union widely celebrated or commemorated, except as a marker for the end of Anglo-Powhatan hostilities. It occurred in ambiguous circumstances, following the seizure of Pocahontas by a party of colonial traders. Revealingly, her future spouse was plagued by self-doubt and spiritual anxiety at the prospect of marrying someone of rude education and barbarous manners, which left him feeling at the mercy of diabolic assault.[9] By Beverley's day the union was uneasily suspended between folklore and history.

For colonists with views that ranged across contrasting images of savagery and civility, cultural attitudes were increasingly influenced by economic development. The upsurge in native hostility towards the creeping territorial encroachment by settlers competing for fertile land along the rivers provoked calls among the latter for the removal of the Indians. In the aftermath of the Powhatan attack of 1622, the start of an insurrection or war depending on perspective, colonial leaders spurned earlier proposals, drawn from Spanish experience, of employing Indians as a cheap labour force. In the face of heavy losses amounting to about one quarter of the colonial population, and under the guise of a just war of retribution, more drastic remedies were called for. As a response to land hunger and ethnic rivalry, the Anglo-Powhatan conflict left a legacy that spread throughout the Bay. In its wake the newcomers resorted to varied, sometimes extreme tactics, exploiting native disunity, to secure their economic interests.[10]

---

pp. 161–7, 190–1.

9 'Letter from John Rolfe to Sir Thos. Dale', *VMHB*, 22 (1914), p. 154; Richter, *Facing East from Indian Country*, pp. 73, 77–8; Karen Ordahl Kupperman, *Indians and English: Facing Off in Early America* (Ithaca, 2000), pp. 196–9; Beverley, *History of Virginia*, pp. 38–9, 233–4.

10 Frederick J. Fausz, 'Patterns of Anglo-American Aggression and Accommodation along the Mid-Atlantic Coast, 1584–1634' in William W. Fitzhugh (ed.), *Cultures in Contact: The Impact of European Contacts on Native American Cultural Institutions, A.D. 1000–1800* (Washington, 1985), pp. 246–52; Horn, *A Land as God Made It*, pp. 264–6; Beverley, *History of Virginia*, pp. 50–4; Melanie Perreault, '"We Washed Not the Ground with Their Bloods": Intercultural Violence and Identity in the Early Chesapeake', in Debra Meyers and Melanie Perreault (eds.), *Colonial Chesapeake:*

The prospective development of separate worlds, defined by difference and distance, was qualified by social practice. Interethnic relations, the focus of intense recent study, included diverse encounters, cultural borrowing, and hybridity. Negotiating the language barrier, contact between natives and newcomers opened opportunities for trade, exchange, and diplomatic gift-giving.[11] During the early years of colonial settlement commerce went some way to offset asymmetrical power relations between the English and the Powhatans. The growth of trade, based on native demand for European goods, was linked with diplomatic goals. But the introduction and spread of commodities, such as metal wares, cloth, alcohol and weapons, had far-reaching, cumulative consequences for Indian society. Beverley lamented the loss of native innocence brought about by new goods and desires. The introduction of 'Drunkenness and Luxury amongst them, … multiply'd their Wants, and put them upon desiring a thousand things, they never dreamt of before'.[12] The attachment of Indian groups to a transatlantic market during the seventeenth century, through direct or indirect contact, was gradual and selective, but it was an important step towards their dependency, which also reflected the growing definition and integration of an English Atlantic.[13]

For the English, as for other Europeans, trade was a vital source of provisions, serving as a lifeline for small, struggling outposts such as Jamestown. It also provided access to supplies of furs. Colonial traders in the Bay, alongside potential competitors in New England, were at the forefront of English efforts to initiate the fur trade in North America. Emerging as a key element of Anglo-Indian relations, it became the focus of volatile intercolonial rivalries.[14] Under these conditions the character and conduct of commerce far outweighed its economic value. As a commercial and cross-cultural enterprise, the fur

New Perspectives (Lanham, 2006), pp. 36–9.

11 Gifts often widened the possibilities for intercultural relations, see for example Richard White, *The Middle Ground: Indians, Empires, and Republics in the Great Lakes Region, 1650–1815* (Cambridge, 1991), pp. 15–17, 98–9.

12 Ibid., p. 233; Kupperman, *Indians and English*, pp. 88–102, 174–7, 206–16; Axtell, *The Invasion Within*, p. 284; Colin G. Calloway, *Crown and Calumet: British-Indian Relations, 1783–1815* (Norman, 1987), pp. 29, 15, 188 on the violent turmoil that came with the fur trade.

13 Ian K. Steele, *The English Atlantic 1675–1740: An Exploration of Communication and Community* (New York, 1986), p. 259; James H. Merrell, *The Indians' New World: Catawbas and Their Neighbors from European Contact Through the Era of Removal* (Chapel Hill, 1989), pp. 5–23, 38–45, 90 and Richter, *Facing East from Indian Country*, pp. 44–5, 53, 174–7 on trade, which was not always detrimental to Indian life; Alfred Goldsworthy Bailey, *The Conflict of European and Eastern Algonkian Cultures 1504–1700* (Toronto, 2nd edition, 1969), pp. 55–71.

14 White, *The Middle Ground*, pp. 94–5 argues that the fur trade was 'embedded in particular social relations'.

trade brought settlers and natives together in face-to-face transactions that required mutual understanding and cooperation. But it operated within an unstable diplomatic and political environment, confusing colonial and native relations and intensifying its competitive character.[15] As a result, it became a catalyst for colonial exploration and expansion, encouraged by the search for new suppliers of an apparently abundant, but ultimately diminishing resource.

Recognizing the existence of different fur trades in North America, in surveying the development of trade within the Bay this study has two central themes. The first is the interlocking relationship between trade and rivalry, both within and among groups of colonial and Indian traders. The second is the wider Atlantic environment which sustained an activity that depended not on colonial, but on native labour. Forming a distinct branch of the transatlantic trade in furs and skins, which grew in volume after 1670 with the establishment of the Hudson's Bay Company, commercial enterprise in the Chesapeake was part of an extensive and complex commodity chain, linking local, regional and international markets, which acquired geopolitical significance.[16] It rested on the inherent unpredictability of relations between labour, production and marketing. Indian hunters and suppliers provided colonial traders with raw or semi-processed materials, mainly beaver skins, which were transported to London where they were made into fine and fashionable headwear. As such, the meaning and value of beaver was transformed as it moved between colonial and metropolitan markets. But the interplay between trade and plantation, which London-based promoters tried to engineer, also fuelled growing concern among some native leaders that interethnic commerce exposed them to the loss of land, cultural disorganization, and impoverishment.[17]

It is probably no coincidence that interest in the North American fur trade occurred at a time of prolonged climate change, including cooler temperatures, widely recognized as the 'little ice age'. This was a global phenomenon, with wide-ranging and varied consequences. Across the northern hemisphere, the period from the mid-1580s to the early seventeenth century experienced an unprecedented cooling as temperatures fell by nearly 1° centrigrade. In Europe,

[15] J. Frederick Fausz, 'Profits, Pelts, and Power: English Culture in the Early Chesapeake, 1620–1652', *The Maryland Historian*, 14 (1983), pp. 14–30; Daniel K. Richter, 'Tsenacommacah and the Atlantic World' in Mancall (ed.), *The Atlantic World and Virginia*, pp. 43–65; Philip D. Curtin, *Cross-Cultural Trade in World History* (Cambridge, 1984), pp. 207–25 for broader reflections.

[16] Defined as a 'network of labor and production processes whose end result is a finished commodity', in Gary Gereffi and Miguel Korzeniewicz (eds.), *Commodity Chains and Global Capitalism* (Westport, 1994), pp. 2–4, 17–18.

[17] Paul Grant-Costa and Elizabeth Mancke, 'Anglo-Amerindian Commercial Relations', in H.V. Bowen et al. (eds), *Britain's Oceanic Empire: Atlantic and Indian Ocean Worlds, c. 1550–1850* (Cambridge, 2012), pp. 374–5, 379.

the cold was accompanied by wet and unseasonable weather, while in parts of North America it was associated with extreme drought. During the winter of 1607 to 1608 the Thames froze, enabling a frost fair to be held on the icy surface of the river. Freezing rivers added to the difficulties facing settlers at Jamestown, though the impact of drought and poor harvests on neighbouring Indians was a more serious issue.[18] Adverse climatic conditions affected material culture, including dress, creating a need for warmer, protective clothing and accessories, especially those made from fur.

The growth of interest in the fur trade was underpinned by fashion and consumption, especially the demand for stylish beaver hats that emerged during the 1570s and 1580s. The decline of beaver populations in Western Europe, and the uncertainty of alternative supplies from Russia, enabled English colonial promoters to trumpet the availability of new sources in North America, demonstrated by the French trade in Canada. It was an appealing argument that drew on images of the New World as a storehouse of valuable commodities.[19] Moreover, it was reinforced by an economic nationalism which sought to reduce England's dependence on European imports, especially from enemies such as Spain. Against this background, chapter 1 surveys the context in which the Chesapeake fur trade emerged. It was embedded in a well-established culture of clothing that acknowledged the virtues of style and fashion, though not without hostility from some. Under these conditions, the market for fashionable headwear was relatively open and responsive to change. Although dress made of specific costly materials, including furs, was limited by sumptuary legislation, its implementation was problematic and increasingly difficult to sustain. Despite subsequent attempts to revive such laws, they were effectively abandoned in 1603.[20] Thereafter the only limits on the market were cost and personal taste.

Within a commercialized and competitive dress regime, clothing and accessories served varied purposes, ranging from the functional to the symbolic. As

[18] Sam White, *A Cold Welcome: The Little Ice Age and Europe's Encounter with North America* (Cambridge, Mass., 2017), pp. 55–63, 77–81, 106–12; Philipp Blom, *Nature's Mutiny: How the Little Ice Age Transformed the West and Shaped the Present* (London, 2017), pp. 35–8, 44–5, 226–7; Geoffrey Parker, *Global Crisis: War, Climate Change and Catastrophe in the Seventeenth Century* (New Haven, 2013), pp. 3, 447–8.

[19] Richard Hakluyt, *Discourse of Western Planting*, eds. David B. Quinn and Alison M. Quinn (Hakluyt Society, Extra Series, 45, 1993), pp. 4, 16–27. Castoreum or musk from the beaver's scent organs was also valued for its reputed medicinal properties, William Beinart and Lotte Hughes, *Environment and Empire* (Oxford, 2007), p. 42; Rachel Poliquin, *Beaver* (London, 2015), pp. 52–3.

[20] Wilfrid Hooper, 'The Tudor Sumptuary Laws', *English Historical Review*, 30 (1915), pp. 433–49. Though the idea was slow to die, Leora Auslander, *Cultural Revolutions: Everyday Life and Politics in Britain, North America, and France* (Berkeley, 2009), pp. 31–3.

chapter 1 argues, the use of headwear was freighted with meaning, reflecting the values of a gendered and hierarchical society. In these circumstances the beaver hat, combining utility with distinction, acquired a special position in late Elizabethan and early Stuart England. Because of its price, however, demand and consumption were limited to a small market, which connected court, city, and country. Its expansion, driven by conspicuous consumption at court and among the aristocracy, led to the establishment of beavermaking in London. As a new industry it was receptive to changes in style, though the structure of the market provoked competition over its control and regulation. From the 1580s to the 1630s the intermeshing between fashion, consumption and manufacturing laid the foundations for the growth of the transatlantic fur trade.

During the same period colonial reconnoitring and settlement paved the way for interethnic trade and exchange. Commercial probing within the Bay and its wider hinterland is explored in chapters 2 and 3. Alongside an increasingly coercive trade in provisions, colonial traders acquired intermittent and often modest supplies of fur. Interest in the trade gained in momentum and ambition with the exploration of the Bay, and the acquisition of information about the region and its resources. Struggling to define an economic function or future for the settlement, the Virginia Company was slow to investigate fur trading opportunities in the Chesapeake, though reports of rival European activity within its claimed jurisdiction briefly galvanized it into action. Under unfavourable, at times hostile, conditions commercial enterprise and exploration passed into the hands of private adventurers, who gained greater freedom of action following the dissolution of the Company in 1624.

Despite the breakdown in Anglo-Powhatan relations, interest in the fur trade grew during the 1620s, paving the way for the creation of innovative transatlantic ventures. War with the Powhatans concentrated attention on the Potomac River, beyond the chiefdom, which became the scene for aggressive competition between colonial traders operating from Jamestown. At the same time, William Claiborne, representative of a younger generation of recent immigrants, whose ambition and hold on office were accompanied by entrepreneurial schemes for expansion, began the commercial penetration of the upper Bay. With the support of a group of London partners, he established a joint stock which combined trade with plantation. The centre of what was envisioned as a far-flung, but coherent commercial network was an island along the Eastern Shore, on which the partnership established a trading outpost in 1631. Known to its native inhabitants as Monoponson, it was renamed Kent Island by Claiborne. From the outset, the success of the venture depended on Indian support and cooperation.

It was an opportune moment. The Susquehannocks, one of the most powerful native groups in the hinterland of the upper Bay, had access to a plentiful supply of fur and were seeking to establish direct commercial contact with European traders. Chapter 3 argues that their support for Claiborne was crucial. In addition, their diplomatic and commercial relations with Indians in the north gave the partnership the opportunity to fulfil its ambition of capturing and diverting south the rich fur trade of Canada. By making use of Indian trade routes along the Susquehanna River, which flowed into the Bay, and of native middlemen at a time when the the northern trades were thrown into disarray as a result of the Anglo-French war, the venture had the capacity to re-configure interethnic trading networks across the north-eastern seaboard.

Claiborne's early success was overshadowed by the establishment of Maryland in 1634. In combining trade with settlement, the Catholic promoters of the new colony almost mirrored the ambition and purpose of the Kent Island partnership. Claiming that the island lay within the bounds of Maryland, the newcomers were soon engaged in a bitter dispute with Claiborne, and Virginia, over trade and territory. The upper Bay became a contested and violent region where Indian groups faced the prospect of becoming entangled in colonial rivalries. Such conditions affected the character of interethnic trade, initially increasing the flow and widening the spread of European goods among native groups. But promoters in England struggled to sustain a regular supply of trading material, which in some cases were also unsuited to experienced Indian traders. These difficulties exposed weak links in a chain of commerce that was vulnerable to cleavages on either side of the Atlantic.

By 1640 both trading ventures had collapsed in confused and conflicting circumstances. Their failure marked a formative stage in the development of the trade. Transatlantic joint stock enterprise was replaced by independent traders, often operating on a part-time basis, and under the regulation of colonial authorities. However, commercial activity during the 1640s and 1650s, which is explored in chapter 4, was badly affected by a succession of crises and controversies. The problems were intensified by the renewal of war with the Powhatans in Virginia, and the outbreak of hostilities between Maryland and the Susquehannocks. Nor was the Bay insulated from the long-distance reverberations of the civil war in the British Isles. The beneficiaries of colonial disunity were rival Europeans, operating from nearby outposts in Delaware Bay. Competing Dutch and Swedish traders began a commercial and diplomatic offensive, seeking to establish trading relations with the Susquehannocks. Consequently, the region between the Bays became a pivot around which wider European and Indian rivalries revolved, reflecting a shifting pattern of cooperation and conflict. These competitive conditions provided native traders with short-term commercial advantage, but they also increased the use of guns and alcohol in interethnic trade.

The disruption of the 1640s and 1650s masked signs of divergence between the Chesapeake colonies, particularly in the direction of commerce, which grew more marked during the late seventeenth century. Chapter 5 surveys the success of frontier explorers and traders in Virginia in pioneering a new, inland trade, compared with the inability of Maryland to resuscitate commerce with the Susquehannocks. The revival of the fur trade in Virginia, reflected in an increase in the volume and variety of exports of furs and skins from the Bay, provoked competition and controversy. Resentment at the regulation and control of interethnic commerce became linked with an enveloping political crisis, culminating in rebellion and metropolitan intervention in 1677. But the widening range of the Indian trade was threatened by new colonial settlement to the south, and the claims of the new colony of Carolina to much of the region in which traders operated.[21] A similar problem emerged in Maryland, following the establishment of Pennsylvania in 1681, which threatened to cut off access to the Susquehanna Valley. Of more pressing concern was the resurgence of raiding by groups of hostile Iroquois from the north. Their long-running conflict with the Susquehannocks, which spilled over to include exposed colonial settlements, seriously disrupted commercial activity, especially in the upper Bay. Despite relying on them as a defensive shield, colonial leaders in Maryland sacrificed their relationship with the Susquehannocks, enabling them to reach an agreement with the Iroquois. By 1700 the fur trade within the Bay was in a parlous condition. The consolidation of an aggressive and exclusionary settler colonialism led to the decline or disappearance of native suppliers and traders, as well as to a fall in local populations of fauna.

These unfavourable colonial conditions were compounded with severe, if short-lived, difficulties in the metropolitan market. Chapter 6, while acknowledging the revival in exports from Virginia during the 1670s, examines the transatlantic context for the decline of the trade. The impact of interrelated problems endangered the limited position of modest and marginal suppliers, such as the Chesapeake colonies, in the fur market of London. At the root of these issues was the inability of domestic demand for beaver hats, which retained their currency as fashionable and costly accessories, to keep pace with a rapid increase in the supply of North American fur. The English seizure of New Netherland, including the rich fur trade of New York, which was accompanied by the formation of the Hudson's Bay Company with access to a vast fur-bearing region, dramatically increased the volume of the transatlantic trade. It led to periodic problems of over-supply during the 1680s and 1690s. Determined to stabilize prices, the company resorted to the re-export of beaver skins to markets in Northern Europe, including Russia. These commercial tactics were of no benefit to dealers in fur from either Virginia or Maryland, nor did they help the hat-making industry, which was faced with internal crises during the same period. These included a bitterly contested dispute between masters and journeymen regarding pay and working practices. By 1699 the leaders of the Feltmakers' Company, which regulated the industry

21 Merrell, *The Indians' New World*, pp. 52–6 for a 'trade war' between the two colonies during the 1680s.

in London, claimed that trade and manufacturing were 'at a full stop'.[22] Collectively these problems raised serious questions about a reviving, but marginal, enterprise in Virginia based on inland supplies of furs and skins. As English imports of beaver skins, mainly from the north, reached more than 40,000 in 1700, interest in the development of the new trade failed to dislodge a metropolitan perception, shared by many colonial planters, that tied and bound the Chesapeake to the cultivation of tobacco.[23]

While this study makes no bold claims about the economic value of the fur trade, it does seek to examine it as a new and distinctive commercial enterprise, reliant on the supply of raw or semi-processed materials by Indian traders, and on the demand for fashionable or fine headwear in England.[24] As a pioneering interethnic trade, within and beyond the bounds of expanding colonial settlements, it presented challenges regarding its character and conduct. From a transatlantic perspective, moreover, it raised problems concerning the structure, organization and control of an extensive enterprise requiring significant investment. Among colonial traders and their native partners, it required some degree of innovation and experimentation which may have contained the seed of an alternative model for the colonization of the Bay. For both groups it created opportunities for the acquisition of knowledge and information that contributed to cultural exchange and diffusion. But this tended to open pathways for colonial as well as commercial expansion. As such, it was always more than a business venture, becoming an often hidden and varied aspect of interethnic relations, which came to serve as a point of contact or demarcation between friends and enemies. But the growth of trade, and the diplomacy that accompanied it, provoked intense rivalry, cutting across ethnic borderlands to the confusion of European and Indian traders. At the same time, of course, cross-cultural commerce served as a vehicle for widespread, irreversible social and environmental change. It helped to create a landscape of new ambiguity. Always at risk from a land-hungry tobacco culture, the fur trade, as this study argues, was nonetheless interwoven into the patchwork fabric of the Chesapeake colonies, while facing the problems and opportunities of a wider Atlantic world.

22 Guildhall Library, London, MS 1570/2, ff.234–5.

23 E.E. Rich, *Hudson's Bay Company 1670–1870*, 2 vols. (London, 1961), 1, p. 231; David Corner, 'The Tyranny of Fashion: The Case of the Felt-Hatting Trade in the Late Seventeenth and Eighteenth Centuries', *Textile History*, 22 (1991), p. 155.

24 John J. McCusker and Russell R. Menard, *The Economy of British America, 1607–1789* (Chapel Hill, 1985), p. 295 noted the lack of a comprehensive treatment of the fur trade. It remains a challenge.

Chapter 1

Fur and Fashion: The Infrastructure of a New Trade

In 1583 the puritan Philip Stubbes denounced extravagant dress in England. During the course of his vitriolic *Anatomie of Abuses*, he fulminated against 'novell Inventions and new-fangled fashions'.[1] One of his targets was the changing style of headwear. Responding to recent developments, he noted that fashion in hats was both rare and strange. They were worn in distinctive ways, dyed in various colours, and made of different materials. The fabric used in the manufacture of headwear included silk, velvet, wool, and fine hair or fur 'far-fetched and dear bought'.[2] Stubbes' concern was provoked by the appearance of the beaver hat in England, which became an essential accessory during the late sixteenth and early seventeenth centuries for rich and fashion-conscious consumers. But the spread of the new fashion provoked moral reformers who insisted that clothing and accessories serve necessity not vanity. Their anger was fuelled by the use of jewellery and feathers, highlighting the distinctive qualities of the beaver, which Stubbes dismissed as unseemly emblems of pride in defiance of virtue.[3] The exaggerated language of complaint reflected a broader battle in early modern England over the regulation and representation of the body. Unintentionally, its impact, as echoed in sermons and drama, may have strengthened the appeal of the new style in headwear across age and gender boundaries as a symbol of wealth, status and power. But the introduction of the beaver hat had unintended and far-reaching consequences. Growing demand revitalized the fur trade, at a time when European supplies were declining, encouraging traders to seek out

[1] Philip Stubbes, *The Anatomie of Abuses* (London, 1583), Bvii. For clerical attack on changes in apparel see John Chandos, *In God's Name: Examples of Preaching in England 1534–1662* (London, 1971), pp. 62–3.

[2] Stubbes, *Anatomie of Abuses*, Bvii.

[3] Ibid., Bvii. Stubbes' work went through four editions by 1595, Louis B. Wright, *Middle Class Culture in Elizabethan England* (Chapel Hill, 1935), p. 458; David Kuchta, *The Three-Piece Suit and Modern Masculinity: England, 1550–1850* (Berkeley, 2002), pp. 65–9 notes the link with fears of effeminacy.

new sources across the Atlantic.[4] It led to the emergence of a new industry, which called for specialized skills and expertise related to wider changes in the structure and organization of feltmaking in London. Based on the domestic market, the growth of consumption and production, linked with marketing and distribution, created the socio-economic infrastructure that sustained the North American fur trade. During an early and experimental phase of seaborne expansion, it served as a driving force for wider commercial and colonial horizons. While acknowledging the deeper roots of change within an established culture of dress, this chapter examines the links between fur, fashion and consumption which established the necessary conditions for the emergence of a new transatlantic enterprise.

Medieval bearings: Clothing, fashion and fur

Clothing and headwear had always served different purposes, ranging from the functional to the aesthetic. As well as providing warmth and protection, dress served utilitarian functions regarding work, including symbolic uses when linked with professional identity and status. It was also ornamental, enhancing appearance and presentation. As such, it was capable of encouraging emotional responses or experiences. But the decorative use of dress was qualified by a biblical tradition that interpreted clothing as a sign of sin, the result of a loss of innocence and expulsion from Eden. Although the body required concealment, if not enclosure, excess in apparel was often seen as the work of the devil. Throughout the Middle Ages churchmen and theologians attacked the growth of luxury and refinement in clothing. Though the clergy directed their attacks against both sexes, the dress and conduct of women generated deeper anxiety and alarm. Images of the whore of Babylon, well dressed in richly-coloured garments, were used to warn women of the dangers of pride and vanity in appearance.[5]

Preaching failed to prevent the emergence of a system of clothing that supported an interest in fashionable wear in parts of Europe during the twelfth century. An essential feature of this system was an appreciation of novelty and an awareness of the pleasure derived from self-presentation and display.

4 Aileen Ribeiro, *Fashion and Fiction: Dress in Art and Literature in Stuart England* (New Haven, 2005), p. 50; Margaret Scott, *Medieval Dress & Fashion* (London, 2009), p. 126.

5 Natasha O'Hear and Anthony O'Hear, *Picturing the Apocalypse: The Book of Revelation in the Arts over Two Millennia* (Oxford, 2015), pp. 158–65; Margaret R. Miles, *Carnal Knowing: Female Nakedness and Religious Meaning in the Christian West* (Tunbridge Wells, 1992), pp. 187–8; Scott, *Medieval Dress*, pp. 13, 37; Ulinka Rublack, *Dressing Up: Cultural Identity in Renaissance Europe* (Oxford, 2010), pp. 77–8, 109, 259–61.

Although recent studies suggest varied chronologies for the origins of fashion, its development demanded a wider audience and a public space for it to have an impact. Under these conditions a concern with the new encouraged the partial commercialization of dress, the use of a greater range of textiles and the appearance of different styles.[6] The scale and range of change should not be exaggerated. The growth of fashion was restricted by wealth, status and custom, expressed to some extent in legislation governing dress codes and materials. Clothing was both a mark of distinction and an obligation of rank, especially among rulers and aristocratic elites.[7] With exceptions among wealthy urban dwellers, most other groups relied on a combination of homespun and re-used garments.

From the twelfth century onwards forms of dress experienced elaboration. The spread of new styles was accompanied by the use of different fabrics and improvements in tailoring and the cut of clothes, informed by the diffusion of knowledge about clothing and materials, as reflected, for example in the influence of foreign fashions and styling.[8] As social elites devoted more of their income to dress, there was a growing awareness of the relationship between clothes, appearance and identity. Within the city-states and republics of Renaissance Italy, under the leadership of Florence, urbanization and changes to lifestyles encouraged the emergence of a more coherent system of apparel and fashion. Economic expansion, reflected in the spending of the rich and well-off, facilitated change, but it was underpinned by a deeper appreciation of clothing and its ability to project honour and wealth. It was demonstrated by the interest in costly and fashionable garments among men and women who possessed the means and motivation to assert their status through sartorial elegance. The occasions and opportunities for personal display bred a more refined understanding of clothes and fashionable dress, associated with new forms of civility and conduct, which included finely calibrated perceptions of excess and restraint. Yet rich clothing and accessories were a significant investment in individual representation which required care and attention. Their purchase had profound implications for patterns of spending and consumption. Clothes were re-sold or re-used, and circulated as gifts and bequests.[9] While change radiated beyond Italy, its impact was irregular and uneven.

[6] Scott, *Medieval Dress*, pp. 8, 35–6; Rebecca Arnold, *Fashion* (Oxford, 2009), pp. 50–3; Miles, *Carnal Knowing*, pp. 187–8.

[7] Scott, *Medieval Dress*, p. 17.

[8] Naomi Tarrant, *The Development of Costume* (London, 1994), pp. 48–9.

[9] Carole Collier Frick, *Dressing Renaissance Florence: Families, Fortunes, and Fine Clothing* (Baltimore, 2002), pp. 77–86, 90, 144–7, 177–8, 223. Up to 40% of the wealth of some families in Florence was accounted for by clothing. Margaret Rosenthal, 'Cultures of Clothing in Later Medieval and Early Modern Europe', *Journal*

As the system of clothing grew more varied and complex, dress reflected not only occupation and status but also social and political power, as well as cultural capital. In some guises it was a mark of ethnicity and difference. Chaucer's merchant, a representative of wealthy urban society, wore a Flemish beaver hat, signifying wealth and respectability.[10] By contrast, pointed hats or caps were indelibly linked by Christian artists with Jewish men. Yet the so-called 'Jewish hat' functioned more as an imaginary symbol, freighted with mixed messages regarding identity and belonging.[11]

In terms of form and function few materials could compare with the use of fur in clothing and headwear. It was a peculiarly appropriate material for a warrior and hierarchical society, imbued with martial and masculine values, while its luxurious and psychological value enhanced its appeal. Throughout the Middle Ages furs were worn for their warmth and appearance. Fur garments and accessories were highly valued by both sexes, possessing a quality and lustre that were difficult to match. Fur also reflected the status of the wearer. Its use in dress was defined and regulated by sumptuary legislation which persisted into the sixteenth century. In England, according to a prohibition of 1337, wearing fur was confined to an elite with an annual income above £100.[12] But it was difficult to enforce codes for clothing, particularly during periods of economic expansion and social mobility. A more effective constraint on the market was cost. Although the use of fur garments apparently reached an unprecedented level in the royal courts of Western Europe towards the end of the fourteenth century, their high price typified an extravagance that was manipulated to display power and wealth.[13]

The early market for fur was limited to rulers, aristocrats and wealthy sections of urban society. Across Europe it was monarchs and military leaders who set the pace of change. Courtly, and to a lesser extent civic, competitiveness fuelled demand for fur clothing, though its use might vary, not least because of the availability of different types of material. Beaver was used in

of Medieval and Early Modern Studies, 39 (2009), pp. 461–5.

10 Geoffrey Chaucer, *The Canterbury Tales*, ed. Paul G. Ruggiers (Norman, 1979), p. 17; Maria Hayward, '"The Sign of Some Degree"? The Financial, Social and Sartorial Significance of Male Headwear at the Courts of Henry VIII and Edward VI', *Costume*, 36 (2002), p. 2.

11 Sara Lipton, *Dark Mirror: The Medieval Origins of Anti-Jewish Iconography* (New York, 2014), pp. 16–45.

12 Scott, *Medieval Dress*, p. 80; Francoise Piponnier and Perrine Mane, *Dress in the Middle Ages* (New Haven, 1997), pp. 58–9, 73–4; Auslander, *Cultural Revolutions*, pp. 32–3.

13 Piponnier and Mane, *Dress in the Middle Ages*, p. 74; Rublack, *Dressing Up*, pp. 58–9.

gloves, cloaks, coats and headwear which were manufactured in Flanders and exported to England during the later fourteenth century.[14]

The English trade in furs and fur clothing fluctuated in accordance with changes in supply and demand. The availability of fur-bearing animals varied according to environment, including climatic conditions, food and water supplies, and reproductive cycle. Some species, such as beaver, were acutely vulnerable to the danger of over-hunting. By the late twelfth century, Gerald of Wales claimed that the beaver population of England and Wales was reduced to a colony along the River Teifi in west Wales, while in Scotland there was one river where they survived, but in small number.[15] Beavers lived on in memory and scholarship, the subject of stories and legend, but by the sixteenth century they were extinct in England. For scholars and antiquarians, such as John Aubrey, the otter served as an 'English beaver'.[16]

The decline of fur-bearing animals within the British Isles forced merchants to rely on international trade for alternative supplies. Fox, bear and beaver, originally from the forests of Scandinavia, Russia and Central Europe, were imported from Bruges, which served as a centre for the trade. Much of the business was in the hands of German merchants, who traded throughout markets in the Baltic and at the leading Russian fur mart of Novgorod. By the late fifteenth century, however, the fur trade was in serious difficulty. The replacement of Novgorod by Moscow as the centre of the Russian trade disrupted the distribution of furs westward. At the same time, the Baltic trade was undermined by political instability. Although beaver, budge and wolf skins were imported from Southern Europe, including Spain, the amount was small and failed to compensate for the decline in supplies from the east. Over-hunting contributed to these problems. By the fifteenth century many of the forests of Central Europe and Russia were stripped of their fur-bearing resources. In the south, the near extinction of the beaver virtually destroyed a regular source of supply for English merchants.[17]

[14] R. Turner Wilcox, *The Mode in Hats and Headdress* (New York, 1952), p. 41; Penelope Byrde, *The Male Image: Men's Fashion in Britain 1300–1970* (London, 1979), pp. 172–6; Janet Martin, *Treasure from the Land of Darkness: The Fur Trade and its Significance for Medieval Russia* (Cambridge, 1986), p. 64.

[15] Gerald of Wales, *The Journey Through Wales and the Description of Wales*, translated by Lewis Thorpe (Harmondsworth, 1978), p. 174; Victor R. Fuchs, *The Economics of the Fur Industry* (New York, 1957), p. 11.

[16] Ruth Scurr, *John Aubrey: My Own Life* (London, 2015), p. 67; Poliquin, *Beaver*, pp. 17, 20; William Harrison, *The Description of England*, ed., Georges Edelen (Ithaca, 1968), p. 145 repeated Gerald's claim.

[17] Elspeth M. Veale, *The English Fur Trade in the Later Middle Ages* (Oxford, 1966), pp. 68–74, 146–7, 166–70; Martin, *Treasure from the Land of Darkness*, pp. 86–109 on Moscow.

The scarcity of fur pushed prices up to such an extent that its use in dress may have declined during the later fifteenth century.[18] At the top end of the market, rich Russian furs became almost too expensive for English consumers. Longer-term changes to style and fashion reinforced this trend. During the 1550s and 1560s certain types of fur began to lose their appeal as a status symbol for the rich, being replaced by lighter, elaborate, but equally expensive fabrics such as velvet and silk. But the depression in the fur market, at least for beaver, was reversed by the new vogue in headwear, originating in France, which spread into England during the 1570s and 1580s.

The Hat: Symbolizing status, style and fashion

The rapidity with which the new style spread was due to the special place that hats and headwear enjoyed in the culture of clothing. Hats were almost universally worn by men and women, and often by children, both indoors as well as outside. In a way that is no longer applicable, headgear was an essential part of the dress of rich and poor, though it varied in form and function. In addition to providing protection, hats were signifiers of occupation, status, privilege and power. Within the public theatre of display, headdress was a supremely suitable prop for expressions of honour and gallantry, affirming differences in rank and hierarchy. Hat honour was an essential part of social conduct, the neglect of which had serious consequences. Hats were particularly valued because in terms of presentation they focused attention on the head and upper part of the body. Within diverse public settings, ranging from churches to courts, they were a striking visual aid for self-presentation and the projection of refinement and respect.[19]

The position and purpose of hats within the wardrobes of fashionable young men, with disposable income to indulge their tastes in clothing and accessories, are illuminated by the extraordinary 'Book of Clothes' kept by Matthäus Schwarz from 1520 to 1560.[20] Schwarz was the head accountant for the firm of Fuggers, a powerful merchant and banking family in Augsburg, in Southern Germany, a commercial and financial centre, with a population that included a

18 Veale, *Fur Trade*, p. 171; Raymond R. Fisher, *The Russian Fur Trade 1550–1700* (Berkeley, 1943), for declining imports of fur from Russia during the 1580s and 1590s.

19 Frick, *Dressing Renaissance Florence*, pp. 85–6, 147, 152, 157–9. On hat honour see Piponnier and Mane, *Dress in the Middle Ages*, p. 41; Anna Reynolds, *In Fine Style: The Art of Tudor and Stuart Fashion* (London, 2013), pp. 101, 260; Penelope J. Corfield, 'Dress for Deference and Dissent: Hats and the Decline of Hat Honour', *Costume*, 23 (1989), pp. 46–79; Richard Grassby, *The Business Community of Seventeenth-Century England* (Cambridge, 1995), pp. 341–2.

20 Ulinka Rublack and Maria Hayward (eds.), *The First Book of Fashion: The Book of Clothes of Matthäus & Vert Konrad Schwarz of Augsburg* (London, 2015).

wealthy group of young men with a shared interest in fashion and new styles. Within this environment, open to the influence of Italian and Spanish styles, the control and management of clothing served multiple purposes. Events and gatherings, as well as seasonal change and life-cycle, provided occasions for innovation in the use of dress and the expression of individuality while fulfilling deeper social and psychological needs.[21] Schwarz's 'Book', compiled with the aid of local artists, portrayed him in varied fashions and settings. He rarely appeared bare-headed. As a young man his headwear included bonnets and caps made of knitted or felted wool and occasionally velvet. Several hats were lined with fur or had covers for the ears. Brims varied in width, and could be slashed or decorated. Colour ranged from flamboyant red to luxurious black, reflecting the occasion and season. In 1512, for example, while 'flirting in the streets' he wore a white felt bonnet with black points as decoration.[22] With age, Schwarz adopted a more plain and sombre style in headwear. The last he was portrayed in, worn to mark the death of his master, had a high crown and, like the rest of his costume, was black. Schwarz's 'Book' is a unique visual record of the distinctive use of headwear, but its capacity to display wealth and style, as a means of aesthetic pleasure and identity, was widely employed by wealthy consumers.[23]

Headdress varied widely in style and substance. An extensive range of hats, hoods, caps, bonnets and related gear were worn, particularly by men. Materials included straw, felt, silk, velvet and fur. By the fourteenth century felt hats, including beavers, were available in different colours as a result of the development of dyeing. Their appearance was enhanced by the addition of feathers and bands. Changes in style and fashion influenced shape, notably height and depth, and the use of wider brims which might be slashed, cocked and studded with jewellery.[24] Because of its felting qualities, malleability and inherent value, the beaver hat acquired a powerful appeal which cut across conflicting views on dress, promoting rapid market expansion in England during the later sixteenth and early seventeenth centuries.

The popularity of the new fashion, and the speed with which it was adopted by men and women, provoked moral outrage and an undercurrent of political concern. Stubbes railed against the confusing 'mingle mangle of apparell', that enabled 'everie Servingman, Countreyman, and other', to wear such hats

[21] Ibid., pp. 1–4, 13–14, 18–19.

[22] Ibid., pp. 69, 239.

[23] Ibid., pp. 19–22; Rublack, *Dressing Up*, pp. 39–76; Scott, *Medieval Dress*, pp. 180–1.

[24] Wilcox, *Mode in Hats*, pp. 42–3, 76–7; M. Channing Linthicum, *Costume in the Drama of Shakespeare and His Contemporaries* (Oxford, 1936), pp. 216–31; James Laver, *Costume and Fashion: A Concise History* (London, 5th edition, 2012), pp. 94–5.

despite their expense.[25] But the literature of moral reform suffered from its own form of exaggeration and excess. As Stubbes was surely aware, during the 1580s the price of beaver hats placed them way beyond the reach of servants, labourers or craftsmen.[26] Yet anxiety at the unregulated spread of new, expensive headwear was widely shared, suggesting the need for more effective sumptuary legislation. According to a report of 1620, James I was prepared to issue a proclamation limiting their use to 'men of certaine quality', led by the royal family and the king's favourite, George Villiers, soon to be the duke of Buckingham.[27] The issue was confused with a moral panic at reports of women taking on male attire. At James' command the Bishop of London instructed clergy in the capital to preach against women for wearing broad-brimmed beaver hats.[28] But the church itself was not immune to the charm of fashionable headwear. In 1632 John Partridge denounced clergymen and their wives for dressing in 'beaver hats of great price' and other vanities.[29] James' successor, Charles I, whose court became a show case for the spectacular, broad-brimmed beaver, considered placing a selective prohibition on its use in 1634. Nearly a decade later, from a very different perspective, the puritan and radical leader, William Walwyn, angrily dismissed the pretensions of religious people, not least for wearing beavers and other costly accessories 'in the very Churches and upon solemne dayes'.[30]

Attempts to regulate headdress foundered on the perceived ineffectiveness of sumptuary legislation which was unable to counter the cultivation of taste

25 Stubbes, *Anatomie of Abuses*, Cii verso, and Walter Cary, *The Present State of England* (London, 1626), pp. 3, 9–12 for similar complaint.

26 Hilda Amphlett, *Hats: A History of Fashion in Headwear* (London, 1974), p. 109; Donald Woodward, *Men at Work: Labourers and Building Craftsmen in the Towns of Northern England, 1450–1750* (Cambridge, 1995), pp. 173–7 for wages; Eleri Lynn, *Tudor Fashion* (New Haven, 2017), p. 106.

27 J.H. Bettey (ed.), *Calendar of the Correspondence of the Smyth Family of Ashton Court 1548–1642* (Bristol Record Society, 35, 1982), p. 56; Susan Vincent, *Dressing the Elite: Clothes in Early Modern England* (Oxford, 2003), p. 125. Until legislation of 1673, in Scotland wearing beaver hats was restricted to the aristocracy and gentry, Alan Hunt, *Governance of the Consuming Passions: A History of Sumptuary Laws* (London, 1996), p. 172.

28 Christopher Breward, *The Culture of Fashion: A New History of Fashionable Dress* (Manchester, 1995), pp. 94–5; Susan D. Amussen and David E. Underdown, *Gender, Culture and Politics in England, 1560–1640: Turning the World Upside Down* (London, 2017), pp. 43–50 on the maintenance of gender boundaries by means of clothing.

29 Kevin Sharpe, *The Personal Rule of Charles I* (New Haven, 1992), p. 400.

30 William Walwyn, *The Power of Love* (London, 1643), A4–A4v; *CSPD, 1634–5*, p. 65 for the prohibition.

and fashion.[31] Within a clothing regime in which hats functioned as a sign of personal honour, the beaver was ideally suited to captivate the interests of the rich and fashionable, as well as their austere critics. The innate quality of the material, after processing and preparation, meant that it could be shaped to a variety of forms, reflecting individual tastes while conforming to current styles. The shape of crowns, in particular, experienced extensive change. During the last quarter of the sixteenth century, when the fashion for wearing beavers caught on, crowns were high and adorned with accessories, including bands, jewellery and feathers, depending on the wealth and status of the wearer. Sometimes known as the copotain or chimney-pot, their elegance and adaptability commanded wide interest. During the ensuing period of market consolidation and expansion, hats grew in height. A surviving example, now in the Victoria and Albert Museum in London, has a crown of 36 centimetres.[32] Unadorned, except for a plain band, they symbolized gravity and dignity. As such they appealed to less flamboyant consumers in the city and country. As a mark of the occasion, Charles I dressed in one for his execution in 1649. John Bradshaw, the president of the commissioners who tried the king, wore a specially constructed version with a metal-plated lining as protection from potential assassins. By contrast, lower-crowned and broad-brimmed beavers gained in popularity during the 1620s and 1630s among courtly followers of fashion. During the civil wars of the 1640s they were emblematic of a royalist and cavalier culture, suggesting a distinctive way of life that was at odds with its rivals and enemies.[33]

Fine and fashionable headwear had a wider cultural impact, resonating in the imaginary worlds of art and drama, which traced the emergence of the beaver hat as an iconic symbol of cultivated fashion. Its use and function were captured in many of the portraits made for wealthy and powerful consumers. By comparison city comedies, a popular genre in late Elizabethan and early Stuart theatre, presented a more ambiguous response to new fashions, while affirming the interest they provoked. Such representations drew on reality, in order to 'show an Image of the times'.[34] While the interpretation of art and

[31] Hunt, *Governance of the Consuming Passions*, pp. 325–52 on the difficulties of enforcement.

[32] http://collections.vam.ac.uk/item/O98558/hat-unknown/?print+1 made c. 1590–1680. On changing styles see Colin McDowell, *Hats: Status, Style and Glamour* (London, 1992), pp. 10–11, 25; Francis M. Kelly and Randolph Schwabe, *A Short History of Costume & Armour Chiefly in England 1066–1800* (London, 1931), p. 42.

[33] Wilcox, *Mode in Hats*, pp. 73–107, 109–14; John Stubbs, *Reprobates: The Cavaliers of the English Civil War* (London, 2011), pp. 4–9, 250, 339.

[34] Ben Jonson, *Every Man in His Humour*, ed. Martin Seymour-Smith (London, 1966), p. 7. Though widely used by fashion historians, portraits can be misleading, see Reynolds, *In Fine Style*, pp. 172–4, 181–2.

drama can be over-determined, especially when dealing with the fluid and contested meanings of fashion, both drew striking attention to the way in which stylish and fashionable clothing contributed to the skills of presentation, and perceptions of identity and individuality.[35]

Portraits presented idealized images. For rich and prominent patrons, including monarchs, they conveyed messages of power and wealth, while capturing the importance of family honour and lineage. The cost of such works, which on average ranged from £20 to £60, made their ownership a mark of privilege. Material and mental representations, including key aspects of physical appearance such as demeanour and dignity, were embedded in clothing, headwear and other worldly possessions. In personalized but also public settings, clothing and headdress enhanced posture and presence. As an eye-catching talisman or trophy, they were highly suited to display style or to record honour and service, including loyalty and allegiance.[36]

Portraits of the 1570s and 1580s illustrate the spread of the new fashion in hats, and its attraction across gender. Coinciding with an increase in the use of decoration by men and women, visual images included a rich array of additional features for headwear. A portrait of Elizabeth Knollys, a well-connected member of Queen Elizabeth's household, by an unknown artist, shows her wearing a stylish hat with a high crown, a jewel-encrusted band and decorated with a striking piece of jewellery and a large ostrich feather. Male images of the 1580s and 1590s demonstrate a similar taste in headwear, with variations in style and ornamentation.[37] Courtly images were accompanied by portraits of country gentry, though their response to fashion was often less showy. The portrait of Fleetwood Burton, c.1610, the wife of Richard Shuttleworth of Gawthorpe Hall in Lancashire, shows her wearing stylish, restrained dress, including a high-crowned hat with a band of embroidery, suggesting an interest in sumptuous, but not necessarily fashionable, sartorial demeanour.[38]

Images from the early seventeenth century affirmed the growing appeal of the beaver as a status symbol. Its adaptability is displayed in a double portrait of Sir Walter Raleigh and his son, of 1602, showing changes to the shape

35 Frick, *Dressing Renaissance Florence*, pp. 203–19; Stubbs, *Reprobates*, pp. 213–6; Rublack, *Dressing Up*, pp. 231–2, 259–61.

36 Stubbs, *Reprobates*, p. 214; Jane Ashelford, *The Art of Dress: Clothes Through History 1500–1914* (London, 1996), pp. 31–3; William Gaunt, *Court Painting in England from Tudor to Victorian Times* (London, 1986), pp. 37–63; Kuchta, *The Suit*, p. 45 on allegiance.

37 Jane Ashelford, *A Visual History of Costume: The Sixteenth Century* (London, 1983), pp. 102–5, 124; Ashelford, *The Art of Dress*, pp. 29, 32; Reynolds, *In Fine Style*, pp. 108–10, 261.

38 Ashelford, *The Art of Dress*, pp. 84–5.

and angle at which it was worn on the head. Raleigh's fashionably-dressed son respectfully holds his hat. Even when not worn, fine headwear exerted a powerful visual appeal. A portrait by Robert Peake the elder, of Prince Henry, son and heir of James I until his premature death in 1612, included a cream or white beaver with personalized jewellery and feather, strategically located on a table. As a display of taste, with overt reference to purity and harmony, the white beaver also appeared in portraits of Henry's brother, Charles, and their mother, Queen Anne.[39]

Portraiture tracked changes in fashion, including new styles and shapes in headwear. The portrait of an unknown cavalier of 1638 by Edward Bower included a wide-brimmed beaver, with a lower crown, as an essential part of fashionable dress. Anthony van Dyck, appointed Charles I's principal painter in 1632, encapsulated the importance of image and appearance at court. In a series of striking works, he presented the refined elegance of the courtly world, capturing the essence of style and texture in clothes and headwear. His portraits of Charles I, *Le Roi à la Chasse,* and of Henrietta Maria with Jeffrey Hudson, the court dwarf, celebrated the elegance and beauty of monarchy. These portraits of the king and queen in rich sartorial outfits, with fashionable broad-brimmed hats and matching feathers, appeared to present the relaxed confidence of well-ordered and harmonious royal authority.[40]

In contrast to the rich and celebratory representation of clothing in portraiture, the theatre seemed to adopt a mocking and derisive tone, especially towards the development of fashion. Elizabethan and Jacobean drama, as a commercialized and popular forum for entertainment, was alive to the theatrical significance of clothing and headwear, and its value as a social and cultural marker. As depicted in city comedies, dress served as a prop for caricature and subversive humour. Such works presented an image of London as a dangerously alluring place, where vanity and vice flourished.[41] City streets were the site of affectation and wit, fed by folly, 'the special gallantry of our time' as noted by Ben Jonson.[42] Civility and manners, often manufactured, failed to conceal impersonation and deception, or confusion and disorder. Although one of Jonson's

39 Ashelford, *Visual History of Costume*, p. 140; Gaunt, *Court Painting*, pp. 53, 56; Ribeiro, *Fashion and Fiction*, pp. 27–9; Christopher White, *Anthony van Dyck: Thomas Howard the Earl of Arundel* (Malibu, 1995), pp. 7–8.

40 Ashelford, *The Art of Dress*, pp. 64. 72, 82; White, *Anthony van Dyck*, pp. 71–2; Christopher Brown and Hans Vlieghe (eds.), *Van Dyck 1599–1641* (London, 1999), pp. 30, 32, 246–7.

41 Jean E. Howard, *Theater of a City: The Places of London Comedy, 1598–1642* (Philadelphia, 2009), p. 120; Ann Rosalind Jones and Peter Stallybrass, *Renaissance Clothing and the Materials of Memory* (Cambridge, 2000), pp. 181–3, 188, 190, 197 on the role of theatre.

42 Jonson, *Every Man in His Humour*, p. 67.

characters might plead 'let the Idea of what you are, be portrayed i' your face', day-to-day practice was more concerned with display and performance.[43] The social and cultural construction of identity, including the way in which dress acted as disguise or costume, blurred gender and status. One of the characters in Thomas Middleton's *No Wit, no Help Like a Woman's*, Mistress Low-water, appears as a gallant gentleman, provoking Master Weatherwise, a gull, to comment on the attraction of a male companion should he fail in his suit to a wealthy widow. In this imagined cityscape, consumption, clothing and conduct worked within an environment of negotiation and manipulation, where cross-dressing generated ambiguous responses. Accordingly, Weatherwise wryly notes that 'Women are wiser than ever they were since they wore doublets'.[44] Dramatic invention, often manifest in bawdy humour, was invested with a deeper anxiety regarding fashion, gender and sexuality. Follywit, a key figure in Middleton's *A Mad World, my Masters,* humorously exposes such concern, when he changes his dress for that of a courtesan. Responding to a query from a comrade about what he will wear on the upper body, he replies that 'the doublet serves as well as the best and is most in fashion. We're all male to th' middle, mankind from the beaver to th' bum. 'Tis an Amazonian time; you shall have women shortly tread their husbands'.[45]

Playwrights such as Jonson and Middleton, as well as Thomas Dekker and Philip Massinger, employed a diverse cast of characters, while exploiting the spread of new vogues in dress, personal appearance and conduct. In the city gallant and his counterfoil, the country gull, they created figures that entertained and teased audiences with their outlandish behaviour and obsession with fashion and self-display. The affectation of the latter left him a prey to mockery and manipulation by the gallant. Yet the attempt of the gallant to impress audiences, partly through his sense of taste, met with satire and wit. For the 'commendably-fashioned gallant ... whose courtly habite is the ... delight of the surveying eye' the beaver was a coveted symbol of status and wealth.[46] 'Good faith', exclaims one of Jonson's characters to a youthful, inexperienced gallant, 'this hat hath possest mine eye exceedingly; tis so prettie, and fantastike: what? ist a beaver'?[47] Though only recently purchased, at a cost of £2, the young gallant is persuaded to exchange it for an old

43 Ibid., p. 21.

44 Thomas Middleton, *A Mad World, My Masters and Other Plays*, ed. Michael Taylor (Oxford, 1995), p. 227.

45 Ibid., p. 39.

46 Ben Jonson, *Cynthia's Revels or, the Fountain of Self-love*, ed. Alexander Corbin Judson (New York, 1912), pp. 138–9. On the importance of the theatre for fashion see Kevin Sharpe, *Remapping Early Modern England: The Culture of Seventeenth-Century Politics* (Cambridge, 2000), pp. 421–2.

47 Jonson, *Cynthia's Revels*, p. 33.

hat from Russia, reputed to have magical qualities.[48] While Middleton and Dekker identified the beaver hat as an emblem of masculinity, the 'beaver gallants' they described in *The Roaring Girl* were 'shallow lechers', whose fashionable dress did little to cover their mercenary motives.[49] By contrast a female character in *The Magnetic Lady*, by Jonson, is offered a 'new brave, four-pound beaver hat set with enamelled studs' to wear, in procession to and from church, before the 'fifty daughters' she delivered as a mid-wife.[50]

As these samples of a wider body of work indicate, art and drama were a form of communication which displayed and advertised stylish or fashionable dress. Portraits did so in appealing and meticulous detail. Although the theatre satirized dress, it also provided a stage for it. From different perspectives the work of artists and dramatists confirmed new trends in fashionable attire. Their audiences may have been limited and distinctive, more so in the case of portraiture than drama, but their reach influenced consumption and the market. As such they formed part of the culture of fashion, in which portraitists registered the spread of new styles among wealthy courtiers and aristocrats, while the satire of dramatists revealed the value of display and presentation within an expanding urban milieu accustomed to change and novelty. From different perspectives they drew attention to the growing market for sumptuous or fashionable dress.[51]

Consumption and the market

Despite the undoubted appeal of the new style in headwear, its economic impact is difficult to gauge, particularly given the lack of evidence for the volume of sales. Little is known about the structure of the market or of patterns of consumption. In 1627 Walter Cary claimed in *The Present State of England* that within the space of eighteen months at least £300,000 was spent on the purchase of beaver hats, despite the availability of cheaper, but less stylish, wares.[52] Based on market values this would suggest that annual sales ranged from 65,000 to 130,000 in number. Such pamphlets rarely provided

48 Ibid., p. 34.

49 Thomas Middleton and Thomas Dekker, *The Roaring Girl*, ed. Paul A. Mulholland (Manchester, 1987), pp. 65, 116; Ribeiro, *Fashion and Fiction*, p. 50.

50 Ben Jonson, *The Magnetic Lady*, ed. Peter Happe (Manchester, 2000), p. 189. It is not clear if this refers to value or weight.

51 Ballads and broadsides also covered the subject of dress, often in an ambiguous manner which was subject to change, see Clare Backhouse, *Fashion and Popular Print in Early Modern England: Depicting Dress in Black-Letter Ballads* (London, 2017), pp. 2–6, 34–5, 47–54, 84, 121–5.

52 Cary, *Present State of England*, p. 10; E.G.R. Taylor, *Late Tudor and Early Stuart Geography 1583–1650* (London, 1934), p. 136.

supporting evidence for their claims, and Cary was no exception. His estimate was exaggerated for effect. It is not supported by surviving customs records, admittedly incomplete and fragmentary, either for the import of beaver skins or of hats. Such an impressive volume of business was beyond the capacity of the emerging beavermaking trade. In focusing on the beaver hat, however, Cary selected an appropriate and highly symbolic article of dress, to attack the 'monstrous prodigality' in apparel which was reducing the country to beggary.[53] By the 1620s, indeed, it was a required item in the wardrobes of fashionable gentlemen, though sales were affected by cheaper, difficult-to-detect imitations, known as demi-castors, made from a mix of beaver and rabbit wool.

During the late sixteenth and early seventeenth centuries consumption rested primarily on the domestic market. Economic expansion and rising incomes, though selective in terms of region and status, encouraged expenditure on clothing and other accessories. Though the timing may vary, it has been widely argued that an increase in personal spending helped to lay the foundations for the subsequent growth of a consumer society.[54] While fashion focused attention on self-display and appearance, interest in personal representation was related to selective improvements in material culture, including housing and furnishings, as well as the elaboration of taste and refinement. Yet investment in rich clothing and headwear was still constrained by cost. The price of beaver hats, ranging from £1 10 shillings to £3 according to Cary, restricted consumption to the royal court, wealthy landowners and urban elites.[55] As a result the market for stylish headwear was segmented and specialized, rather than national, composed of overlapping constituencies at court, in the city and country.[56] These different spaces, which were both physical and mental, fostered varied patterns of spending on costly accessories, ranging from individual, in some cases possibly life-long acquisitions, to multiple purchases. As in the case of other articles of clothing, the market

53 Cary, *Present State of England*, pp. 3, 12–13. For similar comment in Germany, see Rublack, *Dressing Up*, pp. 166–9.

54 Neil McKendrick, John Brewer and J.H. Plumb, *The Birth of a Consumer Society: The Commercialization of Eighteenth-Century England* (London, 1982), pp. 9–33; Linda Levy Peck, *Consuming Splendor: Society and Culture in Seventeenth-Century England* (Cambridge, 2005), pp. 47–52, 348–52 argues for its earlier emergence; Jan de Vries, *The Industrious Revolution: Consumer Behavior and the Household Economy, 1650 to the Present* (New York, 2008), pp. 122–3; Frank Trentmann, *Empire of Things: How We Became a World of Consumers, from the Fifteenth Century to the Twenty-first* (London, 2016), pp. 22–3, 53–4 notes a change in the meaning of consumption but cautions against a national approach.

55 Cary, *Present State of England*, p. 3; Peck, *Consuming Splendor*, pp. 8, 73–7, 162–71, 184–6 on material culture.

56 Breward, *Culture of Fashion*, p. 123.

included the shadowy circulation of second-hand and stolen goods, in addition to gifts and bequests.

The royal court lay at the centre of a widening web of fashionable consumption. Henry Peacham's hostile comment that fashion was like an 'epidemical disease' which first infected the court, underlines its importance for the introduction and spread of new styles.[57] As the site of monarchy, and an arena for politics and patronage, it brought together an unrivalled assembly of wealthy and powerful consumers. Although attendance varied, the hospitality of the royal household combined with a courtly culture of ceremony, entertainment and play was a magnet for ambitious aristocrats and gentlemen. The lifestyle of the court, influenced by competitive display, demanded sustained expenditure on clothing and appearance, despite the risk of crippling financial consequences.[58] For men and women it served as an outlet for the expression of personal capital in the form of fine and fashionable dress. While acknowledging rank and precedence, gorgeously attired favourites, like Robert Dudley, earl of Leicester, during the 1570s and 1580s appeared like peacocks, basking in royal favour. Under the early Stuarts, Buckingham fulfilled a similar role as a model of finery and fashion, arousing admiration and envy. The importance of the court as a beacon for luxury and fashion was reinforced by its accessibility and by the absence of formalized costume.[59] At the same time it was uniquely exposed to overseas influences, even during periods of international rivalry and conflict, as demonstrated by the impact of Spanish styles on the later Elizabethan court. As a reception centre for new modes, it played a vital role in the absorption and diffusion of the beaver hat during the last quarter of the sixteenth century.

Monarchs did not need to dress in the latest fashion, but sumptuous and well-cut clothing was a requirement, reflecting royal wealth, power and taste. Queen Elizabeth acquired an extensive and rich collection of clothes, hats and accessories, although her wardrobe expenditure was carefully managed rather than excessively extravagant. Royal inventories include a range of headdress,

57 Henry Peacham, *The Complete Gentleman, The Truth of Our Times, and the Art of Living in London*, ed. Virgil B. Hetzel (Ithaca, 1962), p. 199; Barbara Burman Baines, *Fashion Revivals from the Elizabethan Age to the Present Day* (London, 1981), p. 108.

58 Peck, *Consuming Splendor*, pp. 73, 112; Valerie Cumming, '"Great Vanity and Excesse in Apparell": Some Clothing and Furs of Tudor and Stuart Royalty', in Arthur MacGregor (ed.), *The Late King's Goods: Collections, Possessions and Patronage of Charles I in the Light of the Commonwealth Sale Inventories* (London, 1989), pp. 322–42. Depending on the time of year, the Tudor court could number 1,000, Lynn, *Tudor Fashion*, p. 141.

59 Tarrant, *Development of Costume*, p. 54; Peck, *Consuming Splendor*, p. 348; Ashelford, *The Art of Dress*, pp. 28–8, 82.

though there is no evidence for the acquisition of beaver headwear before 1585. Three years later the queen received a rich gift of clothes and hats from Elizabeth, Lady Russell, who was seeking support in a personal suit regarding property, which included a white beaver adorned with jewellery.[60] By contrast, according to a hostile observer, the queen's successor, James VI of Scotland, showed little interest in clothing or fashion. Allegedly the king was so constant in his apparel that he rarely changed his clothes, while he was so unconcerned with new styles 'insomuch as one bringing to him a Hat of a *Spanish* Block, he cast it from him, swearing he neither loved them nor their fashions'.[61] Yet wardrobe expenditure increased massively during the first five years of James' reign, reaching £36,377 *per annum,* nearly four times greater than the annual total during the last years of his predecessor.[62] Expenditure and consumption were enhanced by the king's family and his interest in jewellery and fine accessories, including headwear. In 1603 he acquired 18 black beaver hats and one of ash colour, lined and richly embroidered with plumes of black or white feathers. He ordered five elaborately decorated and dyed beavers for his eldest son, embroidered with Venetian gold and silver, and lined with taffeta, also with plumes.[63] Such stylish headwear is displayed in royal portraits of the king and his family. Nicholas Hilliard's miniature of 1604 shows James finely attired, wearing a fashionable white or pale grey beaver.[64]

The position of the court as a centre for the display and consumption of stylish dress reached its apogee under Charles I. Following his marriage to the French princess, Henrietta Maria, the royal couple played a leading role in the development of taste and refinement in personal appearance. Supported by wealthy aristocrats and prominent officials, they represented a small body of cultivated and creative consumers, whose style was circulated and advertised by the court. In March 1627, after dining aboard the earl of Warwick's ship at Blackwall, Henrietta Maria returned to Whitehall accompanied by her ladies-in-waiting, who all wore 'little black beaver hats'.[65] Although growing

60 Janet Arnold (ed.), *Queen Elizabeth's Wardrobe Unlock'd* (Leeds, 1988), pp. 1–3, 97; Arnold (ed.), '*"Lost from Her Majesties Back": Items of Clothing and Jewels Lost or Given Away by Queen Elizabeth between 1561 and 1585* (The Costume Society, Extra Series, 7, 1980), has no references to beaver hats.

61 Anthony Weldon, *The Court and Character of King James* (London, 1650), pp. 180–1.

62 Arnold (ed.), *Queen Elizabeth's Wardrobe*, p. 1.

63 Ibid., p. 200. Purchases of beaver hats by Prince Charles included 64 in 1618, 57 in 1619 and 43 in 1624, Nick Bunker, *Making Haste from Babylon. The Mayflower Pilgrims and Their World: A New History* (London, 2010), p. 241.

64 Gaunt, *Court Painting*, pp. 52–3; Roy Strong, *Artists of the Tudor Court: Portrait Miniature Rediscovered* (London, 1983), p. 145.

65 Thomas Birch (ed.), *The Court and Times of Charles the First*, 2 vols. (London, 1848), 1, p. 206; Amphlett, *Hats*, p. 106. On creative consumers see de Vries, *The*

criticism of court culture focused attention on the moral aspects of fashionable clothing and appearance, expenditure on dress was maintained during the 1620s and 1630s. According to royal household accounts more than £4,000 was spent on the king's apparel from September 1633 to 1634. It included a large number of suits of satin, velvet and other material, cloaks trimmed with silver and gold, embroidered hose, gloves, boots and shoes, and other accessories. Spending on headwear amounted to £130, based on the purchase of 21 beaver hats, gold and silver bands, and three velvet caps. The following year, with an increase in total expenditure of about £600, acquisitions included 32 beavers. Spending on hats and accessories amounted to nearly £150.[66] This volume of consumption was matched by the queen. During the first quarter of 1635 her household was supplied with seven hats, at a cost of £27, including a fine French beaver lined with satin, an earlier example of which appeared in Van Dyck's portrait of 1633.[67] Other purchases for the queen included a white beaver edged with gold and silver lace.

If the scale of royal consumption was unusual and difficult for others to keep up with, the style was adopted by courtiers, ministers and their families. Early in 1632 Sir Thomas Wentworth, recently appointed Lord Deputy of Ireland, promised to bring his son, William, a new beaver hat on condition that he was a 'good boy' and worked at his books.[68] Several years later, in 1636, Francis, Lord Cottington, the Chancellor of the Exchequer, and a prominent follower of the queen, visited the earl of Salisbury at Hatfield, 'bravely horsed … in a white beaver, with a studded hat band'.[69] By these means courtly fashion ranged far beyond the confines of the court, implicitly carrying messages of allegiance, though with mixed, potentially confusing consequences.

The court was essential to the emerging market for beaver hats. Within an environment characterized by extreme variations in income, social differentiation and persistent moral concern regarding dress, it played a pivotal role in the introduction and spread of new fashions. As an institution it represented an impressive concentration of wealthy consumers, whose concern for appearance and display was focused on the fine and luxurious. Well-connected courtiers possessed the resources and leisure, as well as a captive audience,

Industrious Revolution, pp. 46–7.

66 Roy Strong, 'Charles I's Clothes for the Years 1633 to 1635', *Costume*, 14 (1980), pp. 77–89.

67 TNA, LR 5/66, unnumbered. Cumming, '"Great Vanity"', p. 334 argues that Henrietta Maria indulged in 'restrained luxury', but was not unusually extravagant.

68 Sheffield City Archives, Wentworth Woodhouse Muniments, Strafford Papers, 34/13 (I am indebted to Dr Fiona Pogson for this reference). One aristocrat complained of the 'tyranny of fashion' at the Caroline court, Keith Thomas, *In Pursuit of Civility: Manners and Civilization in Early Modern England* (New Haven, 2018), p. 62.

69 *CSPD, 1636–7*, p. 75.

to indulge their tastes in dress. But it was a select market, based on a limited circle of consumer capital and experience that favoured innovation in style and presentation. In terms of the structure and pattern of consumption, it was characterized by depth, or multiple purchases by individuals, rather than width, as reflected in the extent of such acquisitions among a larger group of consumers.

As a market for fine and fashionable headwear the court overlapped with the city and country. Although courtiers tried to maintain their superiority through novelty and variety, in favourable economic circumstances the number of consumers, in London and beyond, who were able to follow courtly trends grew, encouraged by the increasing availability of royal prints and images. The development of London as a national stage for fashionable dress and appearance was closely linked with its role as a centre for conspicuous consumption. Both were underpinned by its staggering growth. The population of London grew from about 145,000 to 200,000 during the second half of the sixteenth century. By 1650 it had reached 375,000. It was eulogized by poets who described it as the sovereign of cities, renowned for its wealth and royalty.[70] But it was a city of growing complexity and contradiction. Urban development strengthened the link between Westminster and the city, nurturing the growth of a fashionable West End, providing a stark contrast to the expanding poorer suburbs of the East End and across the river in Southwark. The influx of large numbers of migrants exacerbated existing social problems, evident in complaints against overcrowding, vagrancy and the existence of an underworld of petty criminals, outcasts and deviants. The speed of change exposed long-lasting fears that London, in the symbolic language of the body, threatened the health of the rest of the kingdom. The contradictions went deeper, of course, and were more personal, intensified by the illusory freedom of city life and its solitude and alienation.[71]

As a capital city and the location of the royal court, parliament and legal institutions, London attracted large numbers of visitors, including wealthy landowners, providing fertile ground for the emergence of an annual season of entertainment and sociability. It was a cosmopolitan environment, home to a growing number of migrants and refugees, temporary or permanent, who

70 The poem 'To London' has been persistently, but dubiously, attributed to William Dunbar according to Priscilla Bawcutt, *Dunbar the Makar* (Oxford, 1992), pp. 44, 82. On London see Peter Hall, *Cities in Civilisation: Culture, Innovation, and Urban Order* (London, 1998), pp. 114–41; F.J. Fisher, *London and the English Economy, 1500–1700*, eds. P.J. Corfield and N.B. Harte (London, 1990) and A.L. Beier and Roger Finlay (eds.), *London 1500–1700: The Making of the Metropolis* (London, 1986).

71 Howard, *Theater of a City*, pp. 162–5; Max Byrd, *London Transformed: Images of the City in the Eighteenth Century* (New Haven, 1978), pp. 5–7; Fisher, 'The Growth of London', in *London and the English Economy*, pp. 174–9.

included artisans, merchants and diplomats. Collectively such groups provided a channel for the influx of new ideas, skills and fashions. At the same time, as Henry Peacham warned, London was 'a quicksand' for rich and inexperienced visitors, whose carelessness could lead to a 'nap upon penniless-bench'.[72] Such a concentration of people represented a varied collection of consumers who sustained a wide range of service industries, educational, legal and financial, as well as commercial enterprises. Not only was London a manufacturing centre, but it was also the largest port in the realm.[73] Enjoying a dominant position in the developing colonial trades, it quickly became the hub for new industries related to staple American products, including the manufacture of beaver hats.

Within contrasting cityscapes, London provided the rich and fashionable with the means and opportunity for personal display. It possessed an extensive range of sites for public appearance and presentation, including theatres, taverns, shops, and parks. Entertainment and ceremony, including fairs and holidays, were occasions for the deployment of the skills of deportment. Churches and courts provided more managed spaces for the presentation of the self. There were alternative and potentially dangerous attractions in drinking, gambling and prostitution, which fed the cause of urban regulation and reform.[74] For locals and migrants London was a world of motion, favouring innovation and novelty, where performance and observation were part of the daily spectacle of civic culture. It contained multiple stages for public-fashioning and presentation, where dress was one of the means of negotiating the challenges and opportunities of city life. Such fluidity aroused mixed reactions and anxiety at the threatened instability of urban identities and the use or misuse of clothing. Although the 'art of living in London' generated advice and conduct books, some of these works exposed mounting concern at the culture of fashion and the addiction of city gallants to public display.[75]

As even critics acknowledged London was a distinctive market for fashionable headwear and clothing. By comparison with the court, however, it was characterized more by its width than depth. The number of individual acquisitions was probably smaller, while the circulation of clothing and hats may have assumed a different pattern, particularly as a result of the trade in second-hand wares and imitations. Structurally the London market was more extensive and layered than the court. It contained an increasingly diverse

72 Peacham, *Complete Gentleman*, pp. 24–5.

73 Fisher, 'The Development of London as a Centre of Conspicuous Consumption in the Sixteenth and Seventeenth Centuries', in *London and the English Economy*, pp. 106–13.

74 Ibid., pp. 114–6; Howard, *Theater of a City*, pp. 6–7, 26, 177; Peck, *Consuming Splendor*, pp. 42–53 on shopping; Breward, *Culture of Fashion*, pp. 52–6.

75 Peacham, *Complete Gentleman*, p. 243; Thomas Dekker, *The Gull's Horn-Book: Or, Fashions to Please All Sorts of Gulls*, ed. E.D. Pendry (London, 1967), p. 88.

body of citizens, merchants, lawyers and other professional figures, as well as visiting and resident landowners. Like the court, it included female consumers. Lady Ann Southwell, the poet, owned at least two beaver hats which were packed in a trunk with other clothes, when she and her second husband moved from Clerkenwell to Aston in 1631.[76] The role of women as civic role models is illustrated by the miniatures and portraits of citizens' wives, showing them wearing high-crowned, black hats with little extra embellishment. The growth of such a dynamic urban market was encouraged by the availability of credit, despite warnings against usurious rates of interest. The fictitious Mistress Spendthrift, who borrowed £3 from a broker to purchase a beaver hat, gold band, yellow feather and other accessories, seemed to portray a growing number of women whose interest in fashionable dress mimicked the conduct of the gallant.[77] Within this multi-layered market the growing commercialization of the culture of fashion, including the rich dress of gentry visitors to the city, held out the prospect of sustained expansion far exceeding the capacity of the royal court.[78]

Beyond London the impact of change and novelty in fashionable clothing and headwear was uneven and irregular. The clergyman and reformer, William Harrison, claimed in his *Description of England* of 1577, that 'the fantastical folly' of the English in their apparel spanned the social spectrum from 'the courtier to the carter'.[79] Suggesting that fashion acquired a wider geographical reach, he complained of 'fickleness … in all degrees', noting that 'nothing is more constant in England than inconstancy of attire'.[80] But the market for fine clothing and headwear in the country, a loose cultural and geographical conception, is difficult to evaluate, particularly given the range of attitudes, including a greater degree of indifference, towards new styles. There is little evidence that rural settlements, like Terling in Essex, experienced much change to clothing in general across the period from 1550 to 1650.[81] The number of clothes owned by individuals may have increased,

76 Jean Klene (ed.), *The Southwell-Sibthorpe Commonplace Book Folger MS. V.b.198* (Renaissance English Text Society, Seventh Series, 20, 1995), p. 97.

77 *Muld Sacke: Or The Apologie of Hic Mulier* (London, 1620), reprinted with an introduction by Barbara J. Baines (ed.), *Three Pamphlets on the Jacobean Antifeminist Controversy* (Delmar, 1978), unpaginated.

78 Ibid., C.

79 William Harrison, *Description*, p. 145.

80 Ibid., p. 146.

81 Keith Wrightson and David Levine, *Poverty and Piety in an English Village: Terling, 1525–1700* (Oxford, 1995), pp. 38–9; Mildred Campbell, *The English Yeoman under Elizabeth and the Early Stuarts* (New Haven, 1942), pp. 253–5 on rural conservatism but also for signs of wealthy yeomen dressing like gentry by the 1650s. On household budgets for workers see Carole Shammas, *The Pre-Industrial Consumer in England and America* (Oxford, 1990), pp. 145–8.

but fashionable dress was of little or no interest among the community of yeomen and labourers with an income that was insufficient to indulge a taste for costly apparel and accessories.

Consequently, the country market was diffuse and dispersed. It was composed of an amalgam of landowners and gentry, and a modest number of urban elites in larger towns, such as Norwich, Bristol and York. At various points of contact this market overlapped with the court and city. Wealthy magnates and gentlemen who were members of the court, or closely associated with it, shared an indulgence towards conspicuous consumption, informed by new styles in dress and headwear. Appointed to a diplomatic mission to Germany in 1603, Lord Robert Spencer drew up a list of necessary accessories which included two beaver hats. One of his daughters, Margaret, regularly visited London between 1610 and 1613, purchasing fashionable wares, including a white beaver and band for £3.[82] During the late sixteenth and early seventeenth centuries some landowners spent between £1,000 and £3,000 annually on their wardrobes, providing a broader base for the expansion of demand.[83] Under these conditions the market rested on a widespread and fragmented pattern of consumption. The volume of acquisitions, with some notable exceptions, was probably modest. While the social and cultural world of the country house furnished opportunities for public display and self-presentation, it was in a confined setting. In some cases, the audience for fashion and consumption was small, possibly less discriminating and lacking in consumer experience compared with the court or city. Nonetheless the country provided opportunities for social gatherings, recreation and entertainment, and for the promotion of fashionable wear. The cultural appeal of fashion might even be detected in such solitary activities as fishing, recommended to gentlemen as an opportunity for contemplation and reflection. The title page of John Dennys' *Secrets of Angling*, of 1613, portrayed a successful gentleman-angler, well dressed and wearing a fashionable, high-crowned hat embellished with a fancy plume.[84]

Communication was vital to the spread of fashion beyond London. Landowners who lacked regular access to the court or city relied on relatives or close associates for information on changes to dress and appearance. Serving

[82] Peck, *Consuming Splendor*, pp. 28–9, 69.

[83] Lawrence Stone, *The Crisis of the Aristocracy 1558–1641* (Oxford, 1965), pp. 185, 565; Felicity Heal and Clive Holmes, *The Gentry in England and Wales, 1500–1700* (London, 1994), p. 316; Breward, *Culture of Fashion*, pp. 52, 59.

[84] Marcia Vale, *The Gentleman's Recreations: Accomplishments and Pastimes of the English Gentleman 1580–1630* (Cambridge, 1977), pp. 52–4; Susan North, '"Galloon, Incle and Points": Fashionable Dress and Accessories in Rural England, 1552–1665', in Richard Jones and Christopher Dyer (eds.), *Farmers, Consumers, Innovators: The World of Joan Thirsk* (Hatfield, 2016), pp. 119–21 on the availability of fashionable clothing beyond London.

as a spur to demand and consumption in the country, correspondents in the city also acted as agents for the purchase of clothing and accessories. Philip Gawdy, a younger son of a landed family in Norfolk, who moved to London, maintained a regular correspondence with his kin. During the 1580s and 1590s he included news of the city and the court, which he attended, as well as reports on the latest fashion, and details of the clothes he purchased for his brother and sister-in-law. A discriminating observer and consumer, in 1587 Gawdy provided the latter with details of the new fashion in gowns at court. Although he reported no change to headwear, two years later styles were changing.[85] From 1587 to 1604 he acquired at least four hats for his wealthier brother, as well as other wares, including lace, buttons and velvet. Writing to his brother in 1597, Gawdy reassuringly expressed his concern to take account of the latest style, choosing articles 'as waryly and well as a theife at the gallowes wold keep himself from hanging'.[86] On another occasion, in despatching a parcel of clothes, he sent a covering letter to explain that if 'anythinge be amysse or not altogether answerable to your sweetest humore blame not mee but Judas that carryeth the bagg'.[87] As some of the correspondence implies, this family network of news and fashion did not always work smoothly. Early in 1604 he informed his brother that he had ordered a hat for him, but was awaiting money to pay for it. Later in the year he purchased three specially prepared feathers, but they were stolen before they could be packed up in a trunk.[88]

A similar correspondence was maintained between Sir Hugh Smyth, one of the largest landowners in north Somerset, and his godson, Stephen Smith, in London. With the wealth to indulge his passion for fashion, as a younger man Smyth relied on the latter for news and information about changes to clothing. He also used him as an agent with his tailor. Acting on his godfather's instructions, Smith purchased clothes and other wares, arranged credit, exchanged goods and advised on current styles. In June 1620 he sent a cassock and canvas doublet, 'now much in request', down to Long Ashton in Somerset.[89] The doublet was only fit for summer, but it was 'buttoned … according to the fashion now in request, [and] is not only suitable to your scarlet hose but will agree as well with any other cloath hose you have'.[90] Several days later he despatched a pair of hangers of the latest style, and 'such as are now

85 Isaac Herbert Jeayes (ed.), *Letters of Philip Gawdy of West Harling, Norfolk, and of London to Various Members of His Family 1579–1616* (Publications of The Roxburghe Club, London, 1906), pp. 28, 34–5, 49.

86 Ibid., pp. 92–3, 97, 101–3.

87 Ibid., p. 80.

88 Ibid., pp. 140, 148; Linthicum, *Costume in the Drama of Shakespeare*, pp. 174–5, 193, 233.

89 Bettey (ed.), *Correspondence of the Smyth Family*, pp. 54, 56.

90 Ibid., pp. 54–5.

in use by men of the best fashion'.[91] Trusting his judgement, Smyth left the choice of a new beaver hat to his godson. In July 1620 he sent 'one as good and fashionable as my credit cold procure', but on condition that his money would be returned if it did not fit.[92] He also advised Smyth of their recent increase in price.[93]

Correspondence ranged beyond England, widening the market for fashionable dress. In January 1635 Sir John Clotworthy, a wealthy English planter in county Antrim, Ulster, requested a 'bever hatt of the best sort' from his friend, John Winthrop the younger, whose father, the governor of the recently established Massachusetts Bay colony, was developing the fur trade in New England.[94] Unusually Clotworthy asked Winthrop, who was on a brief visit to Ireland and England, to 'bestow a word' on an associate, a skinner, for a beaver coat, specifying that it 'bee made very large, and to the length of the calfe of the leg'.[95]

Such personal links bound together fashionable consumers in the court, city and country, strengthening domestic demand, alongside the emergence of overseas markets, including new colonial settlements in North America and the Caribbean. In 1611 George Percy, one of the leaders of Jamestown and brother of the earl of Northumberland, received an assortment of fine clothing, including a Dutch beaver hat, at a cost of £2 16 shillings, which was needed to maintain his status in the colony.[96] John Pory's complaint from Virginia, of 1619, about the wife of a collier from Croydon who wore a rough beaver hat with a pearl band, suggests the impact of fashion in colonial markets, while indicating the availability of cruder versions.[97] An inventory of John Winthrop's estate in Massachusetts of 1649 included an old beaver hat, valued at five shillings.[98] Before the 1660s, however, the development of overseas outlets for beaver hats was limited. The London customs accounts for 1640, though incomplete, record the export of very small numbers to scattered markets, including two to Leghorn in the Mediterranean, six to Hamburg and 15 to Barbados.[99] Yet there was potential for future growth. During the year

91 Ibid., p. 55. A hanger was an accessory that attached the sword to a belt or girdle.

92 Ibid., pp. xvi–xvii, 56.

93 Ibid., p. 56; Peck, *Consuming Splendor*, pp. 39–42 argues that these connections contributed to the growth of a national market in luxury goods.

94 *Winthrop Papers*, 5 vols. (Massachusetts Historical Society, 1929–47), 3, p. 187.

95 Ibid., p. 187.

96 John W. Shirley, 'George Percy at Jamestown, 1607–1612', *VMHB*, 57 (1949), pp. 239–40.

97 *RVC*, 3, p. 221.

98 *Winthrop Papers*, 5, p. 334.

99 TNA, E190/43/1.

from Michaelmas 1662 to Michaelmas 1663, approximately 97 dozen beaver hats, valued at £2,328, were exported from London.[100]

Despite the varied evidence for the growing appeal of the beaver hat, it is difficult to translate this material into convincing estimates for annual rates of consumption. Purchasing patterns differed widely, reflecting wealth, status, and life-cycle. The high price of headwear set limits to the expansion of the market. Inventories and wills from different parts of the country indicate that well-off yeomen and some gentlemen died with estates in which apparel and accessories were valued at £10 or less.[101] For most of the population the acquisition of fur hats was almost an unattainable luxury. As a valuable accessory, moreover, beavers circulated as gifts and bequests. Daniel Hopkinson, a merchant who died during a trading venture to Virginia in 1636, bequeathed seven, which may have been part of a parcel of trade goods he had with him, to members of his family.[102] For some the purchase of such garments may have been a prudent investment in appearance, though consumption was affected by the availability of cheaper imitations, which many consumers were unable to distinguish from the genuine article.

The Beavermakers: craft, competition and control

Domestic demand was sufficient to support the establishment of the manufacture of beaver hats in London during the late sixteenth and early seventeenth centuries. The new industry grew as part of the wider economic response to the spread of consumption. It attracted the interest of feltmakers and traders, as well as projectors keen to exploit the advantages of an expanding and inexperienced market which presented profitable opportunities. In these circumstances the early development of the industry was marked by intense competition, conflicts of interest and jurisdiction, and concern over craft regulation and quality.

The manufacture of beaver hats was a highly skilled and specialized craft. As a process it relied on old and new methods, based on the well-established

[100] Exports included 844 dozen castor hats, Joan Thirsk, *Economic Policy and Projects: The Development of a Consumer Society in Early Modern England* (Oxford, 1978), p. 187. Exports of demi-castors to Maryland during 1664 are listed in TNA, E190/50/1. For later figures see Diana de Marley, *Dress in North America, volume I: The New World, 1492–1800* (New York, 1990), pp. 182–6.

[101] Todd Gray (ed.), *Devon Household Accounts, 1627–59*, 2 vols. (Devon & Cornwall Record Society, New Series, 38–9, 1995–6), 2, p. 158 and *HMC Twelfth Report*, 1, p. 245 for prices; J.A. Atkinson (ed.), *Darlington Wills and Inventories 1600–1625* (Surtees Society, 201, 1993), pp. 163, 179, 190, 198 for examples of estates.

[102] Martha W. Hiden (ed.), 'Accompts of the Tristram and Jane', *VMHB*, 62 (1954), pp. 434–5.

craft of felting and the introduction of overseas expertise and knowledge, and demanded a lengthy apprenticeship. The industry developed in workshops in the city of London and across the river in Southwark. It required technical competence and an ability to work with beaver wool, a scarce raw material that was little known to most craftsmen employed in the making of headwear. If feltmakers were to respond to changes in the market, therefore, they needed new and reliable supplies of beaver skins and an understanding of their peculiar qualities.

The disappearance of the beaver in the British Isles and much of Western Europe left Russia as the most important source of fur during the late sixteenth century. Indeed, the opening up and colonization of fur-rich regions in Siberia might have compensated for the declining resource in the west. As merchants and shippers discovered, trade with Russia was difficult, vulnerable to international rivalry and disrupted by war and diplomacy. In England, control of the new trade was in the hands of the Muscovy Company, established in 1553 with a monopoly over northern trades. Despite instructions to its agents in 1557 to limit shipments of furs, because there was no profit to be gained from them, they became one of the staples of the trade, alongside wax, cordage and tallow.[103] Periodically the company complained of their quality and high prices. It was also concerned at the persistence of a private trade by sailors, claiming in 1566 that they brought back better furs than the merchants. Responding to recent changes in the market, though unsure of its precise requirements, the company requested its agent to acquire supplies of a wool which was very good material for hats and felts.[104] Thereafter varying amounts of beaver, identified as wool, bellies and backs, were imported on its behalf. During 1587 this included 900 beaver bellies and 120 backs. The following year, in addition to 160 bellies and 80 backs, 20 pounds of wool were imported. In 1589 a private trader shipped a consignment of goods which included 50 pounds of wool.[105] But the volume of trade was modest and irregular, subject to the vagaries of state control in Russia and the growth of competition with France. Capitalizing on these problems, in 1620 the Virginia Company claimed that furs which English merchants 'draw from *Russia* with so great difficulty, are to be had in *Virginia* and the parts adjoining, with ease and plenty'.[106]

The acquisition of beaver skins was the first step in an extensive procedure of production involving skilled technique, judgement and the use of specialist

[103] T.S. Willan, *The Early History of the Russia Company 1553–1603* (Manchester, 1956), pp. 1–8, 31.

[104] Ibid., pp. 31, 39, 78–9.

[105] Ibid., pp. 82, 182–3, 203, 263.

[106] E. Waterhouse, *A Declaration of the State of the Colonie and Affaires in Virginia* (London, 1620), in Force, 3, number 5, p. 4; Murray G. Lawson, *Fur: A Study in English Mercantilism 1700–1775* (Toronto, 1943), pp. 1–3.

tools and equipment. In 1666 Robert Hooke, scientist and curator of experiments at the recently established Royal Society, gave a lecture on the feltmaker's trade which described a lengthy and labour-intensive process, though his use of craft terminology to explain the different stages of bowing, planking and blocking may have puzzled rather than enlightened some of his audience. Although Hooke was concerned with the practices and procedures involved in making woollen felts, they were similar to the new craft of beavermaking.[107]

The process rested on several interlinked stages. It began with the preparation of the fur for felting. As in other parts of Western Europe the industry faced a technical problem that was not easy to resolve. The difficulty lay in an inability to remove the fine undercoat of wool that beavers grew during winter, and whose barbs made it excellent for felting, without damaging the skin and a top coat of longer guard hairs. The short-term remedy, adopted by the French was to re-export beaver skins to Russia, where craftsmen were able to comb out the wool for felting without damaging the rest of the pelt. It was subsequently used by the Hudson's Bay Company, following a huge increase in the volume of trade from Canada, though the practice can be detected as early as 1640, with the export of at least 100 beaver skins from London to Russia.[108]

French traders became aware of a partial resolution to the problem, in the availability of two distinct types of peltry in North America. The first consisted of skins, dried and stretched, but not subject to additional processing or wear by the Indians, which they described as *castor sec*. The second covered skins which were prepared and worn for a period by native people, known as *castor gras*. As a result of human wear, they were soft and greasy in condition, and lacked the guard hairs of unprepared skins, enabling feltmakers to remove the wool by shaving. With more experience of the Indian trade, the English also made a similar distinction, between parchment and coat beaver, as demonstrated by reports from the Bay as early as 1620.[109]

By whatever means, once the woollen fur was removed from the skin, the preliminary procedure involved the creation of batts, compressed and loosely shaped raw material, at least twelve of which were required to make one hat. Working on a table or hurdle, the fur was collected into heaps using a bow,

[107] Rosemary Weinstein, *The History of the Worshipful Company of Feltmakers 1604–2004* (Chichester, 2004), pp. xix–xxii.

[108] TNA, E190/43/1; Rich, *Hudson's Bay Company*, pp. 47–9; Ann M. Carlos and Frank D. Lewis, *Commerce by a Frozen Sea: Native Americans and the European Fur Trade* (Philadelphia, 2010), pp. 19–20.

[109] Rich, *Hudson's Bay Company*, pp. 47–8; Joyce E. Chaplin, *Subject Matter: Technology, the Body, and Science on the Anglo-American Frontier, 1500–1676* (Cambridge, Mass., 2001), p. 147. And see below, pp. 69–70.

the vibrations of which 'make it fly like flakes of snow or froth'.[110] These were pressed down by hand, or batted, reducing a heap of ten or twelve inches of material to two or three inches. Separate batts for different sections of the hat, such as crown, middle and brim, were pressed together over a heated bason, moistened by a piece of damp canvas, for about three hours. This enabled the felt to work and shrink together, while also creating a smooth surface. The batts were regularly checked to detect any thin sections which were reinforced with small locks of material. Folded and tied, they were then boiled in a furnace containing a mixture of water and wine or urine, until the felt was soaked and hot.[111]

This initial stage was followed by a laborious procedure known as planking. The softened material was rolled and pressed on planks for between three and five hours. To undertake this effectively, the feltmaker used cuffs, made of shoe soles and a protective piece of felt, tied to the hands. The material was then repeatedly worked and sprinkled with hot wine lees, to encourage shrinking. By the end of this process, known by craftsmen in the trade as the 'working of a felt', it had shrunk to about a quarter of its original size.[112]

The felt was now ready for blocking and the finishing stages. Differences in the height of crowns and the width of brims meant that craftsmen needed to be alert to prevailing styles and fashions. Shaped into a cone with a round top, the felt was soaked and softened as it stood like a bowl filled with hot wine lees. The liquid was thrown out and the damp crown was stretched over a block with the use of a stamping iron. It was then rubbed with a pumice stone and cold water to smooth over any rough sections. A mixture of water and flour was applied to stiffen the crown. A closer fit to the block was achieved using the iron and string. With the crown in an upright position, the brim was stretched and pressed. Still tied to the block, the hat was placed in a vat where it was soaked in dye for eight to 10 hours. Afterwards it was dried in an oven and left to stand for 10 or 12 hours until dry and stiff.[113] During the final stages, the hat was brushed to get rid of any dust. A smoother surface could be achieved by singeing loose hairs over a flame and rubbing it with blacking. Once dry it was lined and edged, trimmed with a band, and ready for sale.[114]

Hooke's report drew attention to a process defined by a succession of complex stages, demanding skill and expertise, and combining craft with art. Deploying technical ability and judgement, feltmakers were able to display their creative virtuosity, particularly if they worked for the upper and stylish

110 Weinstein, *Company of Feltmakers*, p. xix; Judy Vero, *'A Concern in Trade': Hatting and the Bracebridges of Atherstone, 1612–1872* (Warwick, 1995), pp. 13–18.

111 Weinstein, *Company of Feltmakers*, p. xix.

112 Ibid., pp. xix-xx.

113 Ibid., pp. xx–xxi.

114 Ibid., pp. xxi–xxii.

section of the market. But there was also plenty of opportunity for poor or shoddy workmanship, in addition to the manufacture of cheaper imitations which were sold as genuine beaver hats.[115] Despite efforts to regulate the trade, most consumers would have been unable to detect a deception that was difficult to eradicate.

While the development of beavermaking was grafted onto the feltmaking industry, it benefited from the transfer of overseas knowledge and expertise, especially with the arrival of Protestant refugees from France and Flanders during the second half of the sixteenth century. The Huguenots were prominent in the luxury trade in France, and the skills they brought with them may have been essential to the establishment and concentration of the industry in London. In the city, however, they entered a jealously-guarded and competitive craft. In 1584 the Haberdashers' Company complained about various French men who had set up as hat-makers. The company claimed that the number was so great that 'they can scarce lyve one by another'.[116] It became a familiar refrain, especially during periods of high immigration, such as the later seventeenth century. Yet the newcomers possessed the experience and expertise which enabled them to acquire an important role in the industry. A survey of strangers in London for 1593 listed 27 hat-makers, many from France and Flanders, who were in charge of substantial businesses. Robert Bafoire, originally from Falaise in Normandy, for example, maintained ten journeymen and two apprentices, as well as 12 servants in his workshop.[117]

The new industry grew rapidly, albeit from a small base. It was organized in workshops of varying size under the direction of a master craftsman, which included journeymen who had served their time, apprentices and servants or boys. There may have been problems with unregulated labour and piece work, though these were more of an issue later in the seventeenth century.[118] But the assimilation of the industry into the guild structure of London provoked serious rivalry and competition. These problems were aggravated by long-standing divisions within the fur industry between craft and mercantile interests.[119] At

115 The practice of mixing beaver and rabbit or sheep wool persisted throughout the century, Corner, 'Tyranny of Fashion', p. 155.

116 Guildhall Library, London, MS 15842/1, f.8. On the importance of the Huguenots see J.F. Crean, 'Hats and the Fur Trade', *Canadian Journal of Economics and Political Science*, 28 (1962), p. 279.

117 Irene Scouloudi (ed.), *Returns of Strangers in the Metropolis 1593, 1627, 1635, 1639: A Study of an Active Minority* (Huguenot Society of London, Quarto Series, 57, 1985), pp. 131, 138, 148, 160, 180, 220; Lawson, *Fur*, pp. 6–8, 138, 148.

118 See below, p. 118.

119 Veale, *Fur Trade*, pp. 39–40, 190–1, 196–204; George Unwin, *Industrial Organization in the Sixteenth and Seventeenth Centuries* (London, 2nd edition, 1963), pp. 132–3.

the same time, a growing number of mercers and haberdashers acquired a significant stake in the import of fur goods, including hats, and their marketing and sale in the city. Under these conditions, during the late sixteenth century the Haberdashers' Company attempted to control the development of beaver-making. They were thwarted by the establishment of the Feltmakers' Company in 1604. The new body assumed responsibility for regulating the manufacture of beaver hats.[120]

Corporate regulation was unable to prevent widespread abuses. In March 1630 several haberdashers were accused of providing gentlemen with new hats, which were subsequently returned and sold 'as never worne'.[121] The Haberdashers tried to stamp out such practices, but it remained easy for unscrupulous craftsmen or retailers to dress up second-hand stock as new. Complaints against 'corrupt mixtures, false workmanship, and vending old for new' were voiced in 1636.[122] Two years later the Privy Council prohibited the manufacture of demi-castors for the domestic market.[123] In 1639 the prohibition was extended to overseas markets in response to complaints from the Muscovy Company. Nonetheless, the following year Andrew Arnold and five others were summoned before the Court of Star Chamber to answer accusations regarding the manufacture of false or corrupt beavers.[124]

Complaints concerning quality were accompanied by allegations of price rigging. When the cost of beaver hats doubled during the early 1630s, the Privy Council blamed the increase on a combination of merchants, whose control of the trade allowed them to raise prices with the connivance of beavermakers and haberdashers.[125] But the council's intervention had a limited impact. It was also overshadowed by the pressing fiscal priorities of the monarchy. In May 1638 the crown authorized a levy of 12 pence on every beaver hat and cap made by the recently established Beavermakers' Company. Its collection, which was passed on to consumers, was awarded to Sir David Cunningham, the receiver-general of the Prince of Wales' revenue, for an annual rent of £500.[126]

[120] Unwin, *Industrial Organization*, pp. 79, 127–8, 135–6; Harry Duckworth, *The Early History of Feltmaking in London 1250–1604*, www.feltmakers.co.uk/our-history, pp. 25–32.

[121] Guildhall Library, London, MS 15842/1, ff.260–260v.

[122] James F. Larkin (ed.), *Stuart Royal Proclamations Volume II: Royal Proclamations of King Charles I, 1625–1646* (Oxford, 1983), p. 615; *CSPD, 1636–7*, pp. 65–6.

[123] TNA, PC 2/41, f.420.

[124] Larkin (ed.), *Proclamations*, pp. 613–8, 694–7; *CSPD, 1639–40*, p. 414; Sharpe, *Personal Rule*, p. 248.

[125] TNA, PC 2/41, f.420; 2/43, f.444.

[126] *CSPD, 1637–8*, p. 392. Cunningham acted as the 'chief advocate' of the new company at court, Robert Ashton, *The City and the Court 1603–1643* (Cambridge,

Discontent at quality and prices exposed the teething problems of a new, expanding and profitable industry, which left it vulnerable to the regulatory and financial ambitions of a regime desperately seeking new sources of revenue. In 1638 the crown defended its attempt to regulate the trade as a means of combating abuse and deception.[127] It also authorized the establishment of the Beavermakers, incorporated in February 1639, which included a group of feltmakers who were suppliers to the court. The new company, which met at Laramores Hall in Shoe Lane, was granted a monopoly of the manufacture of beaver hats and caps. Its position was reinforced by a prohibition on the import of foreign-made headwear, but it provoked strong opposition. The Feltmakers complained that some of its wealthiest members had joined it.[128] Yet royal intervention was short-lived. Following the collapse of the personal monarchy, the Beavermakers' rivals took advantage of the political crisis to petition parliament, following which the guild's charter was annulled. Although the Feltmakers tried to assert its authority over the industry, it met with mixed success during the 1640s and 1650s, when many hat-makers appear to have operated on their own initiative.

Despite these early difficulties, a flourishing beavermaking industry emerged in London during the early seventeenth century. It was based on the domestic market, and benefited from royal protection. By the 1620s English craftsmen may have been in a position to compete with the French, at least for some types of headwear. In 1629 the Venetian ambassador in Paris asked his counterpart in London to send him a cap of beaver skin, in the French style, because the cost of English hats was less.[129] High prices across the Channel, the result of disruption to the Canadian trade brought about by the English seizure of Quebec, provided a boost to the industry in London and to the trade across the Atlantic. In addition, although corporate rivalry encouraged the spread of abuses in manufacturing and marketing, it may also have allowed the industry to respond more effectively to an expanding market. While craftsmen may have worked directly with consumers for expensive articles of headwear, the growth of retailing, including the emergence of fashionable sites and shops such as the New Exchange, promoted the development of the industry. Within the city, leading practitioners of the craft sought to reinforce regulations covering training and apprenticeship, establishing standards for

1973), p. 75.

[127] Larkin (ed.), *Proclamations*, pp. 613–8, 694–7; George Unwin, *The Gilds and Companies of London* (London, 3rd edition, 1938), pp. 304–9, 320.

[128] TNA, PC 2/48, f.635 and PC 2/50, ff.656–7; Ashton, *City and Court*, pp. 74–6; Unwin, *Industrial Organization*, pp. 145–7.

[129] Allen B. Hinds (ed.), *Calendar of State Papers Relating to English Affairs in the Archives of Venice, Volume 21, 1628–1629* (London, 1916), p. 522.

quality and the use of raw materials, as well as defending their interests against overseas competition.[130]

Unfortunately, the evidence is too fragmentary to estimate the volume of production with precision for this period, though its broad parameters might be suggested. As noted above, an upper limit is provided by Walter Cary's complaint of 1626 regarding expenditure on beaver hats. By contrast a lower limit might be established from the rent of the duty on the sale of hats, which was set at £500 in 1638. This would suggest that annual production ranged from at least 10,000 to 65,000 or even 130,000 hats.[131] Given the degree of exaggeration in the latter, the actual amount probably lay closer to the lower limit, possibly within a range of between 10,000 and 15,000. This crude estimate confirms the rapid, though uncertain growth of beavermaking. It also suggests that demand may have outstripped supply, particularly with wide fluctuations in the volume of imports of beaver skins from North America. This conjecture receives some support from the cost of raw materials in the London fur market. In 1632 Thomas Morton, a colonial adventurer and merchant who was interested in the New England trade, claimed that beaver was the 'best merchantable commodity that can be found'.[132]

Trade served as a dynamo for the pioneering phase of English transatlantic enterprise. With limited state support, the interplay between fur and fashion fuelled the search for new supplies of beaver skins in North America. As this chapter demonstrates, commerce, consumption and craft development combined to furnish one strand of the architecture for an enterprise connecting native American suppliers with European consumers. In effect the character and structure of the market for fashionable headwear shaped the early development of the transatlantic trade. But the counterpoint to this domestic infrastructure had to be established across the Atlantic, within small and struggling colonial settlements, where English commercial ambitions depended on native hunters, traders and middlemen. The development of these connections, part of a wider complex of cross-cultural communication, raised profound questions about the nature and purpose of English overseas expansion.

130 Although the industry was concentrated in London, by 1649 there was at least one beaver feltmaker, William Harris, in Dublin, Henry F. Berry, 'The Records of the Feltmakers' Company of Dublin, 1687–1841: Their Loss and Recovery', *The Journal of the Royal Society of Antiquaries of Ireland*, 1 (1911), p. 28.

131 Based on figures from Cary, *Present State of England*, pp. 3, 10, 12–13.

132 Charles Francis Adams (ed.), *New English Canaan of Thomas Morton* (The Prince Society, 14, 1883), p. 205.

Chapter 2

Commerce and Colonization: The Emergence of the Fur Trade in Chesapeake Bay

Richard Hakluyt the younger was one of the first English commentators to draw attention to the value of the fur trade in North America for commercial and colonial expansion. A clergyman, Hakluyt devoted his career to collecting and publishing accounts of English voyages in an attempt to promote colonization with the support of the monarchy. In 1583 he was sent to Paris by Sir Francis Walsingham, Queen Elizabeth's Secretary, to acquire information on French activity in the New World while serving as chaplain in the residency of the ambassador. During a mission of nine months Hakluyt met merchants and seafarers, providing Walsingham with up-to-date reports on French enterprise. Shortly after his return to London he completed 'The Discourse of Western Planting', a confidential document for the queen and a small group of prominent supporters of American colonization, in which he noted the great quantity of furs available in the gulf of the St Lawrence River.[1] Embroidering eye-witness reportage, Hakluyt portrayed North America as a vast cornucopia, rich with precious metals and stones, spices and drugs, dyes, all kinds of fruits, timber and fish, as well as a multitude of animals that could provide tallow and hides.[2] Here was a land that could compensate England for declining trades in Europe, so long as adventurers were prepared to face hostility from the French and others.[3]

Despite Hakluyt's clarion call for action, English ambitions and enterprise faltered, while French adventurers, responding to the demand for fur in Paris, established an extensive trading network along the St Lawrence. Nonetheless, during a pioneering phase of episodic English overseas expansion, fishermen, traders and settlers developed widespread interests in the trade in beaver skins. At various locations along the eastern seaboard of North America they established small, impermanent and shifting commercial sites, in competition with French and Dutch adventurers. It was an intermittent enterprise, conducted in fleeting, sometimes suspicious, cross-cultural exchanges, which drew various

1 Hakluyt, *Discourse of Western Planting*, pp. 27, 142, 197.
2 Ibid., p. 27.
3 Ibid., p. 27.

Indian groups, eager to acquire trade goods, into contact with Europeans in search of furs. Although the commercial zones that emerged during the late sixteenth and early seventeenth centuries were little more than pinpricks in a vast and unknown continent, they created beachheads for the growth of trade and, in some cases, settlement. Serving as funnels for the introduction into Indian society of new commodities and technologies, they fuelled native desires, but at the risk of social and cultural disruption. At the same time, they acted as entry points for the spread of disease among vulnerable Indian groups. Through intermediaries and middlemen, cross-cultural exchange outran direct contact between natives and newcomers, influencing commercial and diplomatic relations across a wider area.

For the English these trading initiatives ran parallel with the establishment of colonial settlements. Left in the hands of private enterprise, with limited royal support and supervision, small, scattered outposts were implanted along the eastern seaboard from the 1580s to the 1620s. Some, such as Sir Walter Raleigh's settlement of Roanoke, were short-lived. Most struggled to survive under difficult conditions which, as in the case of Jamestown in Chesapeake Bay, included increasing levels of violence and conflict. Collectively, they exposed severe weaknesses in planning, organization and support. But this first wave of the English intrusion into North America was an uncoordinated, improvised process of trial and error, sustained by mixed motives and ambitions. Even in the 1620s it was very much work in progress, as colonial adventurers struggled to give shape to transatlantic settlement and commerce. English enterprise, especially in the Chesapeake, acquired an undercurrent of tension, exposing the potential contradiction between interethnic commerce and colonial planting. Under the auspices of the Virginia Company, early interest in the fur trade was spasmodic, insecurely rooted and overshadowed by the struggle for survival which focused attention on the supply of food.[4] Alert to the success of the French farther north, however, the company made serious attempts to explore the economic potential of the trade in the Bay. Its dissolution in 1624 paved the way for the establishment of more ambitious transatlantic schemes designed to develop commercial enterprise within the region, where competition and rivalry were the driving force for growth. As the outline of a rudimentary economy emerged in Virginia, the integration of trade and settlement, while holding out lucrative opportunities, provoked serious issues regarding the status of native groups. This chapter focuses on English reconnoitring, against a hazardous and hostile background, for commercial openings in the Bay, as the encounter between settlers and natives tested the limits of understanding and the capacity of both groups for cross-cultural

4 For recent discussions of the early years see Kupperman, *The Jamestown Project*, pp. 210–67; Bailyn, *The Barbarous Years*, pp. 49–80.

exchange, creating a pattern of enterprise in which trade, diplomacy and conflict were intermingled.

Native worlds: politics, rivalry and exchange

On the eve of the English intrusion, the native worlds of the Bay region were characterized by disturbing change and instability, the result of challenging conditions that included alterations in the climate, as well as fragile political alliances, diplomatic rivalries and conflict.[5] The resilience of Indian groups concealed points of tension or fault lines that affected key aspects of native politics, external relations and systems of exchange. Such conditions may not have made the inhabitants of the region vulnerable to European colonization, unlike some other groups elsewhere, but their interaction framed early contact and commerce with the English, enabling a small band of settlers to establish a foothold in the lower reaches of the Bay.

It took the English some time to become alert to these opportunities, though early reporters were bewitched by the Bay and its natural abundance. It was a region 'as God made it', a 'place beautified by God, with all the ornaments of nature, and enriched with his earthly treasures'.[6] Insisting that the land was 'little planted, manured, or improved', newcomers were ravished by 'the Beauties of naked Nature'.[7] While allowing for promotional rhetoric, the Bay provided the native inhabitants with the ecological and cultural resources for subsistence, and the development of effective social systems based on locally defined life-cycles, under the canopy of complex spiritual beliefs and practices.

The physical environment sustained human habitation across an extensive region. The Bay contained a rich concentration of marine life, including shell fish, especially blue crab and oyster, and large numbers of local and migratory fish, such as herring, shad and striped bass. At the margin between land and sea, marshland provided the habitat for ducks, curlews, herons and woodcocks. Streams and rivers created feeding grounds for otter, muskrat and beaver. Fertile soil along their banks provided locations for human settlement and potential sites of conflict between natives and intruders. In the surrounding watershed, mixed forests of oak, cedar and cypress protected plants and wild

5 White, *A Cold Welcome*, pp. 121–5.

6 William Stith, *The History of the First Discovery and Settlement of Virginia* (Williamsburg, 1747, repr. Spartanburg, 1965), p. 45; Alexander Whitaker, *Good Newes from Virginia* (London, 1613), p. 37; Smith, *Works*, 1, p. 257.

7 H.R. McIlwaine (ed.), *Journals of the House of Burgesses of Virginia 1619–1658/59* (Richmond, 1915), p. 38; Edward Williams, *Virginia: More Especially the South Part thereof, Richly and Truly Valued* (London, 1650), in Force, 3, No. 11, p. 27; Smith, *Works*, I, p. 45; Beverley, *History of Virginia*, p. 298.

fruits, and supported large herds of deer and other animals including turkey, raccoon, squirrel and bear.[8]

Within the wider context of the eastern woodlands abundant resources of game sustained a versatile hunting culture that was fundamental to native identities, though it varied between its northern and southern limits according to ecology and climate. Among the faunal resources of the Bay, the Indians relied on deer as their primary prey. They were available in considerable number, providing native groups with a supply of food, high in protein, as well as the raw material for clothing, footwear, tools and weapons. For Indians farther north, as Marc Lescarbot, a French visitor to New France, pointed out, beaver took the place of deer.[9] Hunted extensively, probably even before the arrival of Europeans, the beaver furnished natives with a valuable commodity for trade and gift-giving, which was intensified by the arrival of French traders. Its fur, thicker and richer in quality than those farther south, was essential material for native clothing, providing protection and warmth during long, cold winters. Beaver teeth were useful tools for working with wood. Furthermore, it was a nutritious food, of which the tail was prized as the best and most delicate part. Within the hunting culture of the northern Indians, the fur of beavers and other animals were 'all their riches'.[10] But Lescarbot's claim that they were unavailable in Virginia and Florida, where native groups did not rely on fur for dress, owing to the hotter climate, was misleading.[11] Beavers inhabited the streams and wetlands of the Chesapeake region, and fur, sometimes identified as otter by English reporters, was used in mantles or cloaks for winter, and as ceremonial dress by chiefs. But its use in native dress regimes was qualified by the ready availability of deer.

Collectively the natural resources of the region may have supported a native population of about 30,000 around the Bay. Recent studies indicate that the lifestyles and material culture of these people were closely attuned to the use and exploitation of the environment. By the time of the English arrival, native groups had established an adaptable economy and life-cycle based on farming, fishing, foraging and hunting. They cultivated maize and beans, as well as squash, pumpkins and sunflowers in large fields, surrounding open or enclosed

8 J.R. Schubel, *The Living Chesapeake* (Baltimore, 1981), pp. 12, 17–18, 20–5, 28; Stephen R. Potter, *Commoners, Tribute, and Chiefs: The Development of Algonquian Culture in the Potomac Valley* (Charlottesville, 1993), pp. 7–8, 75, 138–9; David Hackett Fischer, *Albion's Seed: Four British Folkways in America* (New York, 1989), pp. 247–52.

9 Marc Lescarbot, *Novia Francia: A Description of Acadia, 1606*, translated by P. Erondelle, 1609 (London, 1928), p. 273.

10 Ibid., pp. 262, 271–3; James Pritchard, *In Search of Empire: The French in the Americas, 1670–1730* (Cambridge, 2004), p. 155.

11 Lescarbot, *Novia Francia*, pp. 274–5.

habitations. The woodland was used for foraging and hunting, while the rivers and Bay provided a plentiful, if seasonal, fishery. This mixed economy rested on a delicate balance between feast and famine, especially during late winter and early spring when corn granaries and the stock of fish were low. Such a life-cycle was vulnerable to new arrivals in search of their own food supply, particularly if crop yields were affected by extensive periods of drought, as during the late 1580s and the period from 1606 to 1612.[12]

As noted by the English, sometimes disparagingly, the division of labour which grew up around this cycle was gender-based and supported by a well-established material culture. While women were responsible for the domestic economy, and played an important role in hospitality and entertainment, they were heavily involved in agriculture, cultivating and tending crops. Men assisted in some of this work, but their main roles lay in hunting and fishing. Hunting was a vital part of native culture, in which prowess conferred status and helped to promote and define masculinity. As in other parts of the eastern woodlands it was linked with ritual and religious ceremonial.[13] The English, who came from a world where deer hunting was a sport reserved for gentlemen, were fascinated by Indian hunting methods. Henry Spelman, a young settler who lived with a native group from 1609 to 1610, described how large numbers of deer were forced into an enclosed space, by setting fire to surrounding thickets, where they were killed, primarily for their skins, with bows and arrows.[14]

Native groups developed a material culture finely attuned to the Bay setting. English observers tended to emphasize its limitations, exaggerating a superior self-image that fuelled belief in a mission to bring civility to the

[12] Christian F. Feest, 'Nanticoke and Neighbouring Tribes', in Bruce G. Trigger (ed.), *Handbook of North American Indians, Volume 15: Northeast* (Washington, 1978), pp. 242, 262; Helen C. Rountree, *The Powhatan Indians of Virginia: Their Traditional Culture* (Norman, 1989), p. 15; Helen C. Rountree, *Pocahontas's People: The Powhatan Indians of Virginia Through Four Centuries* (Norman, 1990), pp. 3–14; Rice, 'Escape from Tsenacommacah', pp. 102, 122; Kupperman, *The Jamestown Project*, pp. 163–76.

[13] Axtell, *The Invasion Within*, p. 158; Rountree, *Powhatan Indians*, pp. 38–9, 79. There has been debate over the role of ritual in Indian hunting. Calvin Martin, *Keepers of the Game: Indian-Animal Relationships and the Fur Trade* (Berkeley, 1978), in examining the north east Algonquians argued that the spread of European disease was blamed by Indians on wildlife, promoting over-hunting with improved weapons. The argument has been subject to critique by Shepard Krech III, *The Ecological Indian: Myth and History* (New York, 1999), esp. pp. 200–6 for ritual, on which see also Matthew Dennis, *Cultivating a Landscape of Peace: European Encounters in Seventeenth-Century America* (Ithaca, 1993), pp. 38–40.

[14] Henry Spelman, *Relation of Virginea*, reprinted in E. Arber (ed.), *Travels and Works of Captain John Smith*, 2 vols. (Edinburgh, 1910), 2, p. cvii; Krech, *The Ecological Indian*, p. 170; P. Seed, *American Pentimento: The Invention of Indians and the Pursuit of Riches* (Minneapolis, 2001), pp. 54–5 on attitudes.

Indians through the introduction of Christianity and commerce. The image was clouded and confused by the dependence of the settlers at Jamestown on native supplies of maize, venison and fish. Experience and closer contact furnished greater insight, though not empathy, into Indian lives and culture. Alexander Whitaker, one of the few clergymen in the settlement, insisted that the Indians were 'a very understanding generation, … exquisite in their inventions'.[15] Observers like Whitaker were alert to the technological expertise and capability of their native neighbours, demonstrated, for example, in the construction of substantial canoes. But the elaboration of this material world was constrained by the availability of effective cutting tools. Weapons and other implements were fashioned from stone and wood or shell and bone. Consequently, native groups were eager to acquire metal tools and weapons, including the cheap stuff described by Hakluyt, such as mirrors and bells, from English and other European traders. Native demand was essential for cross-cultural exchange, but it fuelled widespread rivalry for access to new and powerful goods, some of which were imbued with supernatural meaning.[16]

Commercial competition overlaid pre-existing rivalries within the Bay. Politically this was a world of chiefdoms, marked by varying degrees of structural instability. The power of chiefs, or *werowances*, was decentralized, negotiable and a potential source of weakness, particularly given their role in the re-distribution of prestige goods such as copper and shell beads. Internal tensions were compounded with intergroup rivalry over status and tribute, and anxiety over access to resources. With the sanction of religious leaders, these conditions seem to have engendered endemic conflict, raiding and warfare.[17]

As defined by linguistic affiliation, a large combination of Algonquian groups, known to the English as Powhatans, dominated the lower reaches of the Bay. Though straddling an extensive territory, the Powhatan heartland lay between the James and York Rivers, as named by the newcomers. Its northern fringes, along the Potomac River, were inhabited by the Patawomecks, a powerful group, although they were exposed to raiding from across the

15 Whitaker, *Good Newes from Virginia*, p. 25. There was extensive criticism of culture and customs, see Alden T. Vaughan, *Roots of American Racism: Essays on the Colonial Experience* (New York, 1995), pp. 11–13.

16 Rountree, *Powhatan Indians*, p. 32; Rountree, *Pocahontas's People*, p. 67.

17 Frederic W. Gleach, *Powhatan's World and Colonial Virginia: A Conflict of Cultures* (Lincoln, 1997), pp. 28–43; Rice, 'Escape from Tsenacommacah', pp. 97–140; Helen C. Rountree and E. Randolph Turner III, *Before and After Jamestown: Virginia's Powhatans and Their Predecessors* (Gainesville, 2002), pp. 105–10; Marvin D. Jeter, 'Ripe for Colonial Exploitation: Ancient Traditions of Violence and Enmity as Preludes to the Indian Slave Trade', in M. Carocci and S. Pratt (eds.), *Native American Adoption, Captivity, and Slavery in Changing Contexts* (Basingstoke, 2012), pp. 23–9 on the wider role of violence.

river by their rivals, the Piscataways, and others. The Eastern Shore of the Bay was inhabited by various groups, including the Nanticokes, Choptanks, Pocomokes and Accomacks, some of whom recognized the authority of the leader of the Powhatans. Farther up the Bay lay the Tockwoghs and Wicomiss, who may have served as a buffer against incursions by hostile groups of northern Indians.[18]

The Susquehannocks were the source of much of this hostility in the upper Chesapeake. A large and powerful group of Iroquoian background, they migrated south during the sixteenth century to establish a settlement along the Susquehanna River, close to the head of the Bay. Claiming extensive jurisdiction or territory in the region, they were capable of raiding the Potomac, though they were not a direct threat to the heartland of the Powhatans. Beyond the outer limits of the Bay were a group identified as Massawomecks, who were also aggressively seeking to extend their influence in the area. The inland region to the west was inhabited by Monacans and Manahoacs, Siouan groups, whose uneasy relations with the Powhatans may have been part of a wider reaction to interior disruption and unsettlement.[19]

The fluidity of this political configuration was demonstrated by the emergence of the chiefdom under the authority of Wahunsonacock, who the English named Powhatan and described as an emperor. Such paramount chiefdoms appeared elsewhere, the product of long-term pressures and short-term change and contingency. When the English entered the Bay, Powhatan's leadership was recognized by at least 30 different chiefs and their tribes, with a total population of between 13,000 and 15,000. It covered a region within the lower Bay ranging about 100 miles north to south and east to west. Crucially for the newcomers, it was of recent origin and still seemed to be in the process of formation, by a combination of inheritance, war and coercion. Groups who resisted, such as the Chesapeakes, seem to have been destroyed. In these conditions, although the new chiefdom was organized hierarchically, political integration and consolidation were weak and informal.[20]

[18] On the native configuration of the Bay see the contributions in Helen C. Rountree (ed.), *Powhatan Foreign Relations 1500–1722* (Charlottesville, 1993); Potter, *Commoners*, pp. 1–4, 149–52; Trigger (ed.), *Handbook*, pp. 240–2, 363.

[19] Robbie Ethridge, 'The Emergence of the Colonial South: Colonial Indian Slaving, the Fall of the Precontact Mississippian World, and the Emergence of a New Social Geography in the American South, 1540–1730', in Carocci and Pratt (eds.), *Native American Adoption*, pp. 47–54. Rountree and Turner, *Before and After Jamestown*, pp. 40–2. On the Susquehannocks see Barry C. Kent, *Susquehanna's Indians* (Harrisburg, 1989), pp. 21–8; John Witthoft and W. Fred Kinsey III (eds.), *Susquehannock Miscellany* (Harrisburg, 1959), pp. 19, 29–35.

[20] Potter, *Commoners*, p. 164; Rountree, *Powhatan Indians*, pp. 140–2; Horn, *A Land as God Made It*, pp. 11–20; William Strachey, *The Historie of Travell into Virginia*

The creation of this native structure occurred within a context of intergroup rivalries over status, resources and long-distance trade and exchange.[21] Local or regional competition was complicated by external challenges. These included the threat posed by hostile Indian groups from the north and west, and by the alarming maritime incursions of small bands of Europeans. Although limited in number, and usually short-lived, the arrival of newcomers from the sea was disturbing and destabilizing, not least because they served as a vehicle for the introduction of European sickness and disease. The danger was apparent from the experience of the English at Roanoke, farther south along the coast, during the 1580s. Thomas Hariot, the scientist who was a member of the first colony and the author of a report on the land and people, noted the rapid spread of disease in the wake of English visits to native habitations throughout the neighbouring area. Confounding the expertise of native shamans and healers, who claimed that the newcomers were shooting invisible bullets into their victims, Hariot reported that the death toll between settlements ranged from 20 to more than 100, 'which in truth, was very many in respect of their numbers'.[22] Among native groups this was an unprecedented and harrowing experience, apparently contributing to a belief that the English were gods. Distance may only have delayed the spread of infection into the lower reaches of the Bay. Powhatan's reported claim to John Smith, the president of the Jamestown settlement from 1608 to 1609, that he had witnessed the loss of his people no less than three times, suggests a recent and devastating death rate among some native groups.[23]

The impact of depopulation and endemic conflict, combined with the consequences of drought, may have left native groups in turmoil and disarray. This was fertile soil for the creation of the Powhatan chiefdom. But it came at a cost, as indicated by the experience of the Chesapeake Indians. Within this recently established polity, however, where charismatic leadership and face-to-face authority retained their appeal, centralized control was inevitably nuanced

---

Britania, eds. Louis B. Wright and Virginia Freund (Hakluyt Society, Second Series, 103, 1953), pp. 56–7, 105–8.

21 James D. Rice, *Nature & History in the Potomac Country from Hunter-Gatherers to the Age of Jefferson* (Baltimore, 2009), pp. 48–54 on the emergence of chiefdoms.

22 David B. Quinn (ed.), *The Roanoke Voyages, 1585–1590*, 2 vols. (Hakluyt Society, Second Series, 104 & 105, 1955), 1, pp. 378–9; Henry F. Dobyns, *Their Number Become Thinned: Native American Population Dynamics in Eastern North America* (Knoxville, 1983), pp. 277–8.

23 Smith, *Works*, 1, p. 247; Helen C. Rountree and Randolph Turner III, 'On the Fringe of the Southeast: The Paramount Chiefdom in Virginia', in Charles Hudson and Carmen Chaves Tesser (eds.), *The Forgotten Centuries: Indians and Europeans in the American South, 1521–1704* (Athens, 1994), p. 361 argue that there is no firm evidence to indicate a substantial loss of life due to European disease.

and negotiable. Powhatan's power was limited and possibly dependent on his ability to reward loyal followers. It was even weaker in exposed borderland regions, especially along the Potomac River where the Patawomecks retained considerable autonomy.[24] Moreover the conditions in which the chiefdom was assembled left a legacy of disunity and distrust that might be exploited by the unheralded arrival of disruptive newcomers. Officials at Jamestown were soon aware of the opportunities. Smith resorted to divide-and-rule tactics within the chiefdom, while seeking alliances with enemies of its leader among neighbouring groups. At the same time William Strachey, the colony's secretary, argued that recent additions to it might be tempted to withdraw from Powhatan's authority by the promise of rewards, including plentiful supplies of copper.[25]

Gift-giving, as described by Strachey, was part of a wider native network of trade, exchange and tribute. The Bay provided a very favourable environment for intergroup exchange in various goods, including maize and skins, as well as shell beads, copper and pearls which were also levied as tribute by paramount chiefs. The web of trading relations included groups within and beyond the chiefdom, ranging from the Accomacks along the Eastern Shore to the Piscataways across the Potomac River. At the head of the Bay the Susquehanna River served as an important long-distance trading and military pathway, with a catchment area that extended farther north and south.[26] Much of this activity was water-borne. The Bay and the rivers that flowed into it, navigable by flotillas of canoes, provided access to an extensive hinterland. It also kept transportation costs low. The use of native middlemen enabled prestige goods of high symbolic value, especially copper, to be carried over long distances. Such conditions created wide-ranging networks of commerce and diplomacy which blended tribute and gift exchange along well-established native trails.[27] By the early seventeenth century some Indian groups in the upper Bay possessed iron implements, probably acquired from French traders along the St Lawrence, and carried south along the Susquehanna.[28] At the

24 Rice, *Nature & History*, p. 56.

25 Strachey, *Historie of Travel into Virginia*, p. 108; Rice, 'Escape from Tsenacommacah', pp. 121–3.

26 Christian F. Feest, 'Powhatan: A Study in Political Organization', *Wiener Volkerkundliche Mitteilungen*, 13 (1966), pp. 74–9; Daniel K. Richter, *The Ordeal of the Long-house: The Peoples of the Iroquois in the Era of European Colonization* (Chapel Hill, 1992), pp. 48–9.

27 Rice, 'Escape from Tsenacommacah', pp. 115–17; Hatfield, *Atlantic Virginia*, pp. 9–15. Copper came from western Virginia or the Great Lakes region, Rountree and Turner, *Before and After Jamestown*, pp. 133–6.

28 Smith, *Works*, I, p. 231; James F. Pendergast, *The Massawomeck: Raiders and Traders into the Chesapeake Bay in the Seventeenth Century* (Transactions of the

same time, of course, the deadly connection between commerce and contagion turned trade routes into pathways for the transmission of new infections and disease.

Trade may not have enjoyed the same status among native groups as hunting or warfare, but it was valued and varied in function. Lacking the entrepreneurial character and market of English commercial systems, native trade was rooted in gift exchange and barter. Its importance was reflected in the participation of chiefs, and their concern to regulate or control long-distance commerce. The stability and effectiveness of native exchange seemed to rest on the circulation and re-distribution of goods, as part of the rights and responsibilities of leaders. In addition to its economic value, therefore, exchange was embedded in social relations, diplomacy, and politics. An absence of reciprocity might be interpreted in a hostile manner, while mutuality and respect for trading etiquette promoted peaceful relations and alliances.[29]

It is unclear how far trade and exchange ameliorated the prevalence of conflict, raiding and warfare within the Bay. War was an outlet for aggressive male individualism that included ritual torture such as scalping and dismemberment. Success in battle and other acts of aggression enabled leaders to strengthen their authority and status. It also made them ambitious to acquire and control the supply of European weaponry. As an integral feature of native society, war was motivated by honour and revenge, a need to acquire prisoners or slaves, and to a lesser extent by territorial ambition. It played a part in the assembly of the chiefdom, although it left a legacy of resentment among some groups and aroused alarm among neighbouring Indians anxious about their autonomy. Powhatan was unable to control the Chickahominies, who resided within the heartland of his chiefdom, providing outsiders with potential friends and allies.[30] Nonetheless, the conduct and practice of warfare by native groups, employing guerrilla-style tactics, combined with their local knowledge and expertise, gave them some advantage over the English, though

---

American Philosophical Society, 81, 1991), pp. 33–7 argues that European goods were readily available in the Bay prior to 1607, but there is little evidence to support this, see Kupperman, *Indians and English*, p. 38. The French may have contacted the Susquehannocks during 1615 or 1616 in search of an alliance, David Hackett Fischer, *Champlain's Dream* (New York, 2008), p. 328; Francis Jennings, 'Susquehannock', in Trigger (ed.), *Handbook*, p. 365.

29 Strachey, *Historie of Travell into Virginia*, pp. 62, 65–6, 115; Spelman, *Relation of Virginea*, p. cvii; Ralph Hamor, *A True Discourse of the Present State of Virginia* (London, 1615) reprinted with an introduction by A.L. Rowse (Richmond, 1957), pp. 45–6.

30 Strachey, *Historie of Travell into Virginia*, pp. 44, 68–9, 104; Rountree, *Powhatan Indians*, pp. 84–6, 124; Rountree and Turner, *Before and After Jamestown*, pp. 105, 110, 123.

it was increasingly offset by the newcomers' military technology and their unrelenting use of tactics, employed widely in Ireland, of destroying crops and habitations.[31]

Religious belief and practice went some way to offset internal division and dissension. Leaders recognized the power of priests and shamans, who enjoyed high status within native society. Religious leaders invoked a rich spiritual world to support and strengthen the authority of chiefs, while providing reassurance for the wider community. As guardians of the spirit world, its ceremonial and rites of passage, priests played a role in promoting stability and binding groups together. Their authority, at once mysterious and personal, was deployed in speech, gesture and ritual. The English were soon aware of the importance of such figures in the promotion and defence of native culture. Dismissed by some settlers and clergy as agents of the devil, their removal, either by imprisonment or execution, was ordered by the Virginia Company in 1609.[32]

At the time of the English entry into the Bay, native worlds were in an awkward and transitional stage of development. The creation of a paramount chiefdom, with the imposition of tribute, might have pointed towards further political elaboration, which rested on a mixed economy, blending agriculture with foraging and hunting. But these were not self-contained communities, sealed off from disruption and dislocation in more distant regions. Even before the arrival of the English, native groups within the Bay were exposed to the disturbing impact of the Spanish to the south and the French farther north. The recent birth of the chiefdom was thus overshadowed not only by the persistence of internal disunity, but also by new external dangers. These conditions were crucial in enabling the English to establish a small beachhead at Jamestown. Furthermore, the existence of well-established patterns of trade and exchange allowed the newcomers to acquire a niche for themselves in the Chesapeake. Native demand for commodities such as copper, iron tools and weapons, and glass beads, was ultimately uncontrollable. The commercial nexus that linked natives and newcomers was vital to the maintenance of the settlement during its early years. In the longer term it may have been more significant in fuelling commercial rivalries, dependency and depopulation. Facing fresh challenges both from sea and land, the Indians of the Bay region encountered

[31] Nor was the native interplay between raiding and cooperation understood by the colonists, Rountree and Turner, *Before and After Jamestown*, pp. 27, 123; Gleach, *Powhatan's World*, pp. 43–54.

[32] *RVC*, 3, pp. 4, 15; Strachey, *Historie of Travell into Virginia*, p. 91; Samuel Purchas, *Hakluytus Posthumus or Purchas his Pilgrimes*, 20 vols. (Glasgow, 1905–7), 19, p. 110, a reprint of the 1625 edition; Bernard W. Sheehan, *Savagism and Civility: Indians and Englishmen in Colonial Virginia* (Cambridge, 1980), pp. 46–7; Rice, *Nature & History*, pp. 44–5.

an expanding Atlantic world which they struggled to exploit, with enduring and fatal consequences.[33]

The European intrusion: exploration, colonization and commerce

The English were not the first Europeans to enter the Bay, nor, when they did arrive, was this their first foray into transatlantic settlement. But these early intrusions were of mixed consequence for the prospect of cross-cultural trade leaving, in some parts of the region, a disturbing legacy of mistrust and deep suspicion.

The earliest recorded European entry into the Bay, in 1546, was by a French vessel in search of trade and a route to the South Sea. According to one of the company, the expedition encountered a large trading party of natives in 30 canoes, acquiring furs in exchange for knives, fish hooks and shirts.[34] French interest in the Bay was overtaken by more ambitious, but unsuccessful, schemes to establish an outpost in Florida, to prey on Spanish shipping and serve as a sanctuary for refugee Huguenots. Rival European activity galvanized Spain into action. From the 1560s to the 1580s Spanish officials became intermittently concerned with the Bahia de Santa Maria, as they labelled the Chesapeake. An exploratory expedition of 1561, sent out from Florida, gained the assistance of an Indian, who left with the Spanish and was later baptized as Don Luis. Described as the brother of a 'principal chief of that region', he accompanied another expedition in 1566, though it failed to find the entrance into the Bay.[35] A subsequent attempt to establish a mission in the lower reaches of the Bay in 1570 ended disastrously. With the continued, but ambiguous, aid of Don Luis, nine Jesuits set up a mission house at Chiskiac. Following Don Luis's desertion, the mission was attacked and destroyed. A retaliatory raid in 1572 was followed by an expedition in 1588 which carried out an extensive exploration of the Bay, apparently reaching the mouth of the Susquehanna River. During its course two natives were kidnapped, one

33 Richter, 'Tsenacommacah and the Atlantic World' in Mancall (ed.), *The Atlantic World*, pp. 64–5.

34 An earlier European entry cannot be ruled out according to C.M. Lewis and A.J. Loomie, *The Spanish Jesuit Mission in Virginia, 1570–1572* (Chapel Hill, 1953), pp. 5–13; David B. Quinn (ed.), *New American World: A Documentary History of North America to 1612*, 5 vols. (London, 1979), 1, p. 217. The South Sea was commonly used to refer to the Pacific Ocean.

35 Ibid., 2, pp. 417–20, 475, 478, 556; Lewis and Loomie, *Spanish Jesuit Mission*, pp. 15, 61 suggest that Don Luis may have been related to Powhatan; Gleach, *Powhatan's World*, pp. 142–3; Charlotte M. Gradie, 'Spanish Jesuits in Virginia: The Mission that Failed', *VMHB*, 96 (1988), pp. 148–52.

near the Potomac, the other along the Eastern Shore. But an ambitious plan of 1589 to establish a garrison of 300 men in the region was abandoned.[36]

The inability or unwillingness of the French and Spanish to build on these probes and forays effectively left the Bay open for the English to reconnoitre. Their interest in the Chesapeake grew out of a re-focusing of colonial enterprise during Raleigh's unsuccessful attempt to establish a North American outpost. Beginning with an enchanting vision of an American Eden, from 1585 to 1586 the settlement of Roanoke provided a small band of all-male settlers with a harsh lesson in the realities of transatlantic colonization. The venture coincided with the outbreak of war with Spain, and was authorized by a commission from Elizabeth I, in whose honour the colony was named Virginia. But the experience cast a shadow over the value of a coastal base from which to plunder enemy shipping. It also raised questions about the viability of a settlement that depended on its Indian neighbours for supplies of food. The colony survived for one year, under the military leadership of Ralph Lane, until its hasty abandonment in June 1586. Lane's methods alienated the Indians, culminating in violence and conflict, though casualties among the English were limited. On his return to England, Raleigh's agent in the colony, Thomas Hariot, publicly criticized the conduct of some of the settlers for being too fierce.[37]

Raleigh and his partners despatched a second colonizing expedition during 1587 which, partly based on Lane's advice and experience, was intended for Chesapeake Bay. Under the leadership of John White, a member of the first colony, the settlers, 110 in total, included craftsmen, labourers and a small number of women. Unfortunately, they were effectively marooned at Roanoke by mariners more interested in seeking Spanish prizes in the Caribbean. White returned to England at the end of the year to organize a relief expedition, but he was unable to get back to the colony until 1590. He found the site deserted, but there was no evidence to indicate that the settlers had departed under duress. By this stage, however, Raleigh's interest in a failing venture

36 Lewis and Loomie, *Spanish Jesuit Mission*, pp. 21, 55–6, 167, 185–8; Quinn (ed.), *Roanoke Voyages*, 2, pp. 722–5, 806–11; Stephen Adams, *The Best and Worst Country in the World: Perspectives on the Early Virginia Landscape* (Charlottesville, 2001), pp. 60–71. The attack has been explained as the missionaries' misunderstanding or transgression of a native gift economy by Seth Mallios, *The Deadly Politics of Giving: Exchange and Violence at Ajacan, Roanoke, and Jamestown* (Tuscaloosa, 2006), pp. 37, 44–53.

37 Kenneth R. Andrews, *Trade, Plunder and Settlement: Maritime Enterprise and the Genesis of the British Empire, 1480–1630* (Cambridge, 1984), pp. 9, 31, 36–9, 207–8; Quinn (ed.), *Roanoke Voyages*, 1, pp. 245–6, 257, 260–3, 274–5; Michael Leroy Oberg, *The Head in Edward Nugent's Hand: Roanoke's Forgotten Indians* (Philadelphia, 2008), pp. 31–89 for Indian responses.

had drained away. Abandoned to the mercy of the natives, the fate of the 'lost colonists' remains obscure. It is possible that they dispersed to live with friendly native groups, including the Chesapeakes, potentially spreading new diseases among a wider population. By the early seventeenth century stories of their survival were used to bolster English claims to the region on the grounds of prior discovery and settlement.[38]

Roanoke provided the English with their first real test of transatlantic colonization. It exposed serious weaknesses in structure and organization. Hakluyt's bold vision for the expansion of commerce, Christianity and civility seemed stillborn. Yet the legacy was not all negative. Both Hariot and White presented favourable, possibly too flattering, reports on England's first Virginia, diverting attention away from its violent ending. Their work provided colonial advocates with a window onto a new world where the English would be either welcomed or feared. White employed his skill as an artist to produce a striking set of images which masked the daily harshness and violence of native life. Hariot produced a *Brief and True Report of the New Found Land of Virginia* in 1588, reassuring his readers that the Indians were in such awe of 'the strange weapons and devises' of the newcomers that they were not to be feared.[39] The work of both was published by Theodore de Bry, reaching a wider European audience in his multi-volume collection of material on America of 1590.

Yet neither Hariot nor White seemed to make much of the prospect for cross-cultural trade. English settlers provided gifts for native people, illuminated by White's image of an elite woman of Pomeioc with her young daughter holding a doll and rattle in either hand. The accompanying text indicated that the Indians were delighted with such 'puppetts and babes'.[40] Despite their sensitivity and insight, however, these two reporters on Roanoke struggled to provide a convincing or coherent representation of the natives as trading partners. Hariot's summary of the commodities of the region

38 David Beers Quinn, *Set Fair for Roanoke: Voyages and Colonies, 1584–1606* (Chapel Hill, 1985), pp. 342–75; John Parker, *Van Meteren's Virginia 1607–1612* (Minneapolis, 1961), p. 58; Michael Leroy Oberg, 'Lost Colonists and Lost Tribes', in Kim Sloan (ed.), *European Visions: American Voices* (London, 2009), pp. 102–3; *RVC*, 3, p. 17; Mary C. Fuller, 'Images of English Origins in Newfoundland and Roanoke' in Warkentin and Podruchy (eds.), *Decentring the Renaissance*, pp. 143–6.

39 Quinn (ed.), *Roanoke Voyages*, 1, pp. 460–2, 493–4; Michael Householder, *Inventing Americans in the Age of Discovery: Narratives of Encounter* (Farnham, 2011), pp. 120–3; Shannon Miller, *Invested with Meaning: The Raleigh Circle in the New World* (Philadelphia 1998), pp. 136–49.

40 Theodor de Bry, *Thomas Hariot's Virginia* (Ann Arbor, 1966), unpaginated, plate VIII; Householder, *Inventing Americans*, pp. 119–20.

included reference to furs, though he noted that only two skins were acquired during the year.[41]

Undeterred, Hakluyt drew on the experience of both Roanoke ventures to argue that the best prospect for future settlement lay around Chesapeake Bay. He provided the English with a name for the region in his *Principall Navigations* of 1589, referring to 'Chesepiok' as a 'towne & great bay in Virginia so called by the Savages'.[42] The re-direction of Hakluyt's vision was reinforced by claims, based on Hariot's *Report*, of rich silver mines in the country.

Sixty years after the French incursion, the first English colonizing expedition entered the Bay. It carried a small party of just over 100 men and boys, with instructions from the Virginia Company of London for the establishment of a settlement at a defensible and fertile location along a navigable river. With support from the city, court and country, and with a patent from James I, the company had high ambitions for the success of the venture. Focusing on short-term tactical gains at the expense of longer-term strategic direction, it over-burdened the leaders of the expedition with a lengthy list of instructions that betrayed an alarming lack of knowledge and experience, especially in its attitude towards the natives. Detailed directions for the location and defence of the settlement appeared to anticipate the discovery of a north-west route to the South Sea, while providing for defence against Spanish attack. Advice regarding the exploration of the region included provision for the search for precious minerals in the hills. The leaders were directed to 'have a great care not to offend the naturals', but the company's plans were marked by an unsettling combination of fear and bravado that did not augur well for the future.[43]

Although they contained nothing on the prospects for the fur trade, the instructions included advice about commercial relations with the Indians. The leaders of the settlement were thus enjoined to employ small trading parties to acquire provisions, to avoid the risk of famine during the first year, but this

41 Ibid., p. 120. The English were interested in trade, but it may have lacked clear focus, Oberg, *The Head in Nugent's Hand*, pp. 43–4; Mallios, *The Deadly Politics of Giving*, pp. 60–9 notes a flourishing trade, but also English violations of a native 'gift economy'.

42 Richard Hakluyt, *The Principall Navigations, Voiages and Discoveries of the English Nation* (London, 1589), p. 827; Quinn (ed.), *Roanoke Voyages*, 1, pp. 493–4.

43 E.G.R. Taylor (ed.), *The Original Writings and Correspondence of the Two Richard Hakluyts,* 2 vols. (Hakluyt Society, Second Series, 76 & 77, 1935), 2, pp. 492–4; Ian K. Steele, *Warpaths: Invasions of North America* (New York, 1994), p. 39 argues that the instructions 'made clashes with Powhatan unavoidable'. The failure to find silver or gold influenced the rationale of settlers, J.H. Elliott, *Empires of the Atlantic: Britain and Spain in America 1492–1830* (New Haven, 2006), pp. 27–8.

was to be done before the natives perceived that the English meant 'to plant among them'.[44] At the same time they were to ensure that the terms of trade were not debased by mariners trading with the Indians for their own gain.[45] Consequently commerce was to be restricted to appointees of the president and council of the settlement. Provision for a fortified market place also allowed for the promotion and regulation of trade.

Despite uncertainty and mutual suspicion, there was sufficient interest and need to support the growth of commerce between natives and settlers. Looking back from the vantage of 1705, Robert Beverley noted that so 'strong was the Desire of Riches, and so eager the Pursuit of a rich Trade' among the pioneers that the search for the lost colonists was put aside.[46] Under the distant management of the company, commerce, competition and conflict were laced together. Faced with turbulent, near-chaotic conditions, trade between the English and their Indian neighbours acquired an urgency that lent native leaders greater authority in the acquisition and distribution of new goods.[47] In unfavourable circumstances, exploratory and commercial contacts ranged beyond the Powhatan chiefdom, mapping potential networks for the development of colonial trade in the Bay.

While making allowance for short-term volatility, there were two distinct, if overlapping, phases to the commercial probing of the English during these early years. The first, an exploratory stage in the development of colonial trade within the Bay, lasted from the establishment of Jamestown to the early 1620s. It was succeeded by a short period of expansion and competition, following the dissolution of the company in 1624, which laid the groundwork for the establishment of rival joint stock ventures that sought to combine trade with plantation.

During much of the first phase, a time of weakening corporate control, the prospect of commerce with the Powhatans appeared to recede before the eyes of the colonial community. Struggling to acquire purpose or self-definition, Jamestown was a breeding ground for disorder, disease and rising mortality. The displacement and alienation of a small band of suspicious and fearful settlers, mainly servants of the company, compounded with an acute gender imbalance, threatened the very future of the settlement. The company tried to censor the flow of bad news across the Atlantic, undergoing successive reorganizations based on revised royal charters. But it was forced into expediency in order to keep the settlement supplied with new recruits and provisions. Without a sufficient supply from London, Jamestown became

44 Taylor (ed.), *Original Writings*, 2, pp. 494–5.

45 Ibid., p. 495.

46 Beverley, *History of Virginia*, p. 25; Horn, *A Land as God Made It*, pp. 50–9; Oberg, *The Head in Nugent's Hand*, pp. 123–52 for later interpretations and myth.

47 Richter, 'Tsenacommacah and the Atlantic World', pp. 44–59.

dependent on its native neighbours for food, shaping the early development of the Indian trade.[48]

From the outset, trade and exchange were an expression of intercultural relations.[49] As such there was a series of hurdles that needed to be surmounted by both parties for commerce to proceed. They included practical issues regarding language and translation, which were complicated by the real and metaphorical meanings attached to goods and value. In an environment where English suspicion was confronted by Indian wariness, and lacking a common medium of exchange, natives and newcomers were compelled to negotiate and re-negotiate the terms of trade. The creation of an Anglo-Powhatan market also required a space and structure, literal and imaginative, which raised questions about the role and status of Indians within a small colonial community. Above all, trading with the other challenged preconceptions, particularly among the English, feeding false expectations and misunderstandings.[50]

Early contact and perceptions were mixed. According to a report made shortly after the arrival of the first expedition, which revealingly entwined trade with property rights, the commodities of the country were 'not much to be regarded, the inhabitantes having no comerce with any nation, no respect of profitt, neither is there scarce that we call meum et tuum among them save only the kinges know their owne territoryes & the people their severall gardens'.[51] Yet the description of the resources of the region also included reference to a plentiful supply of rich furs. Contrary to the expectations of colonial promoters, however, conditions at Jamestown fuelled a pressing need for provisions, enabling the Powhatans to retain agency and initiative as the settlers scouted for vital supplies of food. Such dependency exposed a glaring contradiction in the formation of a colonial self-image, cultivated in part by the tension between representations of savagery and civility that found resolution

48 Andrews, *Trade, Plunder and Settlement*, pp. 315–22; H.C. Porter, *The Inconstant Savage: England and the North American Indian 1500–1660* (London, 1979), pp. 339–59; Robert Brenner, *Merchants and Revolution: Commercial Change, Political Conflict, and London's Overseas Traders, 1550–1653* (Cambridge, 1993), pp. 93–6.

49 For a wider perspective, see Grant-Costa and Mancke, 'Anglo-Amerindian Commercial Relations', in Bowen et al. (eds.), *Britain's Oceanic Empire*, pp. 370–406.

50 Potter, *Commoners*, pp. 181–2; J. Frederick Fausz, 'An "Abundance of Blood Shed on Both Sides": England's First Indian War', *VMHB*, 98 (1990), pp. 17–19; Eric Hinderaker, 'Diplomacy between Britons and Native Americans, *c*. 1600–1830', in Bowen et al. (eds.), *Britain's Oceanic Empire*, pp. 222–4 on diplomatic relations. On the language problem see James Axtell, 'Babel of Tongues: Communicating with the Indians in Eastern North America', in Edward G. Gray and Norman Fiering (eds.), *The Language Encounter in the Americas, 1492–1800* (New York, 2000), pp. 15–60.

51 Philip L. Barbour (ed.), *The Jamestown Voyages Under the First Charter 1606–1609,* 2 vols. (Hakluyt Society, Second Series, 136 & 137, 1969), 1, p. 101.

in armed and aggressive tactics.[52] As recent work indicates, ill-feeling was aggravated by misunderstanding and misapprehension at different trading systems and behaviour.[53]

During the two years following the establishment of Jamestown, a critical and confusing period, the settlers struggled to establish commercial relations with the Powhatans. Acting as cape merchant, while relying on his military experience, John Smith visited neighbouring villages along the James River in search of supplies of maize, meat and fish. These contacts were facilitated by gifts, to which native leaders responded in kind, though in an increasingly measured manner. Much of the ceremony and eloquence which accompanied native exchange may have been barely comprehensible to Smith and his companions. Of necessity trade rested on the use of gesture and display. It required gift-giving, which for the English acted as an introduction to barter, a form of exchange to which they were more accustomed, though it required linguistic competence. The verbal sparring and bargaining that accompanied it, as Lescarbot noted for the northern Indians, may not initially have been to the liking of the Powhatans. Their leader used such early encounters to dramatize his authority, claiming on one occasion that 'it is not agreeable with my greatnes in this peddling manner to trade for trifles'.[54] Instead he expected the newcomers to display their commodities for him to make choice of, in return for which he would provide goods of fitting value. With the acquisition of key words and phrases, and the emergence of more accomplished translators, Indian leaders became adept at trading with the newcomers on their own terms.[55] Despite rivalry and occasional hostility, an almost silent process of commercial acculturation was underway, prospectively bringing native groups within the orbit of an expanding transatlantic market.

These positive signs were underpinned by native interest in the newcomers and their commodities. Although European goods entered the Bay during the sixteenth century, and may have enjoyed wide circulation, the amount was limited. Edward Maria Wingfield, the first president of Jamestown, noted that

52 Morgan, *American Slavery, American Freedom*, pp. 37–40.

53 The importance of these differences, and English violations of a native 'gift economy', are emphasized by Mallios, *The Deadly Politics of Giving*, pp. 80–120; Powhatan leaders may also have heard about the English at Roanoke, James Horn, 'The Conquest of Eden: Possession and Dominion in Early Virginia', in Robert Appelbaum and John Wood Sweet (eds.), *Envisioning an English Empire: Jamestown and the Making of the North Atlantic World* (Philadelphia, 2005), p. 29.

54 Smith, *Works*, 1, p. 217; Barbour (ed.), *Jamestown Voyages*, 1, pp. 178–86; Richter, *Before the Revolution*, pp. 125–6 on conduct; Mallios, *The Deadly Politics of Giving*, p. 108.

55 This included the recording of key words by Smith and Strachey, Axtell, 'Babel of Tongues', pp. 18, 38.

in June 1607 an emissary from Powhatan received many trifles, 'which were great wonders to him'.[56] Capitalizing on native demand for tools, trinkets and copper, colonial leaders sent the first supply ships back to London with a cargo of cedar wood, furs, skins and yellow dirt, optimistically believed to contain gold. Responding to these commercial prospects, the company instructed settlers to acquire beaver and otter skins which, if taken in winter, would secure a good profit.[57]

The growth of native demand for English commodities was rooted in a combination of use and function. But it also included symbolic or supernatural meanings that were attached to some goods. Copper, in particular, was highly prized by Indian groups. Its aesthetic quality meant that it was used as personal adornment, and as a form of ritual offering. It was widely employed in gift-giving and exchange, while leaders, such as Powhatan, collected it as tribute. Native elites tried to control the trade in such prestige goods, not only to regulate contact with outsiders, but also to enhance their own power. According to Strachey, the Powhatan leader monopolized the trade in copper, in order to acquire mercenary warriors. The colonists responded by reaching an agreement with the Chickahominies based on the exchange of copper, hatchets and beads for provisions, furs and skins.[58] Even during these early years, however, there was a danger that the increasing volume of trade goods would reduce their value, while weakening the authority of native leaders, who struggled to control access to them.[59]

In response to these teething problems the company encouraged Smith to explore the region, seeking out new trading partners while investigating the existence of a passage to the South Sea. His two expeditions during 1608 opened up native worlds beyond the chiefdom, anticipating the growth of exchange with rivals or enemies of Powhatan. During the first, Smith established contact with the Nanticokes, along the Eastern Shore, who were subsequently described as the greatest traders in the Bay, with access to fine furs

56 Barbour (ed.), *Jamestown Voyages*, 1, p. 215.

57 Alexander Brown (ed.), *The Genesis of the United States*, 2 vols. (Boston, 1891), 1, pp. 385, 395–6; Barbour (ed.), *Jamestown Voyages*, 1, pp. 102, 215. Wingfield's narrative indicates that the settlers were acquiring beaver and deer for provisions from their native neighbours.

58 Strachey, *Historie of Travell into Virginia*, pp. 73, 75, 84, 94–5, 107, 115; Hamor, *A True Discourse*, p. 15; Christopher L. Miller and George R. Hamell, 'A New Perspective on Indian-White Contact: Cultural Symbols and Colonial Trade', *Journal of American History*, 73 (1986), pp. 325–8; Oberg, *The Head in Nugent's Hand*, pp. 45–6; William M. Kelso, *Jamestown: The Buried Truth* (Charlottesville, 2006), pp. 57, 179 on beads.

59 Mallios, *The Deadly Politics of Giving*, pp. 86, 94–96, 103–6, 109–12; Rountree and Turner, *Before and After Jamestown*, pp. 142–5.

and large amounts of roanoke. The English soon became aware of the value of these white beads made from marine shells, which were used for ornamentation and ceremonial purposes. They were to serve as a medium of exchange in cross-cultural commerce. Smith also entered the Potomac which, he noted, supported fur-bearing animals, including beavers and otters. While exploring the river he had a brief and tense meeting with an unidentified Indian group, who may have been seeking to trade with the newcomers.[60]

Later in the year Smith reached the head of the Bay, encountering rival groups of Indians. They included a raiding party of Massawomecks, travelling south in seven or eight canoes, with whom there was an uneasy exchange of goods conducted by sign language. A subsequent encounter with a group of Susquehannocks was friendlier. According to Smith's self-promotional account, they begged him for help against the northern raiders. In exchange they offered 'food, conduct, assistance, and continuall subjection'.[61] But Smith was unable to return the following year, as promised, missing an opportunity to establish an Anglo-Susquehannock alliance that might have opened a pathway to the rich northern fur trade.

Smith's expeditions were milestones in English understanding of the Bay and its native inhabitants. They suggested the possibility of acquiring access to fur-rich regions as yet little known to European traders. The acquisition of new information was recorded in map form, engraved and published after Smith's return to England, in 1612. The first map to portray the Bay and its tributaries with some accuracy, it revealed a seemingly benign landscape, dotted with Indian settlements. It was a powerful tool for ambitious traders, shaping their view of the commercial potential of the region and beyond. The figure of a Susquehannock warrior, imposingly portrayed in 'giant-like' fashion, who dominated the lower reaches of the Susquehanna seemed to act as a barrier against northern raiders while guarding access to supplies of furs.[62] But the map also served an underlying political purpose, affirming English sovereignty over the Chesapeake against European rivals.

60 Smith, *Works*, 1, pp. 123, 227–8; Barbour (ed.), *Jamestown Voyages*, 1, pp. 178–86; Philip L. Barbour, *The Three Worlds of Captain John Smith* (London, 1964), pp. 201–20; Horn, *A Land as God Made It*, pp. 83–98; Richter, *Before the Revolution*, pp. 141–2 on wampum, and see below pp. 104–5.

61 Smith, *Works*, 1, pp. 165–6, 230–2; Pendergast, *The Massawomeck* discusses the origin of these northern Indians; see also Hatfield, *Atlantic Virginia*, p. 12; Frederick J. Fausz, 'English Fur Trade in the Chesapeake', p. 45 argues that Smith 'consistently rejected the advances of the Susquehannocks for trade'; Van Zandt, *Brothers among Nations*, pp. 119–20.

62 Smith, *Works,* 1, pp. 121–3; R.A. Skelton, *Explorers' Maps* (London, 1958), pp. 256–7.

The company tried to exploit Smith's reconnoitring to deal with the enveloping crisis in relations with the Powhatans. In an attempt to safeguard Jamestown, while advancing its commercial ambitions, it sent out a new governor, Sir Thomas Gates, with instructions to establish trading and diplomatic relations with distant native groups, who were known to be enemies of Powhatan. Almost certainly they included the Susquehannocks, who reportedly lived in a large settlement at the head of the Bay known as Cataaneon, near plentiful supplies of copper and furs. Prompted by the profitable prospect of trade and exploration, if undertaken expeditiously, the interests of the company were being directed into the upper reaches of the Bay.[63] By the time Gates reached the colony, however, these plans were surrendered in the face of conflict with the Powhatans.

The commercial results of these early years were uneven. A report by Francis Magnal, an Irishman who spent eight months in Jamestown after arriving with the second supply in 1608, suggested that interethnic commerce was flourishing. Powhatan and his people dealt peacefully with the settlers, with many daily attending a market held at the English fort, where they exchanged native commodities for trinkets, such as mirrors and bells.[64] In more revealing language, Smith claimed that the Powhatans were brought to a 'tractable trade' during these years.[65] Under his leadership a rudimentary commercial infrastructure was established by 1609, which included a small fleet of 10 trading vessels.

But commercial contact failed to promote deeper social interaction. Smith's aggressive and violent tactics, fuelled by the settlers' dependency, led to growing native resentment. The Powhatans reacted in kind by effectively raising rates of exchange. Robert Beverley complained that it was the English who taught the Indians 'to put a value on their Skins and Furs, and to make a Trade of them'.[66] The lack of regulation 'created Jealousies and Disturbances among the Indians, by letting one have a better Bargain than another', consequently they felt 'cheated and abused; and so conceiv'd a Grudge against the English in general, making it a National Quarrel'.[67] Yet the resentment

63 Barbour (ed.), *Jamestown Voyages*, 2, pp. 266–7; Fausz, 'An "Abundance of Blood"', pp. 29–31.

64 Barbour (ed.), *Jamestown Voyages*, 1, pp. 153–4, a rather confused, unreliable, though in places insightful, report translated into Castilian for the Council of State in Madrid in 1610. Archaeological evidence indicates a building 'for storage and trade' with the Indians, which served varied functions from 1607 to 1610, see Kelso, *Jamestown: The Buried Truth*, pp. 81, 96–106.

65 Smith, *Works*, 1, pp. 239, 263, 267; Martin H. Quitt, 'Trade and Acculturation at Jamestown, 1607–1609: The Limits of Understanding', *WMQ*, 52 (1995), pp. 248–50.

66 Beverley, *History of Virginia*, p. 227.

67 Ibid., pp. 29–30.

was by no means one-sided. Henry Spelman, a young settler who served Powhatan as an intermediary and translator, was sent by the native leader to the settlers with a message, promising to supply them with maize in exchange for copper, luring a trading party into a fatal ambush.[68] Suspicion and misunderstanding structured face-to-face contact, to the detriment of commercial and cultural interaction.

Two years after the arrival of the English, relations with the Powhatans deteriorated into open conflict. Jamestown barely survived a desperate period, the 'starving time' of 1609 to 1610, when Powhatan attempted to cut off the native supply of provisions.[69] The crisis encouraged colonial leaders to renew the search for trading partners and allies beyond the chiefdom. Building on Smith's survey of the upper Bay, these initiatives required traders to deal with the twin challenges of navigating native political and diplomatic rivalries, while handling potential competition from other Europeans.

Samuel Argall, a young and ambitious sea-captain, played a leading role in this commercial venturing. He visited Jamestown in 1609 as leader of an expedition to discover a more direct route to the colony. He returned in 1610, when he surveyed the coast from Cape Cod to the Chesapeake and undertook an extensive exploration of the Bay. In search of provisions, he entered the Potomac, where he acquired 400 bushels of maize, beans and peas, in exchange for copper, beads, hatchets, knives, bells and scissors worth about 40 shillings.[70] He returned to Jamestown with Spelman, who had sought sanctuary with the Indians along the river after running away from the Powhatans. His local knowledge and expertise were of considerable value in assisting trading ventures in the region.

Encouraged by Argall's expedition, in May the governor urged the company to send a vice-admiral and mariners to the colony to promote and protect commerce. The charge, he argued, would be made good by developing the fur trade with Indians along the northern rivers, and by the provision of maize and fish for the settlers. At present the growth of trade was limited by Powhatan's concern to act as a middleman, supplying other Indian groups with English commodities. Partly to deal with this and other problems, the Laws of Virginia, subsequently published in London during 1612, prohibited all commercial

68 Spelman, *Relation*, p. civ; Strachey, *Historie of Travell into Virginia*, p. 62.

69 Fausz, 'An "Abundance of Blood"', pp. 31–52; Horn, *A Land as God Made It*, pp. 118–9, 174–80. Different food practices were a point of contact and conflict between natives and newcomers, Robert Appelbaum, 'Hunger in Early Virginia: Indians and English Facing Off over Excess, Want, and Need', in Appelbaum and Sweet (eds.), *Envisioning an English Empire*, pp. 215–16.

70 *RVC*, 3, pp. 106–7, 219; Brown (ed.), *Genesis*, 1, p. 481 and 2, pp. 815–16; Martha W. Hiden (ed.), 'A Voyage of Fishing and Discovery 1609', *VMHB*, 65 (1957), pp. 62–6; Rice, *Nature & History*, pp. 81–5 for the English intrusion into the Potomac.

contact with the chiefdom without lawful authority, and threatened runaways to the Indians with the death penalty.[71]

Argall returned to the Potomac in 1612. He explored the upper reaches of the river and established relations with local leaders. By means of diplomacy and exchange he acquired 1,100 bushels of maize. In a persuasive demonstration of the value of these contacts to the English, with the connivance of the Patawomeck leader, he seized Mataoke or Pocahontas, one of the daughters of Powhatan. In return for his assistance, the native leader was rewarded with a copper kettle and various trifles: 'doubtlesse', Ralph Hamor later remarked, 'he would have betrayed his owne father for them'.[72] Argall's commercial scouting within the Bay continued during 1613 with a visit to the Eastern Shore. According to his account of the voyage, the Accomacks were keen to do business because they had received good reports of his courteous behaviour along the Potomac. After exploring the coastline, he returned to Jamestown with supplies of maize and reports of an abundant supply of fish. Diplomacy and commerce were accompanied by aggressive strikes against European rivals. Later in the year Argall attacked French outposts in the north, at St Croix and Port Royal. Although strategic in purpose, his report on the expedition, including reference to a French vessel with a cargo of furs worth £8,000, was a timely reminder of the economic value of the fur trade.[73]

Yet the contrast between French trade in Canada and English commerce in the Bay was stark. One of Argall's ships returned to London during 1614 with a lading of 175 beaver skins, 18 otter skins, five wild cat skins, two hides of elk and one deer skin.[74] The customs records for London, though incomplete, suggest that shipments of furs from Jamestown during this period were irregular and modest in scale. Nor was the end of the Anglo-Powhatan conflict in 1614, marked by the marriage between Pocahontas and John Rolfe, followed by any significant increase in the volume of trade. Instead the rapid emergence of a booming tobacco culture, in the wake of Rolfe's successful cultivation of a marketable commodity, began the transformation of the settlement, paving the way for the development of a plantation colony in which the status of the Powhatans was open to negotiation.

71 Brown, *Genesis*, 1, p. 493; *For the Colony in Virginea Britannia: Lawes Divine, Morall and Martiall, etc.* ed. David H. Flaherty (Charlottesville, 1969), pp. 15, 20.

72 Hamor, *A True Discourse*, p. 5; Brown, *Genesis*, 2, p. 641. On the mythic creation of Pocahontas see Robert S. Tilton, *Pocahontas: The Evolution of an American Narrative* (Cambridge, 1994).

73 Brown, *Genesis*, 2, p. 644; Hamor, *A True Discourse*, pp. 36–7. Fischer, *Champlain's Dream*, p. 233 for illegal trading along the St Lawrence.

74 A.P. Newton, 'Lord Sackville's Papers Respecting Virginia, 1613–1631', *American Historical Review*, 27 (1922), p. 497; Susan E. Hillier, 'The Trade of the Virginia Colony: 1606 to 1660' (University of Liverpool Ph.D. thesis, 1971), p. 420.

The company struggled to manage this unanticipated change, enabling commercial enterprise in the Bay to be taken over by a small group of officials and well-placed settlers. As governor from 1617 to 1619, Argall began the practice of issuing commissions for the Indian trade. Their primary purpose was to secure supplies of maize and other provisions for the colony. But Argall's authorization of voyages into the upper Bay was also motivated by ambitions to promote the fur trade. The company supported these initiatives, despatching cargoes of trade goods, including shoes, hoes, nails and locks, as well as copper, some of which were intended for native consumers.[75] At the same time, its willingness to allow the establishment of particular and private plantations, though short-lived, created opportunities for commerce with neighbouring Indian groups, especially in provisions.[76]

Colonial leaders struggled to control and safeguard the activities of a growing number of traders and their native partners. During 1618 a party of five colonists went to trade secretly with the Chickahominies. They were attacked by a group of Indians, one of whom was armed with a gun. The leader of the party, Richard Killingbeck, was shot dead. The others were 'all slaine, stripped, and spoyled'.[77] To colonial leaders, Opechancanough, who assumed responsibility for Anglo-Indian relations following the death of Powhatan, sought to excuse the assault by ignorance on the part of the attackers. Symbolically he 'sent a basket of earth, in token of the gift and possession of that Towne where they dwelt, to Captain Argal, desiring him not to revenge the fault of a few, which for feare of revenge were fled to the Woods, on their innocent neighbours'.[78]

Creeping disorder and violence provoked a swift response from the governor and the recently established General Assembly. Initiated by the company as part of a programme of reform and revitalization, the assembly acted as a political forum and a point of contact between the community of freemen and colonial officials. In 1619 John Martin was ordered to appear before it, following a complaint from Opechancanough regarding the conduct of his men during a recent trading voyage.[79] An established settler, and a loyal servant

75 *RVC*, 1, p. 126; 3, p. 79; TNA, E190/22/9; Argall was accused of appropriating the Indian trade to himself according to Stith, *History of Virginia*, pp. 149–51.

76 Walsh, *Motives of Honor*, pp. 30–9, 46–9, 64–5, 83–7; Bailyn, *The Barbarous Years*, pp. 92–6.

77 Purchas, *Hakluytus Posthumus*, 19, p. 120

78 Ibid., pp. 120–1. According to the report of John Rolfe, Powhatan died 15 June 1618. He was succeeded by his second brother, Itopatan (or Itoyatan), but Opechancanough became better known to the English. Together they confirmed 'the league with the Colony' according to Purchas. On attempts to resolve murders by different cultural practices, see White, *The Middle Ground*, pp. 76–7.

79 Smith, *Works*, 1, pp. 269–71; 2, pp. 144–5.

of the company, in November 1616 he received 10 shares of land, known as Martin's Brandon, along the James River. With Argall's approval, during 1619 he sent out a shallop, a small sailing vessel which usually carried oars, to trade in the Bay. It was a difficult and contentious voyage, provoking complaints that Martin's men plundered a canoe, after the Indians refused to trade. The English insisted that they gave copper, beads and other goods in exchange for a supply of maize, but the Indians demanded compensation for their losses. Although the outcome of the dispute is unknown, Martin agreed to provide security to the governor for the good behaviour of his traders towards the Indians, for future voyages in the Bay.[80]

The dangers of disorderly enterprise persuaded the assembly that the Indian trade required regulation. While it opened the trade to all settlers except servants, adventurers had to provide security for their conduct towards the Indians. Furthermore, it warned traders against providing natives with firearms, ammunition and other weapons, 'upon paine of being helde a Traytour to the Colony'.[81] The same concern with security may account for the assembly's attempt to prevent the sale of large hoes, mattocks and English dogs to the Indians. In reality colonial authorities were unable to enforce these controls. To the embarrassment of the company, during the Parliament of 1621 complaints were voiced against colonists who for private gain supplied Indians with weapons.[82]

Responding to changing conditions in the Bay, while urgently seeking to reap profit from the colony, the company's interest in the fur trade revived. It was encouraged by a valuation of commodities available in Virginia, of 1620, which included beaver skins among the more valuable varieties of pelts. The author of the paper was able to distinguish between different types of skins in a manner that seems to have reflected trading activity in the Bay. For example, adult beavers, in season, were valued at seven shillings each. If new, they were not to be bought by the pound, 'because they are thicke and heavy leather, and not so good for use as the old'.[83] By contrast, old skins

80 McIlwaine (ed.), *Journals of the House of Burgesses*, p. 5; William J. Van Schreeven and George H. Reese (eds.), *Proceedings of the General Assembly of Virginia July 30-August 4, 1619* (Jamestown, 1969), pp. 21, 33, 37; Lyon Gardiner Tyler (ed.), *Narratives of Early Virginia, 1606–1625* (New York, 1907), pp. 249–54.

81 *RVC*, 3, pp. 170–1; Van Schreeven and Reese (eds.), *Proceedings*, pp. 55, 59; McIlwaine (ed.), *Journals of the House of Burgesses*, pp. 5, 14–15; Wesley Frank Craven, *The Southern Colonies in the Seventeenth Century, 1607–1689* (Baton Rouge, 1949), pp. 157–8.

82 *RVC*, 3, pp. 494, 535–6; 'Documents of Sir Francis Wyatt, Governor, 1621–26', *WMQ*, 7 (1927), pp. 42–7.

83 *RVC*, 3, pp. 237–9. These valuations were 'rated as they are there worth'.

'in Mantles, gloves or caps, the more worne the better,' were valued at six shillings the pound, if they were 'full of furre'.[84]

The company's commercial ambitions were given greater shape and focus by reports of recent trading and exploratory voyages within and beyond the Bay. They included two expeditions undertaken by John Pory, the colony's secretary. The first, into the upper Bay, led to the establishment of an outpost, reputedly of nearly 100 settlers, 'with hope of a good trade for Furres there to be had'.[85] The second was towards the Chowan River, south of Jamestown, with the primary purpose of securing supplies of maize and other provisions.[86] But such reconnoitring occurred in ambiguous and potentially hazardous circumstances. During a voyage to find a suitable place to make salt, Pory visited the Indian village of Patuxent, where he met the leader and his brother, Wamanato. The latter came aboard Pory's vessel bearing a brass kettle full of oysters. The English were also presented with beaver skins. The visitors responded with a gift of unspecified goods. Wamanato insisted that he would keep them for the rest of his life. However, his brother and others reportedly planned, but failed, to ambush the party in a wood while they were ashore.[87]

In addition to news of Pory's discoveries, the company also heard reports of two voyages by Thomas Savage to the Eastern Shore, and of an exploration along the Atlantic coast, including a brief survey of Delaware Bay and the Hudson River by Thomas Dermer.[88] Savage's news of the great profit made by French fur traders in the north rekindled ambitions that the company could develop a rival trade 'with farr less charge and greater ease'.[89] But their fulfilment demanded urgency, given Dermer's unwelcome information about Dutch activity in the Delaware and along the Hudson. Nonetheless the governor and council agreed that future commercial prospects were very promising.[90]

84 Ibid., p. 239.

85 It was probably situated along the Eastern Shore, though nothing else is heard of it, *RVC*, 3, pp. 549, 587, 641–2; Purchas, *Hakluytus Posthumus*, 19, p. 146; William S. Powell, *John Pory, 1572–1636* (Chapel Hill, 1977), pp. 96–8; Rice, *Nature & History*, p. 86.

86 *RVC*, 3, pp. 641–2; Powell, *John Pory*, pp. 100–2; Purchas, *Hakluytus Posthumus*, 19, pp. 146–7.

87 Ibid., pp. 167–8.

88 *RVC*, 1, p. 504. Dermer provided Samuel Purchas, Hakluyt's successor as the chronicler of English expansion, with a report which included a description of the pandemic afflicting Indians along the coast. Described as plague, it was probably smallpox caught from visiting Europeans, Purchas, *Hakluytus Posthumus*, 19, pp. 129–34.

89 *RVC*, 1, p. 504.

90 *RVC*, 1, p. 504. The company was concerned at reports of a 'rich Trade of Furres' which the Dutch and French had within its 'precincts, and within fiftie leagues of us', Ibid, 3, p. 144.

The company responded energetically to these reports. Within a week it opened a subscription roll for the fur trade, setting a maximum limit of £100, and a minimum of £20, for subscribers. Edward Blaney was appointed factor for the venture. In order to ensure a supply of suitable trade goods for the Indians, later in 1621 it sent captain William Norton and a group of Italian craftsmen to the colony, with instructions to erect a furnace to manufacture glass beads. The governor and council were instructed to limit production, if necessary, to maintain their exchange value.[91] Although the new venture aroused considerable interest, subscriptions were slow to materialize and insufficient to cover the running costs of the first voyage. In mid-September the company sent out two vessels, the *Warwick* and the *Tiger*, with a cargo of goods worth £2,000, but by November only £900 had been collected to underwrite the venture.[92] The company was forced to seek additional support from a syndicate of adventurers, the promoters of one of the largest private plantations in the colony, Southampton hundred, who provided one of the ships. In an attempt to support the voyage, it instructed the governor to hire two or three interpreters, who were 'skilfull in the languages and maners of the Indians, and expert in those places, wherein the trade is to be'.[93]

The voyage ended obscurely. Its failure deepened the financial problems facing the company, weakening corporate interest in the trade. Ceding some of its commercial control to private adventurers, in November 1621 it authorized a partnership, which included aristocrats and gentry, to send out the *Discovery* under captain Thomas Jones, to promote the fur trade. The company acknowledged that the voyage was undertaken by private adventurers, but, identifying it as a public business, officials ordered the governor to provide assistance for Jones.[94] In December it received disturbing reports that two Dutch vessels had recently left Amsterdam, well-stocked with trade goods, bound for the same destination as the *Discovery*. It was subsequently informed that Jones

91 *RVC*, 1, p. 515; 3, pp. 477, 489, 495; Purchas, *Hakluytus Posthumus*, 19, p. 144; Richard L. Morton, *Colonial Virginia*, 2 vols. (Chapel Hill, 1960), 1, p. 67. On glass beads see also George Irving Quimby, *Indian Culture and European Trade Goods* (Madison, 1966), pp. 65, 81; Daniel K. Richter, *Trade, Land, Power: The Struggle for Eastern North America* (Philadelphia, 2013), p. 58.

92 *RVC*, 1, p. 567; 3, p. 527; Frederick J. Fausz, '"To Draw Thither the Trade of Beavers": The Strategic Significance of the English Fur Trade in the Chesapeake, 1620–1660', in Bruce Trigger et al. (eds.), *'Le Castor Fait Tout': Selected Papers of the Fifth North American Fur Trade Conference, 1985* (Montreal, 1987), p. 47 argues that the company made a 'fatal miscalculation' in ignoring trade. The venture is briefly mentioned in Wesley Frank Craven, *Dissolution of the Virginia Company: The Failure of a Colonial Experiment* (Gloucester, 1964), p. 191.

93 *RVC*, 3, p. 527; Richter, 'Tsenacommacah and the Atlantic World', pp. 64–5; A.J. Morrison, 'The Virginian Indian Trade to 1673', *WMQ*, 1 (1921), p. 220.

94 *RVC*, 3, pp. 527–8, 530; BL, Additional 14285, f.77.

re-directed the voyage to New England, where he plundered furs from various Indian groups, until the ship ran aground.

The failure of these ventures, followed by the devastating attack on the colony by the Powhatans in March 1622, effectively ended the company's interest in the fur trade. Nearly 350 settlers were killed during a carefully orchestrated assault which took most of the colonial community by surprise. Across the Atlantic, Edward Waterhouse, the company's secretary, seized the opportunity to denounce Indian treachery. Relying on reports from the settlement, Waterhouse claimed that the colonists had become too familiar and trusting, not least in their commercial interactions, with the Powhatans. On the morning of the attack, small groups of unarmed natives entered their houses to trade furs and provisions for glass beads and other trifles. Under the guise of friendship, the Powhatans indiscriminately killed men, women and children, including those working in the fields, using their own tools to mangle and deface the dead. The violence validated an image of the Indians as savage and bestial who were instigated by the devil, though the hand of God was to be seen in the advance warning of a convert.[95]

The attack was interpreted by the English as a massacre, justifying the most severe response. The advocates of this approach called for a punitive war against the Powhatans and the seizure of their land. Drawing on his earlier experience, John Smith offered to lead a force of 100 soldiers to the beleaguered colony, arguing that it was easier to 'civilize them by conquest then faire means', especially as 'civilizing will require a long time and much industry'.[96] Although Smith's offer was not taken up, the ensuing Anglo-Powhatan conflict contributed to the re-shaping of intercultural relations, confirming the failure of incorporation or assimilation as a means of political negotiation.[97] It also exposed the fragility of trade and exchange, which Opechancanough and other Powhatan leaders seemed to have renounced, to the benefit of rivals along

95 Edward Waterhouse, *A Declaration of the State of the Colonie and Affaires in Virginia* (London, 1622), pp. 13–15, 18–22; John Smith's report was heavily based on Waterhouse, Smith, *Works*, 2, pp. 293–7; Vaughan, *Roots of American Racism*, pp. 120–4.

96 Smith, *Works*, 2, pp. 298, 305–6; Waterhouse, *A Declaration*, pp. 18–25.

97 Andrews, *Trade, Plunder and Settlement*, pp. 323–4; Rountree, *Pocahontas's People*, pp. 73–81; J. Frederick Fausz, 'Opechancanough: Indian Resistance Leader', in David G. Sweet and Gary B. Nash (eds.), *Struggle and Survival in Colonial America* (Berkeley, 1981), pp. 28–32; Richter, *Before the Revolution*, p. 117 comments that the Chesapeake came to resemble Ireland in its aftermath, while Malcolm Gaskill, *Between Two Worlds: How the English Became Americans* (Oxford, 2014), p. 77 regards it as 'primeval chaos'; Dierk Walter, *Colonial Violence: European Empires and the Use of Force*, trans. Peter Lewis (London, 2017), p. 158.

the Potomac.[98] Commerce persisted, but within the confines of an expanding agricultural economy it failed to promote mutual respect or understanding.

As a result, during the early 1620s the colony faced a severe transatlantic crisis. In England, the Powhatan attack hastened the collapse of the company which was dissolved in 1624. The end of corporate control left Virginia in the hands of a monarchy facing major conflicts in Europe. Within the Bay the outbreak of disease and shortages of provisions intensified the revival of Anglo-Powhatan hostilities. The ferocity of the colonial response, lacking external control or regulation, was inflamed by a growing determination to seize the opportunity to root out and remove the Indians.[99] Under the shadow of a savage conflict, the settlers resorted to destroying the crops of their enemies, while aggressively trading for maize with neutral and friendly groups. During 1622 and 1623 the governor, Sir Francis Wyatt, issued commissions to adventurers, including Ralph Hamor, William Tucker and Sir George Yeardley, authorizing trade and the use of force if peaceful methods failed.[100]

The violence accompanying these expeditions spilled over into the Potomac, where it became confused with native rivalries and conflicts. During the latter part of 1622, following an aggressive trading voyage along the river, Hamor returned to Jamestown with the Patawomeck leader and his son as prisoners. Conflict between the Patawomecks and the Piscataways enabled colonial leaders to reach an agreement with the former, anticipating joint action against their mutual enemies. But the violence threatened to spiral out of control. In April 1623 Henry Spelman and his company were killed by the Indians as they traded along the river. According to one report, Spelman's death was an acute loss because he was the best interpreter in the colony. Yet it was also acknowledged to be a just revenge for the English treatment of the Patawomeck leader. Later in the year the governor led an expedition to the region, to punish those responsible, while establishing trade with friendly groups.[101]

Although much of this armed trade was concentrated within the Bay, Wyatt attempted to protect the colony's commercial interests farther north. In October 1622 he granted a commission to captain William Eden to trade for maize

98 Smith noted that Raleigh Crashaw, accompanied by Henry Spelman, were trading along the river during the attack, Smith, *Works*, 2, pp. 304, 308.

99 *RVC*, 4, pp. 9–10; BL, Additional 12496, ff.459–9v: Gesa Mackenthun, *Metaphors of Dispossession: American Beginnings and the Translation of Empire, 1492–1637* (Norman, 1997), pp. 258–9; Horn, *A Land as God Made It*, pp. 264–70.

100 *RVC*, 3, pp. 622, 656–7 and 4, pp. 7, 221–2; 'Documents of Sir Francis Wyatt', pp. 45–7; Bailyn, *The Barbarous Years*, pp. 72, 112–13.

101 *RVC*, 4, pp. 89, 108, 450–1; Morton, *Colonial Virginia*, 1, pp. 80–1; Richard Beale Davis, *George Sandys, Poet Adventurer: A Study in Anglo-American Culture in the Seventeenth Century* (London, 1955), pp. 153–4; Rice, *Nature & History*, pp. 87–90.

and furs in any river or harbour between 33 and 41 degrees. While Eden was authorized to use force if he was unable to trade peacefully with Indian groups, he was also empowered to remove all foreigners from the region.[102] The directive was a clear signal that colonial leaders were prepared to take firm action against rival European traders, particularly the Dutch who were operating in Delaware Bay. It was followed by a voyage to Cape Cod and the Hudson River, promoted by the adventurers of Southampton hundred, who were seeking to gain some return on their investment in plantation.[103]

Trade, rivalry and war

The dissolution of the company left the colonial trade in the hands of private adventurers, under the regulation of the governor and council. Growing demand for beaver skins during the 1620s to supply the market for fashionable headwear, combined with competitive opportunities in North America, fed the ambitions of traders and officials in the Bay, who saw the potential for exploiting hostilities against the Powhatans to promote commercial and colonial expansion. These transatlantic conditions encouraged a sustained attempt to exploit the resources of the upper Bay, as well as along the Potomac, resuscitating ambitions for opening up a trade route farther north. But the rapid growth of trade provoked intense rivalry and competition, cutting across emerging ethnic and cultural borderlands which defined and defended the spread of tobacco culture along the James River and beyond.

In the aftermath of the attack of 1622 there was intense discussion within the colony regarding the future role and status of the Powhatans. In an unpublished paper of December 1622 John Martin argued in favour of subjugating the Indians through the destruction of food supplies and the disruption of trade, without an 'utter exterpation of them'.[104] He also suggested that they could be employed in the colony to make flax, hemp and silk, and to serve as guides on expeditions. Others, such as George Sandys, the colony's treasurer, seemed to be in favour of relying on a well-established strategy of exploiting native divisions, distinguishing between enemies and potential friends or allies.[105] A more radical approach was spelled out by the governor in a letter to John Ferrar, a prominent member of the company, of April 1623. Responding to the renewal of the Anglo-Powhatan war, Wyatt insisted that 'either we must drive them, or they us out of the country, for at one time or other they play

[102] *RVC*, 3, pp. 698–9.

[103] Walsh, *Motives of Honor*, pp. 64–5, 76, 83–7.

[104] BL, Additional 12496, f.459.

[105] *RVC*, 4, pp. 450–1; Sandys had an interest in the Indian trade, Davis, *Sandys, Poet Adventurer*, p. 166.

us false'.[106] In such circumstances he argued that trade with the Indians must cease, while the settlers relied on their own resources. Despite the rhetoric, during the 1620s the colonial community lacked either the resources or will-power to implement such a policy. Most settlers would probably have agreed with Martin's assertion that they needed the Indians, 'least the woods and wilde beasts should over runn them'.[107]

Interethnic commerce persisted, developing two inter-related, but distinct, strands. The maize trade retained its importance as a source of provisions for the colony, despite an undercurrent of concern at its economic consequences, in devaluing rates of exchange. In character it was a subsistence trade driven by local demand. The emerging trade in furs was related to it, often occurring on the same voyage, but it was developing a wider and more distant range of commercial networks. Its structure and organization, moreover, were shaped by a transatlantic market, in addition to local conditions in the Bay. By these means a growing volume and variety of European commodities, including metal wares, cloth and glass beads, circulated among Indian traders and consumers with far-reaching, disruptive consequences for native economies and political systems.

Concerned to safeguard the supply of provisions, Wyatt issued several commissions for the Indian trade during 1623 and 1624. In May 1623 Gilbert Peppet received a commission to trade within or beyond the Bay, with authority to seize maize and other goods. A similar commission was issued to Ralph Hamor in January 1624, though it was restricted to the Chesapeake, and he was instructed to use force only in self-defence.[108] There were others operating without licence. Complaints that traders were willing to 'give any rates for Corne, rather than return emptie', led to a temporary ban on trading activity in September for one year.[109] Although difficult to enforce, at least one trader, Henry Geny, was fined 300 pounds of tobacco for ignoring it. But the prohibition provoked strong opposition from John Pountis, who as vice-admiral of the colony insisted on his right to undertake trading or other voyages as part of his official duties. Pountis also accused traders of seizing and killing Indians, and of trading in bad faith. Their actions, he complained, damaged the reputation of the English among native groups. Formerly they

[106] *RVC*, 4, pp. 9–10; Richter, *Before the Revolution*, p. 201; Vaughan, *Roots of American Racism*, pp. 120–6.

[107] BL, Additional 12496, f.459v. Karen Ordahl Kupperman, *Settling with the Indians: The Meeting of English and Indian Cultures in America, 1580–1640* (Totowa, 1980), pp. 182–3 on colonial dependence.

[108] *RVC*, 4, pp. 189, 447–8.

[109] *RVC*, 4, pp. 275–6.

were 'called Gods, but now through treacherous & inhumaine Cruelty' they were deemed to be worse than devils.[110]

The ambitious and ambiguous character of interethnic commerce was demonstrated by an expedition of 1624, led by captain Raleigh Crawshaw, to the Patuxent River. Crashaw earned recognition for his conduct against hostile Indians during 1622, though admittedly he benefited from 'the helpe of other savages'.[111] At a time of insecurity and scarcity, he offered to go out trading for maize, if the colony's leaders supplied him with a shallop, men, arms and provisions. His subsequent voyage proceeded despite uncertainty over the regulation of trade, exposing the confusion between public and private interests that was characteristic of these years. He sailed with a commission from the governor. Subsequent legal testimony also indicated that George Sandys, acting in his capacity as treasurer, provided commodities for the voyage. But they were allegedly misappropriated by the company.[112] Although the main purpose of the venture was to acquire maize, the mariners devoted as much time to the purchase of furs and skins. Benefiting from his previous contacts along the Potomac, Crashaw provided the leader of the Patuxents with 600 to 800 blue beads, to serve as a guide to Piankatank. During a stay of more than three weeks, the company acquired maize, furs and a canoe in exchange for copper and glass beads. But their conduct provoked official investigation when they returned to Jamestown. Robert Poole, a member of the expedition, denied that any of the mariners used the treasurer's goods for private trade. While admitting that they all traded for furs, he was unable to identify the source of their trucking stuff. Poole's own acquisitions included 29 muskrat skins, nine bear skins, nine otter skins, six deer skins and two wild cat skins, which he handed over to Crawshaw.[113]

Despite its irregularities, Crawshaw's venture registered reviving interest in the fur trade that spanned the Atlantic. Acting in place of the defunct company, in October 1625 the Privy Council authorized colonial leaders to subdue the Indians by force, if peaceful methods failed, while urging their promotion of exploration within the Bay and along the coast, 'whereby also the trade of furs may be upheld'.[114] In the colony such initiatives encouraged the commercial ambitions of an emerging, self-made elite of planters and traders. Some of these men were accused of exploiting difficult conditions, including poor harvests, for personal gain. In January 1627 Richard Crocker, articulating the

[110] *RVC*, 4, pp. 276–7; H.R. McIlwaine (ed.), *Minutes of the Council and General Court of Colonial Virginia, 1622–1632, 1670–1676* (Richmond, 1924), p. 86.

[111] Purchas, *Hakluytus Posthumus*, 19, p. 169; Smith, *Works*, 2, pp. 304–5.

[112] *RVC*, 4, pp. 276, 583.

[113] McIlwaine (ed.), *Minutes of the Council and General Court*, pp. 29–30, 86.

[114] *APC, 1625–6*, p. 220.

view of lesser planters, complained 'that many great men went aboard shipps and bought many goods & sold them againe at unreasonable rates'.[115]

In an attempt to deal with shortages of provisions while implementing the Privy Council's instructions, the governor issued commissions authorizing voyages for trade and exploration. The recipients included leading representatives of younger, entrepreneurial settlers, whose interest in plantation development was allied with a vision for colonial and commercial expansion. In January 1627 Samuel Mathews received a commission to go trading in the Bay for maize. About the same time, his associate, William Claiborne, was awarded a commission for trade and discovery in any part of the colony. Mathews' commission was renewed in March 1629, when Robert Poole was granted a similar licence for the Eastern Shore. The following year Mathews was awarded a monopoly over the maize trade for twelve months, as a reward for his construction of a fort at Point Comfort.[116]

The commercial activities and ambitions of adventurers such as Claiborne were galvanized by the English seizure of Quebec during the Anglo-French war from 1627 to 1629. Undertaken by a private partnership, led by Lewis Kirke and other members of his family, the raid inflicted widespread disruption on the fur trade in Canada. The Kirke syndicate was keen to take over the French trade, estimated by some to be worth at least £30,000 *per annum.* Its success aroused wider interest and competition, strengthened by reports of an inland region, surrounding a great lake, with rich supplies of furs.[117] For ambitious traders in the Bay, the collapse of French Canada appeared to present an opportunity for diverting the rich northern trade south, either through direct contact or by native intermediaries. For Indians in the north, the disruption along the St Lawrence, following a fierce conflict between Mohawks and Mahicans, encouraged a speculative search for new trading partners linked with raiding the upper reaches of the Chesapeake.

Among a growing number of colonial traders, William Claiborne and Henry Fleet played leading roles in prospecting these commercial opportunities. Both men arrived in Virginia just before the attack of 1622. Despite different personal experiences, they shared a keen interest in the Indian trade. While Claiborne used his positions as surveyor, councillor and secretary to acquire extensive property, he also engaged in trading enterprise. In 1629 he led a diplomatic and commercial expedition to the head of the Bay, where he reached an agreement with the Susquehannocks. It provided the colony with powerful supporters, potentially anchoring English interests in a region which

115 McIlwaine (ed.), *Minutes of the Council and General Court*, p. 132.

116 Ibid., pp. 193, 479.

117 Charles Francis Adams (ed.), *The New English Canaan of Thomas Morton* (The Prince Society, 1883), pp. 234–5; Bernard Bailyn, *The New England Merchants in the Seventeenth Century* (Cambridge, Mass., 1955), p. 49.

was exposed to rival Dutch traders operating from an outpost in Delaware Bay. In addition, it enabled Claiborne to press ahead with plans for opening up the upper Bay to colonial development. During the course of the expedition he acquired an island from the Indians. Uncertainly revealed as part of a series of islands on Smith's *Map,* he named it after his home county of Kent. In 1630 he travelled to London, securing the support of William Cloberry and other city merchants for a joint stock venture, focused on Kent Island, with the purpose of combining trade with plantation.[118]

Claiborne's trading interests were shared by his rival, Henry Fleet, whose ambition found an outlet in developing the Indian trade along the Potomac. Fleet's career during the 1620s and early 1630s demonstrates the appeal of the trade, and the problems and opportunities it presented. Shortly after his arrival in the colony, in March 1623, while serving with Spelman on his disastrous expedition to the Potomac, he was captured by Indians. His four years of captivity provided him with an experience that Claiborne lacked. Establishing close relations with his captors, he acquired first-hand information about the inhabitants of the region, and developed his linguistic skills. He subsequently claimed to be more proficient in the native language than his own.[119] Captivity made him aware of the prospects for the fur trade along the river and with the region to the north and west.

On gaining his freedom in 1627 Fleet travelled to London, to secure financial backing for his fur trading schemes. According to a confused, but revealing report, he arrived from Venice, 'being lately ransomed from the Indians, with whom he had long lived, till he had left his own language'.[120] He had curious tales of his captors and reports of 'rare precious stones among them, and plenty of black fox, which of all others, is the richest fur'.[121] Later in the year he seems to have served as captain of the *Paramour* of London, which was sent out with letters of marque against Spain and France by William Cloberry and partners, though no evidence survives for the venture.[122] He returned to the Bay in 1631, acting as factor on a voyage promoted by George Griffith and company, for Virginia and New England.

118 Nathaniel C. Hale, *Virginia Venturer: A Historical Biography of William Claiborne 1600–1677* (Richmond, 1951), pp. 64–128; J. Frederick Fausz, 'Merging and Emerging Worlds: Anglo-Indian Interest Groups and the Development of the Seventeenth-Century Chesapeake', in Lois Green Carr et al. (eds.), *Colonial Chesapeake Society* (Chapel Hill, 1988), pp. 58–65; Fausz, 'Profits, Pelts, and Power', pp. 19–22.

119 Lambeth Palace, London, MS 688, Part 2, f.522v; Rice, *Nature & History*, pp. 93–5.

120 Birch (ed.), *The Court and Times of Charles the First*, 1, p. 238.

121 Ibid., p. 238.

122 *CSPD, 1628–9*, p. 301; Morrison, 'Virginian Indian Trade', p. 222.

Griffith and his partners were mainly interested in the northern fur trade, though Fleet persuaded them to explore the commercial resources of the Potomac. The venture was not a success. In 1634 the merchants petitioned the Commissioners of the Admiralty, seeking redress against their factor, who they blamed for the arrest of their vessel in Virginia.[123]

Remarkably a copy of Fleet's journal of the voyage survives. Despite problems in its interpretation and difficulties in the identification of Indian groups, it is a unique record of the early development of the fur trade in the Bay. It sheds searching light on cross-cultural commerce, and the perceived prospects for its future expansion, based on establishing contact with northern Indians. But his report of conditions along the Potomac confirmed the competitive character of the trade among colonists and natives.[124] As such his return to the region was seen by some as an unwelcome intrusion.

The journal opens in July 1631 with Fleet's departure from London bound for New England. After a brief stay in Piscataqua he sailed on to the Bay, arriving at Yaocomaco, at the mouth of the Potomac, at the end of October. Despite a prior agreement with the Indians, he found that they had burned their beaver skins, owing to his delayed arrival, as was customary.[125] He endeavoured to end the practice, a revealing reflection on the natives' uncertain understanding of a market economy, promising to return the following year. Although he was tempted to sail up-river to trade with an Indian group, identified as 'Mowhaks and Man eaters', with the season advancing, he returned to Piscataqua with a cargo of maize.[126] During the voyage down the Bay contrary winds forced him to seek shelter at Jamestown, where he was challenged by rival traders. Fleet defended himself, claiming that he had a commission to trade along the Potomac. In reality, as he admitted in his journal, it was of doubtful authority.

In preparation for the trading expedition of 1632, Fleet purchased commodities in Massachusetts, though he later claimed that their poor quality led to the failure of the voyage. Sailing up the Bay, accompanied by Claiborne, who was bound for Kent Island, he received disturbing news of complaints to the governor about his activities. On entering the Potomac in May he discovered that a rival, Charles Harman, had preceded him. Claiming that Fleet was

[123] *APC, 1630–1*, p. 364; *APC Colonial, 1603–80*, pp. 251–3.

[124] Lambeth Palace, London, MS 688, Part 2, ff.517–22v; published by Edward D. Neill (ed.), *The Founders of Maryland as Portrayed in Manuscripts, Provincial Records and Early Documents* (Albany, 1876), pp. 19–37.

[125] At this time the Piscataqua River was being investigated by the Laconia Company of London for a route to the inland lake in rich fur country, Bailyn, *New England Merchants*, pp. 49–50; Lambeth Palace, London, MS 688, Part 2, f.517; Rice, *Nature & History*, pp. 95–6.

[126] Lambeth Palace, London, MS 688, Part 2, ff.517–7v.

dead, he made 'an unexpected trade for the tyme'.[127] At a small charge, Fleet complained that he gained 1500 pounds weight of beaver from 14 native towns. This was a substantial haul of fur. It left little for Fleet on either side of the river as far as the Piscataway chiefdom. Surprised at Fleet's re-appearance, the leader of the Piscataways presented him with a gift of 114 beaver skins. He also acquired about 500 pounds of fur from a nearby Anacostan village.[128] He soon discovered that the latter were trying to establish themselves as middlemen with the Massawomecks, whom they supplied with European goods in exchange for protection against raids by the Susquehannocks.

Fleet was determined to insert himself within this native trading network. In June he met a party of northern Indians, including a Massawomeck interpreter, who were visiting the Anacostans. According to the interpreter, the Massawomecks lived in four towns, each with their own leaders, and with a total population of more than 30,000. Their lands were rich with beaver, the skins of which were worn as coats. Eager to establish contact with them, Fleet sent his brother, Edward, and two Indians to their settlements, with a parcel of gifts that included bells, beads, knives and hatchets. The mission went ahead despite opposition from the Piscataways, who had suffered heavy casualties during a recent raid by the northern Indians, and from the Anacostans who were determined to promote their role as middlemen.[129] Fleet's brother returned in July with mixed news. He was accompanied by a large trading party of Massawomecks, with 4,000 pounds of beaver skins, but they had turned back after encountering a group of Anacostans who claimed that the English intended to kill them in revenge for their attack on the Piscataways. When challenged by Fleet, the Anacostans denied all knowledge of the episode. Indeed, their leaders offered to serve as intermediaries with the northern Indians, if the English made a 'firme leage with them', but the offer was rejected.[130]

Despite these difficulties, a small group of Massawomecks made contact with the English. One of the Indians attracted Fleet's attention as he was sailing along the river. With a 'shrill sound [he] cried quo, quo, quo, houlding up a beaver skin upon a pole'.[131] When Fleet went ashore the Indian gave

[127] Ibid., ff.517v–8.

[128] Ibid., f.518v.

[129] Ibid., ff.518v–9, the towns were identified as Tonhoga, Mosticum, Shannetowa and Usserahak; Hatfield, *Atlantic Virginia*, pp. 22–4, 44. Spelman witnessed a conflict between the Massawomecks and Patawomecks in 1609/10, Spelman, *Relation*, p. cxiv. On the role of Indian middlemen, see Harold Hickerson, 'Fur Trade Colonialism and the North American Indians', *Journal of Ethnic Studies*, 1 (1973), pp. 25–6.

[130] Lambeth Palace, London, MS 688, Part 2, ff.519v–9. Reportedly 110 Massawomecks intended to travel south to meet Fleet.

[131] Ibid., f.519.

him the beaver and a hatchet, gesturing in a strange manner and speaking an unfamiliar language.[132] Fleet's response may have been equally strange. He 'cheared him, tould him he was a good man & clapt him on the brest' at which the Indian 'started up and used some complementall speech, leavinge his things' and ran off.[133] Within half an hour he returned with five others, including a female interpreter. With her assistance, Fleet was informed that the group came from Usserahak, and that a larger party travelling in 60 canoes, had been intercepted by the Anacostans. The Massawomecks wanted to trade with Fleet, but they were experienced and discriminating in their selection of commodities. By his own admission, Fleet's goods were poor and unfit for Indians who 'delight in hatchets and knives of a large size, broadcloth & coates, shirtes & Scottish stockings', though he thought that the women might be prepared to accept bells and beads.[134]

He met a similar response during a subsequent encounter with a group of seven Indians claiming to be from the Massawomeck habitation of Mosticum. They were discerning traders, uninterested in toys, but keen to acquire useful goods. Fleet recognized two English axes among their possessions, presumably acquired from the Kirkes' outpost at Quebec. The Indians were unimpressed with Fleet's goods. They left with one of his company, William Elderton, an interpreter, who was to promote contact with the northern Indians. The plan received an unexpected blow when Fleet was informed that the Indian party were Herecheenes, reputedly cannibals, posing as the people of Mosticum. Though they presented Fleet with a gift of two beaver coats, insofar as he understood them, he noted that they were peremptory and inquisitive.[135] They were probably a group of Iroquois who, as rivals and enemies of the Massawomecks, were investigating the opportunities for establishing their own commercial relations with the English.

At such alarming news, Fleet hired 16 Piscataways to rescue Elderton, providing them with some of his best trading goods and a reassuring message for the Indians that he 'came not to wronge them, but to furnish them with such commodities as they wanted'.[136] The rescue party returned three weeks later with 80 beaver skins and news that a large party of Massawomecks wanted to trade with him. But they were unwilling to travel south because of rumours regarding the quality of his goods and reports of the death of Elderton at the hands of the Herecheenes. Widely reported among native groups, this provocative act bore the hallmark of a calculated display of violence, designed to test Fleet's response while disrupting his contacts with the Massawomecks.

[132] Ibid., f.519v; Axtell, 'Babel of Tongues', pp. 19–20 for native etiquette.

[133] Lambeth Palace, London, MS 688, Part 2, f.519v.

[134] Ibid., ff.519v–20.

[135] Ibid., f.520. Pendergast, *The Massawomeck*, pp. 66, 72.

[136] Lambeth Palace, London, MS 688, Part 2, ff.519v–20.

On hearing of Elderton's death, and short of provisions and trade goods, Fleet sailed down the Potomac. He had another brief meeting with a small group of Massawomecks who urged him to stay, offering to return with a larger trading party.[137] These promising, but confused, contacts were cut short by the arrival of John Utie, acting under instructions from the council in Virginia, to arrest Fleet, to answer unspecified charges at Jamestown. The complaints probably came from rival traders. Fleet's arrival at Jamestown seems to have aroused wide interest, generating a scramble among some settlers to become his partner. Following the dismissal of the case against him, as a result of the governor's intervention, he began to prepare for the next trading season with a new and unidentified partner. At this point his journal ends.

Despite the difficulties he encountered, Fleet was convinced that the Potomac trade was ripe for development. On the one hand he had an agreement with Indian groups along the river, by which they would hunt beavers during the winter and retain their skins for him. On the other hand, there was the prospect of establishing trading relations with the Massawomecks, and of exploiting the rich northern fur trade. With an estimated yield of 5,000 to 6,000 pounds of beaver skins from the Potomac and an unspecified and greater volume from the north, future prospects were alluring. But their realization would depend on Fleet's ability to navigate a way through interethnic rivalry and competition, while ensuring a supply of quality trading goods.[138]

By the 1620s Hakluyt's vision for the English fur trade in North America seemed to be on the verge of fulfilment. At favoured locations across the eastern seaboard, rival Indian groups were in search of European trading partners. Traders like Fleet and Claiborne were aware of these opportunities, but also of their dangers and competitive character. In neighbouring Delaware Bay, the Dutch, who claimed the region as part of New Netherland, were trying to establish trading contacts with local groups of Lenapes, who desired European trade, but not settlement. Independent traders operated along the Delaware River, establishing several small, irregularly-occupied outposts. According to Isaack de Rasière, the secretary of the colony, before 1624 their trade amounted to between 2,000 and 2,500 beaver skins each year.[139] Commercial prospects aroused the attention of the Susquehannocks, who sent a mission to Manhattan in 1626, hoping to establish relations with the Dutch. Their ambitions were overcast by the outbreak of war with the Lenapes, which lasted until 1638. In any case, de Rasière complained that Dutch trade faltered, due to the late arrival of ships which lacked duffels, a cloth highly-valued

[137] Ibid., ff.520v–2v.

[138] Ibid., ff.521–1v. After their encounter with Fleet the Massawomecks disappear from English records, Rountree and Turner, *Before and After Jamestown*, p. 40.

[139] Jean R. Soderlund, *Lenape Country: Delaware Valley Society Before William Penn* (Philadelphia, 2015), pp. 17–18, 33.

among native groups.[140] Consequently the Indians diverted their trade towards the English, including traders operating in the upper Chesapeake.

The commercial results were modest, though promising. During 1628 imports of beaver skins into London from Virginia amounted to 1,625. Three years later the total was about 2,390.[141] Other types of furs were imported, but the amount was small. By contrast during the early 1630s the annual volume of Dutch trade from New Netherland ranged between 10,000 and 15,000 beaver skins. The French trade along the St Lawrence, before the English takeover, produced annual shipments, in some years, of between 15,000 and 22,000 skins.[142] For the English in the Bay, who were slower to enter the trade than their European rivals, and who were less experienced, a more meaningful comparison might be with Plymouth Plantation, in New England, which was occasionally sending more than 3,000 pounds of beaver back to England during the 1630s.[143] While such striking European variations reflected different approaches to the exploitation of North America, in the case of the Bay, the volume of trade was also the result of a distinctive and delayed trajectory of enterprise.

As this chapter demonstrates, the English intrusion into the Chesapeake was marked by a disruptive and violent process of colonial development, punctuated by chaos and crisis, which was manifest in intercultural relations. Although the Powhatans played an essential role in supplying Jamestown with provisions, trade did not guarantee their future in an emerging colonial world. Less than two decades after the arrival of the newcomers, they inhabited a contested and shrinking region, vulnerable to violent assault. For many settlers, they were an obstacle in the way of an expanding tobacco culture which threatened to sweep over native tenure and title to land. Despite the end of the second Anglo-Powhatan conflict, in February 1632 the colonial

140 Ibid., pp. 13, 15, 25–6, 32–3. The Dutch post at Swanendael was destroyed in an attack of 1631. Van Zandt, *Brothers Among Nations*, pp. 121–3, 127–30 on overtures to the Dutch.

141 Hillier, 'Trade of Virginia', pp. 289–90, 420–3; TNA, E190/947/8 and 190/1032/13.

142 Adams (ed.), *New English Canaan*, p. 239; BL, Egerton 2395, f.19; Donna Merwick, *Possessing Albany, 1630–1710: The Dutch and English Experiences* (Cambridge, 1990), pp. 70–1; Samuel Eliot Morison, *Samuel de Champlain: Father of New France* (Boston, 1972), p. 125; José António Brandâo, *"Your Fyre Shall Burn No More": Iroquois Policy Toward New France and its Native Allies to 1701* (Lincoln, 1997), pp. 68–9 notes that early French trade was not high in volume, but still profitable, and see pp. 86–8 for Dutch trade.

143 The largest shipment from Plymouth during the 1630s amounted to 3,738 pounds, William Bradford, *History of Plymouth Plantation 1620–1647*, 2 vols. (New York, 1912), 2, pp. 172–3, 190; Bunker, *Making Haste from Babylon*, pp. 339–40, 350, 381–2, 450–1; Francis X. Moloney, *The Fur Trade in New England 1620–1676* (Cambridge, Mass., 1931), pp. 24–9.

assembly decreed that they were irreconcilable enemies with whom trade was prohibited.[144] In these circumstances colonial traders operated opportunistically, while developing a form of enterprise which, in some cases, encouraged a combination of trade with plantation. Outrunning the settled bounds of the colony, they established trading contacts or outposts along the Potomac and in the upper reaches of the Bay. Their apparent success masked deeper structural and contingent problems in the relations between natives and newcomers. Yet adventurers, like Claiborne and Fleet, were attracted by the rich fur resources of these regions, and the prospect of breaking into the lucrative northern trade. Their ambitions anticipated informal commercial expansion, underpinned by a vision of an enlarged Virginia. If tobacco was becoming the economic dynamo of the colony, the fur trade was emerging as its engine of exploration and expansion. By the early 1630s, however, future growth seemed to require transatlantic partners and the provision of capital investment and wider commercial connections. Changing conditions, including international and intercultural rivalries, initiated ambitious and experimental transatlantic ventures for its exploitation.

144 William Waller Hening (ed.), *The Statutes at Large: Being a Collection of All the Laws of Virginia* (Richmond, 1809–23, repr. New York 1923), 1, pp. 173, 176.

Chapter 3

Trade and Rivalry: The Promise of Expansion and Innovation during the 1630s

In 1629 Sir George Calvert, first Lord Baltimore, visited Jamestown seeking a new refuge for a Catholic colony. A former Secretary of State under James I, Calvert resigned office following his conversion to Catholicism. During the early 1620s he established a small outpost on Newfoundland, where he settled with his wife and family in 1628. Defeated by the 'sadd face of wynter', he sought an alternative location in Chesapeake Bay.[1] Robert Beverley subsequently noted that the settlers 'looked upon him with an evil Eye, on account of his Religion'.[2] Despite the hostile reception, on his return to England he secured royal approval for the creation of another colony in the Bay, named Maryland, in honour of Charles I's French wife, Henrietta Maria. Although Calvert died in April 1632, shortly before the charter for the settlement passed under the royal seal, his son Cecil, second Lord Baltimore, proceeded with the venture. By this 'unhappy Accident', bemoaned Beverley, a 'Country which Nature had so well contriv'd for one, became Two separate Governments'.[3] The establishment of Maryland transformed an emerging colonial world. It divided the Bay into rival colonies and competing interethnic trading associations and networks. At the same time the new colony threatened the prospect of colonial expansion in Virginia. Consequently, during the 1630s the Bay became a bitterly contested arena, where religious animosity inflamed the competition over trade and territory. The focal point for much of this rivalry was Kent Island, settled as a satellite of Virginia, but which after 1634 lay within the bounds of Maryland. Claiborne's ambitions to combine trade and plantation in the upper Bay were mirrored by those of the Maryland adventurers along the Potomac. Innovative schemes to develop the transatlantic trade in beaver skins thus occurred under challenging and competitive conditions. Colonial

1 Gillian T. Cell (ed.), *Newfoundland Discovered: English Attempts at Colonisation, 1610–1630* (Hakluyt Society, Second Series, 160, 1982), p. 296; John D. Krugler, *English and Catholic: The Lords Baltimore in the Seventeenth Century* (Baltimore, 2004), pp. 77–103.

2 Beverley, *History of Virginia*, p. 58.

3 Ibid., p. 59.

and native rivalries, which spilled over into Delaware Bay, fuelled commercial expansion, but from the outset there was a danger that these duelling ventures would frustrate the aims and ambitions of the other.

The Kent Island joint stock from 1631 to 1634

Although studied from various perspectives, the Kent Island partnership has yet to be recognized as one of the most ambitious and novel fur trading ventures established by the English prior to the formation of the Hudson's Bay Company in 1670.[4] Its leading promoters were hoping to exploit an unusually favourable environment for commercial enterprise in the Chesapeake. On the one hand, the rapidly growing market for beaver skins during the 1620s aroused the interest of London merchants engaged in Atlantic trade and shipping. On the other hand, the disruption to the Canadian fur trade, as a result of native and European rivalries, presented an opportunity for gaining access to an apparently inexhaustible supply of raw material, by attracting Indian traders from the north into the Bay. Commercial ambitions and prospecting were reinforced by reports of an interior region with an unlimited supply of furs.[5] Gaining access to this region came closer with the seizure of Quebec during 1629. The prospect of securing control of 'a great Trade for furs and Beaver skins' along the St Lawrence provoked the interest of rival groups of city merchants, keen to secure a stake in a new and profitable enterprise.[6]

The partnership established

The partnership grew out of a meeting during 1629 between Claiborne and William Cloberry, a London merchant and ship-owner. Although Claiborne was on an official visit to halt Baltimore's colonizing scheme, he was also seeking support for his ambitions in the upper Bay. Inspired by information from a French fur trader, regarding commercial prospects in the north, Cloberry indicated a 'desire to adventure to Virginia and to Nova Scotia, New England and the parts adjoyninge, to trade with the Indians and English for beaver and corne'.[7] His informant may have been Etienne Brûle, who

4 Brenner, *Merchants and Revolution*, pp. 120–31; Walsh, *Motives of Honor*, pp. 76–83; and contributions by F.J. Fausz and Van Zandt cited in this section.

5 Adams (ed.), *New English Canaan*, pp. 234–5; Donald F. Connors, *Thomas Morton* (New York, 1969), p. 72.

6 Having seized Quebec, the Kirke venture was trading with the Hurons according to a report of 1630, BL Egerton 2395, f.19; Fischer, *Champlain's Dream*, pp. 407–21.

7 TNA, HCA 13/243, Part 1, unnumbered; Van Zandt, *Brothers among Nations*, pp. 132–3; Hatfield, *Atlantic Virginia*, pp. 44, 169 on the intercolonial aspect of trade; Walsh, *Motives of Honor*, pp. 75–83 argues that it was organized along the same lines as 'particular plantations' established under the Virginia Company.

visited England after agreeing to serve the Kirke venture as an interpreter and commercial agent. Following further meetings between Claiborne and Cloberry, a joint stock venture was launched.[8] It was a far-reaching proposal for combining transatlantic with intercolonial trade, based on harmonizing commercial and plantation development. From the outset, the leading partners anticipated that the acquisition of provisions from Indian groups in the Bay would lay the basis for commerce with recently established settlements farther north, effectively competing with Fleet's rival venture along the Potomac. As a business operation it represented an alliance between city and colony. Under the terms of the original agreement Cloberry held a share of two-sixths in the partnership. The remaining stock was divided equally between Claiborne, John de la Barre, Maurice Thompson and Simon Turgis.

With the notable exception of Claiborne, the subscribers to the joint stock were drawn from the so-called 'new merchants' of London.[9] They bore the stamp of a younger generation of traders, distinct from the city's commercial elite, who played a leading role in opening up the transatlantic trades during the first half of the seventeenth century. The partnership assembled a collection of entrepreneurs, of similar age and interests, who were at a formative stage in their careers. Attracted by the profit to be earned from North American commerce, and responsive to market opportunities in England, they were prepared to invest in speculative enterprises, in some cases covering a wide variety of venturing, while also taking advantage of the sea wars with Spain and France from 1625 to 1630, to combine such activity with maritime plunder.[10]

Among the London partners, Cloberry was the linchpin of the joint stock. Born about 1595, he was the second son of Oliver and Anne Cloberry of Bradstone in Devon. He began his city career as an apprentice to Humphrey Slaney, merchant and ship-owner, who played a prominent part in the re-establishment of English trade in West Africa during the early seventeenth century. The connection was enduring. Following in the footsteps of his master, Cloberry gained entry to the Haberdashers' Company in 1620, though he never acquired Slaney's prominence in its affairs.[11] The following year he married one of Slaney's daughters, Dorothy. Throughout the 1620s and beyond, he

[8] TNA, HCA 13/243, Part 1, unnumbered; HCA 24/96, no.278; on Brûle see Bruce G. Trigger, *The Children of Aataentsic: A History of the Huron People to 1660*, 2 vols. (Montreal, 1976), 1, pp. 261–2, 265–6, 287–8, 305–6, 367–75; Fischer, *Champlain's Dream*, pp. 499–500. He may have visited the Susquehannocks in 1615 or 1616, Jennings, 'Susquehannock', in Trigger (ed.), *Handbook*, p. 365.

[9] Brenner, *Merchants and Revolution*, pp. 92–184.

[10] *CSPD, 1628–9*, pp. 289, 293, 301, 306; *CSPD, 1629–31*, p. 156 for examples.

[11] Frederic Thomas Colby (ed.), *The Visitation of the County of Devon in the Year 1620* (Harleian Society, 1872), p. 60; Guildhall Library, London, MS 15842/1, ff.114–4v, 204, 210, 239v, 263, and 15857, f.187.

was a partner with Slaney in a series of ventures to West Africa. Together they pioneered the extension of English commerce to Sierra Leone and Angola. But their activities provoked the hostility of the Guinea Company which was established in 1618 with a monopoly over trade to West Africa. The partners vigorously defended their commercial rights, claiming in a petition to the Privy Council of 1628 that they 'had adventured all their Estates and fortunes, to their great Costs and Charges, in discovering and bringing that Trade to perfeccion'.[12] Their determination to secure such hard-won and costly gains led the council to broker a settlement according to which they were admitted to the company, while retaining the freedom to trade independently.

Although Cloberry was heavily committed to the Guinea trade, he accumulated wide-ranging commercial interests during the 1620s. Dealing mainly in the export of cloth, he traded with Spain, Portugal and the Canary Islands for sugar and wines, supplemented by a sporadic commerce with France and the Baltic region for goods such as wine, vinegar, canvas, tar and iron. In addition, he acquired an interest in transatlantic commerce and settlement, including the rapidly growing tobacco trade with Virginia.[13] As a busy and enterprising merchant, Cloberry was willing to invest in new trades, despite the risks involved. In June 1629 he recorded a significant loss, following the seizure of the *Benediction* of London off the coast of West Africa by a French vessel. Its cargo, of which he was a part-owner, was valued at £13,000.[14] The damage may have been offset by his investment in the business of maritime reprisal. In 1627 he was involved in sending out Henry Fleet, as captain of the *Paramour* of London, against Spain and France. The following year, as a supporter of Sir William Alexander's settlement at Nova Scotia, he sent out two supply vessels, in association with Slaney, which also had commissions to plunder the enemy.[15] For such an adventurous city trader, the Kent Island venture was an inviting opportunity to strengthen and broaden a widespread commitment to Atlantic enterprise. It enabled him to take the lead in a new,

12 *APC, 1628–8*, pp. 149–50; *APC, 1627*, pp. 400, 436. On the Guinea trade see J.W. Blake, 'The Farm of the Guinea Trade, 1631', in H.A. Cronne et al. (eds.), *Essays in British and Irish History in Honour of James Eadie Todd* (London, 1949), pp. 85–106; David P. Gamble and P.E.H. Hair (eds.), *The Discovery of River Gambra by Richard Jobson 1623* (Hakluyt Society, Third Series, 1999), pp. 9–38.

13 Brenner, *Merchants and Revolution*, pp. 110, 122, 187: TNA, E190/25/9, 190/29/4, 190/35/5, 190/36/5 and 7; *APC, 1623–5*, p. 238; *CSPD, 1631–3*, pp. 102, 127.

14 *CSPD, 1629–31*, p. 145; Blake, 'Farm of the Guinea Trade', pp. 103–4.

15 *CSPD, 1628–9*, pp. 289, 293, 301, 306, 439; *CSPD, 1629–31*, p. 156; *APC, 1627*, pp. 376–7; Rev. Charles Rogers (ed.), *The Earl of Stirling's Register of Royal Letters Relative to the Affairs of Scotland and Nova Scotia from 1615–1635*, 2 vols. (Edinburgh, 1885), 1, p. 265; for Alexander 's interest in a fur trading plantation on Cape Breton see, BL, Egerton 2395, ff.23–5.

potentially profitable partnership that drew on his own recent experience and business contacts in London.

Maurice Thompson's membership of the joint stock provided it with unrivalled experience of transatlantic trade with Chesapeake Bay. He was a younger son from a landed family of Watton in Hertfordshire. In 1617, aged about seventeen, he migrated to Virginia, arriving at an opportune time in the development of the colony. The acquisition of 150 acres of land gave him an opening to take advantage of the tobacco boom, probably with the assistance of his brother-in-law, William Tucker, a more experienced colonist.[16] By 1623 Thompson was back in London, though the arrival in the colony of three of his brothers kept his interests in the hands of family members. During the factional in-fighting that preceded the dissolution of the Virginia Company, he defended the colony's leaders against accusations of mismanagement. Thereafter he became one of the leading importers of Virginia tobacco into London. By 1626, in defiance of royal policy and regulation, he was involved in the re-export of colonial tobacco to markets in Northern Europe.[17]

Thompson's transatlantic interests demonstrated an early trend towards diversification. He played a leading role in the colonization of St Kitts in the Caribbean. In 1626, in partnership with Thomas Combes, a merchant of Southampton, he transported 60 slaves to the island, where, the following year, he received a patent for 1,000 acres of land.[18] He combined some of these ventures with seaborne plunder, regularly sending out ships, in association with others, with commissions against Spain and France. By 1630 he was investigating the commercial potential of the fur trade along the St Lawrence, despatching the *Elizabeth* of London which 'traded there with the Savages'.[19] The voyage infringed the monopoly rights of the Anglo-Scottish enterprise led by Lewis Kirke. Consequently, another vessel, sent out by Thompson, John de la Barre and Richard Brereton to trade for beaver skins in Canada, was arrested on its return to London. Against instructions from the Privy Council,

16 Brenner, *Merchants and Revolution*, pp. 118, 195; TNA, HCA 13/60, unfoliated; Annie Lash Jester (ed.), *Adventurers of Purse and Person: Virginia 1607–1625* (Richmond, 1964), p. 49.

17 *RVC*, 4, pp. 245, 257, 557; TNA, E190/29/4; PC 2/42, ff.490, 497; J.R. Pagan, 'Growth of the Tobacco Trade between London and Virginia, 1614–1640', *Guildhall Studies in London History*, 3 (1979), pp. 260–1.

18 V.T. Harlow (ed.), *Colonising Expeditions to the West Indies and Guiana, 1623–1667* (Hakluyt Society, Second Series, 56, 1925), pp. 26–7; *APC Colonial, 1613–80*, p. 122; TNA, HCA 24/102, no.119. There is little evidence that the English were seriously interested in the slave trade at this time, P.E.H. Hair and Robin Law, 'The English in Western Africa to 1700', in Nicholas Canny (ed.), *The Oxford History of the British Empire. Volume I: The Origins of Empire* (Oxford, 1998), pp. 254–5.

19 *APC Colonial, 1613–80*, pp. 168–70, 178–9; TNA, PC 2/42, ff.67–8; *CSPD, 1628–9*, p. 305.

he persisted in sending out vessels to Canada. But in 1632 he was arrested and imprisoned, and forced to submit to the council's ruling in favour of his rivals.[20] Thompson's ambitions to break into the transatlantic fur trade were a compelling motive for subscribing to the Kent Island venture, which reinforced his position in promoting colonial development in the Bay.

John de la Barre provided the joint stock with a more diverse portfolio of interests. Born in London about 1599 or 1600, he was the son of a refugee Huguenot from France. In association with his brother, Vincent, he was one of the leading members of the Huguenot merchant community in the city during the early seventeenth century. Although his interest in the new colonial trades was limited, he was widely involved in overseas trade and shipping. During the 1620s he was a leading importer of wines from France, Spain and the Canary Islands. He exported cloth to markets in France, Flanders, the Netherlands and Spain, with occasional shipments to Russia and Hanseatic ports, such as Hamburg. In 1627 he sent three vessels to the Canary Islands in partnership with Cloberry.[21] They were captured on the return voyage, laden with wine, by an English ship sailing with a commission against Spain. The vessels were later restored, but their cargoes were adjudged as lawful prize by the High Court of Admiralty. Despite the loss, de la Barre's involvement in reprisal enterprise seems to have been modest.[22]

De la Barre's commercial venturing included a substantial interest in the pilchard fishery off south west England and Ireland. He regularly consigned cargoes of fish to markets in the Mediterranean, from which he imported fine textiles, spices and dyes. He also acquired an interest in the transatlantic fishery at Newfoundland, based on a similar pattern of voyaging. Alongside these ventures, during the 1620s he was heavily involved in shipping and contracting for the state, freighting and purchasing vessels for royal service during the sea wars. The scale of this activity is indicated by the reimbursement of £5,700 in July 1628 for his services.[23] His subscription to the Kent Island joint stock marked the emergence of a wider interest in the fur trade, though with mixed

20 *APC Colonial, 1613–80*, pp. 172–3, 185–6; *CSPC, 1574–1660*, p. 156; TNA, PC 2/42, ff.210, 395, 448.

21 John C. Appleby (ed.), *A Calendar of Material Relating to Ireland from the High Court of Admiralty Examinations 1536–1641* (Dublin, 1992), pp. 151, 193; *CSPD, 1625–6*, p. 511; *CSPD, 1627–8*, p. 233; TNA, E190/36/7, 190/38/5; *APC, 1627*, pp. 376–7, 417.

22 *CSPD, 1628–9*, pp. 301, 552; *CSPD, 1629–31*, pp. 43, 116–17, 199, 342–3; *APC, 1628–9*, pp. 104, 394.

23 *APC, 1628–9*, p. 55; TNA, HCA 24/96, no.334; Kenneth R. Andrews, *Ships, Money and Politics: Seafaring and Naval Enterprise in the Reign of Charles I* (Cambridge, 1991), p. 53; Gillian T. Cell, *English Enterprise in Newfoundland 1577–1660* (Toronto, 1969), p. 19; Appleby (ed.), *Calendar*, pp. 191, 245.

results. The Canadian venture with Thompson ended badly with his arrest and imprisonment in 1632. Later in the year, in association with Cloberry and David Morehead, he sent out the *William* of London with passengers and provisions for the Massachusetts Bay colony, intending to establish a fishery at Scituate and trade along the Hudson River for furs. The failure of the venture, as a result of Dutch hostility, left the partners with losses of between £4,000 and £5,000, aggravating de la Barre's financial problems during the 1630s.[24]

The last founder member of the joint stock based in London was Simon Turgis, whose early career bore some similarity to Thompson's. He was from a family of middling status of Petworth in Sussex. Aged about 23, in 1618 he went to Virginia, probably as a servant. According to the muster of 1625, by then he was employed on a plantation owned by Robert Bagwell in West Shirley hundred.[25] During the later 1620s he returned to London, acquiring interests in trade and shipping. In addition, he was admitted to the Haberdashers' Company in 1630. His subscription to the joint stock was accompanied by a growing interest in the colonial provisioning and tobacco trades. Like Thompson he was involved in the re-export of tobacco to Northern Europe. But his modest commercial interests were overshadowed and threatened by Thompson's ambitions to control the Virginia trade, under the terms of a contract of 1633 with the governor and council of the colony. In combination with other lesser traders and planters, he successfully petitioned the Privy Council for permission to continue trading, despite the terms of Thompson's contract.[26]

Although based in Virginia, Claiborne shared a similar background with other members of the joint stock. His father was a merchant of King's Lynn, Norfolk, who moved to London during the 1590s, where he married Sara Smyth. He subsequently settled at Crayford in Kent, where William was born in 1600. As a young man he spent some time at Cambridge University and the Middle Temple in London.[27] In 1620, on the recommendation of Sir Francis

24 *APC Colonial, 1613–80*, p. 173; *Documents of New York*, 1, pp. 71–2, 75; *CSPD, 1636–7*, pp. 368, 409; *CSPD, 1638–9*, p. 241; TNA, PC 2/47, ff.46–7.

25 Jester (ed.), *Adventurers of Purse and Person*, p. 13; Henry St George, *The Visitation of London, 1633, 1634 and 1635*, 2 vols. (Harleian Society, 17, 1883), 2, p. 300; Brenner, *Merchants and Revolution*, pp. 124, 147–8.

26 Ibid., pp. 146–8; TNA, HCA 24/96, no.278; 24/99, no.78; 24/102, no.130; HCA 13/52, f.168; E/190/43/5 and 190/44/1; Guildhall Library, London, MS 15857, f.211v for Haberdashers.

27 Hale, *Virginia Venturer*, pp. 4–8, 45; J. & J.A. Venn, *Alumni Cantabrigienses*, 4 vols. (Cambridge, 1922–27), 1, p. 350; Susie M. Ames (ed.), *County Court Records of Accomack-Northampton, Virginia 1640–1645* (Charlottesville, 1973), p. xxiv; TNA, E190/425/1, 190/426/1, 190/427/8 for trade.

Wyatt, he was appointed the first official surveyor in Virginia.[28] The position launched his colonial career, providing him with a key role in an expanding colonial settlement. His main duties were to survey the lands owned by the company and those belonging to particular or private plantations. He was to receive an annual salary of £30, paid in tobacco or other commodities, and a house with 200 acres of land. He was permitted to work for any settler, on condition that his wages did not exceed six shillings a day. Other positions soon followed. In 1623, two years after his arrival in the colony, he was appointed to the council. The following year he became acting secretary.[29] He retained both posts following the end of company rule. His rapid political ascent allowed him to become a member of an elite group of merchant-councillors who shaped policy in the colony and carefully pursued their own interests.

Claiborne was well-placed to seize the opportunities emerging during the 1620s. With the rewards of office he acquired extensive landed interests amounting to 900 acres by 1625. As secretary he was awarded 500 acres of land, with 20 servants, at Accomack on the Eastern Shore. He used his influence to re-negotiate his annual salary as surveyor, which was raised from 200 to 400 pounds of tobacco. By 1630 his income from office was reputedly worth £1,000 *per annum*. He also acquired a significant interest in the tobacco trade, exporting substantial consignments to London in some years.[30]

Following the collapse of the company, Claiborne and his associates became leading supporters of the war against the Powhatans, while encouraging expansion into the upper Bay. Confident of exploiting native divisions, such men were beginning to formulate a colonial strategy based on conflict with hostile neighbours and peaceful relations with less threatening distant groups. During 1626 Claiborne compiled two papers, including one with Samuel Mathews, which addressed these issues. The first proposed the creation of a palisade across the James and York Rivers to strengthen the colony's defences against Powhatan attack. The second argued in favour of employing trustworthy Indians as guides on trading and exploratory expeditions.[31] He

28 Wyatt, Claiborne and his rival Fleet were all from Kent, James Horn, *Adapting to a New World: English Society in the Seventeenth-Century Chesapeake* (Chapel Hill, 1994), p. 13.

29 *RVC*, 1, p. 494; 3, pp. 477, 486; 4, pp. 69–70, 501–4; Hening (ed.), *Statutes*, 1, pp. 116, 125.

30 *RVC*, 4, pp. 556–8; John Camden Hotten (ed.), *The Original Lists of Persons of Quality Who Went from Great Britain to the American Plantations* (London, 1874, repr. Baltimore, 1983), pp. 271–2, 274; McIlwaine (ed.), *Minutes of the Council and General Court*, pp. 65, 72, 76; Pagan, 'Growth of the Tobacco Trade', p. 261.

31 Hale, *Virginia Venturer*, pp. 113–14; McIlwaine (ed.), *Minutes of the Council and General Court*, p. 111; Ralph T. Whitelaw, *Virginia's Eastern Shore: A History of*

supported his argument by claiming to have developed a means of securing the loyalty of natives so employed. His growing interest in the fur trade enabled him to test these methods at first hand. In 1627 he received a commission to trade with the Indians for furs, skins, maize or any other commodities.[32] Two years later he was appointed to lead an expedition against the Pamunkeys, to destroy their habitations and effectively expel them from the bounds of the colony. His success against these native neighbours was followed by a peaceful mission to the Susquehannocks in the upper Bay, during which he may have heard about their trade with the Hurons in the north, while gaining support for the establishment of an outpost on Kent Island.[33]

Despite common goals and motives, the formation of the joint stock was unsettled by disagreement over its legal foundation. Claiborne subsequently claimed that he urged Cloberry to acquire a royal commission as security against potential opposition from the governor of Virginia, Sir John Harvey.[34] His concern reflected the wider disenchantment of colonial leaders with Harvey's investigation of irregularities committed by officials during the 1620s. Their anxiety included his reluctance to oppose Baltimore's intended settlement in the Bay. Acting on Claiborne's advice, Cloberry acquired a commission during May 1631. But it was issued by Sir William Alexander, subsequently first earl of Stirling, as royal secretary in Edinburgh, under the privy seal of Scotland. It was vague, imprecise and possibly vulnerable to challenge. Issued in Claiborne's name, it was little more than a licence for trade and discovery. It provided authority to traffic for furs, corn and other commodities 'about those Parts of America for which there is not already a Patent granted to others, ... as also to make discoveries for increase of Trade'.[35] It made no mention of the settlement of Kent Island. In response to Claiborne's warning that it was insufficient for the purposes of the joint stock,

Northampton and Accomack Counties, 2 vols. (Richmond, 1951), 1, p. 169.

32 TNA, CO 1/39, f.44, iii–iv; McIlwaine (ed.), *Minutes of the Council and General Court*, pp. 184–5; Fausz, '"To Draw Thither the Trade of Beavers"', in Trigger et al. *'Le Castor Fait Tout'*, pp. 54–7.

33 Hening (ed.), *Statutes*, 1, pp. 139–2; Clayton Colman Hall (ed.), *Narratives of Early Maryland 1633–1684* (New York, 1925), p. 88; Van Zandt, *Brothers among Nations*, pp. 116–36 argues that it established one of the most successful 'intercultural alliances' during the early seventeenth century; Rice, *Nature & History*, pp. 93–4; Denys Delâge, *Bitter Feast: Amerindians and Europeans in Northeastern North America, 1600–1664* (Vancouver, 1993), pp. 54, 145 for Huron trade.

34 TNA, HCA 24/96, no.278; 24/105, no.252.

35 Rogers (ed.), *Earl of Stirling's Register*, 2, pp. 527–8; David Laing (ed.), *Royal Letters, Charters, and Tracts, Relating to the Colonization of New Scotland* (Edinburgh, 1867), pp. 12–4, 37–8, 43, 47, 65–6; Manfred Jonas, 'The Claiborne-Calvert Controversy: An Episode in the Colonization of North America', *Jahrbuch fur Amerikastudien*, 11 (1966), pp. 241–50.

Cloberry promised to procure a more comprehensive commission through the influence of a friend at court. It was a promise he failed to fulfil.

The disagreement had serious consequences following the grant of the Maryland charter in 1632. As Baltimore was preparing the first expedition, he was informed of a division within the joint stock between the London partners and Claiborne. It was reinforced by several proposals from Cloberry which marginalized Claiborne's interest in the venture. Baltimore deferred discussion until he heard from the latter.[36] In protest at the conduct of Cloberry, during 1634 Thompson withdrew from the joint stock. He later accused Cloberry and de la Barre of unfair dealing with Claiborne, declaring that 'he would rather lose all then hold partnership with such men'.[37] His withdrawal was followed by that of Turgis and de la Barre, for unspecified reasons, though both may have been struggling with financial problems, and unhappy with the lack of returns for the venture.[38]

These withdrawals were offset by the recruitment of two new partners. In 1634 David Morehead replaced Thompson, and two years later de la Barre was succeeded by George Evelin. Morehead was a Scottish merchant resident in London. During the 1620s he was heavily involved in Anglo-Scottish trade. At the same time, he developed varied commercial interests mainly within Northern Europe. He imported a range of commodities including French wine, sugar, stockings, salt, grain and Scottish yarn. In some years, grain accounted for much of his business. During 1626 he shipped 3,210 quarters of wheat and oats into London which represented more than two-thirds of his total consignments.[39] In 1632 he was a partner with Cloberry and de la Barre, in an unsuccessful fur trading venture along the Hudson River. During the 1630s he was admitted to the Beavermakers' Company, which may have been intended to enhance the efficiency of the joint stock by improving access to the purchasers of fur.[40]

Little is known of Evelin before his entry into the joint stock. Of a similar age to the other subscribers, he was born in London in 1593. His father joined the Virginia Company in 1609, and his brother, Robert, was involved in several ventures to the colony during 1634 and 1635. His recruitment seemed to signal the reconstitution of the venture. In 1636 he was sent to Kent Island to replace Claiborne.[41] But he later claimed that he was misled by Cloberry, who he

36 As indicated in Baltimore's instructions to his settlers, Hall (ed.), *Narratives of Early Maryland*, pp. 19–20.

37 TNA, HCA 13/243, Part 1, unnumbered.

38 Walsh, *Motives of Honor*, p. 76.

39 *APC, 1629–30*, pp. 228, 242–3; TNA, E190/31/3, 190/35/1.

40 *CSPD, 1640–1*, p. 368.

41 Bernard C. Steiner, *Beginnings of Maryland 1631–1639* (Baltimore, 1903), pp. 62–3; Edward C. Papenfuse et al. (eds.), *A Biographical Dictionary of the Maryland*

described as a 'silly fellow to venture his money soe, and that it was better liveing att Maryland'.[42] It was an attempt to justify his abandonment of the joint stock in favour of supporting Baltimore's claim to the island.

Joint stock enterprise was the favoured mode of operation for implementing this design for trade and plantation. By the late 1620s it was an established means for organizing long-distance commerce, though the failure of the Virginia Company discredited its value for the promotion of colonies or plantations. Under Cloberry's leadership the partnership mobilized city resources, assembling an experienced collection of human capital which included colonial representation, reducing the risks and transaction costs of a new business. The Virginia Company was a warning against the dangers of internal division, to which even small enterprises were prone. But the flexibility and adaptability of the joint stock accommodated the withdrawal and replacement of partners. The experience of the larger company may have provided more instructive lessons regarding the expectations of investors, the problem of distance in delaying or distorting information, and the despatch of regular and appropriate supplies. Yet the success of the joint stock depended heavily on Claiborne's ability to secure supplies of fur from the Susquehannocks. Almost from its inception, however, the ambitions of the partners were overshadowed by the establishment of Maryland. Colonial rivalry and commercial competition politicized the venture, testing its effectiveness at dealing with the challenges of transatlantic faction and disunity.

Trade and plantation

The joint stock met with mixed fortunes. Under Claiborne's leadership the plantation survived a potentially disastrous start. With the support of the Susquehannocks, trade showed greater potential for development, but changing conditions within and beyond the Bay exposed the venture to a succession of threats, provoking fissures between the leading partners which progressively weakened its coherence. Internal division culminated in legal action before the High Court of Admiralty and the collapse of the venture in the later 1630s.

Claiborne led the first expedition, pioneering English settlement in the upper Bay, while also claiming the jurisdiction of Virginia over the region. Before leaving London, in April 1631 he reached an agreement with John Winthrop to supply the Massachusetts Bay colony with 40 tons of maize and fish.[43] The following month he departed aboard the *Africa*. The vessel was laden with supplies valued at nearly £1,320, 17 servants, including one

---

Legislature, 1635–1789, 2 vols. (Baltimore, 1979–85), 1, p. 314; *CSPD, 1625–49*, p. 393.

42 TNA, HCA 13/243, Part 1, unnumbered.

43 *Winthrop Papers*, 5 vols. (Massachusetts Historical Society, 1929–47), 3, pp. 31–2.

woman, and a small, but unspecified number of freemen. By July the ship had reached Kecoughtan or Elizabeth City, where Claiborne had an estate. Before proceeding up the Bay, he acquired livestock, including 20 pigs, 13 ducks and hens, and material for the plantation such as stools, chairs, oven bricks, wheelbarrows and two small cannons, as well as deal boards and a pair of iron rudders for the construction of two trading vessels. In addition, he hired Thomas Savage, a settler with experience of living with native groups, to serve as an interpreter. The stop-over also enabled Claiborne to acquire a licence from the governor and council, authorizing him to trade with Indians in any part of Virginia.[44]

The *Africa* reached Kent Island by late August. Claiborne took formal possession of the island, in addition to two smaller islands nearby. One, situated at the mouth of the Great Choptank River, was named after him. The other, located south of the larger island was known as Popples or Poplar Island.[45] Stocks of pigs were placed on both for the supply of the plantation. Cloberry later defended the ownership of the island on the grounds that Claiborne purchased it from the native owners. According to a detailed account by the latter, which was submitted as evidence to the High Court of Admiralty, in April 1634 he paid £12 to an unidentified 'Landlord in trucke for' it.[46] The reference may be to the Matapeakes, of whom at least 100 lived on the island at the time of the arrival of the English.[47] More likely it referred to the Susquehannocks, who were aggressively asserting their authority over much of the upper Bay, and who would have benefited from being seen as the patrons or sponsors of the newcomers.[48]

During the dying days of summer, the servants, under Claiborne's supervision, constructed a small outpost or fort at the southern tip of the island. At the same time Claiborne turned his attention to establishing commercial contact with the Indians. According to Richard Thompson, who was employed as a trader for the joint stock, in September, 'a littell before the fall of the leaffe', he sailed in the *Africa* to Palmer's Island, at the mouth of the Susquehanna River, where he acquired about 100 beaver skins, amounting to between 400

44 TNA, HCA 13/243, Part 1, unnumbered; HCA 24/96, no.278; CO 1/39, f.44, viii; McIlwaine (ed.), *Minutes of the Council and General Court*, p. 484. On the growth of Kecoughtan see Horn, *Adapting to a New World*, p. 165; and Axtell, 'Babel of Tongues', p. 47 on Savage.

45 TNA, HCA 24/96, no.278. Both islands were subject to considerable erosion, Oswald Tilghman, *History of Talbot County, Maryland 1661–1861*, 2 vols. (Baltimore, 1915), 2, pp. 534–40.

46 TNA, HCA 13/243, Part 1, unnumbered; CO 1/39, f.44, vii.

47 Ibid.; Steiner, *Beginnings of Maryland*, pp. 12–3.

48 Soderlund, *Lenape Country*, pp. 49–50; Richter, *Before the Revolution*, pp. 150–1.

and 500 pounds in weight.[49] Almost certainly the furs were supplied by the Susquehannocks, whose habitations were within easy reach. They also ceded the island to Claiborne, enabling him to establish a small trading post on it.

This promising start did not last. Later in the year, while Claiborne was away, fire swept through the fort, burning down the storehouses and their contents, including the beaver skins. Tools were damaged, clothing was destroyed, and trading goods, including ironware, copper and beads, were reduced to molten lumps. The settlers were left with 10 serviceable muskets to defend themselves. William Coxe, one of the colonists, later claimed that the remaining provisions were so poor, that the servants and freemen were reduced to despair.[50] Shortly afterwards six of the ablest servants died. Claiborne attributed their deaths to the harsh conditions they endured due to the loss of food and clothing. He was also forced to dispose of Richard Haulsey, 'a very untoward youth', whom the survivors accused of deliberately setting the fire.[51]

Informing his London partners of the setback, Claiborne gave them an opportunity to withdraw from the venture. If they persisted, however, he requested an urgent supply, while he re-established the fort and plantation out of his estate in Virginia. Cloberry was reassuring in his reply, urging him to 'proceede cheerfullye and not to be dismayed ... because ... all newe beginnings were difficulte'.[52] But the discouraging news may have had a bearing on the withdrawal of de la Barre and Turgis. Despite Cloberry's confidence, it was more than twelve months before a re-supply was organized, a reflection of the undercapitalized nature of the venture. The delay left the plantation in an exposed and vulnerable situation. Claiborne subsequently complained that the settlers endured misery and want, including the danger of native hostility, through the lack of men and weapons.[53] Without his leadership and support, Thomas Hailes claimed that the servants and freemen would have perished through insufficient provisions.

While acknowledging Claiborne's role, the survival of the plantation during this testing period depended on native acquiescence or cooperation. This may seem paradoxical given the testimony of settlers who were haunted by the

49 Susie M. Ames (ed.), *County Court Records of Accomack-Northampton, Virginia 1632–1640* (Washington, 1954), pp. 34–5. These figures seem too great for the number of skins. The pelt of an 'average adult' weighs between 1½ and 1¾ pounds, Harold A. Innis, *The Fur Trade in Canada: An Introduction to Canadian Economic History* (New Haven, 1930), p. 2.

50 TNA, HCA 13/243, Part 1, unnumbered; HCA 24/96, no.318; Ames (ed.), *Court Records of Accomack*, p. 34.

51 TNA, HCA 13/243, Part 1, unnumbered; HCA 24/96, no.318.

52 TNA, HCA 24/96, no.318; HCA 13/243, Part 1, unnumbered.

53 Ibid. On the wider issue of undercapitalization see Grassby, *Business Community*, pp. 240, 409.

prospect of Indian attack. For example, Hailes reported that they lived 'in danger every day to be cut off by the Indians'.[54] English fears were intensified by news of the recent destruction of the Dutch plantation at Swanendael in Delaware Bay by a group of Lenapes. With limited understanding of the complexities of native politics or diplomacy, there was a tendency for the newcomers to identify all Indians as treacherous and hostile. Thus Thomas Youall, who arrived in July 1634, noted that the outpost 'was always in greate daynger to be lost, and the Men expecting … [to] bee cut off'.[55]

Yet the fort and plantation were re-established unhindered by Indian hostility. Although the English seemed to be taunted and teased by their native neighbours, they faced little overt opposition, at least until the establishment of Maryland. Such conditions were a striking demonstration of the power and policy of the Susquehannocks, and of their association with Claiborne. Whether he was aware of it or not, however, the relationship was structured around clientage and dependency. For the Indians it was driven by long-standing commercial goals, including the search for European trading partners, which were linked with political and diplomatic ambitions. The arrival of Dutch traders in Delaware Bay during the 1620s held out the tantalizing prospect of their fulfilment, but Dutch commercial activity was irregularly maintained. During the late 1620s it was also disrupted by the outbreak of hostilities between the Susquehannocks and the Lenapes.[56] Claiborne's reconnoitring of the upper Bay, which occurred almost in tandem with the Dutch, followed by the settlement of Kent Island, thus occurred at a well-timed moment. Acting as sponsor for the English, the Susquehannocks were determined to protect their interest in the settlement's development.

Under the protection of a native landlord, Claiborne was able to proceed with the venture. Favourable conditions enabled him to lay the foundations for an infrastructure upon which the development of trade and plantation could be accommodated. During its early years the outpost depended heavily on outside supplies for its maintenance. Claiborne acquired much of this material in Virginia, but he relied on his London partners for the provision of trading goods. According to one visitor, under his management the plantation

54 TNA, HCA 13/243, Part 1, unnumbered.

55 Ibid.; C.A. Weslager, *The English on the Delaware: 1610–1682* (New Brunswick, 1967), pp. 38–9; Van Cleaf Bachman, *Peltries or Plantations: The Economic Policies of the Dutch West India Company in New Netherland 1623–1639* (Baltimore, 1969), pp. 82–3, 135–6.

56 Fausz, '"To Draw Thither"' in Trigger et al. *'Le Castor Fait Tout'*, pp. 58–64; Weslager, *English on the Delaware*, pp. 45–6; Francis Jennings, 'Glory, Death, and Transfiguration: The Susquehannock Indians in the Seventeenth Century', *Proceedings of the American Philosophical Society*, 112 (1968), pp. 17–18.

flourished 'better than any such adventures ever did in those parts'.[57] At the same time he mapped the outline of an extensive interethnic network of trade and exchange. Despite its isolated location, the settlement of Kent Island represented an outpost for an expanding, and potentially diverse, colonial world. In a gesture of defiance directed against Baltimore, during 1632 the island community was represented in the House of Burgesses at Jamestown by Nicholas Martiau. The following year the General Assembly proceeded as if it lay within the bounds of Virginia, issuing instructions for the collection of tobacco cultivated on the plantation.[58]

The venture was anchored in a small but growing physical presence on the island. The fort was the nerve centre for the operation of the joint stock within the Bay. It contained a house and several outbuildings used as stores and possibly as accommodation for the servants. As the settlement expanded other structures were added within and beyond its confines. They included a dairy and blacksmith's workshop, a church and several mills. A garden was laid out around the house and land was cleared for the cultivation of tobacco and maize. Yet it remained an improvised and insecure setting. According to William Coxe, one of the freemen, the suspicions of the settlers were easily provoked by visits of large numbers of Indians, who apparently had no business at the fort. A large group of between 60 and 80 visited shortly after the fire, with the reported intention of destroying the fort. Forewarned, Coxe recounted that he 'cutt severall loope holes on everie side & end of the houses'.[59] When the Indians queried their purpose, he replied that they were to 'shoot out att, for he heard they had an intent … to cut off the … plantacion. Whereupon … their trecherie being discovered' they departed.[60]

Buildings, furnishings and other possessions reflected a rough-hewn, adaptable material culture, not dissimilar from other borderland regions. It was informed by Claiborne's experience of colonial life in Virginia. Despite stark living conditions, there were some concessions to domesticity which alleviated the isolation and estrangement produced by space and locality. Although this was a commercial enterprise, driven by a concern for the profit of subscribers not the comfort of servants, Claiborne's accounts record his concern for the health and welfare of settlers, including payments for medical treatment and the acquisition of Bibles and prayer books.[61]

57 TNA, HCA 13/243, Part 1, unnumbered; CO 1/39, f.44, xv–xvii.

58 Hening (ed.), *Statutes*, I, p. 205; Wilcomb E. Washburn, *Virginia under Charles I and Cromwell, 1625–1660* (Williamsburg, 1957), pp. 15–7.

59 TNA, HCA 13/243, Part 1, unnumbered; HCA 13/58, ff.303–3v; Walsh, *Motives of Honor*, p. 70.

60 TNA, HCA 13/243, Part 1, unnumbered; HCA 24/100, no.63.

61 TNA, HCA 13/243, Part 1, unnumbered.

The focal point of the plantation was the house. It fulfilled various functions, serving as a residence and place of worship until the construction of a church in 1636. It was also a physical affirmation of Claiborne's occupation of the island, and a symbol for the new settlement. Although no detailed description survives, it was a timber-framed construction, furnished with glass windows, to which a brick hall and tiled floor were added. The availability of household goods was limited. Domestic furniture was sparse and probably of poor quality. Furnishings, such as bedsteads or wardrobes, were lacking. Sleeping facilities were rudimentary, although Claiborne purchased 30 yards of bed ticking for the servants in November 1633. Household fittings were likewise limited, though supplemented by acquisitions from Virginia. Eating and drinking utensils were of wood and pewter, and were probably shared during the difficult period after the fire. More variety was provided by Claiborne's purchase of drinking jugs and trenchers. A concern for formality and etiquette, within the domestic world of the house, is suggested by the acquisition of table cloths and napkins.[62]

The labour force of the plantation was multi-layered in character. Under Claiborne's control it included officers, indentured and hired servants, as well as freemen and casual labourers. From 1631 to 1637 a total of 77 men and women were employed on the plantation, though the annual number ranged between 22 and 44.[63] It was overwhelmingly male, including less than a handful of women. They were recruited in England and Virginia. Among immigrants, casualties were high. Six members of the first expedition died within months of arrival. A similar number from the supply of 1634, among a party of 28, died before reaching the island. Replacements were hired locally, but they were an additional charge on the running costs of the venture.[64]

The diversity of the labour force was reflected in the age, experience and background of recruits. At least half of the total was made up of unskilled labourers. Skilled craftsmen accounted for another third. The remainder were described as traders, of indeterminate backgrounds, though several had been employed as mariners. The mixture was reflected in the members of the original expedition, which included William Cocke, a bound servant, aged about 19, from Redbourn in Hertfordshire, and William Coxe, a freeman, aged about 46, of Scarcliffe in Derbyshire. Cocke worked as a kitchen hand and labourer. He received no pay, though he was granted 163 pounds of tobacco, valued at £2 14s 4d, to buy clothes on gaining his freedom in September

62 Ibid. On the importance of the house 'as the key to land-ownership' see John R. Stilgoe, *Common Landscape of America, 1580 to 1845* (New Haven, 1982), p. 65; on material culture see Lois Green Carr, Russell R. Menard, Lorena S. Walsh, *Robert Cole's World: Agriculture and Society in Early Maryland* (Chapel Hill, 1991), pp. 90–114; Horn, *Adapting to a New World*, pp. 311–15.

63 TNA, HCA 13/243, Part 1, unnumbered.

64 Ibid.; Walsh, *Motives of Honor*, pp. 80–2 for an analysis of the labour force.

1635. By contrast Coxe was employed as a carpenter and trader, for which he received an annual wage of £20 until September 1636.[65] Servants hired locally included Richard Thompson, who worked on Claiborne's estate at Accomack. Aged about 18 in 1631, and originally from Norwich in Norfolk, he was employed as a trader, accompanying Claiborne on several voyages.[66]

The management of the servants and other workers employed for the joint stock was left in Claiborne's hands, though he was assisted by a small group of officers, including a lieutenant, sergeant, overseer and minister. They all received an annual wage. In March 1632 Claiborne awarded himself £100 to cover the losses, dangers, hardships and 'unspeakable paines' he endured during the year.[67] He received the same amount, at least on paper, annually until March 1637. Arthur Figes, lieutenant from 1631 to 1635, was granted an annual salary of £30. Hugh Heyward was awarded 1,000 pounds of tobacco as sergeant during 1631 and 1632, and the same amount as overseer from 1634 to 1635. The minister Richard James, who replaced Hugh Pink, the prayer-reader in the house, after he broke his leg, received an annual tithe worth £60.[68]

The organization of labour reflected a degree of specialization that was functional in purpose. During the early years of settlement, three overlapping teams emerged. House servants and kitchen hands formed one, field workers and labourers another and traders a third. Their number varied from year to year, reflecting both availability and turnover. Initially three men and a boy were employed in the kitchen to prepare food and undertake other work in the house, in addition to a maid servant, Joan Young, who was responsible for washing linen and clothing. The field hands and labourers included four or five men who were primarily engaged in the cultivation of tobacco and maize. Others were seasonally engaged in fishing and hunting. They were complemented, at various times, by more specialist positions such as rangers, hog-keepers, a gardener and store-keeper.[69]

The traders were the most distinctive group within the work force. Ultimately the commercial success of the joint stock rested on their shoulders. The need for reliable or experienced recruits may explain why at least four of the original five traders came from Claiborne's estate at Accomack. Five men were annually employed in trading voyages, though most served for a period of two years. From 1631 to 1637 about 20 traders and 11 mariners were hired by Claiborne for the joint stock. With one or two exceptions, they were all paid wages in tobacco or beaver skins, and occasionally in cash. Thomas

65 TNA, HCA 13/243, Part 1, unnumbered; CO 1/39, f.44, xvii.

66 TNA, HCA 13/243, Part 1, unnumbered; Gust Skordas (ed.), *The Early Settlers of Maryland* (Baltimore, 1968), pp. 460–1.

67 TNA, HCA 13/243, Part 1, unnumbered.

68 Ibid.

69 Ibid.; Hale, *Virginia Venturer*, p. 167.

Butler received £22 in October 1632 for serving as master of a trading vessel for one year. For some, the rewards were not commensurate with the risks or conditions of service. Thompson left, to set up his own commercial venture, claiming that he was not paid 'such waigs as he thought he should deserve'.[70]

As the plantation took shape, Claiborne began to develop trading relations with the Indians. He made an encouraging start. From 1631 to 1634 he faced little competition, apart from potentially disruptive voyaging by rival traders from Virginia. Conflict with the Lenapes also seems to have restricted the Susquehannocks' access to the Dutch along the Delaware River. From the perspective of colonial traders, however, scouting the upper Bay for Indian trade was a difficult and dangerous business, marked by uncertainty and suspicion. Claiborne claimed that he endured many difficult voyages during which he was forced to lie on the ground in the woods, in extreme heat and cold, while also suffering shipwreck and capture by Indians who threatened to kill him.[71] As a result of such physical hardship, by 1638 he had lost the use of his right arm. Of course, Claiborne's testimony was self-interested. Nonetheless it was supported by other traders who were acutely aware of the asymmetrical power structure of trading encounters. Thomas Youall recounted an occasion when Claiborne and four others, who were in a shallop, were set upon by two or three hundred Indians and 'were like to bee taken … unless God wonderfully delivered them'.[72]

Under these conditions the English were forced to adapt to native practices, maintaining a balance between security and trade. During the early 1630s Claiborne staked out the coordinates for a waterborne network of commerce, focused on a constellation of islands and rivers. It was conducted in a variety of small vessels employing sail and oars, described as boats, shallops and pinnaces. In terms of accessibility and security, locations such as Palmer's Island served as neutral, or at least uncontested, ground for interethnic trade. Traders were responsive to the peculiar demands of the business. Thomas Hailes noted that from March to June it was necessary to have three or four boats trading with the Indians, otherwise 'it will scarce beare charges & not bee worthwhile'.[73] They needed to be manned with at least six or seven men, to avoid the danger of being taken. According to another trader, Thomas Adams, only one man went ashore, to deal with large parties of Indians, otherwise they would not trade.[74] Claiborne claimed that traders were always

70 TNA, HCA 13/243, Part 1, unnumbered; CO 1/39, f.44, xviii; Fausz, "'To Draw Thither'", pp. 57–8. He subsequently moved to south of the Potomac, Horn, *Adapting to a New World*, p. 175.

71 TNA, HCA 24/96, no.318; 13/243, Part 1, unnumbered; CO 1/39, f.44, xviii.

72 TNA, HCA 13/243, Part 1, unnumbered.

73 Ibid.

74 Ibid.; TNA, CO 1/39, f.44, xviii.

in danger and forced to stand their guard with weapons at hand. Two or three men were appointed to look after the truck, though he insisted that much of it was still stolen. In the case of the Susquehannocks, moreover, the English were dealing with experienced trading partners. Commerce began with the provision of gifts for native leaders, or a group described by Claiborne as the 'King's great men'.[75] Thereafter it became customary for colonial traders to display their goods, which the 'Indians wilbe very long and tedious in viewing, and doe tumble it and tosse itt, & mingle it, a hundred times over'.[76] Where verbal communication was limited, close inspection and gesture did the work of speech. Indians refused to exchange with traders who were unwilling to tolerate their behaviour. As a result, Claiborne explained that it was impossible to keep an exact account of transactions. The best that could be achieved was 'to see what is sold & what is gained & what is left' at the end of each voyage.[77]

Despite these concerns Claiborne carefully cultivated relations with native groups. As early suspicions ebbed, in 1633 he sent one of the traders, John Sandis, to live with the Susquehannocks. He stayed four years, acting as an interpreter and intermediary. Claiborne acknowledged that he was instrumental in procuring trade with the Indians, for which he was awarded 1,700 pounds of tobacco as part of his wages in 1637. His success is partly reflected in Coxe's claim that during the early 1630s Claiborne acquired nearly all the trade in the upper Bay.[78] He also secured better returns than his competitors, acquiring 'five skinnes for one more than Mr Harmer or Captain Fleet did, they being in the same bay a traiding'.[79] Despite the shortage of wares after the fire, Claiborne reported that none of his rivals made such good voyages, or acquired so many beaver skins for so little truck.[80] But he was disappointed with the commodities sent with the first supply which arrived at the end of 1632. Consequently, he was forced to purchase additional goods in Virginia and 19 pieces of cloth from the Dutch along the Delaware River.[81]

75 TNA, HCA 13/243, Part 1, unnumbered; Raphael Semmes, *Captains and Mariners of Early Maryland* (Baltimore, 1937), pp. 61–2.

76 TNA, HCA 13/243, Part 1, unnumbered.

77 Ibid. Though it has been argued that the trade developed into a 'profitable, pragmatic complacency' by J. Frederick Fausz, 'The Invasion of Virginia: Indians, Colonialism, and the Conquest of Cant: A Review Essay on Anglo-Indian Relations in the Chesapeake', *VMHB*, 95 (1987), p. 149.

78 TNA, HCA 13/243, Part 1, unnumbered; CO 1/39, f.44, xviii.

79 Ibid.

80 Ibid.

81 Ibid. English traders, c. 1635, were active around the unoccupied Dutch outpost on the Delaware River, Bachman, *Peltries or Plantations*, pp. 141–2.

The poor supply of truck from London constrained commercial opportunities. Initial expectations had to be scaled back as the volume of trade might have been insufficient to cover the unexpected increases in the running costs of the venture. One of the traders, Philip Taylor, estimated that Claiborne acquired 350 beaver skins during 1632. The following year the number increased to between 900 and 1,000. Estimates by Thompson, based on weight, indicate a similar trajectory, rising from 600 or 700 pounds in 1631 and 1632 to 1,400 or 1,500 pounds in 1633.[82]

Claiborne explained his inability to build on this encouraging start by blaming Cloberry for sending inadequate and improper trading goods. The second supply of 1634 contained a miscellaneous collection of truck, some of which seemed more suitable for the Guinea trade. It included 30 duffels, a coarse woollen cloth, 75 pairs of blankets, 126 dozen hatchets and hoes, 2,000 awl blades, 6,184 fish hooks, 80 dozen hawk's bells, 2¼ gross of children's pipes, two gross of trumpets and 20 gross of Sheffield knives.[83] Claiborne maintained that much of it was of little appeal to more discriminating Indian traders, who, in the words of one trader, 'would not meddle with the great kettles nor hoes or verie few of them'. [84] As such, much of it remained unsold three years later.

To maintain the trade Claiborne was forced to purchase additional goods in Virginia. They included cloth, metal wares as well as various forms of wampum, known as peak or *peag,* and roanoke. Identified by the English as both 'Money and Ornament', these small shell beads, usually strung together, were highly valued among Indian groups, fulfilling a variety of functions.[85] They circulated widely within and between colonial communities. While retaining a powerful symbolic value, they served as a medium of exchange between natives and newcomers. From 1631 to 1635 Claiborne purchased at least 60 fathoms of peak in Virginia, at prices that ranged from 10 shillings to £1 for each fathom.[86] Undoubtedly native beads promoted commerce, but

82 TNA, HCA 13/243 Part 1, unnumbered.

83 TNA, E190/38/7; HCA 13/243, Part 1, unnumbered; HCA 24/96, no.318; Soderlund, *Lenape Country*, pp. 32–3 on the need for quality duffels.

84 TNA, HCA 13/243, Part 1, unnumbered.

85 Beverley, *History of Virginia*, pp. 227–8; Smith, *Works*, 2, pp. 107, 168, 249. They were distinct from the wampum employed by Dutch traders, who had access to sources of supply along Long Island Sound.

86 TNA, HCA 13/243, Part 1, unnumbered; William Hand Browne (ed.), *Proceedings of the Council of Maryland 1636–1667* (Maryland Historical Society, 3, 1885), pp. 76–7; Fausz, 'Profits, Pelts, and Power', pp. 28–9. A General Assembly of 1649 set rates for peak, revised in 1652, which established a value of 5s for one fathom and 2s 6d for one yard. It was double these amounts if black (purple or blue), Warren M. Billings, 'Some Acts not in Hening's *Statutes*: The Acts of Assembly, April 1652, November 1652, and July 1653', *VMHB*, 83 (1975), pp. 63, 67. Roanoke was not worth as much,

they were subject to devaluation, and did not compensate for shortcomings in the supply of goods from London.[87] Moreover the purchase of additional commodities was an unexpected and potentially substantial burden on running costs, which Claiborne later estimated at more than £800.

By the mid-1630s the joint stock had made mixed progress. Within the Bay Claiborne had achieved a surprising degree of integration and coordination in managing the plantation and fur trade. But the supply of truck was a weak link in the developing transatlantic infrastructure. In these circumstances he struggled to capitalize on his relationship with the Susquehannocks. One of the traders, Richard Popeley, claimed that the Indians loved him, but they disliked his goods.[88] In such circumstances the joint stock was in danger of losing trade to rival operators. Coxe claimed that if Claiborne had been well supplied from London during the first two trading seasons, he could have acquired an additional 4,000 beaver skins each year. Instead native traders reportedly returned to their habitations with great packs of skins. The Indians informed Coxe that they would take their furs to other traders, English and Dutch. They also indicated that they 'would not kill any more Beaver, or fetch any from other Indians which lived upp in the Country', because of the poor quality of trading wares.[89]

Under the pressure of these problems the partnership showed signs of fraying. In an effort to promote economic diversification, Cloberry despatched a large group of 22 servants and craftsmen, including carpenters, sawyers and millwrights, with the second supply. Claiborne subsequently disclaimed all responsibility for what he dismissively described as new projects of 'mills, rape oil, iron works or the like'.[90] In response, in association with Alexander Mountney and others, he established a separate plantation in the middle of the island. Known as Crayford, it was soon a thriving enterprise. By 1638 the estate was reported to include 16 servants, who cultivated between 50,000 to 60,000 pounds of tobacco, and a large herd of 200 cattle. It was followed by the establishment of several others nearby, including one by John Boteler, Claiborne's brother-in-law, at a place known as the Great Thicket.[91] In these difficult conditions, with the joint stock disorganized and in danger of losing

Rountree, *Pocahontas's People*, pp. 132–3.

[87] Ibid., p. 132, for the estate of a colonist who died in 1691 which included 264 yards of roanoke valued at three pence a yard.

[88] TNA, CO 1/39, f.44, xviii; HCA 13/243, Part 1, unnumbered.

[89] Ibid.

[90] Ibid.; Walsh, *Motives of Honor*, p. 65.

[91] Ibid., pp. 79–80; HCA 13/243, Part 1, unnumbered; HCA 24/102, no.248; Hale, *Virginia Venturer*, p. 177. From 1631 to 1638 Claiborne's herd of cattle increased from 30 to about 150, Garry Wheeler Stone, 'Manorial Maryland', *MHM*, 82 (1987), p. 21; Hall (ed.), *Narratives of Early Maryland*, p. 152.

control over the settlement of Kent Island, it was faced with the challenging consequences of the establishment of a new colony in the Bay.

The Maryland venture from 1634 to 1638

The establishment of Maryland changed the colonial world of the Chesapeake. The introduction of a rival colony threatened the expansion of Virginia into the region, with profound consequences for the Kent Island joint stock. It triggered bitter controversy and competition which spanned the Atlantic.[92] The protracted and unprecedented dispute that ensued spread to both the city and court, compelling royal intervention. At the same time, increasing hostility exposed cleavages within the English Atlantic, aggravated by the confusion between colonial and metropolitan concerns. These rivalries were compounded with the complexities of native politics and diplomacy. As a result, the new colonial settlement of St Mary's represented a serious threat to the plantation and commercial network created by Claiborne.

Charter and adventurers

Maryland was a new departure for English overseas expansion, embodying a vision of Catholic and seigniorial colonialism under royal protection. If the Kent Island joint stock was based on an alliance between city and colonial interests, the Maryland adventure was the result of close connections between a small, resurgent Catholic elite and the court, which experienced a growing number of conversions during the 1620s and 1630s. Yet there were striking parallels between both ventures, notably in the combination of commerce with colonial planting. Reports of the profitability of the fur trade, 'estimated at thirty fold' by Andrew White, one of the clergy who sailed with the first expedition of 1634, encouraged expectations that it would do more than subsidize the costs of settlement.[93] But White's concern that the newcomers avoid the conduct of covetous traders from Virginia, who exchanged 'cloth for nought but beaver', putting commerce before religion, went unheeded.[94] Four years later the head of the Jesuit mission at St Mary's warned Baltimore that

92 The most detailed survey between the new colony and Virginia remains John H. Latané, *The Early Relations Between Maryland and Virginia* (Baltimore, 1895); on the commercial issues J. Frederick Fausz, 'Patterns of Anglo-Indian Aggression and Accommodation along the Mid-Atlantic Coast, 1584–1634', in William W. Fitzhugh (ed.), *Cultures in Contact*, pp. 250–2.

93 Hall (ed.), *Narratives of Early Maryland*, p. 8; Gaskill, *Between Two Worlds*, pp. 138–9.

94 Hall (ed.), *Narratives of Early Maryland*, pp. 7–8, 44; Potter, *Commoners*, pp. 188–91.

the future of the colony was endangered by leaders who neglected planting in favour of a peddling trade with the Indians.[95]

The new settlement was authorized by a royal charter of 20 June 1632 which, despite an early challenge, over-rode the Kent Island commission. It made Baltimore the lord proprietor of an extensive, if ill-defined, region ranging from the Potomac River in the south to Delaware Bay in the north, lying 'between the ocean on the east and the bay of Chesapeake on the west'.[96] It included all islands within these limits. In appearance the charter granted Baltimore the authority and jurisdiction of a feudal lord, providing him with the opportunity to create a manorial society which would serve as a Catholic haven. It granted him extensive commercial rights and privileges, including the power to levy duties on imports and exports. Although the description of Maryland as a 'country hitherto uncultivated' enabled the Kent Island partnership to challenge its legal basis, on the grounds of prior settlement, the charter contained provision for doubts or questions concerning 'the true sense and meaning of any word, clause, or sentence', to be decided in Baltimore's favour.[97]

Opposition to the proposed colony spanned the Atlantic. It brought together a self-interested group, whose members resorted to a campaign of petitioning and obstructive tactics, confirming Baltimore's suspicions of plots orchestrated by his adversaries in England.[98] It included prominent members of the merchant-planter elite in Virginia, led by Samuel Mathews, with the support of Claiborne, and former members of the Virginia Company such as John Wolstenholme, a well-connected city merchant and customs official. In 1633 a group claiming to represent the planters and adventurers of Virginia petitioned Charles I against the charter. Acting independently of the governor, they claimed that the territory of Maryland, including places of commerce,

95 *The Calvert Papers*, 3 vols. (Maryland Historical Society, Fund-Publication, 28, 1889), 1, p. 167; John Bossy, 'Reluctant Colonists: The English Catholics Confront the Atlantic', in David B. Quinn (ed.), *Early Maryland in a Wider World* (Detroit, 1982), pp. 154–5 for missionary impulse.

96 Merrill Jensen (ed.), *English Historical Documents IX: American Colonial Documents to 1776* (Oxford, 1964), pp. 85–6; Hall (ed.), *Narratives of Early Maryland*, pp. 101–12; BL, Sloane 3662, ff.25v-6.

97 Jensen (ed.), *American Colonial Documents*, pp. 90–1; David W. Jordan, *Foundations of Representative Government in Maryland 1632–1715* (Cambridge, 1987), p. 3; Robert M. Bliss, *Revolution and Empire: English Politics and the American Colonies in the Seventeenth Century* (Manchester, 1990), pp. 26–7; Debra A. Meyers, 'Calvert's Catholic Colony', in L.H. Roper and B. Van Ruymbreke (eds.), *Constructing Early Modern Empires: Proprietary Ventures in the Atlantic World, 1500–1750* (Leiden, 2007), pp. 362–6.

98 Hall (ed.), *Narratives of Early Maryland*, pp. 16–7.

lay within the bounds of Virginia.[99] The king referred the petition to the Commissioners for Foreign Plantations who decided in favour of Baltimore. Both parties were instructed to maintain good correspondence with each other, and to avoid any action that might provoke conflict with the Indians. The decision was reinforced by a royal letter of assistance to the governor and council in the colony, supporting Baltimore. But his preparations for the first expedition were disrupted by complaints and discouraging rumours.[100] Later in the year Claiborne and other planters, supported by Wolstenholme, petitioned the Privy Council, in a last-ditch attempt to retain Kent Island. The petitioners also proposed that Baltimore be advised or allowed to select another location for his colony.[101]

In these circumstances Baltimore proceeded cautiously. He recruited subscribers with discretion, relying on established and trusted networks within the Catholic community. Although the venture was dominated by the Calvert family and their close associates, its structure allowed for the wider mobilization of resources and the emergence of distinct, but overlapping, groups of adventurers. They included the promoters of the first expedition, made up of the *Ark* and the *Dove,* among whom Baltimore was the major shareholder, responsible for half of the total investment. His brother, Leonard, the governor of the colony, accounted for a share of one-eighth. Another brother, George, was part of a group of at least 17 'gentlemen adventurers' who sailed with the first expedition.[102] They were entitled to 1,000 acres of land, formed into manors, for every five men they transported into the colony. In addition, 11 members of this group subscribed to a joint stock for the fur trade.

Despite sharing similar commercial goals, this was a larger and more complex venture by comparison with the Kent Island partnership. The subscribers to the joint stock included Baltimore and his brother, Leonard, Jerome Hawley and Thomas Cornwallis, assistants to the governor, John Saunders, Edward and Frederick Winter, Richard Gerard, Henry Wiseman, Henry Greene and Nicholas Fairfax who died during the transatlantic voyage. They agreed an initial subscription of about thirty shares, with an opening value of £20. Although evidence for individual subscriptions is incomplete, Baltimore was responsible for half of the total, while Hawley accounted for

99 TNA, CO 1/6, nos.76–7; Browne (ed.), *Proceedings of the Council of Maryland 1636–67*, pp. 21–44.

100 TNA, CO 1/6, no.84; PC 2/43, f.291 for the stay of both vessels at Tilbury while an official administered an oath of loyalty to the company.

101 TNA, CO 1/6, no.87.

102 Hall (ed.), *Narratives of Early Maryland*, p. 101; Raphael Semmes, 'The *Ark* and the *Dove:* Transcripts from the Public Record Office, London', *MHM*, 33 (1938), pp. 13–22; John D. Krugler (ed.), *To Live Like Princes* (Baltimore, 1976), pp. 12–3; Horn, *Adapting to a New World*, pp. 28, 54–5.

at least three shares.[103] Subscribers made agreements with other adventurers, spreading the cost of their own investments. Hawley reported that several investors 'adventured with him or under his name'.[104] Calvert reached a similar agreement with Sir Richard Lechford, courtier, convert and landowner of Shellwood in Surrey. Together they agreed to subscribe about £400 in the venture, of which Lechford contributed a quarter. These arrangements enabled a group of mostly anonymous adventurers to invest in the joint stock though, like Lechford, they were almost certainly drawn from the ranks of sympathetic Catholic gentry. The difficulties facing such landowners, despite a more favourable environment under the early Stuart monarchy, provided a powerful motive to support Baltimore. In 1634, for example, Lechford was accused of 'sending two of his daughters to the nunneries beyond the seas'.[105] After refusing to take the oath of allegiance he was dismissed from court. On the order of the Privy Council his daughters were placed in the custody of their uncles, 'into such a course of breeding' that it was later reported 'they are become good Protestants'.[106]

As in the case of its rival venture, the joint stock provided for flexibility in membership. Hawley's withdrawal during 1634 was accompanied by the recruitment of new subscribers. They included William Peaselie, the brother-in-law of Leonard Calvert, who contributed £100 for five shares. Appointed treasurer for the venture, Peaselie also collected subscriptions from others, including £20 from Edward Robinson of Lincoln's Inn. Robinson subsequently initiated legal action against Baltimore, claiming that the membership of the joint stock was deliberately exaggerated to draw in new investors.[107]

Within the confines of a carefully defined community, the venture attracted widespread interest and support. Much of it was modest in scale and short-term in duration, based on the provision of varying amounts of capital by silent partners who remained in England. As a result, while the joint stock suffered from undercapitalization, it was left in the hands of a small group of active adventurers led by Baltimore. But his inability to migrate to the new colony,

[103] TNA, C 24/621 deposition of Hawley; HCA 15/1, Leonards contra Hawley, 25 October 1637; Russell R. Menard and Lois Green Carr, "The Lords Baltimore and the Colonization of Maryland," in Quinn (ed.), *Early Maryland*, pp. 167–8, 179–80.

[104] TNA, C 24/621; Jordan, *Foundations of Representative Government*, pp. 12–13 notes the venture did not attract the anticipated number of adventurers.

[105] *Calvert Papers*, 3, pp. 13–14.

[106] TNA, PC 2/43, ff.45–2, 630, 648; *Calvert Papers*, 3, p. 46. Though not unusual, such harsh action seems to have been uncommon during the 1630s, K.J. Lindley, 'The Lay Catholics of England in the Reign of Charles I', *Journal of Ecclesiastical History*, 22 (1971), pp. 210–14.

[107] TNA, C 24/621; L. Leon Bernard, 'Some New Light on the Early Years of the Baltimore Plantation', *MHM*, 44 (1949), pp. 94–7.

as planned, forced him to cede control over the management of the trade to the governor and his assistants.

Leonard Calvert played a key role in developing commercial opportunities within the colony. A young man, born about 1606, he had varied experience of colonial and maritime enterprise. From 1627 to 1629 he was a member of the small colony at Ferryland on Newfoundland. On his return to England he was appointed captain of the *St Claude,* a prize ship loaned by the king, which was sent out during 1629 with letters of marque against France. The end of the war curtailed this potentially lucrative career. In August his father requested Sir Francis Cottington to provide him with £50, the profits on some stock, so that he could return to Newfoundland. With the intimacy that came with friendship, Baltimore admitted that he did not know what to do with his son, 'now that wee have peace with our neighbours', though he had no wish to see his children maintained by the spoils of war.[108] Calvert's appointment as governor of the Chesapeake colony was a turning point in his life. It gave him an unusual opportunity, as the representative for his elder brother, to fashion a role as a colonial leader, securing the rewards of office, land and trade. As governor and one of the leading promoters of the joint stock, he held a strategic position for establishing relations with native groups along the Potomac.

Thomas Cornwallis was the most important investor in the colonial enterprise beyond the immediate family circle of the lord proprietor. Although there is some uncertainty about his background, he was probably the second son of Sir William Cornwallis, from a well-established Catholic and landed family of Norfolk. He may have been distantly related to the Calverts through the marriage of Francis Cornwallis, possibly an uncle, to Katherine Arundel, a niece of Baltimore's wife. Described as one of the 'greatest Propagators and Increasers' of the colony, Cornwallis served as a colonial commissioner until 1637, as a member of the council from 1637 to 1642, while also acting as the commander for military affairs.[109] He acquired extensive interests in the transportation of servants, the cultivation of tobacco and the fur trade. In correspondence with Baltimore during 1638 he claimed to be working for the honour of God and the defence of the church. Scorning tobacco culture, and threatening to leave the colony if he was forced only to plant 'this Stincking weede of America', he emphasized his wider contribution to the colonial community, and his desire for freedom of conscience. By his own admission,

[108] Cell (ed.), *Newfoundland Discovered*, pp. 281, 286–7, 293–4; Papenfuse (ed.), *Biographical Dictionary*, 1, p. 190.

[109] Sebastian F. Streeter, *Papers Relating to the Early History of Maryland* (Baltimore, 1876), p. 207; Russell R. Menard, *Economy and Society in Early Colonial Maryland* (New York, 1985), pp. 27–8; Papenfuse (ed.), *Biographical Dictionary*, 1, pp. 234–5; Jordan, *Foundations of Representative Government*, pp. 38–40.

however, public service was partly designed to counter rumours from England that he was an 'uncontionable Extortioner'.[110]

The interests of the other members of the joint stock were either short-lived or essentially passive and overshadowed by ambitions for the acquisition of land. By 1637 five of the original adventurers, Saunders, Wiseman, the Winters and Fairfax, were dead. Hawley, another leading subscriber, sailed on the first expedition with his second wife, and served as a commissioner in the colony. But he returned to London during 1635, serving briefly in the household of Henrietta Maria. Although he was appointed treasurer of Virginia, he retained links with Maryland, where he acquired at least 6,000 acres, and maintained an interest in the fur trade.[111] The development of these interests provoked Calvert's suspicions, but they were cut short by his death in 1638.

Despite its structural similarity with the Kent Island partnership, there were fundamental differences between the rival ventures. The Maryland joint stock lacked city support and mercantile experience, though it was offset by the royal favour and court connections that Baltimore inherited from his father. Moreover, its leading members were inexperienced in colonial venturing. By comparison with Claiborne, they were newcomers and novices, who lacked expertise in Indian diplomatic and commercial relations. There was thus every reason for the lord proprietor to adopt a cautious strategy within the Bay, while seeking to maintain support for the new colony at court.

Commercial reconnoitring and rivalry

Although Baltimore advised the leaders of the first expedition to avoid Jamestown, they were instructed to inform the governor of their intention to maintain good relations with Virginia. In addition, they were advised to meet Claiborne, to assure him of the lord proprietor's support and encouragement. In another conciliatory gesture, Baltimore expressed a willingness to allow traders to operate within the jurisdiction of his colony, but it was 'by way of courtesy and not of right'.[112] These initiatives met with little success. The arrival of the expedition in the Bay was greeted with widespread suspicion and unconcealed resentment. The establishment of Maryland, and the commercial reconnoitring that followed, provoked competition that was soon entangled with native rivalries.

The prospect of colonial disunity was revealed by widespread disquiet in Virginia at the arrival of the expedition in February 1634. According to White, the newcomers expected the council at Jamestown to prevent them from

110 *Calvert Papers*, 1, pp. 172, 176.

111 Papenfuse (ed.), *Biographical Dictionary*, 1, p. 246; *Calvert Papers*, 1, pp. 179–80, 187–8.

112 Hall (ed.), *Narratives of Early Maryland*, p. 21.

sailing up the Bay, but after a stay of eight or nine days they were allowed to proceed. However, Calvert received alarming news from Claiborne that the Indians were ready to resist him, incited by reports that the expedition was Spanish. These damaging rumours not only expressed deep-seated, if self-serving, colonial suspicions regarding the loyalty of English Catholics, but may also have resurrected long-standing anti-Spanish hostility among native groups which recalled earlier, hostile Spanish incursions into the Bay. Calvert and Cornwallis assumed they originated with Claiborne. He denied the allegation, subsequently insisting that he maintained good correspondence with the newcomers. The claim was contradicted by Cornwallis, who reported that he 'dealt very unworthily and falsely with them' despite being offered the right to trade on the same terms as other settlers.[113]

When the expedition reached the Potomac in March, it was met with distrust and hostility among native groups. Calvert reported that the rumours provoked all the Indian nations of the region in 'a generall alarm, as if they intended to summon all the Indians of America against us'.[114] The leader of the Piscataways reportedly assembled 500 warriors to face the newcomers. As the expedition sailed along the river it encountered Fleet, who was trading in three small vessels. He was persuaded by Calvert to serve as an interpreter and adviser, in exchange for a stake in the joint stock. Under his guidance Calvert established a small settlement, called St Mary's, in the territory of the Yaocomacos, a group with whom he had lived as a captive.[115] Fleet's assistance was contingent and ambivalent. He was described as a firebrand by White, who complained that after talking with Claiborne, 'he revolted … and traded without leave … and incensed the Indians against us'.[116]

St Mary's was established with the approval of the Yaocomaco leadership. To 'avoid all occasion of dislike, and Colour of wrong', Calvert purchased the site with an assortment of axes, hoes, hatchets and cloth.[117] He was soon aware of the hostility between the Potomac River Indians and the Susquehannocks. In response to their raids, which included the seizure of women as well as plunder, the Yaocomacos were preparing to move to a more secure location

113 Hall (ed.), *Narratives of Early Maryland*, pp. 54–55; TNA, HCA 13/243, Part 1, unnumbered; *Calvert Papers*, 1, pp. 142–3.

114 Ibid., 3, p. 20; Rice, *Nature & History*, pp. 53–4, 97–101, on the rivalry and native context.

115 This group, as identified by the English, was part of the Wicomicos, Rice, *Nature & History*, p. 99.

116 Hall (ed.), *Narratives of Early Maryland*, p. 41; James Axtell, *After Columbus: Essays in the Ethnohistory of Colonial North America* (New York, 1988), p. 75; Semmes, *Captains and Mariners*, pp. 63–5; Bailyn, *The Barbarous Years*, pp. 135–7; www.hsmcdigshistory.org/pdf/Forts.pdf.

117 Hall (ed.), *Narratives of Early Maryland*, p. 42.

when the expedition arrived. Despite persistent rumours regarding their identity, they assisted the newcomers. Their support encouraged a flourishing trade, providing the colony with essential supplies of maize, fish, deer and turkey which were bartered for knives, beads and similar goods.[118] Interethnic commerce and cooperation fostered expectations among the Indians that the settlers might act as a counterweight against their enemies.

The new settlement added another layer of complexity to Anglo-Indian relations in the Bay. In an unstable and competitive environment, violent incidents spiralled out of control, creating occasions for the assertion of native agency against rival groups of colonists. The problems and opportunities were illuminated by a report of a violent encounter between hostile parties of Susquehannocks and Wicomiss during a visit to Kent Island. The injury of one of the latter provoked laughter among some of the settlers. The Wicomiss retaliated, ambushing the Susquehannocks on their return home. They then attacked Claiborne's outpost, killing three settlers and cattle. Wicomiss leaders excused the attack as 'the rash act of a few young men, which was done in heate', and insisted that they wished to 'live in peace and love' with the English.[119] Instead of dealing directly with Claiborne, however, they sent a messenger to the governor of Maryland, to offer satisfaction for the violence and harm. Calvert insisted that the Indians restore all the goods they had plundered, and surrender those responsible for trial and punishment. The demand provoked a pointed response. According to the messenger, it was native custom to provide compensation, in the form of wampum, for the loss of life. As the English were strangers, he requested that they conform to the customs of the country, rather than trying to impose their own.[120]

Despite such misunderstanding, and with the tension unresolved, Calvert was eager to explore commercial openings. As St Mary's was taking shape, he sent out a pinnace in search of trade.[121] Calvert's report for Lechford indicated that the expedition arrived too late to participate in the trading season with native groups along the Potomac, during late February and early March, when locally-hunted furs were available. Rival traders from Virginia, including Fleet and Adam Thorowgood, captured most of the trade. Calvert estimated that he lost 3,000 beaver skins to the Virginians. In future he intended to prevent them from trading within the bounds of the new colony. He had more success during the later trading season, in May, when richer furs from the north were

[118] Ibid., pp. 42–3, 75–7; *Calvert Papers*, 3, pp. 21–2; Francis Jennings, 'Indians and Frontiers in Seventeenth-Century Maryland', in Quinn (ed.), *Early Maryland*, pp. 219–37.

[119] Hall (ed.), *Narratives of Early Maryland*, p. 89.

[120] Ibid., p. 90.

[121] *Calvert Papers*, 3, p. 21.

available. The acquisition of 300 skins sustained Calvert's expectations for the profitability of the Indian trade, if he was supplied with truck.[122]

At this stage Calvert was in no position to challenge established traders from Virginia. Inexperience and a lack of knowledge restricted traders from St Mary's to scouting for opportunities along the Potomac, often in the wake of competitors, but there were forays into the Bay, shadowing trading vessels from Kent Island. Calvert instructed a trading party, sent out in March 1634, to 'gather what scattering skins were to be had among the Indians'.[123] Its leader was to keep a written report of the voyage, including descriptions of the places visited and the native groups encountered, as a record for the future.

The operation of the joint stock intensified competition between colonial traders, to the advantage of native suppliers. But the increasing availability of trade goods, particularly along the Potomac, had inadvertent and disturbing consequences. The volume and accessibility of commodities, such as cloth and metal wares, weakened the customary authority of native leaders who struggled to control commercial relations with the English. Archaeological evidence suggests that these conditions created new opportunities for patterns of ownership among Indian groups, disrupting established hierarchies that were also threatened by the unexplained spread of new diseases. Competition among colonial adventurers was thus matched by an intensification of pre-existing native rivalries for access to European goods. The impact of growing competition, among natives and newcomers, ranged far beyond the Bay. The unsettlement of native worlds in the region during the 1630s was aggravated by the commercial ambitions and activities of the Susquehannocks and distant Iroquoian groups, including the Massawomecks, their rivals for access to English traders.[124]

During 1634 Calvert acquired more understanding of native groups and their commercial prospects. Contact with the Susquehannocks was initiated by a trading party led by Cyprian Thorowgood. It was an uneasy, but revealing, encounter at Palmer's Island in late April, which was complicated by the presence of a rival group from Kent Island. According to Thorowgood's report, as soon as the vessel from St Mary's was sighted, Claiborne's men tried to persuade the Indians to take their side. They refused to become entangled in a quarrel not of their own making. Nor were they prepared to 'fight soe neere home'.[125] As a result, having secured a substantial lading of 700 beaver skins, the party from Kent Island departed. In their absence the traders from

122 Ibid., pp. 21–2.

123 Ibid., p. 23.

124 Ibid., pp. 21–2; Stephen R. Potter, 'Early English Effects on Virginia Algonquian Exchange and Tribute in the Tidewater Potomac', in Peter H. Wood et al. (eds.), *Powhatan's Mantle: Indians in the Colonial Southeast* (Lincoln, 1993), pp. 151–3.

125 Enoch Pratt Free Library, Baltimore, Maryland, Young Collection, Document 7.

St Mary's acquired 230 skins. But the contact was short-lived and ended in disagreement. His meeting with an unidentified 'Negroe', who lived with the Susquehannocks 'to learne the language', presumably at Claiborne's direction, was also unwelcoming.[126] Describing the Indians as full of valour, his report of their treatment of prisoners of war, who were slowly burnt alive while their flesh was removed and eaten, may have been intended to deter closer investigation.[127] Thorowgood went on to reconnoitre the Eastern Shore, reporting many deer and turkeys, but 'noe signe of Indians, save certain beaver traps, and one quartering house' which they used during hunting.[128] His report seemed to confirm the commercial promise of the upper Bay, while also shedding light on the trading tactics and resources of the Susquehannocks. During two brief exchanges, lasting possibly less than a week, they disposed of nearly 1,000 beaver skins. Shortly before the arrival of the English, moreover, they sent 40 men laden with skins to the Dutch along the Delaware River.[129]

The encounter with the Susquehannocks was followed by the arrival along the Potomac of a party of distant Indians, reputedly Massawomecks, bearing 2,000 beaver skins. Calvert discovered that they had abandoned trading at Quebec, in favour of securing commercial relations with traders in the Bay. They may have been hoping to renew contact with Fleet. Unfortunately, little evidence survives of their meeting with Calvert, who may have had insufficient or inadequate truck to trade with them.[130]

These early voyages for the joint stock were promising. During the trading seasons of 1634 adventurers from St Mary's acquired at least 540 beaver skins and a small number of other furs which included 53 muskrat, 17 otter and two coats of fox and marten skins.[131] In addition there was the prospect of establishing trading relations with the Massawomecks, who were searching for new outlets for their furs. Convinced of the opportunity for commercial growth, Calvert informed Lechford of his intention to increase his stake in the venture, even at the risk of mortgaging his financial interest in the colony. But these expectations were soon qualified by news of market conditions in London. Following the arrival of the first consignment of fur from the colony, in July 1634 Lechford reported that the price of beaver skins had fallen to one shilling per pound.[132] All of the fur he received was still unsold.

[126] Ibid.

[127] Ibid. Though unnamed, presumably this was John Sandis, referred to above, p. 103. On the use of ritual torture and cannibalism among the Iroquois as a form of 'assimilation', see Dennis, *Cultivating a Landscape of Peace*, pp. 89–90.

[128] Enoch Pratt Free Library, Baltimore, Maryland, Young Collection, Document 7.

[129] Ibid.

[130] *Calvert Papers*, 3, pp. 21–2.

[131] Ibid., pp. 22–3.

[132] Ibid., p. 46; Paul Chrisler Phillips, *The Fur Trade*, 2 vols. (Norman, 1961), 1, p. 121 on prices; Bradford, *Plymouth Plantation*, 2, p. 173.

The underlying problem seems to have been an irregular over-supply for the small and specialized market in London, caused by an upsurge in imports from the North American colonies. It was exacerbated by shipments from France, where merchants may have faced a similar problem. The result was sluggish, at times falling, prices. Nor were other members of the joint stock as sanguine as Calvert about future prospects. Hawley complained that he received 28 beaver skins and some maize as his share. It failed to cover the cost of his investment. Shortly thereafter he withdrew from the venture.[133]

Calvert's optimism was accompanied by concern at the supply of trading goods from London. In words which strikingly echoed Claiborne, he informed Lechford that nothing endangered the development of trade more 'than want of truck to barter with'.[134] In his capacity as treasurer, Peaselie despatched a new supply aboard the *Ark* in September 1634. The company included captain Humber with instructions to trade on behalf of the joint stock.[135] The cargo contained an assortment of implements, tools and trinkets. It included 360 hoes, 600 axes, 45 gross of Sheffield knives, three hundred weight of brass kettles, 480 hawk's bells, 15 gross of glass beads and varied amounts of ivory and horn combs, as well as 1,100 yards of coarse frieze and a separate consignment of cloth for Cornwallis that may have been intended for a separate venture. The inclusion of 50 yards of frieze for Philip Pynchon, a colonist and trader in New England, indicates that Baltimore was hoping to maintain commercial contact with the northern colonies, despite their cool response to the establishment of Maryland.[136] Many of these commodities were similar to those sent to Claiborne during the same year, and which he described as inadequate and of little appeal to experienced Indian traders. Without an improvement in the quality of truck, therefore, it would be difficult for Calvert to establish trading relations with the Massawomecks or other groups from the north.

The progress of the joint stock was beset by further misfortune. Traders from St Mary's acquired beaver skins during the winter of 1634. They were awaiting shipment, as Hawley noted on his departure, but no suitable vessel was available. The *Dove* lay in disrepair, lacking a crew who had deserted following a dispute over pay. It was not until August that the ship was ready and another company had been hired, by which time many of the furs were worm-eaten and decayed due to their prolonged and inadequate storage. Although it departed with a cargo that included 1,000 pounds of

133 TNA, C 24/621; Bernard, 'Some New Light', pp. 97–8.

134 *Calvert Papers*, 3, p. 22.

135 TNA, C 24/621; Bernard, 'Some New Light', p. 98.

136 TNA, E190/38/7 which specifies 'small gross'; Stone, 'Manorial Maryland', p. 15.

skins and a quantity of timber, the vessel was cast away during the voyage across the Atlantic.[137]

Misfortune was accentuated by miscalculation and deepening mistrust between the colony's leaders and Claiborne. Spurning an invitation to take up residence in the new colony, Claiborne subsequently complained that Calvert issued a decree in April 1634 with the purpose of stopping Indians trading at Kent Island. The animosity was inflamed by persistent allegations that he was plotting with the Indians against Maryland. Responding to complaints from Calvert, the governor of Virginia ordered his arrest and detention in the custody of Mathews and John Utie.[138] At the same time commissioners from both colonies, including Mathews, Utie, Frederick Winter and George Calvert, were appointed to investigate the charges, with authority to collect evidence from Indian groups along the Potomac. During their visit to Patuxent they were accompanied by Claiborne and one of his servants who acted as an interpreter. Although the investigation exonerated him, the leaders of Maryland questioned its validity. Cornwallis claimed it was a pretence, the real purpose of which was to 'exasperate the Indians' against the new settlement.[139]

The rhetoric barely concealed the growing intensity of colonial and commercial rivalries. Rival adventurers exploited their connections with native groups, manipulating rumour and reports of plots in an attempt to intimidate competitors. An Indian leader informed the commissioners that he was instructed by Fleet to warn Claiborne that 'the greate men of Pasbehayes would kill him and that it would bee in vaine for him to runne away anywhere, for that if hee goe to the Isle of Kent the greate men can fetch him there'.[140] The investigation exposed deep divisions in the Bay, where rivalries over commerce converged with simmering political and religious tension. In these circumstances, Harvey's attempt to implement royal commands, in support of Baltimore, provoked an angry backlash from Claiborne and his supporters. The confused, chaotic and dangerous conditions were reported by captain Thomas Young to Sir Tobie Mathew, a prominent Catholic convert with court connections, during the course of an expedition to Delaware Bay. Forced into Virginia, Young's report in favour of Baltimore presented an alarming picture of a powerful faction in the colony which seemed ready to challenge royal authority. Mathews was its 'strength and sinews', and a 'great opposer & interpreter of all letters & commands that come from the King & state

[137] TNA, C 24/621; HCA 13/52, ff.373–6; Semmes, 'The *Ark* and the *Dove*', p. 21.

[138] *Calvert Papers*, 1, pp. 142–3; Hall (ed.), *Narratives of Early Maryland*, pp. 56–7; McIlwaine (ed.), *Minutes of the Council and General Court*, p. 481.

[139] Hall (ed.), *Narratives of Early Maryland*, pp. 56–7; TNA, CO 1/39, no.44, x and 1/8, no.74.

[140] TNA, CO 1/39, no.44, x.

of England'.[141] Describing Claiborne as more subtle, he warned of his deep aversion to Maryland.

With the failure of conciliation, in September 1634 Baltimore issued instructions authorizing the seizure of Claiborne and Kent Island. Both sides rallied support at court and in the city. Baltimore sought assistance from Sir Francis Windebanke, the Secretary of State, who instructed Harvey to support Maryland, providing him with a detailed justification for its establishment. In response Cloberry and his partners petitioned the king for protection, complaining that agents for the lord proprietor had shot at their vessels in an attempt to prevent them from trading.[142]

Against this confused backdrop, during 1635 commercial competition in the Chesapeake escalated to confrontation and conflict. With native groups as bystanders, both sides probed for opportunities to test the resolve of their rival. At the start of the new trading season Claiborne despatched a small expedition, under captain Thomas Smith, in the *Longtail,* to trade for fur and maize along the Patuxent. Anticipating an unfavourable response, he provided Smith with a copy of the king's confirmation of his trading licence of 1631. On 5 April, as the company was trading along the Mattaponi River, they encountered a group from St Mary's which included captain Humber and Fleet. Denying the validity of Claiborne's licence, they boarded the *Longtail.* Smith and his men were forced ashore without their weapons and had to spend the night 'in the woods, very dangerously, the natives being up in armes amongst themselves'.[143] The following day, on Fleet's instruction, they were taken to St Mary's. As Calvert was visiting Virginia, Smith was questioned by Cornwallis. He dismissed Smith's complaint at the seizure of the *Longtail*, responding that Fleet was acting on orders to arrest all vessels trading illegally within the colony. On Calvert's return, Smith was forced to sign a note testifying that he was trading for Claiborne. It justified the confiscation of the vessel and its lading of beaver skins and cloth. The company were allowed to leave, without weapons or provisions. Before their departure Calvert had a private meeting with a member of the expedition, Henry Eubanke, who served as an interpreter. He strenuously denied the governor's claim that he was involved in an alleged plot against Maryland. Thereafter, according to Eubanke's subsequent report, Calvert adopted a conciliatory tone, offering him employment and

141 Hall (ed.), *Narratives of Early Maryland*, pp. 59–61; *Collections of the Massachusetts Historical Society* (Fourth Series, 9, 1871), pp. 96–104 for Young's report; Weslager, *The English on the Delaware*, pp. 42–53; Mark L. Thompson, '"The Predicament of Ubi": Locating Authority and National Identity in the Seventeenth-Century English Atlantic', in Elizabeth Mancke and Carole Shammas (eds.), *The Creation of the British Atlantic World* (Baltimore, 2005), pp. 74–80.

142 TNA, CO 1/8, nos.25–7, 32; Hall (ed.), *Narratives of Early Maryland*, p. 58.

143 *Calvert Papers*, 1, pp. 141–2; Steiner, *Beginnings of Maryland*, pp. 197–200.

'good meanes' if he accepted.[144] Eubanke declined the offer, replying that he was bound to Claiborne in service.

Claiborne's response to reports of this rough treatment was swift. After taking sworn depositions from Smith and Eubanke, he sent out two pinnaces, under the command of Philip Taylor, to demand the return of the *Longtail.* If the request was denied, Taylor was authorized to seize vessels belonging to Maryland, though he was to 'proceede without Violence unless it bee in Lawfull necessary defence'.[145] By the end of the month the commercial rivalry had claimed its first casualties. On 23 April the *Cockatrice* of Kent Island clashed with two vessels from St Mary's, with Cornwallis in charge, while they were trading along the Pocomoke River. Responsibility for the ensuing conflict was disputed, though Cornwallis insisted that Claiborne's men attacked as pirates and robbers.[146] One member of his company and three of his rivals were killed or mortally wounded. The *Cockatrice* was seized and taken to St Mary's. A few weeks later Cornwallis was involved in another violent confrontation with Smith at the mouth of the Wicomico River.[147]

The commercial competition and conflict were overshadowed by political drama, with the overthrow and expulsion of Harvey from Virginia in May. The opposition to the governor was fanned by grievances which fed off widespread hostility towards Maryland and anger at his lukewarm response to the seizure of the *Longtail* and *Cockatrice.* His leading enemies blamed him for the confiscation of the vessels, claiming that the Marylanders 'would not have committed such Outrages without … [his] instigation'.[148] Harvey's removal seemed to confirm earlier reports of a powerful faction in Virginia, whose hostility to Baltimore came dangerously close to challenging royal authority. What began as an isolated dispute in a remote colonial region, thus became a matter of serious concern for Charles I.

On his enforced return to England in July 1635, Harvey warned Windebanke that the rebels, as he labelled them, intended the subversion of Maryland.[149] According to his view of recent events Claiborne's men were spoiling for a fight, as they 'sought out the Marylande Boates which were trading among

[144] *Calvert Papers*, 1, pp. 142–3, 146–8.

[145] Ames (ed.), *Court Records of Accomack*, pp. 179–80; Whitelaw, *Virginia's Eastern Shore*, 1, p. 206.

[146] Streeter, *Papers Relating to Maryland*, pp. 34–6, 45; William Hand Browne (ed.), *Judicial and Testamentary Business of the Provincial Court 1637–1650* (Maryland Historical Society, Court Series, 4, 1887), p. 22.

[147] *Calvert Papers*, 1, pp. 170–1; Browne (ed.), *Provincial Court 1637–50*, pp. 21–3.

[148] TNA, CO 1/8, nos.64–5; Michael Leroy Oberg, *Dominion and Civility: English Imperialism and Native America, 1585–1685* (Ithaca, 1999), pp. 177–9.

[149] TNA, CO 1/8, no.73.

the Indians and twice assaulted them'.[150] His opponents tried to defend their conduct, while recommending, as Claiborne did to an unidentified correspondent in London, neither change nor innovation. In a more forthright report for Sir John Wolstenholme, Mathews urged the appointment of 'some worthy religious Gentleman' to replace Harvey.[151]

The crisis in Virginia caught the monarchy off guard. Faced with a confused and contentious dispute, in July the king instructed the attorney general to investigate. Alarmed at the potential threat to Maryland, later in the year Baltimore intervened, requesting the recall of Mathews and his associates, and the return of Harvey with an enlarged and more powerful commission for office. The lord proprietor's alarm was probably triggered by rumours regarding the appointment of a new governor. According to an anonymous report, Sir John Zouch, who was connected with Wolstenholme and like him had been a member of the Virginia Company, was identified as a likely replacement. Reputedly a member of the 'Puritan Sect', he was unlikely to be as favourably disposed towards a Catholic neighbour as Harvey.[152]

The danger of 'further unnaturall broiles' helped to defuse the tension within the Bay, without removing its root cause.[153] In March 1636 John West, the acting governor of Virginia, addressed a conciliatory letter to the Commissioners for Plantations, acknowledging Baltimore's rights and jurisdiction. While the rival parties awaited a royal response, they lobbied for a possible replacement for Harvey. The following year Baltimore tried to turn the tables on his enemies, informing Windebanke of his willingness to serve as governor. The proposal attracted little support, though his influence may be detected in the appointment of Hawley as treasurer, to serve under Harvey who was re-instated as governor. In addition, Mathews and several others were recalled to face charges in the Court of Star Chamber regarding their role in his ejection.[154] At about the same time Claiborne returned to London to defend his interests both within the joint stock and against Baltimore. His account of the conflict in the Bay spurred his partners into action. In February 1638 they petitioned the king, seeking redress and offering to pay a fee to retain Kent Island and Palmer's Island. Charles referred the petition to the Commissioners for Plantations. On 4 April they dismissed it, confirming that the islands and other disputed territory lay within Baltimore's jurisdiction.

150 Ibid., nos.73–4.

151 Ibid., nos.64, 65, 73–4.

152 TNA, CO 1/8, no.85; Zouch was a veteran from the war in the Low Countries who may have had considerable support in Virginia, *CSPC, 1675–6 & Addenda 1574–1664*, pp. 69, 77.

153 TNA, CO 1/9, no.7.

154 TNA, CO 1/8, no.65; PC 2/47, f.452; Browne (ed.), *Proceedings of the Council of Maryland 1636–67*, pp. 42–3.

Consequently, neither trade nor plantation could proceed without his licence. The commissioners refused to consider Claiborne's claim for damages, though he was allowed to seek compensation by other legal means.[155]

These entangled events, threading together commercial competition and political disunity, severely disrupted the operation of both joint stocks. Claiborne complained that his traders made many voyages, but they 'did little good, and had many hindrances from the Marylanders'.[156] Among colonial adventurers, no one seems to have benefited from these disturbed conditions. According to Richard Thompson, rivalry spoiled trade, enabling the Indians to sell their beaver at higher rates of exchange.[157] It also undermined the logistics and legitimacy of commercial networks, weakening the fragile interlacing between natives and newcomers. Among native groups, the rumours and violence may have provoked consternation at the prospect of being caught in an inflammatory conflict that could easily threaten their own interests. Above all, political uncertainty and commercial volatility, combined with the poor supply and quality of trucking stuff, deterred Indian traders to the advantage of rival Europeans. In 1638, at the close of hostilities between the Susquehannocks and Lenapes, representatives from both groups met Peter Minuit, governor of a recently-established Swedish outpost in Delaware Bay, and agreed to the establishment of a fort along Minquas Kill, strategically located close to a native trading pathway.[158] With such powerful native traders seeking other markets for their furs, the commercial ambitions of the English seemed to have stalled under the crippling constraints of competition and conflict.

Reorganization and a reckoning: 1637 to 1640

Events in London justified the seizure of Kent Island and its absorption by Maryland. Claiming huge losses, estimated at more than £8,000, Claiborne began legal action against Cloberry in the High Court of Admiralty. The suit

[155] TNA, CO 1/9, nos.87, 94–5. While in London, Claiborne received a grant of an island in the Bay of Honduras from the Providence Island Company, known as Rich Island (Ruatán Island) in honour of Henry Rich, earl of Holland, brother of Robert Rich, second earl of Warwick, one of the leading members of the company, which comprised a group of powerful puritans. Claiborne's associates in the grant may have included Maurice Thompson, *CSPC, 1574–1660*, p. 275; Karen Ordahl Kupperman, *Providence Island, 1630–1641: The Other Puritan Colony* (Cambridge, 1993), pp. 213, 280.

[156] TNA, HCA 13/243, Part 1, unnumbered.

[157] Ibid.

[158] Soderlund, *Lenape Country*, pp. 55–7, though the grant of land was later disputed.

was unresolved when Cloberry died, foreclosing the opportunity of securing compensation.[159] Across the Atlantic, in what was part of a wider re-ordering in the Bay, Baltimore and Calvert seized the opportunity to reorganize the fur trade, though it was accompanied by detailed discussion within the colony and shadowy negotiation across the Atlantic. The apparent failure of both joint stock ventures raised difficult questions regarding the future organization of interethnic commerce, which were unresolved by 1640.

The prerequisite for commercial reorganization, the takeover of Kent Island, proceeded with the connivance of George Evelin, who replaced Claiborne as the agent for Cloberry and other partners in 1636. During his early weeks on the island Evelin tried to establish good relations with Claiborne and the colonial community. He reportedly ridiculed Calvert and was outspoken in his defence of the joint stock. According to John Boteler, he described Calvert as 'a very dunce & blockhead when hee went to schoole', claiming that his grandfather 'was but a Grazier'.[160] By May 1637, as Claiborne was preparing to return to London, there was a mounting cloud of suspicion hanging over Evelin. When Claiborne refused to assign the plantation to him, as requested, he produced a letter of attorney from Cloberry, authorizing him to take control of the estate of the joint stock. Following Claiborne's departure, his authority was endorsed by the governor and council of Virginia.

During the summer Evelin took control of the plantation and began to re-structure the venture. Acting on instructions from Cloberry, the Indian trade was side-lined in favour of promoting agricultural and related enterprises. While servants and labourers were employed to make pipestaves, the cultivation of tobacco was extended, based on a report of good prices in the Netherlands and Spain.[161] Evelin's conduct deepened suspicion and hostility among settlers who were concerned that he was acting against Claiborne. Failing to get support from the islanders, with the onset of autumn he began

[159] TNA, HCA 13/243, Part 1, unnumbered; Jonas, 'The Claiborne-Calvert Controversy', pp. 241–50. Based on Claiborne's accounts, which were not accepted by the other partners, the total outlay of the joint stock was about £8,800 for which the venture returned £5,200, mainly from the sale of 5,000 beaver skins for £4,500. But there were other opportunities for gains to be made outside of the partnership, which Claiborne exploited, see Walsh, *Motives of Honor*, pp. 78–82; Fausz, "'To Draw Thither'", p. 60.

[160] TNA, HCA 13/243, Part 1, unnumbered; Sebastian F. Streeter, *The First Commander of Kent Island* (Baltimore, 1868), pp. 5–6. On Evelin's actions see Menard, *Economy and Society*, p. 97 and Craven, *Southern Colonies*, pp. 197–8; G.D. Scull (ed.), *The Evelyns in America: Compiled from Family Papers and other Sources, 1608–1805* (Oxford, privately printed, 1881), pp. 23–9.

[161] TNA, HCA 13/243, Part 1, unnumbered; Steiner, *Beginnings of Maryland*, pp. 217, 221.

to transfer his interests and loyalties across the Bay, developing a plantation, known as Evelinton, in the vicinity of St Mary's.

In the light of these actions, Claiborne and his supporters claimed that Evelin incited Calvert to take possession of Kent Island. In reality he may have acted as a precipitant, for it was Claiborne's absence that gave the governor his opportunity. Seeking support, Calvert offered to disregard the islanders' previous contempt for Baltimore's jurisdiction if they submitted peacefully. He also indicated his willingness to accept their nomination for a new commander to replace Evelin. The offer was ignored. Despite misgivings, he was forced to retain Evelin in the post. With a new commission from St Mary's, he returned to the island, summoning all the settlers to a meeting at the fort, where the charter for Maryland was read out. When challenged whether he was acting for Cloberry or Baltimore, he 'answeared he was for both'.[162]

The confusion was clarified by the despatch of an expedition to the island in February 1638. It was justified by the mutinous behaviour of the islanders, and reports that they were conspiring with Indian groups against St Mary's. Led by Calvert and Cornwallis, a force of between 30 and 40 armed men seized the fort unopposed, before sunrise, while the occupants were asleep. Combining coercion with conciliation, Calvert arrested the ringleaders of the opposition, confiscated Claiborne's plantation at Crayford, and implemented a series of measures for the incorporation of the island into Maryland. They included the offer of a pardon for those who submitted to Baltimore's authority, though it excluded Thomas Smith, whose execution for piracy went ahead despite pleas for clemency.[163]

The takeover of Kent Island was followed by the seizure of Palmer's Island in June 1638. At the time of its possession it was manned by four servants equipped with 10 guns and a small herd of cattle and hogs, as well as chickens and hens. They were provided with agricultural tools, fishing material and cooking equipment. Their supply of trading goods included blue beads, kettles, knives, cloth, axes, combs, wampum and two trading pipes. The post also contained a small collection of texts, identified as a Book of Statutes, Sir William Staunford's *Pleas*, a comprehensive exposition of criminal law first published in 1557 and reprinted several times thereafter, and a volume by William Perkins, the puritan divine and theologian.[164] It was a revealing selection of material, emblems of English legal and religious culture, to fortify

162 TNA, HCA 13/243, Part 1, unnumbered; Streeter, *First Commander*, pp. 13–5, 21–2.

163 *Calvert Papers*, 1, pp. 170–1, 183–6; Browne (ed.), *Proceedings of the Council of Maryland 1636–67*, pp. 62–3.

164 Ibid., pp. 76–7. On a request for Staunford's *Pleas* from Virginia in 1621, and the use of law books in the colony, see David D. Hall, *Cultures of Print: Essays in the History of the Book* (Amherst, 1996), p. 118.

the members of such a small outpost on the contested margin of colonial settlement in the Bay.

Competing claims to the island were voiced at a meeting held earlier in the year at Jamestown. Among those present, in addition to Harvey, were Jerome Hawley and John Boteler, a strong supporter of Claiborne's rights. Hawley's weak defence of Baltimore's title prompted Calvert, who was not present, to accuse him of being driven by his own commercial ambition. Brushing aside rival claims, Calvert insisted that the island lay within the bounds of Maryland. He also alleged that Claiborne's servants were supplying guns to the Indians for use in an attack on St Mary's.[165]

But the seizure of the islands, followed by the attainder of Claiborne at St Mary's, threatened to revive the transatlantic dispute, with its wider political ramifications. In June 1638 Cloberry complained to Sir John Coke, Secretary of State, that the joint stock was ruined by the 'many wrongs and oppressions' of the Marylanders.[166] Coke's intervention, possibly with the support of the earl of Stirling, persuaded the king to refer the controversy back to the Commissioners for Plantations. In July he also instructed Baltimore not to disturb the interests of the partners until the complaint was investigated and resolved. No evidence survives of the commissioners' report, if one was made. In any case, by this stage the partnership was in no position to pursue its claim against the lord proprietor. Calvert thus confirmed Claiborne's attainder and the confiscation of his property, summoning him to appear before a court at St Mary's. In August 1640, in a move that appeared to recognize Baltimore's jurisdiction, Claiborne appointed an attorney in Maryland, seeking compensation for his losses through the colony's courts.[167]

The resolution of this protracted dispute gave the leaders of Maryland the opportunity to re-organize commercial activity in the colony. Although fashioned in a piecemeal way, it paved the way for the abandonment of joint stock enterprise in favour of independent traders who operated under licence from the lord proprietor. Intimations of change came with the appointment, during 1637, of John Lewger, a former Anglican clergyman and convert to Catholicism, as secretary and collector of Baltimore's commercial dues and rents. He arrived with draft legislation for the establishment of a revised and more profitable commercial system to replace the increasingly moribund joint stock. Though it survived into the late 1630s, there is scant evidence for its operation. According to Lewger, in January 1638 Baltimore retained half of the stock, and Fleet held a share of one-sixth. Much of the remainder was probably

165 *Calvert Papers*, 1, pp. 187–9.

166 TNA, CO 1/9, no.117; Browne (ed.), *Proceedings of the Council of Maryland 1636–67*, pp. 76–7.

167 TNA, CO 1/9, nos.117, 120; Browne (ed.), *Proceedings of the Council of Maryland 1636–67*, pp. 70, 76–7, 82–3, 92–3.

taken up by Calvert and Cornwallis. Other adventurers may have included Robert Winter who arrived in the colony during 1637 with five servants. The brother of Edward and Frederick Winter, who were subscribers to the original venture, he died the following year with an estate that included two canoes and 40 pounds of beaver.[168]

Trading voyages organized during 1637 and 1638 ranged the upper Bay and beyond in search of maize, beaver skins and wampum. They included a disparate group of adventurers, operating under varying conditions. Cornwallis was granted free licence to trade with any Indian group for maize and wampum, but a separate commission for a fur-trading voyage to Kent Island included provision for a levy of one tenth of the proceeds to the lord proprietor.[169] Traders from the island remained active, sailing with or without commissions issued on behalf of Baltimore. In February 1638 an islander, Thomas Games, received a licence from the council at St Mary's, to trade for beaver skins, maize and other commodities with the Dutch along the Hudson River and Indian groups farther north. Thomas Adams, formerly one of Claiborne's traders, also seems to have maintained an interest in the Susquehannock trade. In addition, Fleet remained active, trading under uncertain conditions.[170]

This varied group included traders acting for the Jesuit mission at St Mary's. Early in 1638 Robert Clarke shipped a cargo of trading goods, including axes, hatchets, hoes, knives and cloth, aboard the *St Margaret*, on behalf of Thomas Copley, the superior. About the same time Copley sent out Cyprian Thorowgood with a lading of cloth to trade with the Indians. He returned three weeks later with 100 pounds of beaver skins.[171] These voyages failed to facilitate closer contact. To the frustration of Copley, for whom 'nothing could have happened more agreeable … than to labor in the Indian harvest', the colony's leaders refused to allow the Jesuits 'to dwell among the savages, both on account of the prevailing sicknesses, and also because of the hostile acts which the barbarians commit against the English'.[172]

The introduction of regulation did not stop illegal trading, particularly from Kent Island. In February 1638 William Brainthwaite, a recent immigrant and kinsman of Baltimore, who served as commander of the island until 1640, was

[168] Browne (ed.), *Provincial Court 1637–50*, pp. 5, 87–8; Papenfuse (ed.), *Biographical Dictionary*, 2, p. 905; Semmes, *Captains and Mariners*, pp. 97–101 on regulation.

[169] Browne (ed.), *Proceedings of the Council of Maryland 1636–67*, pp. 57–9.

[170] Ibid., p. 63; Browne (ed.), *Provincial Court 1637–50*, pp. 91, 99–100.

[171] Ibid., p. 34; Browne (ed.), *Proceedings of the Council of Maryland 1636–67*, p. 63.

[172] Hall (ed.), *Narratives of Early Maryland*, pp. 119, 133, 135; *Calvert Papers*, 1, p. 167. The initial success of converting Indians was not maintained, Axtell, *After Columbus*, pp. 76–85.

authorized to seize all vessels and their cargoes trading without licence. Similar authority was granted to Cuthbert Fenwick and John Holles, former servants of Cornwallis, who developed an interest in the trade during the late 1630s.[173]

According to Cornwallis, closer supervision and regulation provoked a fatal dispute between Baltimore and some of the surviving members of the joint stock.[174] Andrew White claimed it spread wider unease among settlers anxious at the implications for property rights. White warned Baltimore, early in 1638, of a concern that 'if the right of truck bee taken from them … they can have no assurance for the lands you give them: seeing in the declaration and conditions of plantation both share in trade and the land runnes in one and the selfe same tenor, and would bee esteemed so if itt weare brought to any hearinge'.[175] Such feeling persuaded the General Assembly, which met during the year, to pass legislation proclaiming the freedom of the Indian trade. The threat to the authority of the lord proprietor was defused by the intervention of the governor. Following the passage of the act, he informed Baltimore that the members of the assembly had 'wholly exempted themselves from trade with the Indians'.[176] A subsequent meeting of the assembly, in March 1639, accepted without demur the lord proprietor's commercial rights.

Acknowledging Baltimore as absolute lord and proprietor, the assembly recognized the need for regulation and passed revised legislation.[177] It was designed to prevent a 'promiscuous liberty' of trading with the Indians which raised prices and allowed foreign traders to acquire much-needed supplies of maize.[178] In addition it attempted to stop the spread of damaging rumours and false news among native groups by rival adventurers. It was justified by reports of the seizure of arms and ammunition, from weakly-manned trading vessels, by disaffected Indians, which were used against the colony. The new act excluded foreign traders. All others needed a licence, without which their vessels and goods would be confiscated. Security was required to prevent disorderly trading, presumably in muskets and gunpowder. But the need for regulation was qualified by an implicit recognition of the value of interethnic exchange to a rudimentary colonial economy. As such, colonists remained free to trade at their farms and plantations with Indians, 'for two or three Skins or

173 Browne (ed.), *Proceedings of the Council of Maryland 1636–67*, pp. 80–4, 88–9; Papenfuse (ed.), *Biographical Dictionary*, 1, pp. 159–60.

174 *Calvert Papers*, 1, p. 176.

175 Ibid., p. 209.

176 Ibid., p. 190; William Hand Browne (ed.), *Proceedings and Acts of the General Assembly of Maryland, January 1637/8 – September 1664* (Maryland Historical Society, 1, 1883), pp. 307–8.

177 Ibid., p. 42.

178 Ibid., p. 43.

such like small quantity of beaver' and other commodities, including maize and wampum.[179]

Calvert's intervention in the dispute coincided with his negotiation for a new commercial contract to replace the joint stock which was due to expire in 1639. His partner in the new scheme was Cornwallis. The poor performance of the corporate venture strengthened the governor's argument for restricting access. In presenting his case to Baltimore he claimed that 'too many sharers in it' led to the 'destruction both of the trade and traders'.[180] A lack of cooperation, especially Fleet's semi-detached relations with the joint stock, spoiled the market. Competition increased the price of beaver skins to such an extent that subscribers reaped little in return.[181] If Baltimore leased the trade to Calvert and Cornwallis, rent free for several years, it would become more profitable and secure.[182]

Calvert's analysis of the ineffectiveness of the joint stock was supported by White. In a confidential report for the lord proprietor, he noted that 'the concordate' with the original adventurers included 'many who understand little of truck and trade'.[183] Inexperience and misunderstanding were manifest in the response to the failure of early trading voyages, 'in which every body was [sic] losers'.[184] Lacking commercial or city experience, members of the joint stock protested 'against itt as an engine and mystery to undoe' them.[185] It was the prospect of shifting and receding opportunities, however, that lay behind White's proposal for the re-establishment of commerce. Concerned at the loss of trade to rival adventurers, he advised Baltimore to establish three permanent trading posts for dealing with different Indian groups.[186] They were to be located on Palmer's Island for the Susquehannocks, at Anacostan for the Massawomecks, and at Nanticoke for the Wicomiss and others along the Eastern Shore. With each post under the supervision of one trader, and one vessel required to collect furs at the end of the trading season, running costs would be kept to a minimum. Possibly aware of White's report, Calvert presented Baltimore with a similar proposal, if his offer to lease the trade was rejected. Though not as specific, he recommended the establishment of trading posts at convenient shore-based locations, because 'the way of boating it … is very chargeable and uncertaine'.[187]

179 Ibid., pp. 43–4.
180 *Calvert Papers*, 1, p. 190.
181 Ibid., pp. 190–1.
182 Ibid., p. 191.
183 Ibid., pp. 179, 209.
184 Ibid., pp. 209–10.
185 Ibid., pp. 209–10.
186 Ibid., pp. 210–11.
187 Ibid., pp. 190–1.

In the short-term, and for reasons of economy and security, Baltimore left the management of the trade in the hands of his brother and Cornwallis. With the termination of the joint stock, in January 1639 John Lewger reported that the 'trade of beaver is wholly in the Governors and the Captaines hands, without any rival, and they are joined partners in the driving of it'.[188] Although the terms of their agreement with Baltimore are unknown, the partners faced a challenging situation. Competition and conflict disrupted trading activity during the late 1630s. The development of interethnic networks of commerce and exchange was thrown into disarray. Native traders who tried to avoid becoming embroiled in the conflicts between colonial traders were able to raise rates of exchange, effectively setting their own prices, but it was a short-term benefit given deficiencies in the supply of trading goods. In these circumstances there was a real danger of the English losing their commercial position to rival Dutch and Swedish traders in Delaware Bay.[189]

The establishment of an infrastructure during the 1630s, ambitiously linking trade with plantation, thus remained a work in progress, lacking clarity or cohesion. Launched with ambitious expectations, corporate enterprise struggled to maintain momentum. As a result, the Maryland adventurers were unable to take advantage of the collapse of the Kent Island partnership. This seemed to leave the Bay open for independent traders, but they were difficult to regulate and potentially more vulnerable to native hostility and other hazards. During 1638 an adventurer in Maryland was murdered by Indians while 'staying among them for the sake of trading'.[190] About the same time two survivors of an interloping venture from Virginia, which was shipwrecked along the Eastern Shore, were killed by another group of Indians. Their vessel and truck ended up in the hands of the leader of the Patuxents.[191] Under unfavourable conditions even experienced traders, such as Fleet, struggled to make a profit or break even. Early in 1638 he set out from St Mary's in the *Deborah* laden with an assortment of goods including 19 yards of Dutch cloth, 16 pairs of Irish stockings, 74 axes, 26 hoes and two yards of wampum, and a chest containing beads, knives, combs, fish hooks, Jew's harps and looking glasses. He returned within a fortnight, with most of the truck unsold, though he acquired 30 beaver skins in exchange for the cloth.[192]

188 Ibid., pp. 197–8.

189 Soderlund, *Lenape Country*, pp. 52–3. On the development of Dutch trade in the Bay during the 1630s see Christian J. Koot, *Empire at the Periphery: British Colonists, Anglo-Dutch Trade, and the Development of the British Atlantic, 1621–1713* (New York, 2011), pp. 44–5.

190 Hall (ed.), *Narratives of Early Maryland*, p. 119.

191 Browne (ed.), *Proceedings of the Council of Maryland 1636–67*, pp. 73–4, 83, 85.

192 Ibid., pp. 67–8, 75; Browne (ed.), *Provincial Court 1637–50*, pp. 6–7; Helen C. Rountree and Thomas E. Davidson, *Eastern Shore Indians of Virginia and Maryland*

Yet these difficulties were interpreted as the teething problems of a new enterprise which was developing a local and transatlantic dimension. Through interethnic trade and exchange, fur acquired important functions in a small and evolving colonial economy. Lacking an adequate supply of currency, valuable, easy-to-handle and durable material, such as beaver skins, were used as a medium of exchange and credit. Inventories, wills and other legal records demonstrate its use and circulation, with a value, in terms of weight, greater than tobacco. John Baxter a store-keeper of St Mary's, for example, supplied settlers with English goods which were often paid for in beaver skins. Their exchange price could be as much as eight shillings for one pound of fur. Through interlocking networks of exchange, often small-scale and hidden, colonists acquired the means to purchase clothes, shoes, stockings, hats and provisions. At the time of his death Baxter was owed nearly 40 pounds of beaver skins by his customers. The charge for making his coffin was estimated to be two pounds of beaver.[193]

It is impossible to gauge the volume of commercial activity within the Bay during these years or, given the lack of colonial customs accounts, to provide firm estimates for the amount that was shipped across the Atlantic. As London dominated colonial trade, its commercial records might provide an insight into the volume of activity. But the evidence for the 1630s is fragmentary, incomplete or damaged. An account of imports for 1634 contains entries for 940 beaver skins from Virginia and 242 skins from Maryland. A damaged and incomplete volume for 1640 records the import of 132 beaver skins and one bear skin, shipped from Maryland by Cornwallis.[194] These figures can be correlated with other estimates, though they are of varied utility. For Kent Island, Claiborne claimed during his suit against Cloberry that he returned 7488½ pounds of beaver skins for the joint stock between 1631 and 1637. For Maryland a modern estimate, relying on an account for the estate of John Saunders, suggests that the venture traded 3,350 pounds of beaver skins from 1634 to 1637.[195] Based on such patchy evidence, it might be suggested that in good years annual shipments of fur from the Bay ranged from 1,200 to 3,000 pounds of fur, possibly even more.

Although both ventures survived difficult beginnings, and went on to develop encouraging relations with native traders, their promise remained unfulfilled. Competition and conflict disrupted commercial enterprise within

---

(Charlottesville, 1997), p. 87.

193 Browne (ed.), *Provincial Court 1637–50*, pp. 34–5, 76, 103–4; Semmes, *Captains and Mariners*, pp. 67–8.

194 TNA, E190/38/5 (1634); E190/43/5 (1640). On paper the fur was worth about £4,000, Soderlund, *Lenape Country*, p. 52.

195 TNA, HCA 13/243, Part 1, unnumbered; Stone, 'Manorial Maryland', p. 15; Walsh, *Motives of Honor*, pp. 78–80.

the Bay, providing an inflammatory focal point for the rivalry between the two Chesapeake colonies. Trade was also affected by the irregular and inadequate supply of goods from England, the product of inexperience and over-stretched resources. Yet there were some benefits. English merchants acquired experience in the organization of a new trade requiring a market in London. Colonial traders, building on previous contacts, gained an invaluable insight into the conduct and character of interethnic commerce, becoming more confident and familiar in dealing with Indian groups. At the same time, they consolidated and enhanced their knowledge of the region, its people and resources. Benefiting from Indian rivalries, the English established outposts on Kent Island and at St Mary's with the approval or sponsorship of native neighbours. Indian groups were in a strong position to exert a powerful influence over commercial development, as demonstrated by the response of colonial adventurers to complaints regarding the quality of truck. Disappointed with such goods, experienced native traders threatened to abandon the English. Yet the potential rewards of commercial exchange, including the availability of cloth and metal wares, held their attention. By these means a diverse range of goods, including a small number of guns, were dispersed within the upper Bay and beyond. The archaeological discovery of material such as trading pipes and Jew's harps may be open to interpretation, but it demonstrates their diffusion along the Susquehanna Valley, and their re-use and re-invention across an ever-widening hinterland. From this perspective the establishment of competing ventures helped to open the region to colonial exploitation and settlement, spreading European commodities and new patterns of consumption alongside sickness and disease.[196]

[196] For example, a modern estimate suggests that the population of the Lenapes fell from between 7,500 and 9,000 in 1634 to about 4,000 by 1650, Soderlund, *Lenape Country*, pp. 17–18.

Chapter 4

Trade, Rivalry and Conflict during a 'Time of Troubles' from 1640 to 1660

The collapse of the Kent Island partnership left the rival venture in Maryland well-placed to secure control of the fur trade in the upper Bay after 1640. But the prospect of commercial expansion was dashed by the onset of a protracted crisis that threatened the survival of the colony. Civil war in England plunged the Chesapeake into a 'time of troubles', marked by disunity, division and conflict.[1] Surprisingly, the interconnections between English events and the development of the North American colonies during the 1640s and 1650s have rarely been examined in detail, though a recent study argues that they contributed to the establishment and greater definition of an English Atlantic, facilitated by more extensive intercolonial communication.[2] But political turbulence across the colonies, manifest in rebellion or insurrection, was intensified within the Bay by the divisive legacy of the 1630s. Thus, the rapid collapse of royal authority revived the opponents of Baltimore. Seeking to exploit these unsettled and potentially favourable conditions, Claiborne made repeated attempts to recover trade and territory which merged with wider ambitions for the reformation of the region. Colonial rivalry was accompanied by widespread native unrest and dislocation, intensified by the impact of hostilities in the north between Huron and Iroquoian groups. Conflict with the Powhatans in Virginia was paralleled by the outbreak of war with the Susquehannocks in Maryland. During a period of barren confusion much of the fur trade in the upper Bay was diverted to Swedish and Dutch outposts in the Delaware. Colonial traders remained active, despite the rivalry and conflict, but these years represented a turning point in interethnic commerce and exchange. Though masked by the turmoil of war and rebellion on both sides of the Atlantic, the collapse of metropolitan interest in fur trading

1 Russell R. Menard, 'Maryland's "Time of Troubles": Sources of Political Disorder in Early St Mary's', *MHM*, 76 (1981), pp. 124–40; Lois Green Carr, 'Sources of Political Stability and Upheaval in Seventeenth-Century Maryland', *MHM*, 79 (1984), pp. 44–70.

2 Carla Gardina Pestana, *The English Atlantic in an Age of Revolution, 1640–1661* (Cambridge, Mass., 2004), pp. 1–4, 10–13; Bliss, *Revolution and Empire:*, pp. 73–102.

enterprise, combined with a narrowing of colonial opportunities within an embryonic and expanding plantation culture, cast a shadow over the function of native trades. In these circumstances the commercial interruption of the civil war enabled the Dutch to increase their trade in the Chesapeake.[3] The response of the new republican regime in England was to impose regulation over colonial trade and shipping, which pointed towards an exclusionary, imperial direction.

Commerce, conflict and competition during the early 1640s

Commercial enterprise in the upper Bay operated under the constraints of weak economic and political structures characteristic of a small colonial outpost. Although Maryland evaded the 'starving time' that afflicted Virginia, in 1640 its future was heavily dependent on the lord proprietor's support and royal favour. The colony represented little more than a community of several hundred settlers, huddled around St Mary's, whose religious and social make up were a source of potential disunity. Colonial conditions may have favoured entrepreneurial activity, but many settlers lacked the resources, ambition or self-discipline to sustain extensive agricultural or commercial development. Such an improvised and unformed economy, which possessed limited opportunities for diversification, was in the hands of a small group, who represented the first generation of manorial lords. Under the leadership of Leonard Calvert and Thomas Cornwallis, they adopted a hybrid form of enterprise, combining the cultivation of tobacco with commerce and credit broking.[4]

The experience of new arrivals, such as Thomas Gerrard, underlines the importance of family and religion within this economy for the acquisition of land and the resources for entry into trade. From a Catholic and landed background in Lancashire, Gerrard migrated to Maryland during 1638, acquiring an estate of 11,000 acres in the manor of St Clements. Two years later he returned to England, securing a loan of £178 9s 9d from Abell Snowe, his brother-in-law, for the purchase of provisions and trading goods, which was to be re-paid within two years either in tobacco or beaver skins. Snowe also agreed to contribute two pieces of blue trading cloth, valued at £15, to Gerrard's planned venture. John Army made a similar investment.[5] Such extensive lines

3 David B. Quinn and A.N. Ryan, *England's Sea Empire 1550–1642* (London, 1983), pp. 207–10; Koot, *Empire at the Periphery*, pp. 33, 73–6.

4 Aubrey C. Land, *Colonial Maryland: A History* (Millwood, 1981) and Menard, *Economy and Society* on colonial development; Pestana, *The English Atlantic*, p. 229 provides an estimate of 600 for the population.

5 Bernard C. Steiner (ed.), *Proceedings of the Provincial Court of Maryland, 1658–1662* (Maryland Historical Society, 41, 1922), pp. 542–3, 547; Papenfuse (ed.), *Biographical Dictionary*, I, pp. 348–9.

of credit helped to maintain trading activity during a time of change and uncertainty, but they were modest in scale and vulnerable to distance.

As part of the re-organization of the Indian trade, both Calvert and Cornwallis seem to have withdrawn from direct involvement in commercial activity, in favour of licensing or leasing arrangements with freemen and former servants. As governor, Calvert issued trading commissions on behalf of the lord proprietor. At the same time, acting alone or in partnership with Cornwallis, he provided traders with resources, such as vessels and trucking stuff, in return for a share in the profits of their ventures.[6] Both men retained an interest in the trade, while re-defining their roles and economic function. In particular, the provision of credit, in a variety of forms, helped to structure social relations, reaffirming hierarchy and dependency within the colony. By these means colonial leaders were able to use returns from the trade for plantation development. In 1644, for example, Cornwallis paid off a debt of £50, for the purchase of 'two negroes' in Virginia, partly with 97½ pounds of beaver, a peculiarly valuable form of circulating capital.[7]

Although the commercial competition between the two colonies was neither as intense nor as violent as during the 1630s, three distinct, occasionally overlapping and potentially rival groups of traders operated in the upper Bay. The largest was made up of a group based at St Mary's. They included Thomas Boys, Cuthbert Fenwick, John Holles, John Nuthall and George Tailor, most of whom were linked with Calvert or Cornwallis, as well as servants of the Jesuit mission, Henry Bishop and Mathias de Sousa.[8] Across the Bay, on Kent Island, a small band of traders, former servants or employees of Claiborne, such as Thomas Adams, remained active. In addition, interlopers from Virginia, who were supported by and occasionally included local officials from Accomack, ranged farther into the upper Bay, trading without licence.

With the addition of the Swedes and Dutch in Delaware Bay, these traders were rivals for access to the Susquehannocks' supplies of fur. But the

6 Browne (ed.), *Proceedings of the Council of Maryland 1636–67*, pp. 342–3; Stone, 'Manorial Maryland', p. 17.

7 Browne (ed.), *Provincial Court 1637–50*, p. 304; Jonathan L. Alpert, 'The Origin of Slavery in the United States- The Maryland Precedent', in Bruce A. Glasrud and Alan M. Smith (eds.), *Race Relations in British North America, 1607–1783* (Chicago, 1982), p. 139, n.19.

8 Also spelled as either Hallowes or Hollis. There were at least two settlers with the name in the colony. De Sousa was of African and probably Portuguese background, David S. Bogen, 'Mathias de Sousa: Maryland's First colonist of African Descent', *MHM*, 96 (2001), pp. 68–84. The Jesuits were involved in the fur trade in New France, profits from which supported missions, Karen Anderson, *Chain Her by One Foot: The Subjugation of Native Women in Seventeenth-Century New France* (London, 1991), pp. 51–2.

ambitions of colonial leaders in Maryland to establish commercial contacts with them faltered, partly as a result of their relationship with the Piscataways. Long-standing hostility between these Indian groups threatened to include their colonial associates. In 1638 Calvert warned the lord proprietor that the Susquehannocks intended to make war on the colonists, in revenge for their alleged assistance to the latter two years earlier. Calvert denied the allegation, claiming that it was incited by rival traders at Palmer's Island.[9] Seeking to explore the opportunities for commerce and possibly converts, the following year an expedition to the Indians was sent out by the Jesuit mission at St Mary's. It was led by Mathias de Sousa, an experienced trader, who was instructed to hire men at Kent Island for the voyage. It was not a success. After hiring John Prettiman, de Sousa sailed to the head of the Bay, where he had a hostile encounter with a party of Susquehannocks. He later reported that his vessel and company would have been destroyed, but for Prettiman's presence and persuasive powers.[10] The failure of the voyage increased the tension in the upper Bay. For the colony's leaders, Kent Island remained a flash-point of potential hostility. As an outlying and insecure addition to the colony, it was inhabited by resentful settlers whose loyalties were suspect. Its disputed possession drew the attention of Indian groups seeking to take advantage of a divided colonial world. Responding to the perceived threat, in July 1641 the council at St Mary's authorised settlers to shoot Indian visitors to the island. The following year Calvert proclaimed that the Susquehannocks, Wicomiss and Nanticokes, former trading partners of Claiborne, were enemies of the colony.[11]

The governor's declaration was followed by an ill-fated attempt to organize a joint expedition with Virginia against the Indians. It was justified as a response to increased raiding within both colonies, during which settlers were killed and property destroyed. In Maryland the targets for the Susquehannocks included the Jesuit mission with the Piscataways. Calvert requested the governor of Virginia to send 100 militia men to join a similar contingent from Maryland, at a rendezvous on Kent Island. Giles Brent, the captain of Kent Fort, was appointed to lead the expedition. Although Virginia failed to respond, preparations proceeded at St Mary's. In September 1642 the General Assembly

[9] Hall (ed.), *Narratives of Early Maryland*, p. 151; *Calvert Papers*, 1, pp. 179–80, 187–8. The Susquehannocks were under growing pressure from the Iroquois, see Timothy B. Riordan, *The Plundering Time: Maryland and the English Civil War 1645–1646* (Baltimore, 2004), pp. 35–6.

[10] Browne (ed.), *Provincial Court 1637–50*, p. 138: Bernard C. Steiner, *Maryland During the English Civil Wars* (Baltimore, 1906), p. 20; Bogen, 'Mathias de Sousa', pp. 75–7.

[11] Browne (ed.), *Proceedings of the Council of Maryland 1636–67*, pp. 98–9, 106–7, 116–17.

approved a levy of recruits, to be paid from the plunder of Indians. After mustering on the island, the expedition was disbanded until a more favourable time. Brent was subsequently dismissed from office for failing to execute his commission. In his defence he claimed that the inhabitants of Kent Island refused to support military action against the Susquehannocks, claiming it 'would be … [their] undoing'.[12]

The conflict coincided with deteriorating relations between St Mary's and its native neighbours. Fuelled by disputes over land and property, the mounting resentment of the Piscataways provoked alarm that the Susquehannocks were planning to organize a confederation of Indians in the upper Bay against the English.[13] In January 1643 the colony's leaders imposed severe restrictions on native contact with the colonial community. They included a warning that any Indians found in the region around St Mary's, without a white flag or fan, could be shot. This stark measure was later modified to exclude all but the Susquehannocks and their Wicomiss allies who were to be targeted only in self-defence. These initiatives, reinforced by colonial perceptions of Indians as 'barbarous & inhumane pagans', exposed the lives of friendly natives either through misidentification or miscalculation.[14] In February a leader of the Yaocomicos was shot in the neck by John Elkin. Despite his confession, a jury returned a verdict of not guilty. When instructed to reconsider the evidence, it insisted that the Indian leader was killed in self-defence. The case was heard by another jury which found Elkin guilty of manslaughter.[15]

The war against the Susquehannocks, who benefited from Swedish assistance, did not go well for the colonists. Following Calvert's return to London in April 1643, Cornwallis led an expedition up the Susquehanna River during June, in a raid on their largest settlement. While demonstrating the ability of the colonists to enter Indian territory, the party of about 50 volunteers was forced into a disorderly retreat. They abandoned two field pieces and other armaments, though casualties seem to have been limited. John Holles, who served with the expedition, recounted an attack on one of the vessels in the river, during which a member of the company had his throat cut by an Indian with a Dutch knife. Holles, who was in the hold

[12] Browne (ed.), *Provincial Court 1637–50*, pp. 128–34; Browne (ed.), *Proceedings of the General Assembly of Maryland 1637/8–64*, pp. 171–2, 196–8. By the mid-1640s the colony was supplying the Piscataways with weapons to defend themselves against Susquehannock raids, James H. Merrell, 'Cultural Continuity among the Piscataway Indians of Colonial Maryland', *WMQ*, 26 (1979), pp. 564–5.

[13] Browne (ed.), *Proceedings of the Council of Maryland 1636–67*, pp. 148–9.

[14] Ibid., pp. 126, 129; Browne (ed.), *Provincial Court 1637–50*, p. 80; Riordan, *Plundering Time*, pp. 98–9.

[15] Browne (ed.), *Provincial Court 1637–50*, pp. 177, 180–3; Land, *Colonial Maryland*, p. 44.

at the time, responded to a call for help, and 'knocked the Indian on the head with the barrel' of a gun, but he was too late to save his companion.[16] Subsequent unconfirmed reports that 15 members of the colonial force were taken prisoner, tortured and executed were probably part of the atrocity propaganda of interethnic violence.[17]

War and rivalry created an unfavourable environment for the pursuit of trade, encouraging other native groups to test the resolve of the colony, while forcing colonial leaders to introduce strict controls over relations with the Indians. They included a prohibition on the entertainment of natives in the homes of settlers without special licence from the governor.[18] Shifting attitudes among colonists informed and reinforced such regulation. As a result, the opportunity for the creation of a negotiable space, for interethnic commerce and communication, ebbed away. Contact between natives and newcomers continued, but it remained ambiguous or potentially subversive of colonial self-images. Occasionally it raised troubling questions regarding the maintenance of social discipline within contentious communities of settlers throughout the Chesapeake. In 1643 Thomas Parks, a suitor before the county court of Accomack, threatened to appeal to the Susquehannocks if he was denied justice. The following year Mary Edwin complained to the provincial court at St Mary's that widow Whitcliff lay with an Indian in exchange for wampum.[19] Under these conditions trade was in danger of becoming an opportunistic and fugitive enterprise, subject to close but ineffective supervision. Taking advantage of a presumed truce with Indians along the Eastern Shore, in 1643 a group of traders from St Mary's intended to set out on a venture across the Bay, provoking the intervention of the assembly with a warning that all such voyages were prohibited unless licensed by the governor.[20]

Fragmentary evidence illuminates the activities of individual traders, though it casts little light on the scale or extent of commercial enterprise, or on the supply of trading material. John Holles was one of the leading adventurers

16 Ibid., pp. 209–10, 214–15.

17 A.C. Myers (ed.), *Narratives of Early Pennsylvania, West New Jersey and Delaware 1630–1707* (New York, 1912), p. 102; Francis Jennings, *The Ambiguous Iroquois Empire: The Covenant Chain Confederation of Indian Tribes with English Colonies from its Beginnings to the Lancaster Treaty of 1744* (New York, 1984), p. 120; Neal Salisbury, "Native People and European Settlers in Eastern North America, 1600–1783", in Bruce G. Trigger and Wilcomb E. Washburn (eds.), *The Cambridge History of the Native Peoples of the Americas, Volume 1: North America Part 1* (Cambridge, 1996), pp. 413–4. On the Swedes see below, pp. 144–7.

18 Browne (ed.), *Proceedings of the Council of Maryland 1636–67*, p. 129.

19 Browne (ed.), *Provincial Court 1637–50*, p. 258; Ames (ed.), *County Court Records of Accomack*, pp. 313–14, 317.

20 Browne (ed.), *Provincial Court 1637–50*, p. 186.

at St Mary's. He began his career in the colony as a servant to Cornwallis, whom he accompanied on a trading voyage to the Wicomico River in 1635. The connection was maintained after Holles gained his freedom. In June 1639 he married Restituta Tue of Virginia. By 1642 he owned a farm in St Michael's hundred, on which he cultivated tobacco and raised a stock of cattle and pigs. His wife provided much-needed help and assistance, though his absences on trading voyages encouraged damaging rumours of her conduct. In November he was forced to take legal action to defend her reputation against an allegation by Thomas Boys, an associate, 'that he would prove her ... a whore in Court'.[21] His commercial ventures were supported by Cornwallis, who provided him with credit, equipment and commodities in return for supplies of beaver skins and wampum. By the terms of an agreement between the two men at the start of the trading season of 1643, Holles assigned his land and goods to Cornwallis, promising to deliver nearly 270 pounds of good, winter beaver by the end of March 1644.[22] The venture began badly. A small vessel, described as a ketch, freighted by Cornwallis from John Lewger, and sent out under the command of Holles, ran aground shortly after leaving St Mary's. Lewger successfully claimed compensation for freight from Cornwallis, while also seeking damages from Holles of 200 arm's length of roanoke.

Traders on Kent Island, like their rivals, seem to have faced a problem in the supply of trading goods. The inventory of the estate of Thomas Adams, made during 1642, indicates the limited availability of appropriate truck. In addition to personal items, Adams possessed a small amount of trade goods, including three axes, three looking glasses, seven pairs of scissors, an assortment of fish hooks, coloured thread and a piece of new cloth about the size of a towel. He also owned a small shallop, furnished with an old sail and a case containing 'a prayer book, a counting book, a powder-box, some papers, & an old beaver hat', as well as a small parcel of goods made up of seven dagger blades, one hatchet and axe, and 10½ yards of blue trading cloth.[23] Much of this material, the tools and regalia of interethnic commerce, was left over from the joint stock, provided either by Claiborne or his London partners. Of course, the small turnover of trading wares did not preclude profit, either for colonial or Indian traders, but the dearth of evidence for the volume and value of trade makes it impossible to provide an estimate for either.

The early 1640s were a challenging period of adjustment for colonial leaders in Maryland, as they struggled to safeguard their commercial interests under

[21] Browne (ed.), *Provincial Court 1637–50*, pp. 149–50, 169, 225–7; Rountree and Davidson, *Eastern Shore Indians*, pp. 87–8 on Holles and profits; Mary Beth Norton, 'Gender and Defamation in Seventeenth-Century Maryland', *WMQ*, 44 (1987), pp. 3–39.

[22] Browne (ed.), *Provincial Court 1637–50*, pp. 4, 196, 203, 206, 242–3.

[23] Ibid., pp. 99–100.

unfavourable conditions. Rival groups of traders continued to scout the upper Bay in search of native trading partners, while facing intermittent competition from the Dutch and Swedes. Adventurers such as Holles or Adams undertook voyages with small amounts of cloth, metal wares and similar material, supplemented by wampum. In these circumstances, alcohol was incorporated as a commodity into the Indian trade, possibly as a lubricant for the ritual aspects of cross-cultural exchange, and to supplement the limited availability of goods from England. During 1643, for example, John Robinson, a carpenter and trader, and an associate of Holles, acquired 13 beaver skins from an Indian, in return for several bottles of spirits.[24] The growing use of alcohol in interethnic commerce had deeply unsettling long-term consequences for Indian communities, not least because the growth of native addiction gradually shifted the terms of trade in favour of the colonists. Its impact during the 1640s and 1650s was obscured by Anglo-Indian tension and conflict which became part of a wider crisis that plunged Maryland into disorder and rebellion.

Trade and troubles in the upper Bay: The 'plundering time' of the 1640s

The colony's troubles, which brought trading activity to a virtual standstill, were entangled with the transatlantic effects of the political crisis and civil war in England. Unresolved issues regarding religious rivalry, commercial competition and the authority of the lord proprietor were aggravated by Claiborne's ambitions to recover Kent Island. While these conditions provided fertile ground for a renewed attack on Baltimore's charter in London, the disarray in the upper Bay was intensified by interethnic conflict. At its most severe, political leadership within the colony teetered on the verge of collapse. Property was destroyed, land deserted and commerce neglected or abandoned. With the authority of Baltimore at stake, colonial traders were reduced to the role of bystanders as rival Europeans strengthened their contacts in the increasingly sensitive region between the Chesapeake and Delaware Bays.

The turmoil was triggered by a plundering raid on St Mary's by Richard Ingle, a London sea captain. Ingle's rebellion, as some settlers described it, seriously challenged Baltimore's fragile jurisdiction. Looking back on these turbulent times from the vantage of 1649, the General Assembly bemoaned the spoil committed during the 'Heinous Rebellion first put in Practice by that Pirate Ingle'.[25] Supporters of the lord proprietor were plundered and banished.

24 Ibid., pp. 214–5.

25 Browne (ed.), *Proceedings of the General Assembly of Maryland 1637/8–64*, p. 238; Land, *Colonial Maryland*, pp. 46–7. For a detailed narrative see E. Ingle, *Captain Richard Ingle, The Maryland 'Pirate and Rebel' 1642–1653* (Baltimore, 1884), and Riordan, *Plundering Time*, *passim*; Pestana, *The English Atlantic*, pp. 35–7.

Those who remained were forced to live under what they described as an intolerable yoke. Seizing an opportunity, and acting in concert with Ingle, Claiborne launched several attempts to regain Kent Island. He received some support from officials and settlers in Virginia, who were unreconciled with their northern neighbour, and from a group of London merchants determined to protect and promote their interests in the Bay, while advancing the cause of religious reform.

The leading actor in these events, Ingle, had traded with the Chesapeake colonies for about a decade. During the 1630s and early 1640s, when there was little incentive for London vessels to visit St Mary's, he may have acted as a life-line for the small elite of planters and merchants seeking to promote economic development. Cornwallis was described as one of his chief employers and patrons. In 1639 Ingle sailed to London from the Bay, as master of the *Richard and Anne*, with a cargo of tobacco and beaver skins which included a substantial consignment for Cornwallis. He returned with a shipment of cloth for him and others. His commercial contacts included Calvert. In 1640 he agreed to sail to Kent Island, to lade 40,000 pipestaves and transport them to London for the governor. Claiborne intervened in the transaction, claiming ownership of the timber in a suit before the High Court of Admiralty. Ingle was summoned to give evidence before the court in October 1642, but he declined to offer an opinion on the disputed ownership of his cargo, insisting that the case 'doth noe ways concerne him'.[26]

Thereafter Ingle's relations with colonial leaders deteriorated, culminating in a personal campaign of reprisals under the auspices of the parliamentary regime in London. Mutual distrust and suspicion were set in motion by the corrosive consequences of the civil war, providing an outlet for a violent display of anti-Catholicism. Ingle's raid of St Mary's played on deep-seated religious antagonism, while exploiting an appeal for redress in which public interest was opportunistically enfolded with private ambition. As such it proceeded in confused and contested circumstances.

The first sign of trouble emerged during 1643 when Ingle failed to supply the colony with ammunition in accordance with a prior agreement. Ill-feeling was intensified by outstanding debts and obligations. Although the commercial relationship survived, it was weakened by divisions between Ingle's supporters and opponents. His return to St Mary's in January 1644 coincided with the issue of a commission from Charles I to Calvert, reports of which reached the Bay, for the seizure of enemy ships and goods. It targeted vessels from London, the stronghold of the parliamentary cause, though Calvert later admitted that it applied to Virginia only. Shortly after Ingle's return, and while he was dining with Giles Brent, his vessel, apparently re-named the *Reformation,*

26 TNA, HCA 13/58, ff. 278v–9; 13/57, ff. 297–7v; E190/43/5 for trade; Ames (ed.), *Court Records of Accomack*, pp. 162–5, 269–70, 301.

was arrested. It was followed by Brent's attempts to persuade the company to take an oath of loyalty to support the king against parliament. John Durford, the mate, whose brother was a resident of Kent Island, was offered double wages if he agreed to return the ship to Bristol, a royalist stronghold, to which Baltimore moved during the year.[27]

This shadowy manoeuvring was followed by Ingle's arrest at the suit of a settler, William Hardige, for speaking treason and rebellion against the king. At Cornwallis' intervention, legal proceedings were halted. Cornwallis may also have obtained the release of the *Reformation.* Under his protection, Ingle traded without hindrance, gathering in debts and lading tobacco. Acting on behalf of the lord proprietor, John Lewger had Cornwallis impeached before the provincial court. But his attempt to put Ingle on trial for treason was frustrated by Cornwallis' claim, during the course of his own defence, that the accusation was malicious and of no importance. The court imposed a maximum fine of 1,000 pounds of tobacco on Cornwallis. It also took pledges from Ingle, in gunpowder and shot, for his return by 1 February, to answer the charge against him. He departed, followed by Cornwallis who boarded his ship at Accomack, without fulfilling these conditions. At Lewger's request Brent confiscated his goods and outstanding debts in the colony until he 'shall purge himselfe of the said crimes'.[28]

On his return to London Ingle intervened to prevent the arrest of Cornwallis' goods on account of his Catholicism, enabling him to lade cloth, iron and grocery wares, valued at about £200, aboard the *Reformation*. Before his departure, however, Ingle subscribed to the national covenant, a protestation of loyalty to parliament. He also acquired a letter of marque and a copy of a parliamentary ordinance, authorizing the seizure of enemy shipping. Public and private objectives were used to promote the voyage to members of the company. Thomas Greene, who served as boatswain, recounted that he was hired for a trading voyage to Virginia, but on their arrival in the Bay Ingle promised him, and his companions, that if they agreed to sail on to Maryland, 'to roote out the Papists from thence, that they should have a sixte part of what should bee proved prize'.[29]

27 Browne (ed.), *Proceedings of the Council of Maryland 1636–67*, pp. 165–6; TNA, HCA 13/60, unfoliated, examinations of Robert Popelye (26 June 1645), John Durford (27 June), Thomas Greene (10 July); HCA 24/108, no. 21; Hatfield, *Atlantic Virginia*, pp. 76–7.

28 Browne (ed.), *Provincial Court 1637–50*, pp. 233–41, 248–9, 251–6, 261, 457; Browne (ed.), *Proceedings of the Council of Maryland 1636–67*, pp. 166–8; TNA, HCA 24/106, no.265.

29 TNA, HCA 13/60, examination of Thomas Greene (10 July 1645); Browne (ed.), *Proceedings of the Council of Maryland 1636–67*, pp. 165–6; L.F. Stock (ed.), *Proceedings and Debates of the British Parliaments Respecting North America,*

Reprisal and religion re-animated the enemies of Baltimore. According to the surgeon aboard the *Reformation*, when Ingle arrived at Virginia he recruited more men, and during a meeting with Claiborne received news of the issue of a royal commission to Calvert, who was back in the Bay by September 1644. He also heard of the governor's alleged threat to hang him or any Londoner who visited St Mary's. Claiborne's recent visit to Kent Island, in an unsuccessful bid to revive his claim against Baltimore, aroused deep concern in Maryland. In January 1645 the governor appointed William Brainthwaite as commander of the island, and proclaimed Claiborne and Richard Thompson enemies of the colony.[30] Into this threatening environment Ingle signalled his return to Maryland in February with the plunder of a Dutch vessel, *Der Spiegel*, freighted by two English merchants, Henry Brookes and John Glover, resident at Rotterdam. Brookes, a Catholic, served as cape merchant for the voyage. The cargo, valued at between 2,300 and 2,400 guilders, included cloth, silk, hats, shoes and stockings which were to be exchanged for tobacco and fur.[31] Its spoil was an advance warning of the aggressive response of city commercial interests to increasing Dutch activity in the Bay.

Thereafter Ingle's company raided St Mary's. Unable to offer much resistance, settlers were forced to desert their homes and seek sanctuary in the woods. Although property was destroyed, there was little loss of life. The estates of prominent Catholics and the Jesuit mission attracted particular attention. Despite his previous support for Ingle, Cornwallis' house was turned into a temporary garrison and stripped of its furnishings. The raiders seized boats, tools, tobacco and beaver skins, and slaughtered stock. Servants, including four Africans, were confiscated. Some were marooned on a 'shoare upon some place or other amongst the heathens'.[32] Ingle returned to London in March or April with Brent, Lewger and Thomas Copley as prisoners.

1542–1688 (Washington, 1924), p. 178; Craven, *Southern Colonies*, pp. 233–4.

30 Browne (ed.), *Proceedings of the Council of Maryland 1636–67*, pp. 161–2; TNA, HCA 13/60, examination of Robert Rawlins (2 July 1645); Riordan, *Plundering Time*, pp. 125–6.

31 TNA, HCA 13/60, examinations of Havicke Cornelison Cocke (13 June 1645), Gabrant Ockerson (14 June), Michael Albertson (28 June); John R. Pagan, 'Dutch Maritime and Commercial Activity in Mid-Seventeenth Century Virginia', *VMHB*, 90 (1982), p. 491; Riordan, *Plundering Time*, pp. 167–91. International comparisons are difficult, but the Dutch guilder was worth between 2 to 3 English shillings, Francis Turner, 'Money and Exchange Rates in 1632', www.1632.org/1632-tech/faqs/money-exchange-rates-1632/.

32 TNA, HCA 13/60, examinations of Cocke (13 June, 9 August 1645), Henry Stockdon (5 August), John Lewger (6 August), Giles Brent (7 August), Thomas Cornwallis (8 August); Browne (ed.), *Provincial Court 1637–50*, pp. 253–4. Ingle and his company built a fort around Calvert's house, www.hsmcdigshistory.org/pdf/Forts.pdf.

The raid was a serious setback for the colony. Less than a decade after its establishment much of the economic infrastructure was destroyed or dispersed. The loss of boats and pelts was a serious blow to the Indian trade, already badly affected by the war with the Susquehannocks. The collapse of Baltimore's authority seems to have forced Calvert to seek refuge in Virginia, though he regained control of St Mary's and Kent Island during 1647. The victims attempted to recover their losses through legal action. Cornwallis claimed damages of between £2,000 and £4,000.[33] Ingle responded with a suit for compensation, based on the earlier arrest of his vessel. He also insisted that his actions were designed to protect Protestant settlers against tyrannical rule. The raid thus exposed divisions within the colony between the Catholic lords of manors and Protestant freemen. In emotive and partisan speech, Ingle described it as a just war against 'wicked Papists and Malignants'.[34]

Such language demonstrates the importance of the civil war as a necessary context and opportunity for the attack on the colony. Turbulent conditions created a fertile environment in London for the spread of radical ideas, challenging political and religious hierarchies. As parliament's stronghold, the capital became an arena for popular political agency, which ranged from mocking disrespect to outbursts of symbolic and physical violence. In February 1643, for example, the entry of a group of soldiers into Lambeth church, with their hats on, smoking and ridiculing the congregation at worship, provoked a riot with at least one fatality. Across the city the social fabric of the church was subject to sweeping change, with the ejection of suspect clergymen and their replacement by puritan ministers. In the parish of St Mary Magdalen in Bermondsey, where Ingle may still have resided, the incumbent rector, Thomas Paske, was replaced by a prominent puritan, Jeremiah Whitaker.[35] Encouraged by expectations of reform while also trying to comprehend the meaning of

33 TNA, HCA 24/108, no. 21 for Ingle's claim, and C 24/690/14; William Hand Browne (ed.), *Judicial and Testamentary Business of the Provincial Court 1649/50–1657* (Maryland Historical Society, 10, 1891), pp. 253–4; Browne (ed.), *Provincial Court 1637–50*, p. 253; Riordan, *Plundering Time*, pp. 244–57.

34 TNA, HCA 13/60, examination of William Edrupp (5 July, 1645); Joad Raymond (ed.), *Making the News: An Anthology of the Newsbooks of Revolutionary England 1641–1660* (Moreton-in-Marsh, 1993), pp. 259–60; Pestana, *The English Atlantic*, pp. 37, 203 for division between servants and masters.

35 *Mercurius Aulicus, The Eighth Week*, 22 February 1643; *HMC, Fifth Report, Appendix*, 1, p. 73; House of Lords Journal, 5, 21 February 1643, www.british-history.ac.uk/lords.jrnl/vol5/ pp. 613–619. There is a vast literature on the civil war – recent contributions include Michael Braddick, *God's Fury, England's Fire: A New History of the English Civil Wars* (London, 2008), pp. 115, 175–82, 222–4, 252 on London, and Keith Lindley, *Popular Politics and Religion in Civil War London* (Aldershot, 1997), pp. 258–9, 262, 302 for Lambeth; John Morrill, *The Nature of the English Revolution* (London, 1993), especially Part 1 on religion.

such stirring times, as the parliamentary cause gained the upper hand during 1644 soldiers, seafarers and other working men and women were emboldened and radicalised. The experience of civil discord reinforced hostility towards Catholicism, routinely expressed in the language of anti-popery, providing Ingle and his supporters with a powerful, ready-made mission that struck at the privileges of well-connected Catholic aristocrats, such as Baltimore.

In these circumstances the defeat of the royal cause dangerously weakened the ability of the lord proprietor to defend his charter against attack. A petition from the colony, complaining of oppressive rule claimed that Protestants were 'not only seduced but forced … from their religion'.[36] It led the House of Commons to declare, in November 1646, that the charter should be repealed. The house also requested the appointment of loyal Protestants to replace the lord proprietor's officers. Baltimore appealed to the House of Lords, seeking time to prepare a defence. His intervention provoked a swift response from a group of London merchants, including Maurice Thompson, a leading radical in the city, and Oliver Cloberry, brother of William, who accused Baltimore and his agents of committing 'horridd things in that province as Papists and Enemyes'.[37] But the attack on Baltimore was overshadowed by the political crisis that accompanied the renewal of the civil war, followed by the execution of Charles I and the abolition of the House of Lords. When the issue came to the attention of the Council of State in December 1649, therefore, it was under even less favourable conditions for the lord proprietor.

As Baltimore struggled to retain his charter, the political disorganization in the colony continued. Leaders of the disaffected seem to have acted in anticipation of the arrival of a new governor, or the return of Claiborne with an armed force 'to support the Rebellion of Kent'.[38] However Claiborne's plan to use the island as a springboard for an assault on St Mary's generated little support. By April 1647 Calvert had re-asserted his authority over the recalcitrant community. But his death in June robbed Baltimore of his strongest supporter. In difficult circumstances, he nominated William Stone, a Protestant of Accomack, whose uncle was a prominent city trader and an associate of Maurice Thompson, to replace his brother as governor. The appointment was followed by the replacement of Catholic officials with Protestants. These carefully weighted concessions enabled Baltimore to ward off critics in London, but they failed to deal with enemies in the Bay. In an 'upbrayding,

36 Stock (ed.), *Proceedings*, pp. 171–2, 183–4; Browne (ed.), *Proceedings of the Council of Maryland 1636–67*, pp. 173–4.

37 Ibid., pp. 180–1; Stock (ed.), *Proceedings*, pp. 194–5.

38 Browne (ed.), *Proceedings of the Council of Maryland 1636–67*, pp. 175–9; Gaskill, *Between Two Worlds*, pp. 163–4; Rice, *Nature & History*, p. 104.

insolent, threatening manner', Claiborne warned the new governor of his determination to 'renew his former pretended Claymes' in the colony.[39]

Although Maryland survived the plunder and destruction of the 1640s, it remained in an exposed condition. Colonial leaders struggled to maintain the lord proprietor's authority. Baltimore's attempts to revive the colonial project were weakened by his depleted financial situation and political isolation. Divided and disorderly, the colony seemed to be encompassed by hostile forces. Across the Bay, Kent Island suffered repeated raiding by the Nanticokes and Wicomiss. Falling back on well-established colonial tactics, in July 1647 the governor appointed captain John Price to lead an expedition, with the purpose of 'destroying the said Nations ... by killing them, taking them prisoners, burning howses' and crops.[40] It was offset the following year by a raid along the Potomac by a group of Susquehannocks, who attacked native allies of St Mary's and seized the leader of the Patawomecks.[41]

The Swedes and Dutch were the main beneficiaries of division and disorganization in the upper Bay. The close proximity of rival trading posts fuelled intense competition during which English traders steadily lost ground. With the assistance of the Lenapes, the Swedes at Fort Christina established close commercial relations with the Susquehannocks. Their success aroused deep concern among the Dutch and resentment by the English in both Chesapeake colonies, who linked trading rights with territorial claims. In 1643 the governor of Virginia warned the leader of New Netherland of English interests in Delaware Bay, and requested the prohibition of trade in arms and ammunition with native groups because it was 'contrary to the lawes of Nations'.[42] But Anglo-Dutch rivalry diverted attention away from the Swedes, who it was later claimed crept into the Bay where they acquired a 'great and secret trade of furs'.[43]

In reality these concerns were exaggerated. Although two vessels left New Sweden in 1644 with 2,142 beaver skins, Swedish trade with the Indians was intermittent and limited by the provision of trading goods from Europe. In part

39 TNA, CO 5/728, ff. 31v–2; Browne (ed.), *Proceedings of the Council of Maryland 1636–67*, pp. 187–91, 201–9; Jordan, *Foundations of Representative Government*, pp. 49–55; Stone's wife was the sister of Claiborne, Hatfield, *Atlantic Virginia*, pp. 107–8; Riordan, *Plundering Time*, pp. 321–3.

40 Browne (ed.), *Proceedings of the Council of Maryland 1636–67*, pp. 191–2.

41 Rice, *Nature & History*, p. 105.

42 Jennings, *Ambiguous Iroquois Empire*, pp. 117–23; S. Dahlgren and H. Norman (eds.), *The Rise and Fall of New Sweden: Governor Risingh's Journal 1654–1655* (Uppsala, 1988), pp. 45–7; Bailyn, *The Barbarous Years*, pp. 277–307; Grant-Costa and Mancke, 'Anglo-Amerindian commercial relations', in Bowen et al. (eds.), *Britain's Oceanic Empire*, p. 390.

43 *A Perfect Description of Virginia* (London, 1649), p. 9.

the deficiency was remedied by the use of wampum, though its employment in interethnic exchange within the region increased its colonial value, despite its decline farther north. Johan Printz, the governor of the settlement, reported that he was 'obliged to pay … a double price in good beavers' for supplies of wampum from traders in New Amsterdam and New England.[44] The Swedes sought to strengthen their position by erecting a trading post in the precincts of Fort Beversreede, the Dutch outpost. Like their competitors, the Dutch experienced difficulties in the supply of trading material. While the Indians had plentiful supplies of beaver skins during the late 1640s, they were dissatisfied with the availability of European commodities. On occasion, indeed, the Susquehannocks used native middlemen to sell surplus furs farther north in New Amsterdam.[45]

The problems got worse for the Swedes after 1648, when the settlement was effectively abandoned by its promoters. Commercial activity revived in 1654, with the arrival of a supply expedition and a new governor, Johan Risingh. Soon after his arrival Risingh met Susquehannock leaders, providing gifts to promote friendship and trade. Competing overtures from colonial leaders at St Mary's, who were keen to take advantage of their recent peace with the Indians, met with suspicion and mistrust. According to Risingh, the Indians drew a distinction between the English, who were 'accustomed to shooting them to death wherever they find them', and the Swedes, with whom they maintained friendly relations and commerce.[46] In June 1655, at a ceremony at Fort Christina, the Indians granted the Swedes land which St Mary's had hoped to acquire. It was conditional on the provision of cloth, firearms and other goods, as well as the availability of craftsmen to assist in the repair and maintenance of guns. Alarmed at the revival of Swedish competition, the governor of New Netherland, Pieter Stuyvesant, despatched an expedition to the Delaware which seized control of New Sweden and neutralized the threat of its alliance with the Susquehannocks.[47]

European rivalries were a catalyst for the growing use of weapons in interethnic commerce. The Swedes were accused by their rivals of initiating

[44] Dahlgren and Norman (eds.), *Governor Risingh's Journal*, pp. 74–5; B. Fernow (ed.), *Documents Relating to the History of the Dutch and Swedish Settlements on the Delaware River* (Albany, 1877), p. vii; Myers (ed.), *Narratives of Early Pennsylvania*, p. 127. Richter, *Before the Revolution*, pp. 259–60 on the declining value of wampum in New Netherland from 1641 to 1658.

[45] Fernow (ed.), *Documents*, p. 43; Myers (ed.), *Narratives of Early Pennsylvania*, pp. 122–3; *Documents of New York*, 12, pp. 43, 47.

[46] Dahlgren and Norman (eds.), *Governor Risingh's Journal*, pp. 78–9, 179.

[47] Ibid., pp. 199, 237–9; Karen Ordahl Kupperman, 'Scandinavian Colonists Confront the New World', in Carol E. Hoffecker et al. (eds.), *New Sweden in America* (Newark, 1995), pp. 105–6; Richter, *Trade, Land, Power*, pp. 102–5.

the trade with the Susquehannocks, but they were soon dealing in arms with other native groups. Intercolonial competition provided experienced native traders with opportunities to exploit. In July 1647 Susquehannock leaders advised Stuyvesant that the Swedes had agreed to supply them with guns, powder and lead. Almost by way of response, the governor of New Sweden complained that the Dutch were furnishing the Indians with weapons in order to capture their trade. Such competition qualified the prohibition on the trade in arms and ammunition which the General Assembly at St Mary's passed in 1650.[48]

Although the military capability of trade guns varied, their increasing availability had wide-ranging consequences for interethnic trade and politics. The supply of firearms by the Swedes bolstered the predominance of the Susquehannocks within the upper Bay. But it also intensified their hostility with the Iroquois, who were armed by the Dutch during the 1640s. The rapid impact of guns on native diplomacy, trade and warfare is demonstrated by the experience of the Susquehannocks and their neighbours. In 1634 they were reportedly fearful of European weapons, having no protection against muskets, swords or pikes.[49] Ten years later they were able to overawe native rivals and enemies 'with the sight of guns only', while holding their own against an expedition from St Mary's.[50] But native demand for firearms intensified the more violent aspect of interethnic relations. Two Swedish traders were killed in September 1648 while trading with a group of Indians in arms and ammunition. In July 1653 a party of four Piscataways raided the estate of Daniel Gookin in Maryland, seeking firearms. They killed an African servant and his son, escaping with three guns, powder and shot. The acquisition of European weapons emboldened hostile Indians, exposing the insecurity of outlying colonial settlements. In 1652 settlers on Kent Island complained of Indians who were so well supplied with guns, powder and shot that they haunted their dwellings, day and night.[51] During recent months they had

48 For contested allegations, see Edward Williams, *Virgo Triumphans: or Virginia Richly and Truly Valued* (London, 1651), pp. 18–9; Amandus Johnson (ed.), *Geographia Americae with an Account of the Delaware Indians Based on Surveys and Notes Made in 1654–1656* (Philadelphia, 1925), p. 227; Dahlgren and Norman (eds.), *Governor Risingh's Journal*, pp. 67–8; Fernow (ed.), *Documents*, pp. 59–61; Browne (ed.), *Proceedings of the General Assembly of Maryland 1637/8–64*, pp. 233, 250–1. By the mid-1640s the Iroquois had between 300 and 400 muskets, Richter, *Before the Revolution*, p. 147.

49 Beauchamp Plantagenet, *A Description of New Albion* (London, 1648), in Force, 2, no.7, p. 22.

50 Ibid., p. 24; Kent, *Susquehanna's Indians*, pp. 253–7.

51 Browne (ed.), *Proceedings of the Council of Maryland 1636–67*, p. 279; Plantagenet, *New Albion*, p. 29; Browne (ed.), *Business of the Provincial Court 1649/50–57*, pp. 52, 293–5, 353–4; Dahlgren and Norman (eds.), *Governor Risingh's*

killed two settlers and wounded another. Reports that the Indians had either purchased or plundered a large quantity of weapons from a Dutch vessel forced settlers to abandon the island in fear for their lives.

Interest in interethnic trade within the upper Bay survived this difficult period, though commercial activity may have ground to a halt. The disruption of the transatlantic trade and the metropolitan market for fur overlaid the dislocation of colonial trading networks, including the diversion of the Susquehannock trade to the Swedes and Dutch. Under the pressure of events the delicately woven infrastructure for cross-cultural commerce was in danger of unravelling. Yet the situation was not irretrievable. In an effort to promote its revival, in 1650 the General Assembly opened up the fur trade to all settlers of Maryland. Traders were cautioned to avoid giving offence to native groups, and advised not to set out on voyages 'too weake in strength', to deter the danger of Indian attack.[52] According to previous practice, the financial interests of Baltimore were protected by the levy of one tenth, in weight or value, on all fur and skins. But this initiative to encourage the recovery of the fur trade, by exploiting the weakness of New Sweden, was soon obscured by the re-emergence of rivalry with Virginia.

Trade, war and colonial rivalry in the lower Bay

Distance shielded Virginia from much of the disorder in the upper Bay. Even so, with the exception of the Eastern Shore, fur trading enterprise within the colony was in decline during the 1640s. An expanding plantation culture, boosted by the influx of a new wave of migrants, threatened the survival of native groups with a re-shaping of the land and its ecology.[53] As such the Indian trade appeared to be in danger of being reduced to marginal significance. Yet the intersection between commerce and war continued to lend it political and diplomatic significance. At the same time the rivalry between Virginia and Maryland ensured that interest in the trade survived, enlivened by hope for the recovery of Kent Island. Unavoidably, therefore, it remained connected with territorial and religious issues which assumed growing importance within a wider transatlantic context of political crisis and civil war in England. The

Journal, p. 67; Fernow (ed.), *Documents*, p. 43.

52 Browne (ed.), *Proceedings of the General Assembly of Maryland 1637/8–64*, pp. 278, 307–8. The Susquehannocks trade with the Dutch also attracted the attention of the Iroquois, Paul A. W. Wallace, 'The Iroquois', in Glasrud and Smith (eds.), *Race Relations in British North America*, pp. 9–11.

53 Adams, *The Best and Worst Country*, pp. 214, 226–8; James Axtell, *The Indians' New South: Cultural Change in the Colonial Southeast* (Baton Rouge, 1997), pp. 40–1; Darrett B. and Anita H. Rutman, *A Place in Time: Middlesex County, Virginia 1650–1750* (New York, 1984), pp. 45–7 for native displacement.

linkages were illuminated by a petition to the House of Lords in 1641 by Anthony Panton, minister and agent for the clergy in Virginia. With rumours circulating in London of an alleged popish plot at court, Panton accused Sir John Harvey, re-instated as governor in 1637, of ruling under an 'arbitrary law', and of supporting 'popery and the popish faction' in Maryland.[54] Among the leaders of the colony, political and religious concerns merged with complaints regarding the loss of trade and territory. Thus Panton informed the Lords that Catholicism was 'audaciouslie professed and practised in a whole plantation, within the former verge and limittes of Virginia, to the great scandell and disturbance of religion, [and] the interdiction and interception of the richest and choicest trade with the natives'.[55]

Confronted with rebellion and political disunity within the British Isles, Charles I sought to retain support in Virginia with the appointment of a young courtier, Sir William Berkeley, as governor. A staunch royalist, nonetheless after his arrival in the colony during 1642 Berkeley pursued a moderate course throughout the civil war, preferring consensus to confrontation. In an important gesture of political accommodation, the following year he appointed Claiborne as treasurer of the colony. Sir Edward Hyde, later earl of Clarendon, was critical of his political caution, but commended his stewardship. Under his leadership, Virginia 'in a short time was more improved in people and stock, than it had been from the beginning to that time'.[56] As a royal appointee Berkeley's position was finely balanced. It was threatened by parliament's decision to allow the colony to appoint its own governor, which came with a strong recommendation for Samuel Mathews, one of Harvey's leading opponents, and a 'man of approved affection to the good of that plantation'.[57] In the short term this intervention aroused little interest among colonists whose ambitions were focused on access to land and its acquisition from suspicious native groups.

Despite Berkeley's efforts to encourage economic diversification, by the 1640s the planter elite were tied to the cultivation of tobacco, with self-evident implications for Anglo-Powhatan relations. As a profitable commodity, benefiting from an expanding market in England and Northern Europe, it fuelled the spread of colonial settlement with little metropolitan supervision

[54] Stock (ed.), *Proceedings*, pp. 123–4.

[55] Ibid., pp. 123–4.

[56] W.D. Macray (ed.), *The History of the Rebellion and Civil Wars in England in the Year 1641, by Edward Hyde, Earl of Clarendon*, 6 vols. (Oxford, 1888), 5, p. 263; Warren M. Billings, *Sir William Berkeley and the Forging of Colonial Virginia* (Baton Rouge, 2004), pp. 51–7; Fischer, *Albion's Seed*, pp. 210–15; Williams, *Virgo Triumphans*, B2v provides a flattering portrait of Virginia, including the claim it was near the passage to China.

[57] BL, Stowe 184, f.124; Pestana, *The English Atlantic*, pp. 34, 51.

or control. By the time of the new governor's arrival colonists were moving north and inland, along the James and York Rivers, disrupting the insecure relationship with the Powhatan chiefdom and threatening the revival of interethnic trade following the restoration of peace with the Indians in 1632. Commercial activity during these years was subject to sporadic regulation. Alarmed at the sale of cloth and other goods, while many settlers were in need, in 1633 the General Assembly prohibited commerce without licence from the governor. It also outlawed the trade in arms and ammunition, on pain of life imprisonment. Berkeley's instructions from Charles I of 1641 included a clause prohibiting the Indian trade without special licence, to 'avoid and prevent treachery of the Savages'.[58]

Cross-cultural commerce had failed to safeguard the position of Indian groups within the colony, or to promote their interests in a wider Atlantic world. The exchange of manufactured goods, particularly cloth, for supplies of maize and varying amounts of furs did little to curb the hardening of mutual suspicion. Undoubtedly the trade grew rapidly during the late 1620s and early 1630s, with annual exports of between 2,000 and 3,000 beaver skins at its height. But it was followed by decline and irregular shipments, ranging from about 350 to 1,200 skins, which narrowed the economic function of native groups in an expanding settlement determined to exploit the availability of land.[59]

By the early 1640s the Powhatans were aware of their tenuous status in a colonial landscape characterized by the spread of commercialized agriculture and increasing numbers of livestock. Although change often went unrecorded, the cumulative impact of the newcomers on the native environment and ecology was extensive. It had disruptive implications for the supply of the fur trade. Intensive tobacco cultivation destroyed or disturbed established habitats for native fauna. Because of their life-cycle and slow reproductive rate, local populations of beavers were under severe pressure, even if they were not the victims of intensive native hunting.[60] English traders and colonists may have remained unaware of the damaging consequences of their intrusion into the

[58] Hening (ed.), *Statutes*, I, pp. 219, 255–6, 353–4; Gleach, *Powhatan's World*, pp. 172–3. He was authorized to grant commissions for discovery of the country, Warren M. Billings (ed.), *The Papers of Sir William Berkeley, 1605–1677* (Richmond, 2007), p. 26.

[59] Hillier, 'Trade of Virginia', pp. 289–90, 420–2, for a peak total of 3,291 beaver skins in 1631.

[60] David J. Wishart, *The Fur Trade in the American West 1807–1840* (Lincoln, 1979), pp. 27–33; Carlos and Lewis, *Commerce by a Frozen Sea*, pp. 107–11; Chaplin, *Subject Matter*, pp. 202, 220–8 for changes to the landscape and removal of the Indians. The loss of wildlife affected native diets, Axtell, *The Invasion Within*, pp. 161–3; Bailey, *The Conflict of Cultures*, pp. 55–7.

Bay, but across the eastern seaboard, at different entry points for Europeans, an irreversible process of ecological disruption and depletion was underway.

Subject to regional variation, the consequences were illustrated by a report of Adriaen Van der Donck on New Netherland during the 1640s and 1650s. Drawing on his experience as a fur trader, Van der Donck noted that beavers shunned human habitations, preferring isolated and unsettled environments. As hunting intensified, native bands travelled longer distances and devoted more time to the acquisition of skins. They combined traditional methods of hunting with European technology, using lances to force beavers from their lodges. He also reported a more ruthless approach to hunting, which included young animals whose skins were of little value. Estimating that about 80,000 beavers were killed each year in New Netherland and adjacent territory, he acknowledged that the scale of destruction provoked unease at the consequences for future trade. But he dismissed such concern as unnecessary. Native traders seemed to have access to an inexhaustible supply of fur, 'worth tons of gold, which may be increased, and is like goods found'.[61] While the volume of the fur trade in the Chesapeake never approached this figure, which was in any case exaggerated, native hunting still inflicted a heavy toll on the population of beavers. By the early 1640s thousands of animals may have been killed in Virginia and its hinterland to supply the fur market in London. At the same time, the irregular nature of the trade, a reflection of persistent ambiguities in Anglo-Indian relations, may have provided some protection for the survival of more inaccessible beaver lodges.

These ambiguities were clarified by the renewal of hostilities during 1644 when the Powhatans launched a series of raids on exposed farms and plantations. Under the leadership of Opechancanough, whose life bore witness to a receding native world, the Indians inflicted heavy casualties on the colonists. Estimates vary, but between 400 and 500 settlers were killed. It was a violent rejection of the culture of the newcomers, and a denial of commercial cooperation or integration within an emerging transatlantic economy.[62] But the balance of power was now much less favourable to the natives. Colonial militias led by experienced Indian traders, such as William Claiborne and Henry Fleet, and Berkeley, inflicted severe damage on disorganized native groups, burning villages and corn. The colonists suffered a

61 Adriaen Van der Donck, *A Description of the New Netherlands*, ed. Thomas F. O'Donnell (Syracuse, 1968), pp. 97–8, 114–18, this over-estimated the volume of trade; Brandâo, *"Your Fyre Shall Burn No More"*, pp. 86–9.

62 Gleach, *Powhatan's World*, pp. 175–9; Helen C. Rountree, 'The Powhatans and the English: A Case of Multiple Conflicting Agendas', in Rountree (ed.), *Powhatan Foreign Relations*, pp. 194–5. It was accompanied by rumours that the Powhatans were seeking to take advantage of the civil war in England, of which allegedly they had been informed by Sir Francis Wyatt, Pestana, *The English Atlantic*, p. 66.

reversal of fortunes when they ran out of gunpowder, enabling the Powhatans to retaliate with raids on outlying farms. It was a brief setback, remedied by the purchase of additional supplies of powder from visiting London ships. As the colonists gained the upper hand, forts were constructed to protect access along the James and Appomattox Rivers, symbols of an emerging and expanding frontier, and representative of new methods of power and authority. By March 1646 Opechancanough had been taken prisoner. He was subsequently murdered in colonial custody. His successor, Necotowance, and other Indian leaders, had little option but to accept the treaty which brought the conflict to an end in October.[63]

Defeat marked the disintegration of the chiefdom. Dismissed by the General Assembly as 'noe longer a nation', the Powhatans acknowledged their tributary status with an annual gift of 20 beaver skins to the governor.[64] Colonial leaders claimed they 'had reduced the Indians to very good neighbourhood'.[65] In practice native survivors were forced to surrender territory between the York and James Rivers. The north side of the York was designated an area for native habitation, though colonial settlement was not prohibited. In future Anglo-Powhatan contact was to be strictly controlled and regulated. Indians wishing to enter the colony, for trade or other purposes, were now required to wear badges of striped cloth. The projection of separate worlds was qualified in favour of Indian children aged up to 12 years, who voluntarily wished to live with the English. The treaty was thus part of a broader cultural re-negotiation, increasingly expressed in Indian dislocation and dependency. Within five years of the Powhatan attack, one report noted that most Indian groups in the colony had been destroyed or driven away.[66] Those who remained struggled to survive in an inhospitable environment of lost or wasted assets.

Native displacement opened up new areas for colonial occupation. Lacking metropolitan oversight, ambitious and aggressive planters speculatively combined the acquisition of land with trade by means of the plantation and

63 Hening (ed.), *Statutes*, 1, pp. 323–6; Gleach, *Powhatan's World*, pp. 178–83; Steele, *Warpaths*, pp. 48–51; Rountree and Turner, *Before and After Jamestown*, pp. 151–6. On forts and trade see, Douglas C. Comer, *Ritual Ground: Bent's Old Fort, World Formation, and the Annexation of the Southwest* (Berkeley, 1996), pp. 90–3 and Merrell, *The Indians New World*, pp. 28–9.

64 Stock (ed.), *Proceedings*, p. 182; Rountree, *Powhatan Indians*, pp. 87–9, 92.

65 *A Perfect Description*, p. 6; Macray (ed.), *History of the Rebellion*, 5, p. 263; E. Randolph Turner, 'Socio-Political Organization Within the Powhatan Chiefdom and the Effects of European Contact, A.D. 1607–1646', in Fitzhugh (ed.), *Cultures in Contact*, pp. 194–217.

66 And few were willing to adopt colonial culture, Rountree and Turner, *Before and After Jamestown*, pp. 161–6; Gleach, *Powhatan's World*, pp. 184–5; Billings (ed.), *Papers of Berkeley*, pp. 71–3.

the sailing vessel. They included established settlers and leaders, such as Claiborne, and more recent migrants, like Edmund Scarborough, who settled along the Eastern Shore following his arrival in 1634. Claiborne and his former trading rival, Fleet, were in the vanguard of expansion into the northern neck, soon known as Northumberland County. But with further movement checked by Maryland, it soon became an unruly borderland, sheltering rebellious and disaffected settlers from Kent Island and St Mary's.[67]

Nonetheless, the peace with the Powhatans enabled Claiborne to renew his campaign against Maryland. It merged with a metropolitan assault against Baltimore's charter. Proprietorial authority survived, as noted above, but it was severely weakened, and faced acute problems. The influx of several hundred Protestant settlers from Virginia during 1649, part of Baltimore's response to anti-Catholic rhetoric in England, badly misfired. Under the leadership of William Fuller, the newcomers established a settlement at Providence, along the Severn River, which became a focal point for hostility against his rule.[68]

The consequences of war and colonial rivalry strengthened a perception that Virginia had lost the initiative in the fur trade to its rivals. In 1650 Edward Williams complained that the colonists were 'so supinely negligent to permit the Dutch and French to carry away most of this pretious Commodity, to trade in our Rivers, under-sell us' and provide the Indians with firearms.[69] A small group of traders along the Eastern Shore maintained a foothold in the trade, but little evidence survives of their ventures. They included Jenkin Price, John Westlock and John Nuthall, formerly an indentured servant who ran away to live with a group of Indians, from whom he was purchased by William Jones. But all three re-located to Maryland, where Nuthall acquired two manors and 12 slaves, while retaining an interest in interethnic commerce.[70] The activities of such men were overshadowed by the ambitions of Scarborough. With a commission of 1651, authorizing him to establish a trading post on Palmer's Island, he made repeated attempts to break into the Susquehannock trade, in competition with the Dutch and Swedes. One of his traders, John Fisher, reported in 1651 that he had undertaken five voyages along the Susquehanna River and into Delaware Bay. Four years later, the last governor of New Sweden complained that the competition had ruinous consequences for

67 Ibid., pp. 185–7; Horn, *Adapting to a New World*, pp. 174–6; Oberg, *Dominion and Civility*, pp. 184–5 for Scarborough (or Scarburgh); Rice, *Nature & History*, pp. 121–8 on the 'land rush' and declining Indian autonomy.

68 Hall (ed.), *Narratives of Early Maryland*, pp. 255, 263–5; Bernard C. Steiner, *Maryland Under the Commonwealth: A Chronicle of the Years 1649–1658* (Baltimore, 1911), pp. 62–5.

69 Williams, *Virgo Triumphans*, pp. 18–9.

70 Rountree and Davidson, *Eastern Shore Indians*, pp. 91–2, 101; Menard, *Economy and Society*, p. 187.

the trade. While Scarborough offered the Indians seven or eight pounds of gunpowder for one beaver skin, the Swedes were 'accustomed to give at the highest from 3 to 4 *lbs.* and cannot give over 5 *lbs.* except at a loss'.[71]

Scarborough's commercial activities were encouraged by political and diplomatic change, under the impact of distant developments across the Atlantic. In England, Baltimore's weakened position, following the execution of Charles I and the establishment of a republican regime, created unexpected opportunities for such ambitious entrepreneurs in the upper Bay. At the same time Berkeley was dismissed as governor and replaced by commissioners, who included Richard Bennett and Claiborne. In September 1651 they were instructed to reduce the Chesapeake plantations to parliamentary obedience, and empowered to use force if they met resistance.[72] By March 1652 they had imposed their authority over Maryland. Legally Baltimore's charter remained in force, but in practical terms he had lost control of the colony. With the support of the General Assembly, they also used legislation to establish a commonwealth regime in Virginia.[73]

Political change was accompanied by diplomatic initiatives which included peace between the Susquehannocks and Maryland. Both sides were keen to end their long-running conflict. For the Indians it was an opportunity to retain their commanding position in the region as they struggled to deal with sustained population losses, in part the legacy of severe smallpox epidemics of 1636 and 1637. The revival of raiding by Iroquoian groups from the north, following their success against the Hurons, intensified the pressure on the Susquehannocks. Although native rivalries were reinforced by the availability of European weapons, both sides were less concerned with inflicting casualties on their opponent than with taking captives. These 'mourning wars' were being re-cast as a result of contact and commerce with Europeans. As such the recent success of the Susquehannocks, who were reported in 1650 to have taken 200 Iroquoian prisoners, was unlikely to end the raiding from the north.[74]

[71] Myers (ed.), *Narratives of Early Pennsylvania*, p. 187; Billings (ed.), *Papers of Berkeley*, p. 101; Rountree and Davidson, *Eastern Shore Indians*, pp. 88–9, 92–3 for traders on the Eastern Shore.

[72] Thomas Birch, *A Collection of the State Papers of John Thurloe*, 7 vols. (London, 1742), 1, pp. 197–8; *CSPC 1574–1660*, p. 361; Hening (ed.), *Statutes*, 1, p. 364; Stephen D. Crow, '"Your Majesty's Good Subjects": A Reconsideration of Royalism in Virginia, 1642–1652', *VMHB*, 87 (1979), pp. 170–2; Pestana, *The English Atlantic*, pp. 91–2, 115–16, 118.

[73] Billings (ed.), 'Some Acts not in Hening's *Statutes*:, pp. 22–76, though much of it re-enacted previous laws; Billings, *Papers of Berkeley*, pp. 109–12.

[74] The Iroquois may have suffered population losses of 60% as a result of a smallpox epidemic in 1634, Jeter, 'Ripe for Colonial Exploitation', p. 42; Richter, *Trade, Land, Power*, pp. 70–6; Delâge, *Bitter Feast*, pp. 85–93; George T. Hunt, *The Wars of the Iroquois: A Study in Intertribal Relations* (Madison, 1940), pp. 9–14; A.W.

For their part the leaders of Maryland saw the peace as a means of dealing with Dutch and Swedish activity in Delaware Bay. According to a report from a recently established, and short-lived, settlement by traders from the northern colony of New Haven, who laid claim to part of the bay, the Dutch were stirring up the Indians against the English. It was followed by alarming rumours that they were behind a wider Indian conspiracy ranging from Virginia to New England. Such barely concealed hostility aggravated Anglo-Dutch commercial rivalry, preparing the ground for the Navigation Act of 1651, and the outbreak of the first Anglo-Dutch war the following year. But metropolitan ambitions to exclude them from the colonial trades threatened to provoke a backlash in parts of the Bay, where Dutch traders were 'the Darling of the People of Virginea', despite the concern of some that their commercial and territorial claims threatened to cut across English ambitions.[75]

Faced with interlocking problems and opportunities, representatives for the Susquehannocks and Marylanders concluded a treaty of peace and friendship in July 1652. The agreement was negotiated by parliament's commissioner, Richard Bennett, and other Protestant leaders, with a party of Indian rulers who included Aurotaurogh. The presence of an agent for the governor of New Sweden indicates that other interests were at stake in the negotiations. It may also illuminate the ability of Susquehannock leaders, based on prior experience, to adapt to European-style diplomacy. The treaty proclaimed that 'all former Injuries [were] buried and forgotten'.[76] It made provision for future reparation in case of damage committed by either party or their allies, and for the return of runaways, colonial and native. Indian leaders recognized the colony's claim to territory in the upper Bay, though much of it was not in their possession, and they affirmed Claiborne's ownership of Kent and Palmer's Islands. They also agreed that either side could construct on the latter a 'House or Fort for trade or any such like use'.[77] The treaty thus appeared to provide the English with a key to unlock the Susquehannock trade, possibly based on

---

Trelease, *Indian Affairs in Colonial New York: The Seventeenth Century* (Ithaca, 1960), pp. 118–200; Richter, *Long-House*, pp. 58–60, 232–3; Plantagenet, *Description of New Albion*, p. 203; Dean R. Snow, *The Iroquois* (Cambridge, 1994), pp. 110–4.

75 *A Perfect Description of Virginia*, p. 8; Pagan, 'Dutch Maritime and Commercial Activity', pp. 486–95; Victor Enthoven and Wim Klooster, 'The Rise and Fall of the Virginia-Dutch Connection in the Seventeenth Century', in Bradburn and Coombs (eds.), *Early Modern Virginia*, pp. 99–107; D. Pulsifier (ed.), *Records of the Colony of New Plymouth in New England*, 2 vols. (Boston, 1859), 1, pp. 188–9, 199, 211. They included Augustine Herrman, Christian J. Koot, 'The Merchant, the Map, and Empire: Augustine Herrman's Chesapeake and Interimperial Trade, 1644–73', *WMQ*, 67 (2010), pp. 612–15.

76 Browne (ed.), *Proceedings of the Council of Maryland 1636–67*, p. 278.

77 Ibid., p. 277; Jennings, *Ambiguous Iroquois Empire*, p. 121 suggests that the Susquehannocks ceded land for arms; Rice, *Nature & History*, p. 105.

an unwritten expectation regarding the availability of arms and ammunition. But the reference to Claiborne's rights suggested that commercial ambitions continued to be threatened by an undercurrent of rivalry between Maryland and Virginia.

The unresolved issues between the two colonies were laid bare by a pamphlet war during the mid-1650s, during which authors appealed to audiences on both sides of the Atlantic. The controversy was triggered by *Lord Baltemore's Case* of 1653, a defence of the charter which presented Maryland as a barrier 'to prevent the Dutch and Swedes from incroaching any nearer to Virginia'.[78] Two years later a rejoinder portrayed the colony as a nursery for Jesuits, threatening the security of its neighbour. Exploiting recent events and previous objections, it claimed that Maryland was ill-founded and badly-managed. The colony was little more than a 'factory for Trade', where firearms were sold to the Indians while the land lay void of settlers.[79] Although Baltimore had taken over the trade, he was unable to manage it effectively. A commercial enterprise 'discovered and begun by the Virginians', had thus fallen into the hands of the Swedes and Dutch, with the 'profit of many thousand pounds yeerly'.[80] The war of words grew more intense with Leonard Strong's account of *Babylon's Fall in Maryland*. Representing the puritan community of Providence, Strong depicted the saints as struggling against the forces of anti-Christ. Claiborne refrained from entering the controversy, though he was portrayed as a villainous Judas by John Hammond in one of the last contributions to it.[81]

The interweaving of colonial rivalry and war, and the decline of the Powhatans, had uneven consequences for interethnic commerce within the Bay. While trading activity in many parts of the region may have stalled, changing conditions strengthened the activities of Eastern Shore traders in a contested space for trade and plantation. The collapse of Baltimore's authority also provided Claiborne with an opportunity to renew contact with the Susquehannocks. At the same time, the defeat of native groups in Virginia may have helped to focus attention on the potential resources of regions beyond the area of colonial settlement. Such interest was fuelled by the revival of transatlantic schemes for the colonization of Carolina, which was promoted

78 Hall (ed.), *Narratives of Early Maryland*, pp. 167–80; Steiner, *Maryland Under the Commonwealth*, pp. 62–5; Land, *Colonial Maryland*, pp. 53–5.

79 Hall (ed.), *Narratives of Early Maryland*, pp. 187–230.

80 Ibid., p. 190; Carl Bridenbaugh, 'The Old and New Societies of the Delaware Valley in the Seventeenth Century', *Pennsylvania Magazine of History and Biography*, 100 (1976), pp. 151–2 for the Dutch.

81 Hall (ed.), *Narratives of Early Maryland*, pp. 235–46, 261–2, 281–308.

in London as possessing 'all manner of provision for life', including profitable commercial commodities, such as deer and beaver skins.[82]

Colonial rivalry and commerce during the 1650s

The turmoil of the 1640s distracted but did not destroy interest in the Indian trade. In the upper Bay peace with the Susquehannocks encouraged its revival, while creating a more favourable environment for challenging the Dutch and Swedes. Such conditions re-awakened ambitions for the capture of a rich, though possibly faltering, trade in fur. Although the prospect attracted attention in both colonies, breathing new life into an old dispute, divergent patterns began to emerge during the 1650s. As traders in Maryland sought to establish commercial contact with their former enemies, in the lower Bay frontier middlemen and explorers began to scout for new Indian trading partners inland and along coastal regions to the south. Partly a reaction to the corrosive impact of war and rivalry, these differences may also have been an opportunistic response to the damaging consequences of competition for interethnic trade.

Rivalry with the Swedes and Dutch failed to inhibit the growth of intercolonial contacts between the Bays. The end of hostilities with the Susquehannocks provided greater security for commerce and migration, enabling the transfer of knowledge, skills and experience. Despite metropolitan ambitions to exclude the Dutch from colonial commerce, even during the first Anglo-Dutch war, they retained access to the Chesapeake. In 1653 a Dutch vessel laden with Virginia tobacco and 'a good quantity of beaver skins', reputedly worth £5,000 in total, was seized by an English ship, while returning to the Netherlands.[83] By contrast traders from Maryland supplied New Sweden with provisions in exchange for furs. Although regulated by the issue of licences at St Mary's, intercolonial commerce was overshadowed by competing territorial claims which assumed greater importance following the Dutch seizure of New Sweden during 1655.[84]

Commercial activity was also threatened by persistent tension between the Chesapeake colonies, complicated by political change in England, where a commonwealth regime gave way to the protectorate of Oliver Cromwell. In the

82 Stock (ed.), *Proceedings*, p. 132; Raymond (ed.), *Making the News*, p. 269.

83 George F. Steckley (ed.), *The Letters of John Paige, London, Merchant, 1648–1658* (London Record Society, 21, 1984), p. 89; Delâge, *Bitter Feast*, p. 268 for Dutch interest in furs from Virginia; Browne (ed.), *Business of the Provincial Court 1649/50–57*, pp. 166, 496.

84 Steiner, *Maryland Under the Commonwealth*, p. 74; Pagan, 'Dutch Maritime and Commercial Activity', pp. 494–7; Koot, *Empire at the Periphery*, p. 46 argues for the emergence of 'an interimperial world' among English and Dutch colonists during the 1640s.

upper Bay a temporary agreement of 1652 enabled William Stone to resume office as Baltimore's governor. Across the Atlantic, however, the colony's charter came under renewed attack. In 1654 political compromise collapsed. Amid disruptive and violent circumstances, Bennett and Claiborne, with the support of the Protestant community, replaced Stone with William Fuller. By means of legislation passed by General Assemblies in 1654 and 1657, the new leadership sought to root out Catholic influence with the intention of undermining Baltimore's authority in the colony. Yet Cromwell was reluctant to become involved in a distant and distracting dispute. In January 1655 he warned Bennett, then serving as governor of Virginia, not to interfere in the affairs of Maryland until the issue was resolved in London. Edward Digges, who briefly served as Bennett's successor, effectively disowned the campaign against the lord proprietor, implying it was the work of a small faction, acting without the approval of the council and assembly.[85]

Despite signs of local disengagement, Baltimore's enemies were not so easily deflected. In October 1656 Bennett and Samuel Mathews, the younger, who replaced Digges as governor, lobbied John Thurloe, Secretary of State for the protectorate, against a proposed agreement to end the dispute. Their case was supported by evidence ranging back to the 1630s, designed to demonstrate Baltimore's unfitness to remain in charge of Maryland. Claiming that he had authorized Stone to oppose the settlement imposed by the parliamentary commissioners, they argued that military defeat had deprived the lord proprietor of his colony. Little of the rest of this material was new. But it articulated an interpretation of Maryland's origins, 'founded upon the rights and labours of other men, and begun in bloodshed, robbery, and all manner of cruelty', which attracted wider support, while serving the interests of Claiborne and his supporters.[86] Yet the intense partisanship of their case wrecked the opportunity for compromise in London, enabling Baltimore to survive as lord proprietor until the restoration of the monarchy in 1660.

Colonial disunity, combined with persistent fears of native hostility, delayed the revival of trading activity and weakened the ability of colonial leaders to seize the military initiative. In Maryland a planned expedition of December 1652 against hostile Indians on the Eastern Shore, in response to complaints from Kent Island, was deferred and later abandoned. In March 1653 Thomas Gerrard was appointed to lead a force against suspect Indians at Portobacco or Choptico, but with uncertain result. It was followed by alarming reports of the appearance of an unknown Indian group, identified as Mathues, on the

[85] Land, *Colonial Maryland*, pp. 51–3; Meyers, 'Calvert's Catholic Colony', pp. 375–8; Birch (ed.), *State Papers of John Thurloe*, 1, p. 724; Pestana, *The English Atlantic*, pp. 150–4.

[86] Birch (ed.), *State Papers of John Thurloe*, 5, pp. 482–7.

colony's borderland, who were reportedly trading with the native neighbours of St Mary's.[87]

In these circumstances Maryland was unprepared to respond to the Dutch takeover of New Sweden. With their experience of the fur trade, manifest in commercial expertise and efficient organization, the Dutch were able to translate trading advantage into political influence. Faced with weak competition, they soon developed close connections with the Susquehannocks. In October 1658 Indian leaders travelled to Fort Albany to serve as intermediaries in a conflict between the Dutch and native groups along the Hudson River. They also agreed to return the following year 'with all their beavers, to ... trade there and with nobody else'.[88] Anticipating that the Dutch would provide them with munitions, they offered to supply more fur in return for generous allowances of gunpowder.

Unable to compete on these terms, the leaders of Maryland laid claim to Delaware Bay, insisting that it came within the colony's charter. Intercolonial diplomacy grew more aggressive with the reviving authority of the lord proprietor, marked by the arrival of his brother, Philip Calvert, who served as secretary until his appointment as governor. In September 1659 Nathaniel Utie, a representative from St Mary's, presented the claim to the council at New Amstel, warning that the English would be 'guiltless of the vast quantity of innocent blood that may be shed', if they failed to leave.[89] Playing on the threat, he also recruited several Dutch settlers with the offer of favourable conditions in Maryland. Others followed, including Jacob Clausen, a trader and interpreter. In response, a Dutch delegation, led by Augustine Herrman, visited St Mary's. Advising Calvert of the recent arrival of 100 soldiers, he warned that the Dutch would 'defend the river to the last man'.[90] Although Herrman challenged the legality of Maryland's claim, he suggested that the dispute could be resolved by arbitration. Discretely he offered Calvert 'an intimate

87 Browne (ed.), *Proceedings of the Council of Maryland 1636–67*, pp. 279, 282–90, 293–4.

88 *Documents of New York*, 13, p. 95; Jennings, *Ambiguous Iroquois Empire*, pp. 123–4; Richter, *Trade, Land, Power*, pp. 108–9.

89 *Documents of New York*, 2, pp. 73–4; 3, p. 344; C.A. Weslager, *Dutch Explorers, Traders and Settlers in the Delaware Valley 1609–1664* (Philadelphia, 1961), pp. 233–6. New Amstel was established by Amsterdam in 1657, but it never flourished, Jaap Jacobs, 'Dutch Proprietary Manors in America: The Patroonships in New Netherland', in Roper and Ruymbreke (eds.), *Early Modern Empires*, pp. 323–4.

90 *Documents of New York*, 2, p. 89; Francis Jennings, 'Jacob Young: Indian Trader and Interpreter', in Sweet and Nash (eds.), *Struggle and Survival*, pp. 347–9. On Herrman, see Hatfield, *Atlantic Virginia*, pp. 98–99 and Koot, 'The Merchant, the Map, and Empire', pp. 603–44, who notes that the mission to St Mary's persuaded him to prepare a new map of the region.

correspondence and confederation for reciprocal trade and intercourse'.[91] Yet the offer was thrown into relief by Herrman's plan to visit Virginia, in order 'to create some diversion between them both'.[92]

Despite these diplomatic overtures, the rivalry between English and Dutch settlements grew more threatening with the re-establishment of peace between Maryland and Indian groups of the Eastern Shore. While creating more favourable conditions for trade, it opened up the region to colonial expansion. Its key provision allowed colonists to settle Indian territory 'without molestation or Trouble'.[93] By 1659 settlers from St Mary's were surveying land in the region, and traders were ranging into the Delaware, operating almost under the shadow of New Amstel. Dutch plans to remove the intruders only seem to have exposed their own vulnerability. According to one report the claims of Maryland provoked 'such fright and disturbance' among the inhabitants of the Dutch settlement 'that thereby all work has been stopped and everyone endeavours to fly'.[94]

The revival of interest in the Indian trade, coinciding with the restoration of proprietorial authority in Maryland, led to the return of commercial regulation. During the late 1650s the council at St Mary's issued commissions for trade with Indian groups, in beaver skins and other goods, within and beyond the colony. In addition, Nathaniel Utie was authorized to seize traders operating along the Eastern Shore without licence.[95] But the imposition of regulation threatened the activities of Virginia traders, such as Scarborough, who were struggling to deal with native hostility. Acting on behalf of the governor, in August 1659 Scarborough appealed to the leaders of Maryland for assistance in combined action against the Assateagues and others. After due consideration the governor and council at St Mary's declined to participate in the proposed expedition.[96]

If the restoration of peace within the upper Bay gradually created more favourable conditions for a revival of interethnic trade, in Virginia it favoured the exploration of regions beyond the colony. In 1649 Berkeley, who was authorized to issue commissions for the discovery of the country, led a brief scouting expedition inland. Although Edward Bland's well-publicized

[91] *Documents of New York*, 2, pp. 92–4, 96.

[92] Ibid., pp. 98–9.

[93] Browne (ed.), *Proceedings of the Council of Maryland 1636–67*, pp. 362–4; Paul G.E. Clemens, *The Atlantic Economy and Colonial Maryland's Eastern Shore: From Tobacco to Grain* (Ithaca, 1980), pp. 39–47 on the development of the Eastern Shore.

[94] *Documents of New York*, 2, p. 248; 3, pp. 345–6; Browne (ed.), *Proceedings of the Council of Maryland 1636–67*, pp. 363, 378–80.

[95] Ibid., pp. 342–3; Rountree and Davidson, *Eastern Shore Indians*, p. 91.

[96] Browne (ed.), *Proceedings of the Council of Maryland 1636–67*, pp. 378–80.

exploratory venture the following year exposed the dangers of such enterprise, it failed to dampen the ambitions of explorers and traders. Commercial interest was reinforced by the decline of local Indians, who complained that they were unable to subsist, either 'by plantinge or huntinge', as a result of their loss of land.[97] In 1653 the General Assembly awarded a commission to Claiborne, Fleet and others for the discovery of new trades in unknown regions, with the authority to take out patents for land, though it seems to have remained dormant. About the same time Francis Yeardley and Nathaniel Batts were investigating the region around Albermarle Sound, where colonial enterprise became interlinked with native raiding and slaving.[98]

Exploration and expansionist ambitions were freighted with enhanced meaning, reflecting the development of the frontier as a distinct and de-regulated space. But they also bore the burden of the past. Contact with unknown Indians was qualified by anxiety, fear and a concern to maintain the identity of the colonial community. Commerce and control were thus entwined with images of distant and potentially dangerous relations. From this perspective 'fair and far off is best with Heathen Indians; and fit it is to reduce all their trading to five Ports or Pallisadoed trucking houses, and to kill all straglers and such spies without ransome'.[99] Action against traders who dealt in arms and ammunition would not only safeguard the colonists, but also enable the Indians to be 'sooner ruled, civilized and subjected'.[100] Consequently when the General Assembly received reports in 1655 of the arrival of a large party of Indians, reportedly from the mountains in the west, near the falls of the James River, it despatched an expedition under Edward Hill for their removal.[101] Described by the colonists as Richahecrians, they were subsequently known as Westos.[102] According to Lionel Gatford they arrived with a large quantity of beaver skins which they wished to trade with the English, but the commercial

97 Billings (ed.), 'Some Acts not in Hening's *Statutes*', pp. 72–3.

98 C.W. Alvord and L. Bidgood, *The First Explorations of the Trans-Allegheny Region by the Virginians 1650–1674* (Cleveland, 1912), pp. 48–50; McIlwaine (ed.), *Journals of the House of Burgesses*, p. 85; Hatfield, *Atlantic Virginia*, pp. 24–6; Hale, *Virginia Venturer*, pp. 291–2. The grant may reflect Claiborne's loss of interest in the upper Bay, Rice, *Nature & History*, pp. 106–7. And see below, pp 170–1.

99 Plantagenet, *Description of New Albion*, p. 25.

100 Ibid., p. 25.

101 Hening (ed.), *Statutes*, 1, pp. 402–3; Wesley Frank Craven, *White, Red, and Black: The Seventeenth Century Virginian* (New York, 1977), p. 60; Rountree (ed.), *Powhatan Foreign Relations*, p. 110.

102 W. Neil Franklin, 'Virginia and the Cherokee Indian Trade, 1673–1752', *East Tennessee Historical Society*, 4 (1932), pp. 5–6; John R. Swanton, *Early History of the Creek Indians and their Neighbors* (Washington, 1922), pp. 294–7; Alan Gallay, *The Indian Slave Trade: The Rise of English Empire in the American South, 1670–1717* (New Haven, 2002), p. 41. They were suppliers of native captives to the colonists.

opportunity was missed. Although Hill's expedition, supported by a contingent of Pamunkeys and their leader Totopotami, failed to dislodge the newcomers, they seem to have been defeated by another force the following year.[103]

Within the broader compass of interethnic relations, colonial legislation was used to impose regulation and order on the Indian trade. Seeking to reinforce earlier initiatives, in 1656 the assembly prohibited Indians from visiting 'fenced plantations without a ticket from some person to be nominated on the head of each river'.[104] Trade was restricted to forts and outposts or other locations designated as Indian markets. If enforced, these provisions enabled frontier entrepreneurs, such as Abraham Wood at Fort Henry, to act as colonial gatekeepers for native traders seeking access to the colony. Although focused on the location of commerce, subsequent legislation addressed its character, in an attempt to prevent the growth of disorderly and deceitful practices by colonists. In 1660 the assembly tried to limit the amount of truck offered by unscrupulous traders, on the grounds that it led to native indebtedness and imprisonment. Legislation of the following year also attempted to prohibit the supply of Indians with firearms and ammunition by 'ill-minded, idle, and unskillfull people'.[105] In future the governor was requested to issue trading commissions only to 'persons of knowne integrity'.[106]

Surviving evidence sheds little light on colonial traders or their ventures during these years. Undoubtedly the number of colonists engaged in interethnic commerce fluctuated. In many cases trade was combined with planting, which provided the working capital for small-scale and localized enterprise. Within Maryland a small group of established traders based at St Mary's included William Lewis, John Nuthall and possibly John Holles, who moved across the Potmac in 1647 to establish a small farm and trading post close to the Indian village of Matchotic.[107] They were joined by John Batemen, a London merchant who migrated in 1658 or 1659 with his wife and eight servants. He acquired 1,000 acres of land near Palmer's Island, known as Perry Point or Neck, which may have been intended partly as a trading location with the Susquehannocks. An appraisement of his estate in January 1665 suggests

[103] Hatfield, *Atlantic Virginia*, p. 25; Hening (ed.), 1, pp. 402–3; Gleach, *Powhatan's World*, pp. 186–91.

[104] Hening (ed.), *Statutes*, 1, p. 415.

[105] Ibid., pp. 20, 415.

[106] Ibid., p. 20.

[107] The site, along the shore of Currioman Bay in Virginia, has been subject to archaeological investigation which strongly suggests that Holles was engaged in local trade in venison and ceramics, among other goods, see D. Brad Hatch, 'Venison Trade and Interaction between English Colonists and Native Americans in Virginia's Potomac River Valley', *Northeast Historical Archaeology*, 41 (2012), pp. 22–3, 28–31.

that his interests in the Indian trade were modest.[108] It included an old case containing a parcel of Indian truck, such as bells and Jew's harps, valued at 100 pounds of tobacco, as well as a trading gun and two otter skins. A more disparate group of traders was located along the Eastern Shore, where adventurers from both Chesapeake colonies competed with the Dutch and Swedes. Conditions in the region facilitated intercolonial movement, enabling the crossing of boundaries for trade and settlement. Such local migrants included Nathaniel Utie, who re-located from Accomack to Maryland during 1656. This collection of Bay traders was complemented, within Virginia, by the emergence of a small, well-connected group of explorers and adventurers, such as Abraham Wood, who were seeking to establish commercial contact with inland Indians.[109]

The volume and profitability of the fur trade during these years are impossible to estimate. In 1656 John Hammond reported that good returns were to be made 'by trading with Indians for Skins, Beaver, Furres,' and other commodities.[110] But he was promoting settlement in the Bay and failed to provide any supporting material. Under prevailing conditions, returns were probably modest in scale. Yet within the confines of a developing colonial economy, where currency and specie were scarce, beaver skins were a valued commercial commodity, circulating widely as a medium of exchange and a marker of reciprocity or dependency. They formed part of a web of credit and personal obligation linking traders, settlers and suppliers. William Lewis, for example, left an estate in 1658 that included 70 arm's length of roanoke, valued at £350, as well as an assortment of debts in beaver skins and other goods. He owed 15 pounds of beaver to Thomas Cornwallis. But he was also a creditor with the leader of the Piscataways for 12 skins, though their collection was described as uncertain.[111] Vincent Atcheson, who seems to have traded in the upper Bay, died in 1661 with a greater range of obligations, including debts of more than 170 pounds of beaver.[112] The transactions hinted at by such evidence

108 J. Hall Pleasants (ed.), *Proceedings of the Court of Chancery of Maryland 1669–1679* (Maryland Historical Society, 51, 1934), pp. 86–7, 93–4, 381–2; J. Hall Pleasants (ed.), *Proceedings of the Provincial Court of Maryland 1663–66* (Maryland Historical Society, 49, 1932), pp. 3–6, 366; Rountree and Davidson, *Eastern Shore Indians*, p. 91.

109 Bernard C. Steiner (ed.), *Proceedings of the Provincial Court of Maryland 1658–62* (Maryland Historical Society, 41, 1922), pp. 319, 322; J. Hall Pleasants (ed.), *Proceedings of the County Courts of Kent (1648–1676), Talbot (1662–1674), and Somerset (1665–1668) Counties* (Maryland Historical Society, 54, 1937), pp. xix–xx; Papenfuse (ed.), *Biographical Dictionary*, 2, p. 848.

110 Hall (ed.), *Narratives of Early Maryland*, p. 299.

111 Steiner (ed.), *Proceedings of the Provincial Court of Maryland 1658–62*, pp. 69–70, 115.

112 Ibid., pp. 535–6.

served important economic and social needs, though the extension of credit to native leaders and traders was more problematic, sowing confusion and misunderstanding over the meaning of debt. In such cases credit was rarely mixed with gratitude.

The persistence of a small group of colonial traders maintained the fur trade during the 1650s. Operating under de-centralized conditions, with limited regulation, they met native traders in a variety of local and temporary markets, which included outlying forts in Virginia. Against a background of European rivalries, many of these encounters occurred in conditions of competitiveness and mutual suspicion. The perceived consequences of this difficult period were summed up in a report on Virginia which Berkeley presented to the Privy Council in 1662. Complaining of the 'dismembring of the Colony' as a result of the establishment of Maryland, he drew attention to the success of the Dutch in enriching themselves on English discoveries.[113] With a degree of hyperbole, he claimed that within the precincts of Virginia they had 'settled a trade of Beaver with the Indians, amounting to 2 hundred thousand skins a yeare', while supplying enemies of the colony 'with Ammunition and Guns in greater proportion then wee have them ourselves'.[114]

As this chapter indicates, a dangerous cocktail of political and religious disunity, war and international rivalry, severely disrupted the development of the fur trade during the 1640s and 1650s. Within the context of a wider trans-atlantic crisis, which threatened supply routes and markets, colonial traders struggled to maintain a significant stake in a difficult, demanding and dispersed commercial enterprise. These conditions denied Maryland the opportunity of exploiting the collapse of the Kent Island joint stock, though at the same time they prevented Claiborne from recovering the island and reviving his ambitions for commercial and colonial expansion. Interethnic commerce persisted, in an intermittent and hazardous manner, but it was subject to change and re-structuring. The abandonment of transatlantic corporate ventures left commercial organization and strategy in the hands of local adventurers, reinforcing emergent colonial identities. Responding to rivalry with the Dutch and Swedes, traders employed firearms and alcohol as commercial commodities.[115] It was a key change with unpredictable consequences for interethnic relations. Guns and

[113] William Berkeley, *A Discourse and View of Virginia* (London, 1663, repr. Norwalk, 1914), p. 6.

[114] Ibid., pp. 6–7. He also expressed resentment against the metropolitan regulation at commerce, according to which 40,000 colonists could be impoverished to enrich little more than 40 merchants.

[115] Hatfield, *Atlantic Virginia*, pp. 25–6; Brandâo, *"Your Fyre Shall Burn No More"*, pp. 88–9; Peter C. Mancall, *Deadly Medicine: Indians and Alcohol in Early America* (Ithaca, 1995), pp. 43–4; Pestana, *The English Atlantic*, pp. 10–3 and Bliss, *Revolution and Empire*, pp. 100–2 for wider implications regarding identities.

spirits, imbued with supernatural, in some cases hallucinatory, associations, provoked competition and conflict, re-shaping Indian diplomacy and warfare. Their increased commercial use laid the basis for corrosive contests within some native groups, especially over the addictive impact of alcohol. At the same time, reports of the availability of such powerful trade goods penetrated inland, widening the catchment area for commerce and facilitating the investigation of new territory by explorers and colonial traders. Collectively these changes represented a turning point in the erratic evolution of the fur trade in the Bay, though their full impact would not become apparent until after 1660.

Chapter 5

Commercial Change and Conflict: Contrasting Experiences after 1650

In 1679 John Banister, minister and naturalist, informed one of his correspondents that the Indian trade in Virginia, 'once great & good', had 'dwindled almost into Nothing'.[1] Dismissing the opinion of many settlers who identified interethnic commerce as the source of recent troubles in the colony, he claimed it was 'rightly considered our Vinculum Pacis', or a bond of peace, with the Indians.[2] Writing from the fort located at the falls on the James River, where William Byrd was developing commercial relations with inland groups, Banister envisioned a commercial pathway based on native demand for 'many Things which they wanted ... for their use & ornament'.[3] Despite this appealing prospect, twenty years later a proposal to launch an ambitious fur-trading venture in Virginia failed to gather support on either side of the Atlantic.[4] The response in London indicated that the primary propose of the colony was the cultivation of tobacco. Such a perspective reflected the consolidation of the Chesapeake colonies as agricultural economies sustained by an expanding transatlantic trade. Shipments of tobacco into London, which amounted to two million pounds in 1640, reached seven million in 1663, and climbed to 11 million by 1676. Commercial expansion, based on servant and slave labour, was accompanied by population growth. Sir William Berkeley claimed that the colonial population of Virginia was at least 40,000 by the mid-1670s, while that of its northern neighbour was about 20,000 by 1685. Socio-economic change increased the hunger for land, intensifying the pressure on native communities, leading to a sharp demographic decline in neighbouring groups. In combination with the ever-widening impact of

1 Joseph and Nesta Ewan, *John Banister and His Natural History of Virginia 1678–1692* (Urbana, 1970), p. 41.

2 Ibid., p. 42.

3 Ibid., p. 42.

4 Henry Hartwell, James Blair and Edward Chilton, *The Present State of Virginia and the College*, ed. Hunter Dickinson Farish (Williamsburg, 1940), p. 7; W. Neil Franklin, 'Act for the Better Regulation of the Indian Trade, Virginia, 1714', *VMHB*, 72 (1964), pp. 141–5; John C. Rainbolt, *From Prescription to Persuasion: Manipulation of Eighteenth Century Virginia Economy* (Port Washington, 1974), p. 146.

interethnic trade, it encouraged Indian re-location and re-structuring, with the association of survivor or refugee groups, or their assimilation by others, reflected in re-naming and cultural adaptation.[5]

The development of a colonial tobacco culture, alongside the cultivation of grain and the raising of stock, were accompanied by changes to the fur trade. As commerce within the confines of the Bay declined, trading ambitions were either re-directed to regions beyond or re-shaped by Indian hostility and conflict. At the same time, the gradual disengagement of former colonial rivals was both cause and consequence of the emergence of divergent patterns, demonstrated by exploration and expansion in Virginia and stagnation and conflict in Maryland. Traders in the upper Bay struggled to revitalize relations with the Susquehannocks, in the face of Dutch competition and hostile raiding by Iroquoian groups. Lower down the Bay, however, frontier adventurers initiated the commercial reconnoitring of the interior. As a result, diplomatic and commercial relations beyond the Chesapeake, part of the increasing density of intercolonial communication which has received recognition in recent work, assumed greater importance, provoking controversy regarding the control and regulation of commerce.[6] Cumulatively the experience of these years exposed the ambiguity of the Indian trade in colonial economies where traders faced the decline or disappearance of local native suppliers and the fur-bearing resources on which they depended.

Virginia: Exploration and exchange

The exploration of regions beyond the colony helped to break down unfavourable images of the interior, paving the way for an overland trade with distant and little-known Indian groups. Commercial initiatives were encouraged by the ready availability of skins, the product of vast herds of deer, and a variety of furs, beyond the area of colonial settlement. It included an aggressive trade in native captives and slaves, which has until recently been unduly neglected.[7] During the 1660s and 1670s the scale of

5 On colonial development, see Morgan, *American Slavery, American Freedom*, pp. 203–4, 231–4; Land, *Colonial Maryland*, pp. 59, 67–71, 119; Menard, *Economy and Society*, pp. 156–8; Russo and Russo, *Planting an Empire*, pp. 63, 107, 120; Rountree and Turner, *Before and After Jamestown*, pp. 170–5; Rice, *Nature & History*, pp. 108–21, 130 which notes that by 1675 most of the native people of the Potomac region were gone, while many of those that remained were in reservations.

6 It is an important theme in Hatfield, *Atlantic Virginia*; Pestana, *The English Atlantic*; and Van Zandt, *Brothers among Nations*.

7 Gallay, *The Indian Slave Trade*, *passim*, and more widely Andrés Reséndez, *The Other Slavery: The Uncovered Story of Indian Enslavement in America* (Boston, 2016).

activity was relatively modest. Yet its potential strengthened the interests of older frontier traders, like Abraham Wood, and attracted the ambitions of a younger generation, who exploited and developed an existing infrastructure of native trails and middlemen, inaugurating a new phase of commercial investigation and expansion. It led to a striking revival in exports of fur from the colony as demonstrated by the surviving customs records for London. But charting new inland trades was a risk-laden enterprise, dependent on extensive lines of supply and credit. As such it was vulnerable to Indian rivalries and competition with traders operating in the recently established colony of Carolina in which Sir William Berkeley, re-instated as governor of Virginia, was interested. In September 1663 the promoters of the new settlement agreed that the governor, nominated by Berkeley, should enjoy the sole trade in furs for three years. Under these conditions the widening range of commerce was accompanied by discontent at its regulation which merged with concern at Berkeley's Indian policy.[8]

Exploration and trade

Serious interest in the exploration of the interior revived during the 1650s. It was limited to small groups of traders and explorers, acting under the authority of commissions issued by Berkeley. Such adventurers were motivated by the search for trade and territory, mingled with a quest for precious metals and a passage to the South Sea. For the governor and his supporters, colonial expansion was linked with the promotion of Christianity and civility among neighbouring Indians. One scheme of the 1650s offered native leaders a cow, in return for the heads of eight wolves. While designed to eradicate unwelcome and feared predators from the environs of the colony, it was also seen as a 'step to civilizing' natives and 'making them Christians'.[9]

Yet the reconnaissance of new regions was defined by a colonial context characterized by the inability of the English to establish close or harmonious relations with their Indian neighbours, though they retained a role as interpreters and translators. Experience and fear persuaded explorers and traders to adopt a suspicious, potentially hostile, attitude towards other native groups. Left in the hands of private enterprise, the probing of the interior was erratic, uncoordinated and distracted by other problems. But it was facilitated by widespread Indian unsettlement, the product of native rivalries complicated by the reverberations of contact, direct or indirect, with Spanish traders and

[8] Hatfield, *Atlantic Virginia*, pp. 26, 34–6; Billings (ed.), *Papers of Berkeley*, pp. 203–4; Billings, *Berkeley*, pp. 75, 201–2.

[9] Hening (ed.), *Statutes*, 1, p. 395; Anderson, *Creatures of Empire*, pp. 107–8. Bounties were also offered to natives in New England, but with limited effect, Jon T. Coleman, *Vicious: Wolves and Men in America* (New Haven, 2004), pp. 59–61.

missionaries in Florida, overlaid by reports of the English presence in the Bay. The impact of such unsettling change varied. In some cases, it re-directed Indian diplomacy in favour of direct access to European trading partners and suppliers of firearms. In these circumstances native traders were drawn to the border of Virginia by the prospect of commerce with the colonists.[10]

Adventurers like Wood were well-placed to take advantage of these emerging opportunities. Part of an earlier generation of migrants, which included Claiborne, he arrived in the colony in 1620, entering the service of Samuel Mathews. By the 1640s he had acquired extensive interests in land and trade. Like other self-made leaders, his status was reflected in public office and service in the militia. Anglo-Powhatan hostilities during the 1640s enabled him to become established as a prominent frontier trader. The treaty which ended the conflict confined the Indian trade to a small number of forts, including Fort Henry which was under his command.[11]

It was from this base that Wood sent out a small expedition, in August 1650, to explore the region to the south west. It was led by Edward Bland, accompanied by four colonists and an Appamattuck guide, Pyancha. During the course of a week, the party covered about 120 miles. Bland's report, published in London during 1651, presented a favourable portrait of the region, though it also betrayed confusion regarding its people. Claims that the country would support the cultivation of tobacco and sugar were enlivened by descriptions of Indians who wore copper about their necks and smoked tobacco pipes tipped with silver. If Bland was prospecting land for colonial expansion, he was also keen to establish commercial contact with native groups. He informed the leader of the Nottoways, Chounterounte, that the expedition was in response to an invitation to trade from the ruler of the Tuscaroras, and to investigate reports of two English people who lived with them. Likewise, the Meherrin leader was told that the party came in search of friendly exchange, hoping to acquire skins, furs and other goods.[12]

10 Hatfield, *Atlantic Virginia*, pp. 25–6.

11 Alvin Vance Briceland, *Westward from Virginia: The Exploration of the Virginia-Carolina Frontier 1650–1710* (Charlottesville, 1987), pp. 14–15, 23–7 sees him as the 'Frontenac of Virginia'; Alvord and Bidgood, *First Explorations*, pp. 34, 37–44; Merrell, *The Indians' New World*, pp. 28–9; Morton, *Colonial Virginia*, 1, pp. 158–9, 200.

12 Alexander S. Salley (ed.), *Narratives of Early Carolina 1650–1708* (New York, 1911), pp. 5–7, 11; Briceland, *Westward from Virginia*, p. 44; Adams, *The Best and Worst Country*, pp. 237–9. On the survival of the Appamattucks as guides, see Rountree and Turner, *Before and After Jamestown*, p. 171. English traders long recognized the value of Indians as guides, and their superiority in the woods, J. Long, *Voyages and Travels of an Indian Interpreter and Trader* (London, 1791), pp. 27–8.

Lacking reliable information, the party was dependent on their guide to navigate a way through a maze of native rivalries and suspicion. The Nottoway leader tried to dissuade Bland from further exploration. Denying reports of English residents with the Tuscaroras, he warned that the route was long and impassable owing to heavy rain. Moreover, his people were opposed to the expedition proceeding. During a visit to Bland's camp, expressing discontent and scorn towards the colonists, he warned their guide that he would 'be knockt on the head'.[13] As Bland was determined to continue, he offered the assistance of his brother, Oyeocker, as a guide. But the progress of the expedition was hindered by damaging rumours that frustrated hopes of establishing direct contact with the Tuscaroras. At the Meherrin settlement Bland received encouraging news that they were keen to trade with the colonists, despite native reports of English hostility and bad faith. He later dismissed such talk, claiming it was common practice for the Indians not only 'to villefie one another', but also to 'tell nothing but lies to the English'.[14]

During his stay with the Meherrins, Bland secured the services of a native who was reputedly a member of the Tuscaroras, to arrange a meeting with his leader. On reaching a pre-arranged location, however, the colonists became alarmed that they had been lured into a trap. After a brief survey Bland named the territory New Brittaine. Further exploration was cut short by Oyeocker's refusal to lead the party any further. He also informed their other guide that the local inhabitants were angry with them, as a result of the spread of alarming reports regarding their purpose. At the same time their new recruit, whom Bland had hoped to use for contacting the Tuscaroras, ran away, spreading stories that the colonists 'came to cut them off'.[15] Unable to counteract such dangerous rumours, Bland returned to Virginia. A small group of Tuscaroras caught up with the expedition, but they were unable to persuade it to turn back. Although both parties agreed to meet again, the Indians failed to appear.

The expedition had mixed results. Bland's report of a region ready for colonial settlement, including the prospect of gold and other precious metals awaiting discovery, though formulaic, may have reaffirmed interest in expanding horizons. But it was tempered by evidence of native rivalries for commercial access to the English. The conduct of the Nottoways was intended to promote their role as middlemen between colonial traders and the Tuscaroras. The hostility of the Weyanocks, who reportedly possessed firearms, also seems to have been motivated by an attempt to disrupt English efforts to establish commerce with more distant groups. John Banister subsequently interpreted

13 Salley (ed.), *Narratives of Early Carolina*, p. 11.

14 Ibid., p. 12; Merrell, *The Indians' New World*, pp. 9–18 on Siouan groups of the piedmont region.

15 Salley (ed.), *Narratives of Early Carolina*, pp. 16–18; Hatfield, *Atlantic Virginia*, pp. 27–30.

the reluctance of Indians to act as guides for explorers too far inland as an expression of policy rather than fear.[16] In these uncertain circumstances Bland's report of unreliable and unpredictable natives may only have encouraged Wood to develop Fort Henry as a secure trading outpost, instead of trying to negotiate direct access to the Indians of the interior.

These problems strengthened interest in coastal exploration south of the Bay, as a means of finding an alternative route to the Tuscaroras. A combination of raiding and trading during the 1640s led to the establishment of informal settlements along the Chowan and Roanoke Rivers, in the region around Albermarle Sound. Thereafter the declining population of local native groups, combined with their demand for European commodities, exposed the vulnerability of accessible coastal areas to an increasing influx of settlers from Virginia.[17]

One of the leading promoters of this enterprise was Francis Yeardley, son of a former governor of the colony. In 1653 he sent an expedition to Roanoke Island in search of land and trade. It comprised four men, including Nathaniel Batts, an enterprising trader and interpreter. According to Yeardley, they were welcomed by an Indian ruler, who gave them a tour of the ruins of Raleigh's fort, a relic from the colonial ventures of the 1580s.[18] They purchased land along the Pasquotank River for which they agreed, in part, to construct an English-style house for the native leader. The latter also agreed to provide guides to conduct two members of the party to the Tuscaroras. After travelling for several days, they met a large group of Indians at a hunting lodge. Although the colonists were courteously received, they declined the opportunity of returning to their settlement, because their interpreter was sick. When the expedition returned to Virginia, however, it was accompanied by a group of Tuscaroras and the leader from Roanoke with his wife and son, who was subsequently baptized in Yeardley's household.

Building on this promising contact, in 1654 Yeardley sent an expedition to Albermarle Sound. One of its purposes was to build a trading post for Batts, represented on Nicholas Comberford's map of 1657 at the mouth of the Roanoke River. From this base, Batts established trading relations with

16 Ewen and Ewen, *Banister*, pp. 92, 229–30; Briceland, *Westward from Virginia*, pp. 76, 90; Salley (ed.), *Narratives of Early Carolina*, pp. 13–17.

17 William G. Stannard (ed.), 'The Indians of Southern Virginia, 1650–1711', *VMHB*, 8 (1900), pp. 1–2; William S. Powell (ed.), *Ye Countie of Albermarle in Carolina: A Collection of Documents 1664–1675* (Raleigh, 1958), pp. xviii–xxii.

18 Salley (ed.), *Narratives of Early Carolina*, pp. 25–8; William L. Saunders (ed.), *The Colonial Records of North Carolina*, 10 vols. (Raleigh, 1886), 1, p. 18; Gregory McPherson (ed.), 'Nathaniel Batts, Landholder on Pasquotank River, 1660', *North Carolina Historical Review*, 43 (1966), pp. 66–81; Craven, *Southern Colonies*, pp. 317–18.

Indian groups which he continued to develop despite Yeardley's death in 1655. He emerged as the leader of several small, scattered communities which grew up along the river and beyond. According to George Fox, the Quaker leader who travelled through the region in 1672, he was 'a Rude, desperate man who has great command over the countrie, especially over the Indians', acting as unofficial governor of the settlers, who lived by fishing, hunting, farming and trading.[19] His relations with native groups, including the Tuscaroras, subsequently acquired legendary status, although little evidence survives of his activities except for the widespread use of his name to describe coastal features.[20]

The development of interethnic trade, as an offshoot from Virginia, was frustrated by the establishment of Carolina, whose promoters formed a well-connected and powerful group of Lords Proprietors in England. Although Berkeley granted patents of land to settlers in Albermarle during 1663, the new colony soon laid claim to the region. Furthermore, the proprietors were keen to promote the Indian trade, within an environment of cheap land and religious tolerance, to encourage immigration. Consequently, traders operating from Virginia were excluded by legislation passed by the Carolina assembly of 1670.[21] The establishment of Charles Town fostered the rapid growth of trade in deer skins, as traders ranged deeper inland, supplying firearms and other goods, to Indian groups. Their commercial activities cut across those of their rivals in Virginia. The competition, which became increasingly violent during the early eighteenth century, had a disruptive and destabilizing impact which included an increase in native slaving and raiding. At the same time, it endangered the extensive trading network of frontier traders, such as William Byrd.[22]

19 Journal of George Fox, https://docsouth.unc.edu/csr/index.html/document/csr01–0085; Powell (ed.), *Countie of Albermarle*, p. 19; Lindley S. Butler, 'The Early Settlement of Carolina: Virginia's Southern Frontier', *VMHB*, 79 (1971), pp. 24–5; W.P. Cumming, 'The Earliest Permanent Settlement in Carolina: Nathaniel Batts and the Comberford Map', *American Historical Review*, 45 (1939), pp. 85–6.

20 Peter Linebaugh and Marcus Rediker, *The Many-Headed Hydra: Sailors, Slaves, Commoners, and the Hidden History of the Revolutionary Atlantic* (London, 2000), p. 138.

21 Saunders (ed.), *Colonial Records*, p. 187; Billings, *Berkeley*, pp. 163–72; Hatfield, *Atlantic Virginia*, p. 187 notes it was widely ignored.

22 Butler, 'Early Settlement of Carolina', pp. 27–8; Briceland, *Westward from Virginia*, pp. 187–95; L.H. Roper, 'Conceiving an Anglo-American Proprietorship: Early South Carolina History in Perspective', in Roper and Ruymbreke (eds.), *Early Modern Empires*, pp. 390, 397–9; *CSPC, 1661–8*, pp. 125–6, 154–5; Etheridge, 'The Emergence of the Colonial South', pp. 54–5 and Gallay, *The Indian Slave Trade*, pp. 49–53 on slaving.

These commercial probes from Virginia produced mixed results. Although the General Assembly issued commissions for the investigation of regions to the west and south, there is little evidence of their implementation. For many settlers, whose daily interaction with Indians was declining, the bounds of the colony were less of an open frontier, inviting commercial penetration, than an insecure and uninviting border, at the edge of a dangerous wilderness. Native rivalries and hostility, provoked in part by competition for direct access to the English, underlined the risks to colonial explorers and traders. Yet there were also opportunities as some groups, such as the Occaneechees, moved closer to the borderland of the colony to cultivate commerce with the colonists.[23]

For much of the 1660s interest in colonial and commercial expansion was diverted by a succession of problems. A prolonged dispute with Maryland was compounded with the failure of intercolonial negotiations to limit the cultivation of tobacco. More alarmingly during the second Anglo-Dutch war an enemy expedition raided the Bay. In June 1667 four Dutch warships under Abraham Crijnssen entered the James River, dramatically exposing the vulnerability of the colony to seaborne invasion. Berkeley informed the king that Crijnssen 'sailed off with his prizes without a blow' after five days.[24] The raid coincided with attacks on outlying settlements by northern Indians, supported in some cases by neighbouring groups. Native hostility intensified unease about colonial defence, provoking concern at the regulation of interethnic commerce. During the summer of 1667 complaints were registered against the 'Governor licensing some to trade with the Indians, and not timely suppressing their incursions'.[25]

As these problems receded, interest in exploration revived. In May 1669 Berkeley intended to lead a large party of 200 gentlemen in search of silver mines and a route to the South Sea, but unusual and heavy rainfall prevented their departure.[26] Concerned at the Spanish response, later in the year he solicited a commission from the king for the expedition, which included a grant of land from the head of the James River westward to the sea. Under this authority, the following year he sent out John Lederer to explore the interior.

23 Ethridge, 'The Emergence of the Colonial South', p. 54; Briceland, *Westward from Virginia*, pp. 93–4; Alvord and Bidgood, *First Explorations*, pp. 103–4; Hatfield, *Atlantic Virginia*, p. 26; Merrell, 'The Indians' New World', pp. 552–3; Phillips, *The Fur Trade*, 1, pp. 166–74. The Occaneechees acquired a 'trade jargon' to enhance their commercial role, Axtell, 'Babel of Tongues', pp. 38–9.

24 Billings (ed.), *Papers of Berkeley*, p. 319; *CSPC, 1661–8*, pp. 474–5, 490, 494, 502; Enthoven and Koot, 'The Rise and Fall of the Virginia-Dutch Connection', pp. 108–9.

25 *CSPC, 1661–8*, p. 484; Billings (ed.), *Papers of Berkeley*, p. 322.

26 Ibid., p. 358; *CSPC, 1669–74*, pp. 26, 69, 71; Rainbolt, *From Prescription to Persuasion*, pp. 77–8.

A German doctor, and a recent immigrant into the Bay, Lederer undertook three expeditions during 1670, searching for a route through the Appalachians, prospecting a pathway to 'unlimited Empires' and opening up new supplies of furs.[27] His report, published in London following his re-location to Maryland, contained guidance for colonial traders with ambitions to exploit the commercial potential of new regions.

The scale of these expeditions suggests that the governor's ambitions were not widely shared in the colony. Lederer was accompanied by three Indians on his first foray towards the north and west. The second attracted a larger party of 20 colonists and five natives, though after travelling west for more than a week he was abandoned with only one Susquehannock guide. He went on to reach a native settlement, identified as Usheree or Iswa, where he acquired information of a hostile group farther west, and of a 'powerful Nation of Bearded Men' to the south west.[28] Such reports, including the reference to the Spanish, persuaded him to turn back, though he seems to have found an entry way through the mountains near a Cherokee habitation. His final expedition, which included 10 settlers and five natives, proceeded north-westerly along the Rappahannock River and one of its tributaries. Faced with mountainous peaks in the distance, the party returned with most of its members convinced that there was no way through such a seemingly impenetrable barrier.[29]

By contrast Lederer articulated a more favourable outlook for exploration and trade, based on his acquisition of native information and knowledge of Indian pathways. Drawing on such experience, he argued there were two routes through the mountains. But he advised that future expeditions should be made up of between six and 10 members, as the Indians were suspicious of larger groups of colonial traders. Regarding interethnic commerce, he distinguished between local and long-distance trade, arguing that the latter was more profitable. With more understanding of trading with Europeans, neighbouring groups were experienced and discriminating traders and consumers. They required cloth, metal wares and firearms, though the trade in arms was officially prohibited. Yet Indian behaviour was arbitrary and unpredictable. As such Lederer advised colonial traders to disparage native wares as part of their bargaining tactics. The use of alcohol assisted these transactions. Employed with care, it disposed the Indians to 'giving … ten times the value'

27 W.P. Cumming (ed.), *The Discoveries of John Lederer* (Charlottesville, 1958), pp. 4, 15–19; Alvord and Bidgood, *First Explorations*, pp. 63–9, 135–71; Adams, *The Best and Worst Countries*, pp. 240–6; Billings (ed.), *Papers of Berkeley*, pp. 368, 374.

28 Cumming (ed.), *Discoveries of Lederer*, pp. 19–22, 31–2; Merrell, *The Indians' New World*, p. 47 for English ignorance and confusion regarding Indian life and place names.

29 Cumming (ed.), *Discoveries of Lederer*, pp. 34–7; Hatfield, *Atlantic Virginia*, p. 31.

of English goods.[30] By comparison distant native groups were easily satisfied with cheap trinkets and toys, including mirrors, beads, glass bracelets, knives and scissors. This encouraging evaluation was accompanied by a warning that traders should not operate on their own. Under prevailing conditions 'many ought to joyn and go in company'.[31]

This sporadic reconnoitring included a small expedition for the discovery of a route to the South Sea sent out by Abraham Wood in September 1671. Assisted by Perecute, an Appamattuck leader and guide, Abraham Batts and Robert Fallam traversed the Appalachians, reaching a tributary of the Ohio River. Yet the ruggedness of the trail suggested that a colonial trade route might not be commercially viable. As they travelled west Batts and Fallam also became aware of widespread native disruption and re-location as a result of an increase in Iroquoian raids against the Susquehannocks. Seeking encouragement from London, Berkeley reported that further exploration of the mountains and beyond 'shall certainly find a great trade of furs', while raising the prospect of the discovery of precious metals.[32]

In 1673 Wood sent out Gabriel Arthur and James Needham, accompanied by Indian guides, on two expeditions of discovery. The first accomplished little, but the second led to the establishment of contact with a group known as Tomahitans. They had experience of trading with the Spanish in Florida, though it ended violently when some of the members of a native trading party were killed, and the survivors were enslaved. While the English explorers noted that the Indians had 60 guns, as well as a miscellaneous collection of brass pots and kettles, they were unsure if they were acquired through peaceful exchange or plunder.[33]

Although Needham was subsequently murdered by an Indian guide, Arthur stayed with the Tomahitans for nearly one year. Accompanying them on raiding expeditions, he was captured by a rival group. According to Wood's report, Arthur turned his captivity into a commercial opportunity. Witnessing the Indians prepare a beaver for cooking, he used signs to inform them of the value of their skins to the English. Despite the difficulty in communication, the Indians resorted to the language of gesture to ask how many skins would

30 Cumming (ed.), *Discoveries of Lederer*, pp. 39, 41–3; Mancall, *Deadly Medicine*, pp. 49–50.

31 Cumming (ed.), *Discoveries of Lederer*, pp. 42–3; Merrell, *The Indians' New World*, pp. 31–2 comments on Lederer's breaches of etiquette, and discriminating native traders.

32 Billings (ed.), *Papers of Berkeley*, p. 399; *CSPC, 1669–74*, pp. 270–1; Briceland, *Westward from Virginia*, pp. 126–46; Adams, *The Best and Worst Countries*, pp. 247–9.

33 Ibid., pp. 249–51; Verner W. Crane, *The Southern Frontier, 1670–1732* (Durham, 1928), pp. 14–6; Craven, *Southern Colonies*, pp. 370–2; Briceland, *Westward from Virginia*, pp. 131–46.

be needed for the acquisition of a knife. Arthur 'told them foure, and eight for … a hatchet and made signs that if they would let him return, he would bring many things amongst them'.[34] With this promise, they allowed him to return to the Tomahitan settlement. From thence he returned to Virginia in June 1674. He was followed by the leader of the Tomahitans who, after a meeting with Wood, agreed to send a large trading party to the colony later in the year. But the development of these contacts was threatened by colonial competitors, described by Wood as self-interested operators who he accused of planning to intercept the Indians on their return.[35] Complaining of the lack of encouragement and support in Virginia, he was forced to seek the 'countenance of some person of honour in England to curb and bridle the obstructers here'.[36]

Despite these challenges, by the early 1670s colonial traders established commercial relations with inland Indian groups who enjoyed access to abundant supplies of furs. In addition to Wood and his associates, they included William Byrd, a recent arrival who inherited the estates and trading interests of his uncle, Thomas Stegge, as well as Henry Hatcher, who was trading with the Occaneechees by 1673. The promise of these ventures encouraged traders farther inland, despite the danger of armed rivalry with colonial competitors and native middlemen.[37]

As a result, the development of the new trade was vulnerable to a variety of external and internal threats. It was disrupted by the third Anglo-Dutch war which revived widespread concern at the colony's land and sea defences. The invasion of the lower Bay by a Dutch fleet of eight men-of-war caught a convoy of merchant ships on the eve of its departure. Despite the presence of two royal frigates, the Dutch inflicted significant damage on shipping and property. According to Berkeley's report to the king, the raid revealed the 'particular disadvantages and disabilities' of the colony during war, fuelling fears of frontier insecurity and apprehension at the lack of suitable coastal defences.[38] It also focused attention on a potential enemy within. Berkeley

34 Alvord and Bidgood, *First Explorations*, p. 223; Axtell, 'Babel of Tongues', p. 26. The Tomahitans, who disappear from the colonial record, have been identified as forming part of the Yuchis by Swanton, *History of the Creek Indians*, pp. 187–9

35 Alvord and Bidgood, *First Explorations*, p. 225.

36 Ibid., pp. 225–6; *CSPC, 1669–74*, pp. 604–5.

37 Ewen and Ewen, *Banister*, pp. 48–9, 91–2; Briceland, *Westward from Virginia*, 148, 171–9 notes that competition reduced the number of traders; Merrell, *The Indians' New World*, pp. 28–9, 36–7; Alvord and Bidgood, *First Explorations*, pp. 76–7; Gary C. Goodwin, *Cherokees in Transition: A Study of Changing Culture and Environment Prior to 1775* (Chicago, 1977), pp. 86–90. Traders from Virginia may have been crossing the Appalachians during the 1670s to trade with Indian groups along the Ohio valley, Ethridge, 'The Emergence of the Colonial South', pp. 58–9.

38 Billings (ed.), *Papers of Berkeley*, p. 423.

informed Charles II that the absence of men with estates and families, to defend the frontier, engendered widespread concern that poor, indebted and single freedmen would seize the opportunity to aid the Dutch in the plunder of the country.[39] Although the Dutch threat receded, it was followed by native hostility and colonial rebellion during 1676. In its early stages the rebel leadership exploited growing concern and complaint at Berkeley's control of the fur trade which rapidly turned into an implicit attack on his Indian policy.

Commercial reconnoitring survived the turmoil of war and insurrection, though it ended Berkeley's career in the colony. But the competition between colonial traders in Virginia and Carolina, matched by rivalry among native groups, shaped the character and conduct of interethnic commerce and diplomacy. It fuelled the rapid influx of European goods across an expanding commercial hinterland, disrupting native relations and diplomacy. In 1674, following a visit to the Westo habitation along the Savannah River, Henry Woodward, trader, slaver and interpreter for Carolina, noted that the Indians were well-supplied with arms, ammunition, cloth and other goods from the north, for which they traded deer skins, furs and young native slaves.[40] Travelling towards the head of the Ashley River, he noticed that some Indians 'had drawne uppon trees (the barke being hewed away) the effigies of bever, a man, on horseback & guns'.[41] Intrigued, he interpreted them as a sign of their desire for trade and friendship with the English. But the message may have contained mixed meanings, resistant to outside interpretation. Inadvertently, moreover, it drew attention to the real and symbolic consequences of colonial exploration and expansion during the 1660s and 1670s.

Commercial regulation: Disorder and defence along a trading frontier

The growth of the inland trade raised in acute form the issue of commercial regulation. As part of piecemeal initiatives to control interethnic encounters, legislation was used to accommodate and manage trading relations with native groups. While seeking to maintain the defence of the colony against Indian raiders, the law was also employed to curb the disorderly conduct of colonial

39 Ibid., pp. 423–4; *CSPC, 1669–74*, p. 524; Morgan, *American Slavery, American Freedom*, pp. 241–3.

40 *The Shaftesbury Papers: South Carolina Historical Society* (Stroud, 2000), p. 460; Ethridge, 'The Emergence of the Colonial South', p. 59; Gallay, *The Indian Slave Trade*, pp. 55–7; William L. Ramsey, *The Yamasee War: A Study of Culture, Economy, and Conflict in the Colonial South* (Lincoln, 2008), pp. 35–7; Swanton, *Early History of the Creek Indians*, pp. 64–9, 306–7 on Woodward.

41 *The Shaftesbury Papers*, p. 457. Pictographs were used as messages, possibly for commercial (and other) reasons in cross-cultural communication, see Birgit Brander Rasmussen, *Queequeg's Coffin: Indigenous Literacies and Early American Literature* (Durham, 2012), pp. 18–27, 32–4, 40.

traders. Growing concern at the control of commerce, combined with anxiety about the security of the frontier, reinforced resentment against Berkeley's rule which culminated in disunity and rebellion during the 1670s.

Licensing lay at the heart of the regulation of interethnic trade, though it was weakened by ineffective policing. In 1661 the General Assembly barred colonists from trading with native groups without a commission from the governor, the issue of which was restricted to reputable traders. The following year, however, when the prohibition was renewed, the assembly admitted that 'many underhand and unlicensed traders' continued to operate.[42] It was particularly concerned at their role in the development of the trade in native slaves. As a result, it banned the sale of Indians either as slaves or servants if, in the latter case, the term of service exceeded that for Europeans. The need for such measures was demonstrated by the recent acquisition of a Powhatan Indian, identified as Metappin, by Elizabeth Short. Purchased from the leader of the Weyanocks, it emerged that Metappin spoke 'perfectly the English tongue' and wished to be baptized into the church.[43] He was freed in 1662 by order of the assembly. In 1670 it also prohibited the purchase of Indian captives, though it remained lawful to sell native prisoners as servants. Qualifying its earlier restriction, terms of service were fixed at 12 years for adults, while children could be employed as servants up to the age of 30. Following widespread native disturbances and hostility, in 1682 the distinction between servants and slaves was removed. Thereafter captives purchased from neighbouring Indians were to be identified as slaves.[44]

The regulation of colonial traders was accompanied by attempts to control the activities of Indians who frequented the outer regions of the colony. According to a report of 1661, they included large numbers of Susquehannocks. Alarmed at the threat to livestock and concerned at the potential disruption of relations with the colony's tributary and neighbouring Indians, Berkeley published a proclamation imposing limits on frontier commerce. It prohibited northern Indians, as well as settlers from Maryland, from trading with Virginians or natives farther south.[45] Its enforcement was left in the hands of Abraham Wood, whose promotion of the inland trade was threatened by the forays of the Susquehannocks and others along the upper reaches of the colony's rivers.

The spread of such disturbances led to further attempts to control native groups and their contact with settlers. Violence along the James River was

[42] Hening (ed.), *Statutes*, 2, pp. 20, 140–3; Gleach, *Powhatan's World*, p. 193.

[43] Hening (ed.), *Statutes*, 2, p. 155.

[44] Ibid., pp. 283, 491–2. On the growth and impact of slaving see Eric R. Bowne, 'Southeastern Indian Polities of the Seventeenth Century: Suggestions Toward an Analytical Vocabulary', in Carocci and Pratt (eds.), *Native American Adoption*, pp. 71–8.

[45] Hening (ed.), *Statutes*, 2, p. 153; TNA, CO 5/1376, f.89.

blamed by local Indians on the Tuscaroras and other distant groups who were reportedly 'sculking about the English plantations for private sinister commerce'.[46] It prompted the revival of an earlier scheme prohibiting the entertainment of visiting natives, unless they wore badges of identification. Under this new code of conduct Berkeley assumed the right to appoint Indian leaders within the colony. Failure to accept these conditions would be interpreted as a sign of rebellion and enmity. In addition, responsibility for the murder of a colonist by an Indian was extended, in an unprecedented fashion, to include native communities. In practice the General Assembly acknowledged that the provision was too severe to be implemented across the colony, though it made an exception for Henrico County, an exposed frontier region.[47] In 1666 the assembly authorized settlers to kill Indians who entered the county in force. But the practical impact of this desperate measure was doubtful. In 1671, at the request of local burgesses, it was repealed.

Collectively these initiatives, and the responses to them, exposed the tension between security and commerce which was intensified by the sale of firearms to Indians. The trade was banned in 1658. Within a year it was overturned on the grounds that traders in Maryland and Delaware Bay were supplying native groups with weapons, drawing away the trade in fur to the great loss of Virginia and the profit of its rivals. The prohibition was re-imposed in 1664 following the seizure of New Netherland.[48] Offenders faced a fine of 10,000 pounds of tobacco or imprisonment for two years. Despite these sanctions, traders continued to supply Indians with guns. By the mid-1670s the assembly was so concerned at the quantity of weapons being sold, that it introduced the death penalty for transgressors.[49] But implementation was overtaken by the resurgence of raiding by groups of Doegs, possibly survivors of the Powhatan chiefdom, and Susquehannocks, who had re-located to a new habitation within Maryland, along the Potomac. Under these threatening conditions the assembly issued a declaration of war against hostile natives, empowering the captains of outlying forts to provide firearms for tributary Indians to serve as a defensive shield for the colony.[50]

46 Hening (ed.), *Statutes*, 2, pp. 185, 202–3; TNA, CO 5/1376, f.31v.

47 Ibid., ff.40v–51v; Hening (ed.), *Statutes*, 2, p. 289; Rountree and Turner, *Before and After Jamestown*, p. 173.

48 Ibid., 1, pp. 441, 470, 525; 2, p. 215; Gleach, *Powhatan's World*, pp. 192–3.

49 Hening (ed.), *Statutes*, 2, p. 336.

50 TNA, CO 5/1376, ff.60–2v, 63v; William Hand Browne (ed.), *Proceedings of the Council of Maryland 1671–81* (Maryland Historical Society, 15, 1896), pp. 47, 57. *Strange News from Virginia; Being a Full and True Account of the Life and Death of Nathanael Bacon Esquire* (London, 1677), p. 3 described it as an Indian insurrection. Richter, *Before the Revolution*, p. 266 and Rice, *Nature & History*, p. 137 for Doegs, an unsettled and elusive group.

The escalation of Indian hostilities triggered a political crisis that challenged Berkeley's rule in the colony. Deteriorating economic conditions, as a result of falling tobacco prices, provoked the concern of colonial leaders at the problem of unemployment and indebtedness, particularly among single freedmen.[51] The tension between a wealthy elite and a large, disaffected body of poor planters and servants, identified by the governor and his supporters as a rabble, exposed alarming signs of disunity, as the colony stood on the threshold of civil war. The conflict with the Susquehannocks, coloured by reports of Indian hostilities in New England, deepened the crisis, strengthening suspicions that Berkeley was more concerned about the profit from the fur trade than the defence of outlying settlements. Despite its multifarious aspects, rebellion revealed widespread anxiety at colonial Indian policy, which focused attention on the control and regulation of interethnic commerce. Although Robert Beverley, whose father was a loyal supporter of the governor, later argued that the political upheaval was not the work of 'Two or Three traders only, who aim'd at a Monopoly of the *Indian* Trade, as some pretend to say', frustrated commercial ambitions and resentment helped to stitch together a wider range of grievances against the colony's leadership.[52]

Raiding by the Susquehannocks and their allies brought these issues to a head. In August 1675 the governor and council received alarming reports that a large party of Indians crossed the Potomac and killed several settlers, destroyed cattle and cut up fields of tobacco and corn.[53] Berkeley responded by authorizing John Washington and Isaac Allerton to attack hostile Indians with the local militia. Later in the year he also prohibited the Indian trade to all except traders acting under his commission. The raiding persisted. According

[51] Billings (ed.), *Papers of Berkeley*, p. 423; Billings, *Berkeley*, pp. 211–14 notes his declining health and argues he was out of touch; Gaskill, *Between Two Worlds*, pp. 255–6, 301–3; Bailyn, *The Barbarous Years*, pp. 508–9, 522; Horn, *Adapting to a New World*, pp. 157–8.

[52] Beverley, *History of Virginia*, pp. 74, 78–95; Hatfield, *Atlantic Virginia*, p. 26; Morgan, *American Slavery, American Freedom*, pp. 255–69; on local grievances against taxation and officials see Brent Tarter, 'Bacon's Rebellion, the Grievances of the People, and the Political Culture of Seventeenth-Century Virginia', *VMHB*, 119 (2011), pp. 15–33. The most detailed account remains Wilcomb E. Washburn, *The Governor and the Rebel: A History of Bacon's Rebellion in Virginia* (Chapel Hill, 1957), pp. 153–62 on causes, but see also James D. Rice, *Tales from a Revolution: Bacon's Rebellion and the Transformation of Early America* (New York, 2012). Stephen Saunders Webb, *1676: The End of American Independence* (New York, 1984), pp. 67, 82, 409–10 argues that it was an anti-imperial revolution.

[53] Billings (ed.), *Papers of Berkeley*, pp. 485, 504; Matthew Kruer, 'Bloody Minds and Peoples Undone: Emotion, Family, and Political Order in the Susquehannock-Virginia War', *WMQ*, 74, (2017), pp. 410–36 argues that different emotional regimes both set the stage for, and shaped patterns of conflict.

to a report of February 1676, settlers were killed during raids at the head of the Rappahannock. At the same time an attack on William Byrd's trading post and plantation led to the loss of two men. The scale and intensity of native hostility stoked fears of a general Indian combination against the English across the eastern seaboard. They were reinforced by rumours that the Susquehannocks were trying to hire Indians two or three hundred miles away.[54] Berkeley was convinced that their enmity was linked with the war in New England. He was acutely aware of colonial vulnerability because planters 'covet more Land than they are safely able to hold from those they have disposest of it'.[55]

In these testing circumstances opposition to the governor coalesced around Nathaniel Bacon, a young, ambitious settler, who arrived in the colony in August 1674. He rapidly acquired land in Henrico County, an interest in the Indian trade under licence from Berkeley, and appointment to the Council of State. He emerged as the leader of a coalition of disaffected settlers. Though dismissed by a report published in London as 'Runnagado English', to whom Bacon added 'his own Slaves and Servants', it included planters and traders, such as William Byrd, whose commercial interests were under threat.[56] Unwilling to wait for advice or instructions from Jamestown, Bacon assumed the command of an irregular force of volunteers who attacked a group of Appamattucks accused of stealing corn. This unauthorized action provoked an angry reprimand from Berkeley, who described it as 'a rash heady action and dishonourable'.[57] Bacon's swift response, in which he tried to repair relations with the governor, exposed his fur trading ambitions. During the course of his apology, he reminded Berkeley of a joint proposal with Byrd to farm the Indian trade. Under existing arrangements, he claimed that the governor was defrauded of half of his commercial dues. While willing to surrender his trading licence, he renewed his bid for the farm of the trade, offering 800 beavers for the first year and 600 annually thereafter. Acknowledging heavy losses, Berkeley seemed prepared to take up the offer, though he advised prudence and caution in its execution. But the proposed reorganization, 'by putting the trade into responsable hands', was a casualty of the Indian war.[58]

54 Billings (ed.), *Papers of Berkeley*, pp. 504, 509.

55 Ibid., p. 509; Billings, *Berkeley*, pp. 229–35; Walsh, *Motives of Honor*, pp. 368–9; Rice, *Tales from a Revolution*, pp. 30–6; Parker, *Global Crisis*, p. 453.

56 *Strange News from Virginia*, p. 5; Angelo T. Angelis, '"By Consent of the People": Riot and Regulation in Seventeenth-Century Virginia', in Meyers and Perreault (eds.), *Colonial Chesapeake*, p. 133; Wesley Frank Craven, *The Colonies in Transition 1660–1713* (New York, 1968), p. 131.

57 Billings (ed.), *Papers of Berkeley*, pp. 486–7.

58 Ibid., pp. 492–3; *Collections of the Massachusetts Historical Society*, p. 166; Washburn, *The Governor and the Rebel*, p. 29; Richter, *Before the Revolution*, pp. 265–79 notes the personal dispute between Bacon and Berkeley.

Alarm at the prospect of a wider native combination against the English was used by Bacon to justify indiscriminate and unauthorized action along the frontier, which led to his suspension from the council. In May 1676 he and his followers set up camp near Fort Henry. Acting on their leader's instructions, a small party seized Jack Nessom, an Indian, who was in Wood's custody, and transferred him to the county gaol, claiming he was a murderer and a proclaimed enemy to the English.[59] Wood's account of the episode included a disturbing report that two leaders of the Occaneechees had been killed by the volunteers during a raid on their habitation about 100 miles away. Although Bacon admitted that the Indians 'will reproach us', he justified his conduct to Berkeley, claiming that the Occaneechees were allied with the Susquehannocks, and together they 'killed the King of the Tuskarores and disobliged almost all the Indians in those parts'.[60] Other information acquired by Berkeley presented Bacon's conduct in a very different light. This indicated that the volunteers were welcomed by the Occaneechees who agreed to attack a nearby camp of Susquehannocks on their behalf. In the aftermath the colonists quarrelled with the Indians over their claim to the booty, which included beaver skins and a large amount of wampum. The Occaneechees retired to the security of their fort, forcing the volunteers to retreat, but the plunder and violence inflicted on the Indians seriously damaged their role as middlemen.[61]

Bacon defended his actions to Berkeley, seeking to deflect accusations of mutiny and rebellion. His claim that he acted in defence of the colony 'against all Indians in generall for that they were all enemies' collapsed the distinction between friendly and hostile natives on which Berkeley's policy rested.[62] Under the pressure of events, the governor was forced into a similar direction, issuing instructions to militia leaders, including William Claiborne's son, to reinforce forts and to range the woods for enemies. Convinced that

59 Billings (ed.), *Papers of Berkeley*, pp. 522–4.

60 Ibid., p. 529. Wilcomb E. Washburn, 'Sir William Berkeley's "A History of Our Miseries"', *WMQ*, 14 (1957), pp. 403–13. The accessibility of friendly Indian groups made them a common target for colonial violence, Walter, *Colonial Violence*, pp. 93–4.

61 Billings (ed.), *Papers of Berkeley*, p. 569; Washburn, *The Governor and the Rebel*, pp. 43–6; Rice, *Tales from a Revolution*, pp. 41–9; *Collections of the Massachusetts Historical Society*, pp. 166–7; Oberg, *Dominion and Civility*, p. 202. They were replaced by Tuscaroras according to Ethridge, 'The Emergence of the Colonial South', p. 56.

62 Billings (ed.), *Papers of Berkeley*, p. 523; Kruer, 'Bloody Minds and Peoples Undone', pp. 424–9.

the colony's neighbours were supporters of the Susquehannocks, he instructed commanders 'to spare none that has the name of an Indian'.[63]

Bacon's arrest in June halted this irregular frontier war. But his submission to the General Assembly and reconciliation with Berkeley did not last. Later in the month, amid growing anger at the levy of taxes to pay for colonial defences and accusations that the governor 'was a greater frend to the Indians than to the English', he returned to Jamestown with a following of about 400.[64] He forced the assembly to grant him a commission as general of the volunteers, with the promise of Indian plunder as a reward. According to Beverley, it was 'in effect a Power to secure a Monopoly of the *Indian* Trade to himself and his Friends'.[65] Under this authority Bacon and his party seized horses and arms, threatening and abusing county officials who opposed them. Others plundered ships and settlers along the James. The violence culminated in an attack on a group of Pamunkeys during which women and children were killed. Following Berkeley's unsuccessful attempt to regain control, from the sanctuary of the Eastern Shore, the rebels set fire to Jamestown.

In seeking to rally support and defend his actions, Bacon issued a Declaration and Manifesto in which, among other grievances, he attacked the governor's interest in the fur trade. Renouncing his interest in the business, he insisted that interethnic commerce was fatal to the security of the colony. Not only did it enable neighbouring Indians to gain information on the 'manner of living and discipline of warr' of the colonists, but also it allowed them to acquire expertise in the use of firearms, so that 'they have almost lost the use of their bowes & arrows'.[66] Bacon admitted he was tempted by the profit from the Indian trade. But he lost interest in it, and became an avowed enemy of the Indians, claiming that by the means of commerce they were able 'to furnish themselves with instruments to destroy us'.[67] By contrast Berkeley's 'love to the Beaver', threatened the future survival of the colony.[68]

63 Billings (ed.), *Papers of Berkeley*, p. 521. According to *Strange News from Virginia*, p. 6, Bacon had William Claiborne and his son 'degraded for ever bearing any Office' military or civil; *Collections of the Massachusetts Historical Society*, pp. 167–70; Eric Hinderaker and Peter C. Mancall, *At the Edge of Empire: The Backcountry in British North America* (Baltimore, 2003), pp. 49–52.

64 Billings (ed.), *Papers of Berkeley*, p. 537.

65 Beverley, *History of Virginia*, pp. 74, 81; BL, Egerton 2395, f.551.

66 C.M. Andrews (ed.), *Narratives of the Insurrection 1675–1690* (New York, 1915), pp. 59, 109; BL, Egerton 2395, f.551.

67 Andrews (ed.), *Narratives*, pp. 59, 109; BL, Egerton 2395, ff.551–1v; Billings, *Berkeley*, pp. 245–6.

68 Andrews (ed.), *Narratives*, pp. 109–10; Washburn, *The Governor and the Rebel*, p. 42; Webb, *1676*, p. 14.

Bacon's testimony represented the wider fears and frustrations of poor and less wealthy planters, particularly in outlying and exposed regions. He exploited their resentment against the colonial elite, while manipulating a deep underlying fear of Indians. The self-interested and inflammatory language clarified competing views of interethnic relations and trade. Following the decision of the General Assembly to arm friendly groups, Bacon demonized them as violent enemies of the colonists.[69] Fear and insecurity were exaggerated by lurid rumours of native barbarity. They were coloured by the resurgence of popular anti-Catholicism, fuelled by reports from across the Atlantic, which were associated with renewed hostility towards Maryland. They included reports of settlers who were the victims of Indian torture and cannibalism. Seduced by a 'popish Divell', it was alleged that Baltimore was using northern Indians in an attempt to overthrow the Protestant establishment in Virginia.[70]

The political crisis was curtailed by the death of Bacon in October 1676, though the unrest persisted. Stability was restored with the arrival of troops from England and the appointment of commissioners, one of whom, Herbert Jeffreys, replaced Berkeley as lieutenant governor. This unprecedented intervention was partly designed to investigate colonial complaints, and to re-establish peaceful relations with the Indians. But it also presented an opportunity for the Stuart monarchy to implement plans for a more centralized and integrated empire.[71]

The crisis in Indian policy and relations was less easy to resolve, though it had far-reaching implications for the maintenance of the fur trade. In an attempt to restore trust and unity among colonists who were either unable or unwilling to distinguish between friendly and hostile groups, the General Assembly authorized a levy of militia to prosecute the war against a common enemy. Prisoners taken during the conflict were to be enslaved for life. At the same time, with the exception of trade with neighbouring Indians for supplies of maize, interethnic commerce was prohibited. Such conditions compelled settlers to abandon outlying regions of settlement. It also left a legacy of mutual mistrust, manifest in occasional acts of violence. In March 1680, for example, William Byrd was involved in the deaths of several Indians, whose

69 Andrews (ed.), *Narratives*, p. 109; BL, Egerton 2395, f.551.

70 TNA, CO 1/36, ff. 231–8; John Davenport Neville (compiler), *Bacon's Rebellion: Abstracts of Materials in the Colonial Records Project* (Jamestown, 1976), pp. 50, 205; Rice, *Tales from a Revolution*, pp. 155–8.

71 Ibid., pp. 103–5 on the persistence of unrest; Billings, *Berkeley*, pp. 249–61; Parker, *Global Crisis*, p. 455 on policy. The arrival of the commissioners seems to have encouraged Claiborne and his son to revive the claim to Kent Island, H.R. McIlwaine (ed.), *Journals of the Burgesses of Virginia 1659/60–1693* (Richmond, 1914), pp. 98–9 and Hale, *Virginia Venturer*, pp. 312–15.

partners and children were imprisoned, because they were suspected of the recent murder of several colonists.[72]

As the commissioners discovered, in the aftermath of Bacon's rebellion native groups became a focal point for colonial hostility. Concern at the expense of maintaining frontier forts, which it was claimed were of no military value, merged with a call for continual war against the Indians. The complaints were dismissed by the commissioners as either impractical or dangerous. Responding to a demand for the prohibition of the trade in firearms, they pointed out that its success depended on cooperation with Maryland. In addition, they urged colonial leaders to resist the pressure for a 'war to extirpate the Indians. It would be madness', they cautioned, 'to destroy the friendly Indians who are their best guards on the frontiers against the incursions of the barbarous Indians … who still continue their implacable enemies'.[73]

Despite widespread hostility, the commissioners served as peace brokers, facilitating a treaty with neighbouring Indians in May 1677. It included Nansemonds, Pamunkeys and Weyanocks, to whom others, such as Meherrins and Monacans, were added three years later. According to its main terms, native leaders acknowledged their subjection to the English monarchy, agreeing to provide an annual tribute of three Indian arrows and 20 beaver skins for land and protection.[74] Provision was made for the re-establishment of trade, the regulation of which was left in the hands of the new governor. The assembly tried to impose tighter control over commerce, limiting it to designated markets and fairs, held twice each year in the counties. A record of transactions, including a register of the sale of firearms, was to be kept by the clerks of county courts. But the impracticality of the scheme was recognized in 1680 with the authorization of a 'free and open trade, for all persons at all tymes and places with … friendly Indians'.[75]

Indirectly the assembly's action acknowledged the importance of the inland trade, which grew rapidly during the 1680s and 1690s with little oversight or regulation. Its character and the challenges it presented to colonial entrepreneurs are illuminated by the correspondence of William Byrd, who survived his participation in Bacon's uprising to emerge as one of the leading Indian traders in its aftermath.[76] Byrd employed a group of traders, supplying them

[72] Hening (ed.), *Statutes*, 2, pp. 343–6; Andrews (ed.), *Narratives*, p. 110; Neville (ed.), *Bacon's Rebellion*, pp. 88, 92, 96; *CSPC, 1675–6*, pp. 398–9.

[73] TNA, CO 5/1371, ff.59v-60; Neville (ed.), *Bacon's Rebellion*, p. 258; Rice, *Tales from a Revolution*, pp. 213–14 concludes that 'the Baconites' won the battle over the issue of dealing with the Indians.

[74] Rountree, *Powhatan Indians*, pp. 100–1; Gleach, *Powhatan's World*, pp. 196–7.

[75] Hening (ed.), *Statutes*, 2, p. 480; TNA, CO 5/1376, f.85v.

[76] Rice, *Tales from a Revolution*, pp. 98, 116, 120; Louis B. Wright, *The First Gentlemen of Virginia: Intellectual Qualities of the Early Colonial Ruling Class* (San

with truck and credit in exchange for skins and furs, for long-distance overland ventures covering hundreds of miles. Encompassing an extensive network of supply and demand, it required careful management, knowledge of markets on both sides of the Atlantic, and diplomatic contacts and skills, not least because these trading expeditions were exposed to native hostility. Frontier diplomacy, often improvised, thus played a part in enabling trade to proceed. In April 1684, for example, Byrd met a group of 50 Senecas, about 12 miles from his residence, securing a promise that they would behave peacefully towards the English. Yet the dangers remained. In May 1686 two of his traders were killed during an expedition about 400 miles inland, while other members of the party lost their horses and trading commodities.[77]

Byrd's correspondence with his London suppliers, who included Micajah Perry and Thomas Lane, one of the leading city partnerships involved in the tobacco trade, indicates a persistent problem with the provision of suitable goods for native consumers, though transatlantic huckstering may also have been an attempt to drive down costs. The problem was exacerbated by intense competition among colonial traders, which led to the Indian market becoming over supplied with some commodities. In February 1684 he informed the Londoners of complaints against their supply of duffels and other cloth, described as cottons, claiming that they were the worst he had ever seen. One month later, he reported similar complaints about their stockings, hats and linen, expressing irritation at the absence of beads and trinkets. He was also concerned at the limited information they provided about the metropolitan market. Frustrated at the lack of news, by the end of the year he complained of 'being in the darke', as a result of which he was a 'considerable looser within this twelfe moneth'.[78]

As the new trading season got underway, in February 1685 he repeated his concern about the quality of duffels and cottons, complaining that rival adventurers were supplied with better material. According to reports from his traders, the Indians preferred dark blue cloth, instead of the lighter material

Marino, 1940), pp. 315–17. Traders included Cadwallader Jones see, Fairfax Harrison, 'Western Explorations in Virginia between Lederer and Spotswood', *VMHB*, 30 (1922), pp. 323–40.

[77] Marion Tinling (ed.), *The Correspondence of the Three William Byrds of Westover, Virginia 1684–1776*, 2 vols. (Charlottesville, 1977), 1, pp. 16, 59; Stephen Saunders Webb, *Marlborough's America* (New Haven, 2013), p. 332. The Seneca (confusingly used for the Iroquois more generally) may have been in search of new sources of furs, as well as captives, Merrell, *The Indians' New World*, pp. 41–2; John Lawson, *A New Voyage to Carolina*, ed. Hugh Talmage Lefler (Chapel Hill, 1967), pp. 60–1.

[78] Tinling (ed.), *Correspondence*, 1, pp. 10, 14, 28; Morrison, 'The Virginia Indian Trade', p. 226 for similar complaint.

provided by Perry and Lane. Despite these difficulties, in April he sent six hogsheads of fur and skins to London. He subsequently advised his London agents that though the beaver was rough in appearance, as a result of being wet, it had been dried and was generally good. Seeking an improvement in the supply chain, in June he reminded Arthur North, one of his metropolitan factors, of the need for care and discrimination in the selection of goods for native consumers. In particular, he was alarmed that his supply of beads was more expensive and of poor quality compared with others. At the same time, he appealed for an early, and potentially advantageous, despatch of goods from London.[79]

In March 1686 Byrd provided North with a brief review of the previous trading season, in an attempt to improve the quality of supply. While acknowledging that his gunpowder and brandy were cheaper than that of others, he complained that the hoes were too small, and did not sell. By contrast, gun locks from Perry and Lane had sold well. As his traders had only recently departed, he lacked information on the current state of the market for duffels and other goods. Consequently, he advised Perry and Lane that he was compelled to order his 'Indian trucke by guesse, not yet knowing how the last proved'.[80] But he was worried that the native market was overstocked, with rival traders 'indeavoring to eat out another'.[81] Reporting the ill success of one of his trading expeditions in May, he warned of the likelihood of a small return of beaver, as there was little to be purchased from the Indians he traded with. He requested a supply of guns and powder, repeating complaints about the quality of cloth and kettles, which reportedly contained holes. In July he admonished Perry and Lane for sending large, instead of small, white beads, which remained unsold. Although he sent North a parcel of furs and skins, packed in a barrel and a hogshead, he renewed his request for information on the market in London.[82]

Two years later, he had hopes of profiting from the disruption to the fur trade of New York. In July 1688, with a supply of furs and skins ready for London, he anticipated an increase in their price, as the northern trade was 'quite spoild by the French warring with their Indians'.[83] Yet he faced an unexpected difficulty in trying to lade them aboard a ship. Despite securing space for a cargo of tobacco, the master departed without four hogsheads of pelts, reneging on a promise to take them. With a large parcel of skins on hand, perplexed and angry, in March he was unwilling to order any trade goods from London. During July, however, he requested a variety of truck, including

79 Tinling (ed.), *Correspondence*, 1, pp. 29, 37–8, 41–2.
80 Ibid., pp. 41, 57–8.
81 Ibid., p. 58.
82 Ibid., pp. 58–60, 64, 66.
83 Ibid., p. 86.

blue cloth, plain belts, Jew's harps, tobacco tongs, scissors and shears, and 18 'Indian guns'.[84] Early the following year he informed Perry and Lane that he was well stocked with goods. But trade was dull, with 'little beaver & skins to bee had, the Indians att war with each other, & troubles on all hands'.[85] They included a prohibition placed on the Indian trade by the General Assembly. It was rescinded by June 1691, when he sent a parcel of furs to his London agents. In anticipation of the forthcoming trading season, he also ordered a supply of white and black wampum, from Stephanus Van Courlandt, an associate and prominent trader in New York. But he was concerned and pessimistic at future prospects, warning Perry and Lane that the assembly had imposed such an imposition on the trade, that he feared it would never be worthwhile.[86]

In combination with rebellion and war, interethnic commerce contributed to a re-structuring of native worlds within and beyond Virginia. But the emergence of the inland trade coincided with an intensification of raids by Iroquoian groups who were ranging further into the Bay as a result of their long-running conflict with the Susquehannocks. At a time of growing concern with colonial borders and boundaries, the uninhibited movement of native groups provoked widespread concern. Against such external threats colonial leaders hoped to use local Indians, linked more closely to the colony, as a protective buffer.[87] Although Iroquoian raiding disrupted the fur trade during the 1690s, it failed to halt the commercial drive into the interior. During the late seventeenth century as many as 50 or 60 colonial traders may have been engaged in such commercial expeditions.[88] But the crisis of the 1670s demonstrated that, in the face of widespread hostility towards native groups, the colonists struggled to formulate a coherent, widely supported, Indian policy. The experience of Virginia during these years suggested that the alternative to regulation was plunder and violence along a frontier where planters and traders, like Byrd, saw themselves as living at 'the end of the world'.[89]

[84] Ibid., pp. 88, 93, 97, 101, 106, 109.

[85] Ibid., p. 118.

[86] Ibid., pp. 153–4, 163–4. Profits were sometimes marginal due to high investment and Indian raiding according to Briceland, *Westward from Virginia*, p. 172. Significantly, during the 1690s Byrd developed his interests in the Atlantic rather than the frontier, Rice, *Tales from a Revolution*, pp. 185–6.

[87] Hatfield, *Atlantic Virginia*, pp. 191–3, 196–7, 209–14, 219–28.

[88] Merrell, *The Indians' New World*, pp. 28–9; Ramsey, *The Yamasee War*, pp. 129–31 for the persistence of the trade.

[89] Tinling (ed.), *Correspondence*, 1, p. 136; Hatfield, *Atlantic Virginia*, p. 37; on frontiers see Elliott, *Empires of the Atlantic World*, pp. 265–6 and on the widening range of Virginian traders, rivalry with Carolina and regulation see Gallay, *The Indian Slave Trade*, pp. 102–3, 161, 203, 208–9, 305–6. Byrd's son was to acquire a patent for 100,000 acres of land along the Roanoke River in 1735, Kulikoff, *Tobacco and Slaves*, pp. 143–4.

Maryland: trade, diplomacy and war

The experience of Maryland contrasted with that of its southern neighbour. Although the end of the Susquehannock war favoured the revival of commerce, it was plagued by interconnected colonial and native rivalries. While the lord proprietor's territorial claims were the source of antagonism with Dutch competitors in Delaware Bay, his promotion of colonial settlement along the Eastern Shore damaged commercial relations with Indian groups. Increasingly the Susquehannocks were in no position to compensate for the decline in local supplies of fur. Under the prolonged pressure of Iroquoian raiding, moreover, they were forced to seek assistance from the colonists. The conflict undermined their commanding position at the head of the Bay, curtailing hunting and trading. As a result, interethnic commerce was overshadowed by the demands of war and diplomacy. Confronted with the prospect of becoming a target for the northern Indians, during the 1670s, colonial leaders sacrificed native allies and trading partners in the interests of defence and security.

Commercial revival and regulation

Reviving interest in the fur trade was registered by George Alsop in *A Character of the Province of Maryland* published in 1666. Drawing on his experience as a servant in the colony during the late 1650s and early 1660s, as well as other sources, Alsop portrayed a land of natural plenty, supporting large herds of deer and a variety of fur-bearing fauna which provided native groups with a valuable exchange commodity. He understood that interethnic commerce rested on Indian expertise. Furs and skins were 'first made vendible by the Indians of the Country, and sold to the Inhabitant, and by them to the Merchant, and so transported into England and other places where it becomes most commodious'.[90] Alsop's treatise on the Susquehannocks, the 'most Noble and Heroick Nation of Indians', included a description of native hunting and trading which demonstrated their adaptation to a colonial market.[91] At the onset of the season in November, the most skilled hunters travelled to remote parts of the woods, where they remained in temporary shelters for three months, in search of game to provide for their families during the summer. Although hunting remained a high-status, masculine activity, undertaken with native weapons and firearms, women, who served as carriers on such expeditions, played a vital role in preparing skins for trade. The prey included deer, bear and elk, as well as beaver and otter, whose skins were 'brought down to the English at several seasons in the year', and exchanged for 'Blankets, Guns, Powder, and Lead, Beads, small Looking-glasses, Knives, and Razors'.[92] Alsop described

90 Hall (ed.), *Narratives of Early Maryland*, p. 363.

91 Ibid., p. 365.

92 Ibid., pp. 371, 377.

a world where custom and commerce co-existed. While the Indians possessed firearms, men continued to present gifts of beaver and otter skins to their future spouses, receiving a kettle of boiled venison or bear in exchange.

Alsop provided no estimate for the scale of commercial activity, but the number of traders operating during the late 1650s and early 1660s seems to have been limited and subject to regulation. Traders required licences, reserving 10% of the weight or value of pelts to the lord proprietor, but the number issued was small. They were granted to Nathaniel Utie and John Bateman in May 1658, and to William Hollinsworth in January 1661.[93] Undoubtedly there were others, for which no evidence survives. But the recovery of proprietorial authority under the new governor, Charles Calvert, Baltimore's son and heir, was followed by a determined effort to control interethnic commerce. In December 1661 the council prohibited the Indian trade within and beyond the colony without licence. A subsequent proclamation cancelled all former commissions and authorized the seizure of vessels and cargoes owned by illegal traders.[94]

Baltimore's ambitions to revive and regulate the fur trade were qualified by the growth of a small farm and plantation economy based on the cultivation of tobacco. According to Alsop 'Tobacco, Furrs, and Flesh' were the main exports of the colony, but he acknowledged that the first was their 'only solid Staple Commodity'.[95] As in Virginia, the development of commercialized agriculture, including the introduction of stock and draught animals, had serious consequences for Indians and their native habitats. The impact of the colonists was acutely felt within the environs of St Mary's, where native groups were drawn into dependent relations with the colonial community during the 1660s. Such changes provoked anxiety and dislocation. Faced with encroachments on their territory, in 1665 the leader of the Mattawomans complained to the governor and council, seeking permission to remain on their land, warning that otherwise they would re-locate in the woods.[96] At the same time, the spread of settlement across the Bay endangered relations with other groups, disrupting interethnic commerce, to the advantage of Dutch traders who were operating near Kent Island.[97]

93 Browne (ed.), *Proceedings of the Council of Maryland 1636–67*, pp. 342–3, 382–3, 386–7, 443–4.

94 Ibid., p. 443; William Hand Browne (ed.), *Proceedings and Acts of the General Assembly of Maryland October 1678–November 1683* (Maryland Historical Society, 7, 1889), p. 417.

95 Hall (ed.), *Narratives of Early Maryland*, p. 363.

96 Pleasants (ed.), *Proceedings of the Provincial Court of Maryland 1663–1666*, pp. 512–13; Rice, *Nature & History*, pp. 139–41. Disease intensified the problems facing Potomac River Indians, Rice, *Nature & History*, pp. 131–4.

97 Browne (ed.), *Proceedings of the Council of Maryland 1636–67*, pp. 452–3.

Under the revised regime of regulation, from 1661 to 1681 the governor and council issued at least 34 licences for the Indian trade. About three-quarters of this total were granted during the 1660s.[98] With no evidence to suggest a significant increase in illegal trading after 1670, such a pattern points to a dramatic decline of interest in interethnic commerce. It reflected the inherent weakness of a business which was undermined by changing conditions, marked by the growing vulnerability of the Susquehannocks to their Iroquois enemies.

Structurally the Indian trade remained an opportunistic enterprise, the regulation of which did little to promote sustained interest or investment. Evidence for the recipients of trading commissions indicates that many were small-scale adventurers, operating in an intermittent or part-time manner. Among a total of 27 licensed traders, only three seem to have received more than one licence. They were usually valid for one year, and included provision for the payment of one tenth of the proceeds to the lord proprietor, though profits might be boosted by the authority to seize illegal trading vessels and their ladings. Traders were expected to take out bonds, ranging from £500 to £1,000, for their good behaviour. The only significant exception to these terms was contained in an unusual commission awarded to John Lederer in March 1671, authorizing trade with native groups in the south west for 14 years.[99] But Lederer did not stay long enough to exploit it. By 1674 he was resident in Connecticut.

In these circumstances many traders were primarily concerned with the acquisition of land. Andrew Cooke, a merchant of London, who received a licence in 1661, patented 1,000 acres before returning to England. Among the recipients of commissions during 1662, Francis Wright owned 500 acres, while Robert Slye was building up an estate of at least 2,500 acres with 11 servants and 14 slaves. William Boreman, a mariner during the 1640s, received licences in 1662 and 1663, and was heavily involved in land acquisition and speculation. He owned 3,000 acres in 1671, which had more than doubled by the time of his death. John Allen, granted a licence in 1669, owned a water mill and smithy, and an estate of 1,050 acres. Among other recipients, William Calvert, possibly the illegitimate son of the governor, owned 9,000 acres in 1682, when he was drowned while trying to cross the Wicomico River.[100]

98 Ibid., pp. 443–9, 453, 455, 467–8, 472, 488–90, 513–14, 526, 555–6. A small number of separate licences were issued to trade for maize, including one for widow Hannah Lee, Ibid., pp. 448–9.

99 Ibid., pp. 445–6, 472; William Hand Browne (ed.), *Proceedings of the Council of Maryland 1667–1687/8* (Maryland Historical Society, 5, 1887), pp. 84–5.

100 Ibid., pp. 38–9; Browne (ed.), *Proceedings of the Council of Maryland 1636–67*, pp. 453, 472, and n. 95 above.

There were exceptions to this pattern which indicates more extensive engagement with the Indian trade. They included a small group of Dutch migrants from the Delaware. Jacob Clausen established a trading post at the head of the Bay, where he maintained close relations with the Susquehannocks during the 1660s and 1670s. Harman Cornellison and Peter Groendyck, who retained an interest in the Delaware trade, received licences in 1672. John Nuthall, one of the leading traders among the English, was awarded commissions from 1661 to 1664. On his death in 1668, his estate included 570 pounds of beaver skins, valued at more than £140, a sloop and a substantial amount of wampum. His successors included Thomas Jones, an ambitious and disorderly trader, who received a commission in April 1672 appointing him the 'sole Indian Trader' in the colony, with the authority to seize the ships and goods of anyone trading without licence.[101] It was withdrawn after he plundered Dutch merchants at the Whorekill in the neighbouring Bay, and ransacked a vessel of 350 beaver skins owned by Richard Ackworth, a trader who lived along Manoakin River.[102]

Although the regulation of the Indian trade remained in force, there was a sharp reduction in the issue of licences. Eight were awarded during the late 1660s and 1670s, only three of which seem to have been for resident colonists. In addition to Cornellison, Groendyck and Jones, the recipients included Samuel Groome, captain of the *Globe* of London, and James Moll of Bristol. Groome used his commission to appoint agents to act on his behalf in the colony.[103] Under these conditions it seemed likely that much of the trade would fall into the hands of semi-resident and resourceful Dutch merchants, adapting to the takeover of New Amsterdam in 1664.

The activities of the Dutch, exemplified by the career of Jacob Clausen, exposed the difficulty of regulating commerce, especially when it lay between rival colonial jurisdictions. Clausen was an experienced trader who served as an interpreter for New Amstel during the late 1650s, employing or earning the name of 'Jacob, My Friend' among native groups.[104] A report of 1660 claimed that he 'lived as a savage among' the Susquehannocks, marrying a native woman, reputedly causing 'great damage, diversion of trade and trouble'.[105]

[101] Browne (ed.), *Proceedings of the Council of Maryland 1671–1681*, pp. 106–7, 114, 312–3; Browne (ed.), *Proceedings of the Council of Maryland 1667–1687/8*, pp. 86–7, 115–16.

[102] Elizabeth Merritt (ed.), *Proceedings of the Provincial Court of Maryland 1670/1–1675* (Maryland Historical Society, Court Series, 65, 1952), pp. 41–2, 56.

[103] Browne (ed.), *Proceedings of the Council of Maryland 1671–81*, p. 352.

[104] Jennings, 'Jacob Young', p. 26; *Documents of New York*, 3, p. 344.

[105] *Documents of New York*, 12, p. 317; Browne (ed.), *Proceedings of the Council of Maryland 1636–67*, p. 462; Pleasants (ed.), *Proceedings of the Court of Chancery of Maryland 1669–1679*, pp. 86–7, 93–4, 381–2.

In 1661, and on subsequent occasions, he was employed by the council at St Mary's as an interpreter and intermediary with the Indians. Under the name of Jacob Young, he was licensed to trade with the Indians. His establishment of a trading post at the mouth of the Susquehanna helped to revive interest in the region for colonial commerce and settlement.

Most of Clausen's trade with the Indians went unrecorded and apparently unlicensed after 1662. There was little that the colony's leaders could do to control the activities of an independent frontier trader who enjoyed the protection of powerful native partners. But the weakening of the Susquehannocks during the late 1670s exposed his vulnerability as an outsider who challenged the self-identity of the English colonial community. In 1682 he was impeached before the General Assembly. The charges included allegations regarding his relationship with an Indian woman. Clausen vigorously defended himself. Professing great influence with the natives, he issued a thinly-veiled warning to those who were responsible for his arrest. He was a maverick trader, whose defence of the Susquehannocks as 'an innocent and harmless People' was seen as a further provocation, and the assembly offered to pay his fees if he departed for the Netherlands, and never return to America.[106]

It may be no coincidence that the action against Clausen occurred at a time when the activities of rogue traders were the source of mounting concern. In September 1679 two Indian leaders, Hatsawapp and Tequassino, were so alarmed at the spread of drunkenness within their communities that they successfully appealed to the governor and council for a ban on the use of alcohol in interethnic trade. But it was a problem which afflicted native leaders. Two years later Hatsawapp was summoned to appear before a commission of inquiry into the murder of several colonists, but 'he being something in drink refused to come and made answer that he staied away for his pleasure'.[107] Other traders ignored the ban on the sale of firearms, gunpowder and swords. In 1680 Thomas Jones was identified as a 'dangerous and contemptuous person for dealeing and tradeing with Indians' in powder and shot.[108] During the course of a discussion on trade in 1682, members of the General Assembly expressed concern at the spread of rumours and false reports by some traders, as they visited native towns, which produced such disquiet that it threatened the public peace.

As this record indicates, the re-imposition of regulation after 1660 met with mixed success. The collection of a levy of one-tenth on the proceeds from

[106] Browne (ed.), *Proceedings of the Assembly of Maryland 1678–83*, pp. 370–2, 475–6, 591. Clausen stayed in the colony, possibly because of his skills as an interpreter, Jennings, 'Jacob Young", pp. 349–52; Brandâo, *"Your Fyre Shall Burn No More"*, p. 113 for difficulties of the Susquehannocks.

[107] Browne (ed.), *Proceedings of the Council of Maryland 1671–81*, pp. 260, 413.

[108] Ibid., p. 312.

trading voyages was a burden on commerce. A proposal presented to the lower house of the assembly in 1682, to open the Indian trade to colonists, included provision for it to be halved. But the plan failed to find support in the upper house.[109] Regulation may have acted as a deterrent for licensed enterprise, while failing to deal effectively with irregular and illegal commerce. By the 1680s, however, the activities of all traders were severely disrupted by native hostilities, stifling the uncertain revival of the Indian trade in the upper Bay.

Diplomacy, rivalry and conflict

In December 1660 a delegation of Piscataway leaders visited St Mary's to renew their peace with the colony. During the course of negotiations with the governor they warned of the dangers they faced from the Senecas, a generic term used by the English for the Iroquois.[110] Five of their men had recently been killed during an attack on their fort, because they were friends of the English and Susquehannocks. The following year, in May, four colonists were killed by a party of unidentified Indians as they returned to their homes after a visit to a trading post near the Whorekill. Two suspects were arrested and put on trial for murder at New Amstel, but the case collapsed. The Dutch governor warned that further legal action could trigger war, and defended his conduct to the leaders of Maryland, claiming that the 'Ignorant cannot suffer for the Guilty'.[111] Such violent episodes illuminate the obstacles in the way of the revival of interethnic commerce within and beyond the Bay. They also re-awakened concern that the colony was in danger of encirclement by rivals and enemies. Responding to the perceived threat, colonial leaders embarked on a programme of assertive diplomacy. Its primary purpose was to maintain security and defence, but it was also motivated by a concern to promote commercial and colonial expansion. These goals were progressively overshadowed and endangered by the widening range and intensity of Iroquoian hostility.[112]

The Susquehannocks lay at the centre of this colonial network of diplomacy and commercial relations. By a treaty of 1661 Calvert and his councillors agreed to despatch a force of 50 men to reinforce the Indians' fort. In return, Dahadaghesa and six other leaders promised to supply the colony

[109] Browne (ed.), *Proceedings of the General Assembly of Maryland 1678–1683*, pp. 271, 293, 301, 425.

[110] Richter, *Long-House*, p. 98.

[111] Browne (ed.), *Proceedings of the Council of Maryland 1636–67*, pp. 412–16; *Documents of New York*, 3, p. 345; Daniel K. Richter, 'Ordeals of the Longhouse: The Five Nations in Early American History', in Daniel K. Richter and James H. Merrell (eds.), *Beyond the Covenant Chain: The Iroquois and Their Neighbors in Indian North America, 1600–1800* (Syracuse, 1987), pp. 21–4 on the Iroquois.

[112] Rice, *Nature & History*, pp. 144–57 for wider ramifications.

with provisions. It may have been presumed that such assistance would also facilitate the growth of the fur trade, but the results were discouraging for both parties. John Odber was appointed to lead the expedition, with detailed instructions regarding its purpose and conduct. They included strengthening the native fort with the addition of European-style spurs and flankers. While Odber was instructed to gather intelligence on the relationship between the Susquehannocks and the Dutch, he was also authorized to provide assistance during enemy raids. If the Indians were slow to prosecute the war against the Iroquois, he was to urge them to greater action.[113] By mid-October, however, Odber and his men had returned to St Mary's, claiming that the Indians were either unwilling or unable to furnish them with provisions according to the terms of the treaty. A different perspective was provided by a Dutch report, indicating that they were reeling from the devastating impact of a smallpox epidemic, while 'hard beset by the Sinnecus, which makes the trade bad'.[114]

Despite this setback the governor and council at St Mary's continued to rely on diplomacy to exert and extend their influence over native groups. A treaty with the Passayonkes of September 1661 dealt with issues regarding the protection of livestock and the return of runaways, and included provision for dealing with Indians accused of killing settlers. It served as a model for an agreement with three representatives of the Lenapes, made at Fort Amstel in August 1663. The Dutch were involved in the treaty, possibly as intermediaries.[115] But commercial and territorial rivalries were thinly veiled. In a local agreement brokered at Monoakin plantation the previous year, the Nanticokes had agreed to stop trading with the Dutch, on condition that the colony provided them with necessary supplies.[116] As native diplomacy and Dutch rivalry became confused with the threat of raiding from the north, the colony's leaders responded with more forceful measures, sending out scouting parties to seize Indians who were not recognized allies, with authority to kill any who resisted.

The Susquehannocks bore the brunt of Iroquoian hostility. During the summer of 1663 they were besieged in their fort by a large raiding party, reportedly made up of 800 warriors. According to a Jesuit report, the Iroquois were seeking captives and glory. Surprised at the improved defensive works of the fort, they 'abandoned their projected assault, and after some light skirmishes, resorted to their customary subtlety, in order to gain by trickery

113 Browne (ed.), *Proceedings of the Council of Maryland 1636–67*, pp. 417–8; Jennings, *Ambiguous Iroquois Empire*, pp. 127–8.

114 *Documents of New York*, 12, p. 357; Browne (ed.), *Proceedings of the Council of Maryland 1636–67*, pp. 434–5, 441; Richter, *Before the Revolution*, p. 151.

115 Browne (ed.), *Proceedings of the Council of Maryland 1636–67*, pp. 433, 486.

116 Ibid., p. 452.

what they could not accomplish by force'.[117] Following their overtures for a parley, a group of 25 Iroquois were allowed into the fort. They were seized, mounted on scaffolds and burned alive before their followers and companions. The Susquehannocks, 'by thus declaring war more hotly than ever, gave the Iroquois to understand that this was merely the prelude to what they were going to do in the latter's country'.[118] Insulted and humiliated, the raiders withdrew. They were expected to return in the autumn with reinforcements. But the Susquehannocks were not in a strong position to take the offensive without support from the colonists. Shortly after the siege was lifted, one of their leaders, Wastahandaw, appealed to the General Assembly for assistance. Relying on Jacob Clausen and Simon Carpenter as intermediaries, the governor and council responded with supplies of gunpowder and lead, as well as two artillery pieces with four men to manage them. The supply did nothing to compensate for the alarming decline in the population of the Susquehannocks, whose number of adult male warriors may have fallen by nearly half over the previous 15 years.[119]

During 1664 the leaders of Maryland missed an opportunity to make contact with the Iroquois, inadvertently revealing differences over Indian policy and diplomacy between frontier traders and settlers. It followed the seizure of the leader of a party of Indians during a visit to a trading post operated by Francis Wright along the Patapsco River, 'under pretence & Colour of a friendly trade'.[120] Although the colonists were uncertain about the identity of their prisoner, he was recognized by several visiting Susquehannocks as a renowned war-leader of the Senecas, the first to be taken by the English.[121] They urged Wright to burn him, but he refused claiming that it was not an English custom to torture their enemies.

The Indian prisoner made a declaration while in Wright's custody, possibly interpreted with the aid of Clausen, a written copy of which was sent to the governor. He claimed to be on a peaceful mission to both the colonists and the Susquehannocks. As a sign of his good intentions he brought a gift of 40 beaver skins for the former and belts of wampum for the latter. In the nuanced language of native diplomacy and metaphor, he informed the English that 'if

117 Reuben Gold Thwaites (ed.), *The Jesuit Relations and Allied Documents: Travels and Explorations of the Jesuit Missionaries in New France 1610–1791*, 73 vols. (repr. New York, 1959), 48, pp. 77–9; Jennings, 'Glory, Death, and Transfiguration', p. 28; Richter, *Before the Revolution*, pp. 262–3.

118 *Documents of New York*, 12, pp. 431, 434, 439; Oberg, *Dominion and Civility*, pp. 196–7.

119 Browne (ed.), *Proceedings of the General Assembly of Maryland 1678–83*, pp. 471–2.

120 Browne (ed.), *Proceedings of the Council of Maryland 1636–67*, pp. 498–50.

121 Ibid., p. 500.

he had been taken by the Sasquehanoes, that he should not have beene put to death by them, that all the Joynts of his Body is Belts of peake that he hath laid out for … peace and quiettnes'.[122] Blaming recent casualties among the colonial community on another group of natives, he proclaimed that the Senecas did not seek war with the English. But he was in search of revenge or compensation for the death of his son and two others, who had been taken and killed by the Susquehannocks.

For Indian traders such as Wright and Clausen this was an unexpected opportunity to gain influence with the Senecas. Wright proposed the return of the prisoner, with gifts from the governor, in expectation of establishing peace. Clausen offered his services as a mediator and interpreter, claiming that Civility, a Susquehannock leader, was prepared to join such a mission if there was a prospect of ending the conflict. But the proposal came to nothing, following the transfer of the prisoner to St Mary's. Amid angry accusations that the Senecas were responsible for attacks on the colony, some settlers cast doubt on his truthfulness, predicting further raids on vulnerable farms and plantations.[123]

These doubts seemed to be confirmed by the aggressive incursions of Iroquoian groups during the summer. They included a party of Oneidas, reportedly 60 in number, who raided the Potomac in search of targets. Two of the group were seized by the Piscataways. Tortured in the presence of Thomas Mathews, a trader and interpreter, one of them confessed that they came to make war on the colonists and their allies. They were acting in association with another raiding party who set out to attack the Susquehannocks and the English at the head of the Bay. The prisoners warned that others would follow later in the summer, on a mission to kill the English, if they were undetected by friendly Indians.[124] Following further raids, during which several settlers were killed, in June 1664 the governor declared war against the Senecas. Rewards of wampum were offered to anybody, Indian or English, who brought in a prisoner or the ears of one who had been killed.[125]

The outbreak of hostilities exposed the limits of diplomacy and placed a severe burden on the resources of the colony and its allies. Faced with renewed raiding during 1665, the governor and council levied recruits to defend exposed settlements on both sides of the Bay. Commanders were instructed to range the woods with the help of friendly Indians. But the effectiveness of these expeditions was limited, particularly as the main focus of Iroquoian enmity remained the Susquehannocks. In June 1666 Wastahandaw and two other leaders informed Calvert that they had lost a considerable number of

[122] Ibid., pp. 499–50.
[123] Ibid., pp. 498–9.
[124] Ibid., p. 501.
[125] Ibid., pp. 501–3.

men at the heads of the rivers, in the defence of English plantations against the raiders. Weakened and alarmed at reports of an impending attack on their fort, they signed a new treaty with colonial leaders. Reflecting their declining status and position in the upper Bay, its main terms were modelled on the earlier agreement with the Passayonkes, though it covered more specific issues, including the transfer of prisoners into colonial custody.[126]

The impact on commerce of sustained raiding from the north, combined with the short-term consequences of the second Anglo-Dutch war from 1665 to 1667, was devastating. The Indian war turned the Susquehanna River into a pathway for Iroquois raiders. By means of its tributaries and other rivers which flowed into the Chesapeake and the Delaware, the violence and disorder spread across a wide area. At the same time the war with the Dutch had unanticipated consequences for the colony's leaders and the lord proprietor. The seizure of New Netherland was followed by the establishment of New York, based on former Dutch territory which included Delaware Bay. The transfer of the jurisdiction of the new colony to James, duke of York, the king's brother, effectively denied Baltimore's territorial ambitions in the region. Sir Robert Carr, acting for the duke, seized New Amstel, renamed Fort Delaware, in 1664, though his presence was an unwelcome intrusion for Baltimore and his representatives at St Mary's. As the leaders of New York sought to take over and develop Dutch trade with the Iroquois, Carr attempted to mediate in their conflict with the Susquehannocks. The intervention aroused little interest from the leaders of Maryland who were deeply suspicious of his motives.[127]

During the late 1660s the threat of Iroquoian raiding was aggravated by the revival of conflict among Eastern Shore native groups. They included the Wicomiss who were held responsible for the murder of John Odber and a servant. Expeditions were despatched across the Bay in July 1667 with instructions to 'destroy, kill, burne and take all such Indians as shall be declared' enemies of the colony.[128] Captains were authorized to keep native captives for their own benefit. In August four Wicomiss prisoners were condemned to death for their role in Odber's murder. Aided by the continuing loyalty of the Piscataways, which was confirmed by the renewal of treaties, the colony's leaders exploited native disunity to deal with their enemies across the Bay. By an agreement of March 1668 the Nanticokes promised to deliver up the Wicomiss and any other Indians who protected the murderers of Odber.[129] It was followed by a similar arrangement with the Assateagues. In both cases,

126 Ibid., pp. 523, 530–2, 549–50.

127 *CSPC, 1661–8*, pp. 236–7, 245–6, 339–40, 567; Michael Kammen, *Colonial New York* (Oxford, 1975), pp. 74–5; Percy Lewis Kaye, *English Colonial Administration Under Lord Clarendon 1660–1667* (Baltimore, 1907), p. 150.

128 Browne (ed.), *Proceedings of the Council of Maryland 1667–1687/8*, p. 10.

129 Ibid., pp. 11–12, 29–30; Rice, *Nature & History*, pp. 139–42 for Piscataways.

these native groups also agreed neither to make war nor peace without the approval of the lord proprietor or his representative.[130]

Diplomacy was intended to promote settlement and trade along the Eastern Shore, while protecting the interests of the colony in contested and strategic regions. According to a scheme drawn up by Baltimore in 1669, the region to the north was to be re-named Durham County. In order to attract settlers, parcels of 50 acres of land were offered at a rent of one shilling, but the plan met with a poor response.[131] The wider strategy, of which it formed a part, also suffered an embarrassing setback in 1672 when the trader Thomas Jones raided the Whorekill, where the Dutch and English operated rival trading posts, with an irregular force of 30 men. Under cover of a commission to seize the vessels and goods of unlicensed traders, he and his followers plundered the Dutch of substantial amounts of fur and truck. A supply of gunpowder, awaiting sale to a group of visiting Indians, was destroyed. Jones defended his actions as lawful, but the provincial court decreed that he had exceeded the limits of his commission. By Calvert's own admission, he was 'a little too rough in the Horekeele'.[132] Consequently his licence was revoked, and he was ordered to provide compensation for the Dutch.

The third Anglo-Dutch war from 1672 to 1675, during which the Dutch regained control of New York, provided an opportunity to revive these more aggressive tactics. In 1673 the colony's leaders sent out captain Thomas Howell and 40 men to raid the Whorekill. Houses were burnt, stock was destroyed and settlers, Dutch and English, were plundered. Harman Cornellison, a Dutch trader, claimed he was tortured until he revealed where his furs were hidden.[133] Witnessing the participation of native allies in the attack, apparently Indians at the Whorekill wept at the cruelty of 'their owne native Country men'.[134] Although the expedition inflicted considerable damage, its strategic purpose was cancelled by the recovery of New York in 1674. The re-establishment of the authority and jurisdiction of the duke of York ended any serious effort to enforce Baltimore's claim to the region.

130 Browne (ed.), *Proceedings of the Council of Maryland 1671–81*, pp. 170–4; Feest, 'Nanticoke and Neighbouring Tribes', in Trigger (ed.), *Handbook of North American Indians*, p. 243.

131 By 1672 there were more than 1,000 settlers on the Eastern Shore, Clemens, *The Atlantic Economy*, p. 49.

132 Merritt (ed.), *Proceedings of the Provincial Court of Maryland 1670/71–1675*, pp. 40–1, 54–5; Jennings, 'Glory, Death, and Transfiguration', pp. 31–2.

133 Browne (ed.), *Proceedings of the Council of Maryland 1671–81*, pp. 27–9; Leon deValinger, Jr, 'The Burning of the Whorekill, 1673', *Pennsylvania Magazine of History and Biography*, 74 (1950), p. 480; *Calvert Papers*, 1, pp. 289–90.

134 Ibid., p. 477.

The dispute over the Whorekill contributed to a radical revision of the colony's diplomatic programme. With the Susquehannock alliance, its centrepiece, under strain, in June 1674 the General Assembly voted in favour of peace with the Iroquois. It was justified by reports that the Susquehannocks were responsible for the murder of colonists and other outrages in Baltimore County. Both sides seem to have met at Mattaponi, though the date of the meeting and its business are unknown. With their current position in jeopardy as a result of the cumulative impact of war and disease, it is likely that the re-location of the Indians to a more secure habitation within the colony was raised. In February 1675 leaders of the Susquehannocks appeared before the upper house of the assembly, and 'being asked their Business they Desired to know what part of the Province should be Allotted for them to live upon'.[135] When the issue came before the lower house, the response of some members betrayed deep unease and suspicion at their motives. After further discussion they were offered an abandoned fort, formerly used by the Piscataways, along the upper Potomac.[136]

The removal of the Susquehannocks had rapid and dramatic consequences. During a period of widespread anxiety at Indian relations in both Chesapeake colonies, the migrants were in danger of becoming a target for the displaced aggression of settlers, for whom they were uninvited and unwelcome neighbours. Following an alarming increase in violent incidents in Virginia during the summer of 1675, which contributed to the ensuing political crisis, a group of Doegs were pursued by the militia into Maryland. A subsequent skirmish led to the deaths of several Susquehannocks and Doegs. The former responded with attacks on isolated farms and plantations on either side of the Potomac. As the violence escalated colonial leaders agreed to send out a joint expedition against the Indians. In September, under siege in their new habitation, five Susquehannock leaders were taken prisoner, during a parley, and executed, despite previous guarantees for their safety. The governor and council at St Mary's laid responsibility for the incident on the shoulders of John Washington, the commander of the militia from Virginia. Confounding their enemies, after a siege of six weeks, during the night the survivors slipped through a cordon of militia, seeking safety in the woods.[137]

135 William Hand Browne (ed.), *Proceedings and Acts of the General Assembly of Maryland April 1666–June 1676* (Maryland Historical Society, 2, 1884), pp. 428–9.

136 Ibid., pp. 428–30; Jennings, 'Glory, Death, and Transfiguration', pp. 33–4; Hatfield, *Atlantic Virginia*, pp. 198–200.

137 Proceedings were initiated against the leader of the Maryland militia for his role in the killing of the Indian leaders, Browne (ed.), *Proceedings of the Assembly of Maryland 1666–1676*, pp. 483–6, 493–494, 500–4; Browne (ed.), *Proceedings of the Council of Maryland 1671–81*, pp. 49, 56–7; *CSPC, 1675–6*, pp. 365–6; Andrews (ed.), *Narratives*, pp. 19–20, 107; Rice, *Nature & History*, pp. 145–8.

The escape of the Susquehannocks signalled the start of a bitter and confused conflict which was aggravated by intercolonial rivalry and diplomacy. Seeking to act as a broker for a wider settlement with the Indians, the new governor of New York, Edmund Andros, offered sanctuary to the Susquehannocks. The leaders of the northern colony were concerned to defend their strategic and commercial interests against French competition and native hostility. In August 1676 the governor at St Mary's was informed that, through the mediation of Andros, a group of Susquehannocks had reached an agreement with the Iroquois. But they also requested the return of peace and trade with Maryland.[138] The dispersal of their former allies left the colony's leaders in the difficult position of maintaining a costly war while searching for a diplomatic solution. In April 1677 the governor sent a mission to New York, under Henry Coursey, who also represented Virginia, to make peace with the Indians.[139] As he travelled north, along the Delaware River he met Jacob Clausen, who reported the scattering of the Susquehannocks. One group of eight warriors had recently fled to the Senecas. A larger party of about 30, who were 'hunting to make a present' for the governor, had been captured by other Iroquois.[140] In New York, Andros was encouraging the survivors to settle with the Mohawks, as reinforcements against the French.

The agreement that Coursey and other colonial delegates reached with Indian leaders at a conference in July 1677 was a striking, if flawed, achievement. Responding to native protocol and ritual, the colonists agreed that the past was buried and forgotten. Representatives at the meeting acknowledged a covenant of peace so strong that 'the very thunder ... would not break it asunder'.[141] Coursey received gifts of beaver and elk skins, and belts of wampum, confirming the words of native speakers. But the Susquehannocks, who were not covered by the treaty, remained free to continue their conflict with the colonists and their native allies. Supported by the Senecas they continued to raid parts of the upper Bay. They were reportedly of 'such a

[138] Browne (ed.), *Proceedings of the Council of Maryland 1671–81*, pp. 120–1; Browne (ed.), *Proceedings of the Council of Maryland 1667–87/8*, pp. 152–4; *CSPC, 1677–80*, pp. 7–8; Hatfield, *Atlantic Virginia*, pp. 201–4.

[139] Hinderaker, 'Diplomacy Between Britons and Native Americans', in Bowen et al. (eds.), *Britain's Oceanic Empire*, pp. 229–32; Browne (ed.), *Proceedings of the Council of Maryland 1671–81*, pp. 246–8, 251–2; Webb, *1676*, pp. 377, 382–91.

[140] Browne (ed.), *Proceedings of the Council of Maryland 1671–81*, pp. 246–7; Jennings, 'Jacob Young', pp. 352–3; Kruer, 'Bloody Minds and Peoples Undone', pp. 420–1, 425 on the dispersal.

[141] Browne (ed.), *Proceedings of the Council of Maryland 1671–81*, p. 65; Richard L. Haan, 'Covenant and Consensus: Iroquois and English, 1676–1760', in Richter and Merrell (eds.), *Beyond the Covenant Chain*, pp. 43–4; Oberg, *Dominion and Civility*, p. 215.

turbulent bloody mind that they will never cease doeinge mischief both to the English & Pascattoway Indians soe long as a man of them is left alive'.[142] Under the pressure of continued raiding, the Indian trade seemed to be in terminal decline. In 1678 Baltimore informed the Committee of Trade and Plantations that tobacco was the colony's main product and export, except for 'some few skins of Beasts sometimes brought from the Indian Neighbours which are not considerable'.[143]

Unintentionally, these conditions encouraged the commercial ambitions of Pennsylvania, established by William Penn as a refuge for Quakers, who faced intense persecution in England. Penn's charter of 1681, which was probably issued to offset a long-standing royal debt to his father, included land in the Delaware ranging as far as the head of Chesapeake Bay. Because of its strategic and commercial value, the region was a focal point for competing claims between Maryland and New York, as well as native groups including the Lenapes, survivors of the Susquehannocks and Iroquois. Penn tried to mollify the former while relying on diplomacy and trade to deal with the latter. Opposition from Baltimore's agents in London, who expressed concern at the boundary of the colony, and demanded a prohibition on the trade in arms and ammunition, met with little success.[144]

Penn's interest in the Indian trade was manifest in his attention to commercial regulation. Drawing on past practice, he acknowledged the tendency of 'Planters to Overreach the poore Natives of the Country in Trade' by the provision of commodities of little value.[145] To prevent such abuse, all trade in goods for export was to be restricted to a public market. It was a well-intentioned, if impractical gesture, which also led him to decline a tempting

[142] Browne (ed.), *Proceedings of the Council of Maryland 1671–81*, pp. 240, 242 for a warning that if the colony did not supply them with powder and shot, they would be forced to make bows and arrows, 'wherein for want of practice they have not that experience as formerly'. Rice, *Tales from a Revolution*, pp. 141–6; Eric Hinderaker, *Elusive Empires: Constructing Colonialism in the Ohio Valley, 1673–1800* (Cambridge, 1997), pp. 12–3, 25.

[143] Browne (ed.), *Proceedings of the Council of Maryland 1667–87/88*, p. 266; Gloria L. Main, *Tobacco Colony: Life in Early Maryland, 1650–1720* (Princeton, 1982), pp. 87–95 *passim*. Nor was there much immediate interest in commercial activity beyond the frontier. Rice, *Nature & History*, pp. 174–83 for the slow expansion inland from Maryland.

[144] Richard S. Dunn and Mary Maples Dunn (eds.), *The Papers of William Penn*, 5 vols. (Philadelphia, 1981–7), 2, pp. 33, 43, 85–7, 261; Andrew R. Murphy, *William Penn: A Life* (Oxford, 2013), pp. 137–40. At this time the dispersal of the Susquehannocks seems to have left the lower Susquehanna Valley virtually empty of native people, though small groups of the former and some Senecas returned c. 1690. They became known to the colonists as Conestoga Indians, Hinderaker, *Elusive Empires*, pp. 25–6.

[145] Dunn and Dunn (eds.), *Papers of Penn*, 2, p. 99.

offer for the farm of the Indian trade. The proposal, for a company of traders to enjoy monopoly rights within a region spanning the Susquehanna and Delaware Rivers, included a payment of £6,000 and a rent of 2½%, but Penn was unwilling to 'defile what came to me clean'.[146] Nonetheless he agreed to the establishment of a Free Society of Traders, made up of London Quaker merchants, with James Claypoole as its treasurer, which was empowered to develop the fur trade along the rivers. Before leaving England, he wrote to the 'Emperor of Canada' in an attempt to promote commercial expansion in the north.[147]

Following his arrival in the colony, in October 1682, Penn took control of the purchase of land from native groups, alongside promoting and regulating commerce. He banned the sale of alcohol to Indians because of its dangerous and disruptive consequences. In July 1683 he informed Robert Spencer, second earl of Sunderland, one of his leading political supporters in London, that the Indians were 'an extraordinary people', but 'the Dutch, Sweeds & English learn'd them drunkenness in which condition they kill or burn one another'.[148] The problem was selective, but corrosive. Although Penn noted that many old and some younger men avoided spirits, within a year the ban was repealed in response to a petition from native leaders. Yet commercial activity in the colony was rapidly overshadowed by rivalry with Maryland and New York. Within a few years the dispute with Baltimore, concerning the lower counties of Pennsylvania, seemed to have irredeemably damaged the prospect of neighbourly relations. Claiming that 'American rights are so wilde, that the labourers is 99 parts of the 100 of any such title', Penn purchased large tracts of native territory with an array of goods, including guns, cloth and clothing, axes, knives and fish hooks, as well as beads and wampum.[149] While his attempt to buy land in the upper Susquehanna Valley from the Iroquois was blocked by the governor of New York, who was determined to protect the colony's fur trade at Albany, the purchase of territory farther south inflamed relations with Baltimore. Faced with resistance and rebellion from non-Quaker residents in the lower counties, in August 1684 Penn returned to England to defend his colonial rights. With the Free Society of Traders nearly moribund, the fur trade was taken over by independent traders, including Claypoole who migrated to the colony in October 1683. It subsequently came under the effective control of James Logan, Penn's colonial secretary and agent.[150]

146 Ibid., pp. 110–11.

147 Ibid., p. 261.

148 Ibid., p. 417.

149 Ibid., pp. 262–3, 345, 381–437.

150 Ibid., pp. 248, 422–5, 441, 467–521 *passim*; Gary B. Nash, 'The Free Society of Traders and the Early Politics of Pennsylvania', *Pennsylvania Magazine of History and Biography*, 89 (1965), pp. 158–60; Murphy, *Penn*, pp. 157–69, 179–80; Hinderaker,

Penn's prolonged absence coincided with the revival of anti-Catholicism in England, the transatlantic reverberations of which contributed to renewed turmoil in Maryland. Pent-up Protestant resentment compounded with wider economic and political grievances led to the overthrow of Baltimore in 1689 and the end of proprietary rule. In these circumstances colonial interest in the Indian trade ebbed away. The beneficiaries seem to have been traders in the colony's new neighbour. But the early growth of interethnic trade in Pennsylvania was modest and marked by considerable fluctuations. Colonial traders were also confronted with declining supplies of fur-bearing animals, and the disappearance of Indian groups who began migrating westwards during the 1720s.[151]

As this chapter demonstrates, during a period of rapid and wide-ranging change, after the 1650s the fur trade followed different paths in the Bay colonies. Exploration and expansion in Virginia were paralleled by conflict and contraction in Maryland. But the revival in the volume of exports of fur from Virginia mainly originated from inland groups, some of whom were far removed from the colony. As such the overland trade was vulnerable to native rivalries and hostility, as well as to competition with traders based in Carolina. During the 1680s it was also attracting the attention of French adventurers, 'latelie seated at the back of Virginia', who 'will in a short time be absolute Masters of the Beaver trade'.[152] Despite its prospects, the challenges of inland commerce provided little incentive for a community of planters attached to the cultivation of tobacco. According to the authors of *The Present State of Virginia* of 1697, there 'might be a vast *Indian* Trade for Skins and Furrs carried on there,' but because 'tobacco swallows up all other Things, everything else is neglected'.[153] In Maryland, which followed a similar economic trajectory, expectations for the growth of trade with the Susquehannocks faltered in the

Elusive Empires, p. 22; James H. Merrell, *Into the American Woods: Negotiators on the Pennsylvania Frontier* (New York, 1999), pp. 32, 62–3, 83–7, 118–20; Arthur L. Jensen, *The Maritime Commerce of Colonial Philadelphia* (Madison, 1963), pp. 7, 90.

151 Hinderaker, *Elusive Empires*, pp. 20–5, 28–45; Richter, *Long-House*, p. 244; Jane T. Merritt, *At the Crossroads: Indians and Empires on a Mid-Atlantic Frontier, 1700–1763* (Chapel Hill, 2003), pp. 24–9, 50–67.

152 Alvord and Bidgood, *First Explorations*, pp. 194–5; Hinderaker, *Elusive Empires*, pp. 9–10, 13, 34–5; Rice, *Nature & History*, pp. 181–2 on French and a small number of colonial traders mainly interested in deer skins; Hornsby, *British Atlantic, American Frontier*, pp. 208–9.

153 Hartwell et al., *Present State of Virginia*, p. 7. The claim was repeated by Blair in a paper for John Locke, with a proviso, 'if it were reduced into Rules under a Company', Michael G. Kammen (ed.), 'Virginia at the Close of the Seventeenth Century: An Appraisal by James Blair and John Locke', *VMHB*, 74 (1966), p. 154; Harrison, 'Western Explorations', pp. 329–35 for limited interest in a proposal for a fur trading venture put forward by Cadwallader Jones in 1699.

face of competition with the Dutch, conflict with the Iroquois, and rivalry with Pennsylvania.[154] The decline of commercial activity within the Bay reinforced a loss of interest among colonial communities in native groups who were faced with an unending struggle against disease and dislocation. The implications were noted by John Banister in 1679, who regretted the collapse of interethnic commerce because it bound together natives and newcomers.[155] By the late seventeenth century those bonds were stretched to breaking point.

154 Rice, *Nature & History*, pp. 161–73 for the decline and re-location of Potomac River Indian groups.

155 Ewen and Ewen, *Banister*, p. 42; Merrell, *The Indians' New World*, pp. 46, 66; James H. Merrell, '"Their Very Bones Shall Fight": The Catawba-Iroquois Wars', in Richter and Merrell (eds.), *Beyond the Covenant Chain*, pp. 116–18 on the threat of Iroquoian raiding. Rice, *Tales from a Revolution*, pp. 191–2, 212 for the native experience. In 1691 the assembly in Virginia passed legislation banning marriages between whites and non-whites, Rountree and Turner, *Before and After Jamestown*, p. 169.

Chapter 6

Trade, Consumption and Industry: Transatlantic Constraints on the Bay Trade

In November 1700 the Board of Trade in London received an alarming report that the fur trade of New York and Boston had 'sunk to little or nothing, and the market is so low for beaver in England that 'tis scarce worth the transporting'.[1] The author, Richard Coote, first earl of Bellomont, governor of the province of New York, was concerned at the wider consequences of the fall in the price of beaver skins, from fourteen to five shillings per pound, in the London market. While the declining value of beaver discouraged the Iroquois, the main suppliers of fur to the colony, it also reduced the incentive for distant native groups to trade with the English. Playing on the threat from the French in Canada, Bellomont argued that New York was a frontier province where relations with the Indians had to be managed in the interests of the monarchy. Ignoring the situation at Boston, he requested the removal of customs duties on fur in New York and England. Early the following year, he urged the board to secure parliamentary support to encourage the fur trade. Drawing on the example of France, he appealed for legislation requiring all hatters to use a certain amount of beaver wool in the manufacture of headwear. Such intervention would 'help the consumption of Beaver which at present is grown almost out of use in England, since Carolina hats have been so much and Beaver hats so little in fashion'.[2] Although demand for the latter revived, Bellomont's concerns illuminate the state of the transatlantic fur trade at the close of the seventeenth century. Colonial networks on which commerce depended seemed to be under threat, not least as a result of changes in the supply of raw material. This included the opening up of a vast

1 *Documents of New York*, 4, p. 789; Cathy Matson, *Merchants and Empire: Trading in Colonial New York* (Baltimore, 1998), p. 96. Steele, *The English Atlantic*, pp. 239–40 for Bellomont's letter writing.

2 *Documents of New York*, 4, pp. 789, 834; Thomas Elliot Norton, *The Fur Trade in Colonial New York 1686–1776* (Madison, 1974), pp. 22–3, 100. Carolina hats were made of deer skins. The damage to the fur trade of New York and New England by French privateering was noted by Daniel Defoe in *A Review of the Affairs of France*, vol. 22, 20 May 1704, pp. 131–7. For the impact of the falling price of beaver during the 1730s, see Richter, *Facing East from Indian Country*, pp. 178–9.

commercial zone awarded to the Hudson's Bay Company in 1670. As studies of the company demonstrate, the rapid growth of the northern fur trade, based on seemingly limitless supplies of thicker and more valuable pelts, created problems in the metropolitan market, which was one of the sources of the governor's alarm.[3] But an over-supply of beaver skins also exposed the deep vulnerability of the Chesapeake Bay trade to intercolonial competition. Despite an unexpected recovery in the export of fur from Virginia during the 1670s, the development of the transatlantic market raised a question over its sustainability, which this chapter explores through the connections between trade, consumption, and industry.

Trade and traders

The fur trade formed part of an arc of commerce, communication and consumption that spanned the Atlantic. The assembly of a succession of discrete stages was initiated by native hunting and the preparation of skins for colonial traders, followed by their export. In London they were sold or auctioned to furriers, who supplied feltmakers with the raw material for the manufacture of headwear. Fur accumulated value as it moved between these markets. But the increasing volume of trade during the later seventeenth century presented challenges for fur trading enterprise across the eastern seaboard of North America. Coinciding with problems in the feltmaking industry, from a transatlantic perspective such conditions created a bottleneck in the development of the business, leaving colonial traders, and officials like Bellomont, struggling to deal with the consequences of falling prices.

Within the Chesapeake, the fur trade was an adjunct to the cultivation of tobacco. By the 1640s the collapse of joint stock ventures in both colonies left interethnic commerce in the hands of varying numbers of independent traders. In many cases they were frontier farmers or planters who were willing to explore the economic potential of the region beyond. As such, their commercial activities lacked the specialism or coherence of the northern trades, particularly in Hudson's Bay. With limited resources they created an irregular and loosely woven pattern of small-scale, improvised enterprise, which was in theory subject to colonial regulation. There were similarities, as well as differences, in the structure and organization of ventures across these widely scattered commercial areas. Operating during distinct trading seasons, traders collected skins from native suppliers, which required careful handling to retain their quality. Bound or bundled together, they were probably

3 For example, Michael Wagner, *The English Chartered Trading Companies, 1688–1763: Guns, Money and Lawyers* (New York, 2018), pp. 48–9; E.E. Rich, 'Russia and the Colonial Fur Trade', *Economic History Review*, 7 (1955), pp. 319–25; Rich, *Hudson's Bay Company*, 1, pp. 40–6.

packaged for protection against damp and insects. Trading agents who were supplied with credit by specialist traders in New England, such as John Pynchon of Springfield in Connecticut, seem to have emerged in the Bay during the 1640s.[4] They were employed in the emerging, long-distance, inland trade promoted by adventurers like William Byrd, though evidence for their organization is scant. As in New York, some colonial traders were not directly involved in the shipment of furs to England. Instead they appear to have exchanged skins for trading goods and provisions, or to pay off debts, with local merchants, factors and visiting ship masters. By these means small or modest parcels of beaver and other furs were acquired for London merchants, including Micajah Perry, one of the preeminent tobacco traders in the city.[5]

The lack of ports in the Bay meant that furs, like tobacco, were stored in warehouses with access to the rivers along which visiting vessels traded. Both commodities required careful packing and stowage for shipping across the Atlantic. The quality of pelts, some of which may have retained particles of blood and fat, exposed them to the risk of decay or bacterial infection on long sea voyages. Consignments of beaver skins were usually packed in hogsheads and stored in the hold. If need arose, they were stowed in other places. Two Dutch travellers, returning from Boston to London in 1680, discovered a large parcel of skins in the powder room. It also contained a substantial amount of dry fish which began to rot after the sea burst in during a blustery squall. The stench in the adjacent gunner's room was such that the Dutchmen 'could hardly stay there day or night'.[6] Although they initially blamed it on a wounded and incapacitated passenger, who was unable to care for himself, once the source was discovered, the fish were brought up on the deck to be dried or thrown overboard.[7] A number of new cloaks were spoiled and several gloves had to be washed in fresh water, but the damage to the fur, if any, went unrecorded.

Although the transatlantic trade was disrupted by the vagaries of weather and war, it developed in an open and unregulated manner. Such conditions provided a fertile environment for the growth of intense rivalry, particularly with the Dutch. Exploiting opportunities presented by the civil war, during the 1640s they made deep commercial inroads in the Bay. In response, the republican regime passed a Navigation Act in 1651, for commercial control and regulation, aimed at excluding Dutch traders and shippers from Anglo-American

4 Ruth A. Mcintyre, 'John Pynchon and the New England Fur Trade, 1652–1676', https://www.colonialsociety.org/node/814#rch04, pp. 8–9; Moloney, *Fur Trade in New England*, pp. 49–64; Hinderaker and Mancall, *At the Edge of Empire*, pp. 39–40.

5 Norton, *Fur Trade*, pp. 83–4; Jacob M. Price, *Perry of London: A Family and a Firm on the Seaborne Frontier, 1615–1753* (Cambridge, Mass., 1992), pp. 47–8, 105.

6 Jasper Dankers and Peter Sluyter, *Journal of a Voyage to New York in 1679–80*, ed. Henry C. Murphy (Brooklyn, 1867, repr. 1966), pp. 403–4.

7 Ibid., p. 404.

trade. Building on previous piecemeal initiatives, the act was too ambitious and impossible to enforce, even among colonial leaders who were responsible for its implementation. In December 1653, for example, William Claiborne and others successfully petitioned for the restitution of tobacco laden aboard a Dutch ship taken as prize, despite the imposition by the colony's assembly of a customs duty of ten shillings for each hogshead of such shipments.[8] The Navigation Act was renewed, in modified form, by the restored monarchy in 1660. Subsequent legislation strengthened its provisions, creating a regulatory framework for the growth of transatlantic commerce.[9]

This emerging navigation system was partly designed to protect the colonial trades with North America and the Caribbean. It specified a variety of commodities which had to be shipped to England, and in vessels of English or colonial origin. These enumerated goods included tobacco, sugar, cotton wool and dyes. The legislation allowed for the re-export of such products, including the return of a proportion of customs duties in the form of a drawback. Beaver skins were not included among the enumerated commodities. Consequently, they could still be exported from the colonies direct to other European ports. By these means, despite the English takeover of New Netherland, the Dutch retained a significant stake in the fur trade of New York, which they had developed at Albany. In some years exports of fur to Amsterdam ranged between 20,000 and 30,000 skins.[10] There was little incentive for the Dutch to maintain an interest in the trade farther south, but shipments from the Bay may have provided a cover for smuggling tobacco into the Netherlands. Lacking sufficient naval and administrative resources until the early eighteenth century, the English state was unable to prevent this illicit trade. It was probably small scale and occasional in character, particularly given the widespread cooperation of merchants and shippers based on the growing efficiency of English transatlantic enterprise. As in the past, however, commercial regulation was threatened by war. Anglo-French conflict during the 1690s, accompanied by an upsurge in piracy, severely disrupted overseas commerce in general, while putting the system under intense pressure. Metropolitan control was extended with legislation to limit the development of manufacturing in the colonies, introduced at the end of the seventeenth century, and with the subsequent

[8] *CSPC, 1575–1660*, p. 395; Billings (ed.), 'Some Acts not in Hening's *Statutes*', pp. 26, 73–4.

[9] Ralph Davis, *English Overseas Trade 1500–1700* (London, 1973), pp. 29, 35–7, 48–9; Charles Wilson, *England's Apprenticeship 1603–1763* (Harlow, 2nd edition, 1984), pp. 61–2, 135–6, 163–4, 168–9; Bliss, *Revolution and Empire*, pp. 58–9, 109–12.

[10] Carlos and Lewis, *Commerce by a Frozen Sea*, p. 27.

inclusion of beaver skins among the enumerated commodities during the early 1720s, in an attempt to support hat-makers.[11]

The figures in Table 1 provide a snapshot of the fur trade from the Bay, based on the surviving customs records for London during the 1670s.[12] At this time the capital dominated the transatlantic trades, while also acting as the centre of the English fur market and the feltmaking industry. Among the provincial ports only Bristol was periodically involved in the trade, but imports were limited in volume and variety, and in some years amounted to little, as Table 2 indicates. Small quantities of pelts may have been illicitly landed in Scottish and Irish ports, and shipped to the Netherlands, but the bulk of fur from the Bay was destined for London.[13]

The customs records furnish striking evidence for the mixed fortunes of fur trading enterprise during the later seventeenth century. Collectively they confirm the decline of the trade in the upper Bay, as reflected in the virtual collapse of exports from Maryland, and its recovery in Virginia. In 1677 an assorted shipment of furs from Maryland included beaver skins, but they amounted to fewer than 450 in total. Estimates for exports from the colony during the late 1690s, based on the collection of a small duty, indicate that the volume of trade remained low. It was mainly made up of the skins of small fur-bearing fauna, with annual shipments of fewer than 100 beaver skins, complemented by larger numbers of mink, muskrat and raccoon.[14] Most of these exports came from colonial settlements along the Eastern Shore, where small farmers supplemented their income with occasional hunting. Confronted by native hostility and dislocation, and the rival claims of Pennsylvania to the Delaware and Susquehanna Rivers, there was little interest among colonists in prospecting new sources of supply. According to a report from the governor to

[11] Ibid., pp. 26–7; smuggling by the Dutch persisted during the 1660s and 1670s, but was over by the 1690s, Enthoven and Klooster, 'The Rise and Fall of the Virginia-Dutch Connection', pp. 111–4; Koot, *Empire at the Periphery*, pp. 89, 112–22, 185–7; Zahedieh, *The Capital and the Colonies*, pp. 6–7, 38–41, 179–8, 280–1; Bliss, *Revolution and Empire*, p. 222; *CSPC, 1700*, pp. 301–2, 327–28 for complaints of pirates infesting the coast of Virginia.

[12] See Appendix 1, p. 253.

[13] For table 2 see Appendix 1, p. 254; Zahedieh, *The Capital and the Colonies*, pp. 193–4; Bristol interest in the trade can be detected in instructions, of August 1659, for a factor to sell commodities 'for good beaver and sound Virginia Tobacco', Patrick McGrath (ed.), *Merchants and Merchandise in Seventeenth-Century Bristol* (Bristol Record Society, 19, 1955), p. 255. Shipments into other ports were irregular and very small. During 1688 the *Resolution* of Whitehaven landed tobacco and 21 beaver, 99 deer, 60 cat and 8 otter skins, in its home port, TNA E190/1448/8.

[14] Margaret Shove Morriss, *Colonial Trade of Maryland 1689–1715* (Baltimore, 1914), pp. 12–14; Rountree and Davidson, *Eastern Shore Indians*, p. 121.

the Board of Trade, they were too fearful of the western Indians to establish commercial contact with them.[15]

Although the recovery of the trade in Virginia is difficult to date with precision, it was linked to the development of new sources of supply with inland Indian groups who were keen to acquire European goods at first hand. Indirectly the figures in Table 1 may therefore reflect a decline in the beaver population within settled areas of the colony. In his *History of Virginia* of 1705, Beverley reported the presence of beaver, otter, muskrat and mink in marshy grounds and swamps, but noted, with qualification, that the 'Inner Lands want these Benefits, (which, however, no Pond or Slash is without)'.[16] Moreover, while the Indians in the colony, who were 'almost wasted', continued to employ 'many pretty Inventions, to discover and come up to the Deer, Turkeys and other Game undiscern'd', they were forced to go 'Hunting into the Out-lands to do so'.[17]

In these circumstances most of the beaver skins shipped into London during 1672, as recorded in Table 1, originated from the interior, beyond the range of colonial settlement. The evidence also suggests that this trade was growing, at least until 1675, and included deer skins and a variety of other furs, especially muskrat, raccoon, fox and otter. Thereafter it was thrown into disarray by the political disturbances associated with Bacon's rebellion. Partly provoked by animosity against the allegedly self-interested control of the fur trade by the governor, the insurrection led to attacks on Indian traders and middlemen, which severely disrupted the supply of furs. Imports into London of beaver skins and most other types of pelt fell by more than half, and remained at this level at least until 1680, after which the volume of trade began to recover.[18]

The commercial recovery in Virginia needs to be set within a wider context. While the volume and variety of trade during the early 1670s compared very favourably with the 1620s and 1630s, across the intervening period the colony's share of the transatlantic fur trade fell. This relative decline was due to the acquisition or development of new trading regions, including New York and Carolina, covering areas that traders from the Chesapeake colonies were seeking to exploit. Although the New York fur trade experienced difficulty during some of these years, annual exports of beaver skins still ranged between 9,000 and 14,000. The trade of Carolina was smaller, but growing in volume. During 1676 shipments of beaver skins amounted to nearly 900. Two years later they had increased to about 1,500. At the same time, the fur trade of New

15 Morriss, *Colonial Trade of Maryland*, p. 14.

16 Beverley, *History of Virginia*, p. 153.

17 Ibid., pp. 155–6, 232.

18 TNA, E190/90/1. There were occasional years during the early eighteenth century when there was a surge in exports based on inland supplies, see Crane, *Southern Frontier*, p. 328.

England also showed signs of growth, possibly as a result of the re-direction of pelts from New York. Between 1672 and 1676 exports of beaver skins ranged from 4,000 to nearly 19,000. The volume of trade remained high in 1677 and 1678, when 12,000 and 16,500 skins were shipped to London.[19] Above all, the emergence of the rich Canadian trade under the auspices of the Hudson's Bay Company inaugurated a new phase in the transatlantic trade. By 1700 more than 40,000 beaver skins were imported into London, most of which were thicker quality material.[20] With access to a vast region of supply, the scale of the Company's operations re-shaped the fur market in London, with unfavourable consequences for rival traders and suppliers.

Few of the merchants involved in the transatlantic fur trade with the Bay were specialists. The customs accounts for the 1670s reveal that shipments of pelts were concentrated in the hands of five or six traders, whose interests varied from year to year. In 1672, 21 merchants imported fur into London from the Chesapeake. The volume of individual shipments ranged from large consignments for George Richards, amounting to 680 beaver skins, 178 wild cat and 68 otter skins, to small parcels of 12 beaver, 39 raccoon and seven otter skins for John Tilsley. A small group, including Thomas Grindon, Thomas and John Harding, William Renshawe and George Richards, accounted for 83% of beaver and 79% of deer skin imports. A similar pattern prevailed for other types of skins, though the traders were not always from this group and the amounts were generally smaller.[21]

Although more merchants were involved in the trade during succeeding years, it continued to be dominated by a small number of shippers. In 1676, from a total of 48, Robert Cooe, John Ede, John Gardner, Thomas Grindon and Richard Yeardley accounted for 1,975 beaver and 5,896 deer skins, representing 69% and 75% of the annual total for each. Within this group Yeardley imported 1,247 beaver and 1,720 deer skins, while Cooe shipped 230 beaver and 2,480 deer skins. A larger number of merchants accounted for small consignments of assorted furs and skins. Micajah Perry imported 139 deer, 46 muskrat, 11 beaver, four black bear, three wild cat and three otter skins. Despite some variation in the number of merchants, in 1680 the trade remained concentrated in a small number of hands, though less so than in preceding years. Out of a total of 29 traders, Thomas Grindon, George Richards, Robert Sole and Samuel Story were responsible for the import of 822 beaver and 2,952 deer skins, or 57% and 70% of the annual totals. Richards also imported 304 fox

19 TNA, E190/56/1; 190/64/1; 190/68/1; 190/75/1; Matson, *Merchants and Empire*, pp. 95–6; Ramsey, *The Yamasee War*, pp. 61–3 for the changing Indian trade in Carolina.

20 Rich, *Hudson's Bay Company*, 1, pp. 45–6, 56 231; Corner, 'The Tyranny of Fashion', pp. 154–5; Elizabeth Ewing, *Fur in Dress* (London, 1981), pp. 67–8.

21 TNA, E190/56/1. Isa Savidge was the other member of this group.

and 356 raccoon skins, accounting for 45% and 62% of total shipments for these types of peltry.[22]

These characteristics indicate that the interests of merchants in the fur trade were either modest or small-scale, irregular and often marginal to the shipment of tobacco.[23] Unusually, Giles Blizard, a fur trader of Maryland, claimed to have successfully developed the manufacture of beaver hats and castors in the province, suggesting the local integration of commerce and manufacturing.[24] But colonial traders, including Thomas Grindon, who regularly shipped significant quantities of skins during the 1670s, operated within the context of a developing plantation culture. A cousin of William Byrd, and one of his suppliers of furs, Grindon was described as a merchant in 1677, though he also possessed a substantial landholding in Charles City County.[25] Structurally, the revival of the fur trade in Virginia seemed to rest on fragile foundations. It was ill-suited to face the buffeting of falling prices and an over-stocked and competitive market in London.

The market, fashion and consumption

The problem of over-supply was compounded with the nature of the metropolitan fur market. Apart from small clothing accessories, such as muffs and gloves, this was tied to demand for headwear. The beaver retained its appeal among wealthy and fashionable consumers during the second half of the seventeenth century. Within a changing clothing regime, it remained an important vehicle for the expression of taste. Despite the growing use of periwigs, in terms of function and form the beaver hat remained an important part of the wardrobes of the wealthy elite. Its quality allowed for accommodation to individual choice or creativity, spanning a wider market of consumers. In June 1659, for example, Sir Edward Hyde, a leading royalist during the civil war, ordered a 'good English beaver hat' from his refuge in the Netherlands.[26] Nearly thirty years later John Locke, the political philosopher, living in exile in Rotterdam, requested a 'good beaver hat made as high as the fashion will

22 TNA, E190/64/1; 190/68/1; 190/90/1.

23 On tobacco see Jacob M. Price and Paul G.E. Clemens, 'A Revolution of Scale in Overseas Trade: British Firms in the Chesapeake Trade, 1675–1775', *Journal of Economic History*, 47 (1987), pp. 1–43.

24 Browne (ed.), *Proceedings of the Council of Maryland 1667–87/8*, pp. 471–2.

25 TNA, CO 5/1371, ff. 177–7v. Or Grendon. His wife, Sarah, provoked Berkeley's anger while he was away, speaking indiscretely during Bacon's rebellion when she showed a 'great deale of Feare and a great deale of Folly' according to the report by the commissioners into the colony's grievances.

26 Rev. O. Ogle et al. (eds.), *Calendar of Clarendon State Papers*, 5 vols. (Oxford, 1872–1970), 4, p. 226. On wigs see Alice Morse Earle, *Two Centuries of Costume in America 1620–1820*, 2 vols. (New York, 1903, repr. 1970), 1, pp. 323–48.

bear' from friends in London.[27] Within a divided society, headwear possessed a powerful symbolic value while furnishing an essential prop for a developing culture of civility and politeness in which a coherent ensemble of dress and bodily carriage was seen as a reflection of character.

The restoration of the monarchy in 1660 prompted the revival of the market for fur hats. Fashionable presentation was curtailed by the civil wars and the establishment of a republican regime. The defeat of the royalists led to the decline of a cavalier lifestyle, for which the broad-brimmed beaver was emblematic. At the same time the closure of the theatres and the decline of ceremony and entertainment reduced the opportunities for public display, despite the emergence of a shadow court under the protectorate of Oliver Cromwell. The unfavourable environment included industrial disorganization. The Beavermakers' Company, which had acquired control of the new industry during the 1630s, was a casualty of the pre-war political crisis. Hat making survived under the regulation of the Feltmakers' Company, but it was forced to adapt to a more sober and smaller metropolitan market and scattered fashionable consumers among provincial landowners and exiled royalists.[28]

Against this background, the restoration paved the way for the return of a fashionable courtly culture, though the reconstitution of monarchy occurred in an ambiguous and increasingly divisive environment. Its potential appeal was illuminated by the coronation of Charles II in April 1661, commemorated in print by John Ogilby, with engravings by Wenceslaus Hollar. As depicted by the latter, the lengthy procession bore the appearance of a fashion parade. Mounted ranks of knights, officials and aristocrats wore high-crowned and broad-brimmed hats, adorned with feathers, demonstrating visual links to the reign of Charles I.[29] It was political theatre on a grand scale, a dazzling display of the cultural power of restored monarchy, and a timely reminder of the role of the royal court as a centre for fashionable and conspicuous consumption. Among the spectators, Samuel Pepys and his companions were overcome by the glorious and sumptuous parade, though the day ended with unsettling storms and drunkenness.[30]

[27] Bridget Clarke, 'The Wider World of Locke's Landlady Rasby Smithsby', *Locke Studies*, 16 (2016), pp. 195–213 at https://doi.org/10.5206/ls.2016.642.

[28] Breward, *Culture of Fashion*, pp. 77, 82–3; Ashelford, *The Art of Dress*, p. 85; Auslander, *Cultural Revolutions*, pp. 59–64 argues for a puritan clothing code during the 1640s; Peck, *Consuming Splendor*, pp. 230–76 claims that luxury consumption was not curtailed during these years.

[29] John Ogilby, *The Entertainment of His Most Excellent Majestie Charles II* (London, 1662); Kevin Sharpe, *Rebranding Rule: The Restoration and Revolution Monarchy, 1660–1714* (New Haven, 2013), pp. 49, 93, 103–4, 153–60.

[30] Robert Latham and William Matthews (eds.), *The Diary of Samuel Pepys*, 11 vols. (London, 1970–83), 2, pp. 81–4, 87–8.

Headwear continued to serve a variety of practical, personal and public purposes. Hat honour, which acquired greater formality after the 1590s, was widely accepted as a marker of status and respect. It assumed different forms depending on context and gender. Men doffed headwear to acknowledge social superiors, while women retained theirs as a sign of subordination. Advice and conduct books indicate that the use of gesture and etiquette included room for personal expression, though it required a respectful and graceful manner. However, it also provided an opportunity for irreverence, disrespect and dissent. In extreme cases religious radicals refused to doff their hats to bishops or to remove them in church. Their number increased during the 1640s and 1650s, with the growth of radicalism and religious sects. As Charles I was conducted to and from his trial in Westminster during 1649, he faced spectators who retained their hats, while soldiers railed at those who attempted to remove them. Later in the year Gerard Winstanley and Robert Everard, the leaders of a group labelled True Levellers or Diggers, refused to remove their hats when they met the general of the army, claiming that 'hee was but their fellow Creature'.[31] For similar reasons, if expressed in a different light, the Quakers, who grew rapidly during the 1650s under the leadership of George Fox and others, also denied hat honour. But the issue of removing or retaining headwear during worship subsequently became a deeply divisive issue within the movement.[32]

Given its cultural significance the use of headwear was a sensitive barometer of concern about personal conduct and character. Under a far from universally popular royal regime, it may have served a wider function, representing a reassuring return to a traditional hierarchy. Consequently, the Quakers, identified as fanatics by Anglicans and Royalists, faced opprobrium, legal proceedings or physical assault for failing to remove their hats. In 1661 John Boyer of Leicester, who refused to doff his hat to Lord Gray, was cudgelled so severely by a servant, that he lost his sight and shortly after died.[33] A

31 *The Declaration and Standard of the Levellers of England* (London, 1649), p. 3; Krista J. Kesselring, 'Gender, the Hat, and Quaker Universalism in the Wake of the English Revolution', *The Seventeenth Century*, 26 (2011), p. 302; Corfield, 'Dress for Deference and Dissent', pp. 64–70; Thomas, *Pursuit of Civility*, pp. 36–7, 321–2; John Rees, *The Leveller Revolution: Radical Political Organisation in England, 1640–1650* (London, 2016), pp. 270–310 for a recent treatment of the changing fortunes of the radicals.

32 Kesselring, 'Gender, the Hat, and Quaker Universalism', pp. 299–302; Barry Reay, *The Quakers and the English Revolution* (London, 1985), pp. 44, 53, 58 which notes the objection to titles.

33 Joseph Besse, *A Collection of the Sufferings of the People Called Quakers*, 2 vols. (London, 1753), 1, pp. 332, 347, 366–7, 388, 408; Reay, *The Quakers and the English Revolution*, pp. 95–100 for fears. Tim Harris, *Restoration: Charles II and his Kingdoms, 1660–1685* (London, 2005), pp. 48–52 on mixed responses to the restoration.

decade later, George Heathcote, a Quaker ship's captain of London, was jailed in Massachusetts for refusing to take his hat off in the presence of the colony's governor.[34] The day-to-day social value of hat honour was reflected in Pepys' anger 'at a proud trick' of his servant, Will, 'to keep his hatt on in house', which provoked concern that he would 'be troubled with his pride and lazinesse'.[35] At the same time, in 1663 he was alarmed at the possible offence he caused to James, duke of York, the king's brother, for failing to acknowledge him from a distance in St James' Park.[36]

The importance of headwear in social interaction was strengthened by the association between deportment and newer forms of civility and decorum. It was sustained by the ubiquitous use of hats, which continued to be worn in and out of doors. The practice began to change during the late seventeenth and early eighteenth centuries, partly as a result of material improvements to domestic interiors, though it survived at court and ceremonial events.[37] Indeed the persistent potential for violence, associated with the 'Ceremony' of the hat, provoked Daniel Defoe into proposing a 'Court of Honour, for preventing, punishing, and making Reparation for such villainous cases', in the *Review* of 1704.[38]

If the restoration of monarchy prompted the revival of the market for fashionable headwear, its expansion rested on socio-economic development. The scale and pace of change varied, but was interrelated and incremental in character. Economic growth and social change proceeded within a context of stationary population growth. Estimates for England even suggest a slight fall from 5.23 million in 1651 to 5.06 million by 1701. Although Scotland and Wales seem to have followed a similar trend, the population of Ireland appears to have recovered from a decline during the 1650s, increasing to 2 million by the 1690s. These figures mask a significant demographic redistribution, drawing on extensive patterns of internal and external migration, which was reflected in a striking increase in urban centres, particularly in England, where nearly one-third of the population lived in towns and cities by the start of the eighteenth century, providing the foundation for a more uniform market for dress. London dominated this urban landscape, with a population of about 575,000 in 1700. Dublin and Edinburgh also grew, but from a smaller base

34 Dunn and Dunn (eds.), *Papers of Penn*, 2, p. 321, n. 1. Failure to doff hats remained an issue in Virginia until the 1790s, Rountree and Turner, *Before and After Jamestown*, p. 163; Harris, *Restoration*, pp. 76–7, 302–3 for use of the law against Quakers.

35 Latham and Matthews (eds.), *The Diary of Pepys*, 2, p. 199.

36 Ibid., 4, p. 252.

37 Corfield, 'Dressing for Deference and Dissent', pp. 11–14; Thomas, *Pursuit of Civility*, pp. 326–8.

38 *A Review of the Affairs of France*, vol. 22, 20 May 1704, p. 104.

and at a slower rate, reaching populations of about 60,000 and 40,000 by the same date.[39]

This demographic structure formed part of an environment favouring economic growth and consumption. It included agricultural improvement and specialization, underpinned by increasing productivity, which led to stable or falling food prices. In association with the expansion of domestic and overseas trade, agricultural advance stimulated the development of infrastructural facilities, especially in communication and distribution. In addition, an increase in domestic and overseas markets, including the North American and Caribbean colonies, encouraged manufacturing and industry. These changes were linked with improved standards of living and changing lifestyles. Modest increases in wages, in parallel with rising landed and commercial incomes, provided the bedrock for improving prosperity, though wage earners in London seem to have experienced little real advance. Generally, a growing proportion of the population had more to spend on clothing and other goods, which were beginning to include fashionable dress and furnishings. The falling price of former luxuries, like tobacco and sugar, extended the market, while encouraging wage earners to sacrifice leisure time in favour of increased spending power.[40]

The growth of expenditure and consumption threatened to provoke a moral backlash. It fed a wider debate on luxury which gained momentum during these years. For the Quaker, William Penn, writing as a prisoner in the Tower of London in 1668, luxury was a 'mischief … to mankind', a disease which 'creeps into all stations and ranks of men'.[41] Attacking 'sumptuous apparel, rich unguents, delicate washes, stately furniture, costly cookery, and such diversions as balls, masques, music-meetings, plays' and the like, he

[39] Keith Wrightson, *Earthly Necessities: Economic Lives in Early Modern Britain* (New Haven, 2000), pp. 229–30; David Scott, *Leviathan: The Rise of Britain as a World Power* (London, 2013), pp. 229, 265–6.

[40] Wrightson, *Earthly Necessities*, pp. 232–48; Russell R. Menard, 'Colonial America's Mestizo Agriculture' in Cathy Matson (ed.), *The Economy of Early America: Historical Perspectives and New Directions* (Philadelphia, 2006), p. 122; McCusker and Menard, *Economy of British America*, p. 122 on productivity gains in Virginia; John Styles, 'Product Innovation in Early Modern London', *Past & Present*, 168 (2000), pp. 124–8; Jeremy Boulton, 'Food Prices and the Standard of Living in London in the "Century of Revolution", 1580–1700', *Economic History Review*, 73 (2000), pp. 472–9; de Vries, *Industrious Revolution*, pp. 177 ff for the 'new consumption regime'.

[41] William Penn, *No Cross, No Crown: A Discourse, Shewing the Nature and Discipline of the Holy Cross of Christ* (London, 1682), pp. 168–9, 174; de Vries, *The Industrious Revolution*, pp. 58, 149–51.

condemned a culture as much as personal conduct.[42] In decrying rich and superfluous dress, he denounced the use of clothing for display and pleasure. Linking apparel with character, Penn warned that 'dressing for a market' was an 'ill sign of loving and living well at home'.[43]

Yet such critics were challenged by the champions of an emerging commercial society who acknowledged the economic benefits of consumption, and defended the new world of fashion in material possessions. Emphasizing the importance of competition and emulation, in 1690 Nicholas Barbon argued that fashion should be encouraged. A prominent business man and building speculator in London, he claimed that the 'alteration of Dress is a great Promoter of *Trade',* which employed a large number of craftsmen, including hatters, hosiers and glovers.[44] His psychological and practical insights were echoed and elaborated by Bernard Mandeville in the early eighteenth century. Of Dutch background, Mandeville settled in London, practising as a doctor and publishing satirical observations on the paradoxes of a commercial culture. His *Fable of the Bees*, published anonymously in 1714, drew a storm of protest from the church and legal establishment for its unflinching anatomy of the apparently contradictory, but essential interrelationship between private vices and public virtues. It included a commentary on luxury, the 'greatest Excesses' of which were to be found in clothing, furniture and building, concluding that with 'wise Administration all People may swim in as much foreign Luxury as their Product can purchase'.[45] Reflecting on his experience of living in the largest city in Western Europe, Mandeville noted that society demanded close attention to changing modes and fashion. Clothes and accessories bestowed honour on individuals. From the 'richness of them we may judge of their Wealth, and by their ordering of them we guess at their Understanding'.[46] But they also enabled strangers to dress above their rank, and 'have the Pleasure of

42 Ibid., pp. 169; John Brewer, '"The Most Polite Age and the Most Vicious": Attitudes Towards Culture as a Commodity, 1660–1800', in Ann Bermingham and John Brewer (eds.), *The Consumption of Culture 1660–1800: Image, Object, Text* (London, 1995), pp. 342–9; John Brewer, *The Pleasures of the Imagination: English Culture in the Eighteenth Century* (New York, 1997), pp. 82–6.

43 Penn, *No Cross, No Crown*, pp. 139, 174; Reay, *The Quakers and the English Revolution*, pp. 117–20 for the Quaker aesthetic.

44 Nicholas Barbon, *A Discourse of Trade* (London, 1690), p. 35; Paul Slack, 'Perceptions of the Metropolis in Seventeenth-Century England', in Peter Burke et al. (eds), *Civil Histories: Essays Presented to Sir Keith Thomas* (Oxford, 2000), pp. 175–9; Peck, *Consuming Splendor*, pp. 345–7 on the 'new mentality'.

45 Bernard Mandeville, *The Fable of the Bees*, ed. Phillip Harth (Harmondsworth, 1970, repr. 1989), pp. 144, 148; Maxine Berg, *Luxury and Pleasure in Eighteenth-Century Britain* (Oxford, 2005), pp. 31–6. Others like Sir Dudley North attacked sumptuary laws as a bridle to trade and industry, Parker, *Global Crisis*, pp. 623–4.

46 Mandeville, *Fable*, pp. 152, 154.

being esteem'd by a vast Majority, not as what they are, but what they appear to be'.[47] From this perspective, social competition and emulation served as a spur to industry and improvement.

Barbon and Mandeville drew attention to the creative connection between fashion, consumption and production, and its applicability to clothing and headwear. The former observed that 'tho' the Trader or Maker is the Inventor of the Shape, yet it is the Fancy and Approbation of the Buyer that brings it into Use, and makes it pass for a Fashion'.[48] According to Mandeville new styles rarely lasted more than ten or twelve years. Within a culture of fashion, he noted 'how mean and comically a Man looks that is otherwise Well Dress'd in a Narrow Brim'd Hat when every Body wears Broad ones, and again, how monstrous is a very Great Hat, when the other extreme has been in Fashion for a considerable time'.[49] Yet staying in fashion required sustained and significant investment in personal appearance.

These ideological interventions drew on the expansion of the market for fashionable clothing and headwear. But the practical consequences are difficult to gauge. The difficulty is compounded with the lack of a national or uniform market for costly accessories, particularly beaver hats. Nonetheless during the later seventeenth century there was a re-configuration of patterns of consumption based on the connections between court, city and country. At its centre there was a shift in favour of London and provincial urban centres at the expense of the court and country. The growth of consumption among urban middling and professional groups, which included office holders such as Pepys, was probably characterized by width rather than depth. While the number of consumers was increasing, beyond the wealthy and fashionable elite, individual purchases may have remained limited in number. To some extent this reflected the development of consumer choice, benefiting from the growing availability of a variety of commodities which Mandeville described as the 'necessary Comforts of Life'.[50] But fashionable consumption was also influenced by broader social and cultural change, manifest in the growth of a

47 Ibid., p. 152; Beverly Lemire, *Dress, Culture and Commerce: The English Clothing Trade Before the Factory* (London, 1997), pp. 1–8.

48 Barbon, *Discourse*, p. 13; Peck, *Consuming Splendor*, pp. 345–7.

49 Mandeville, *Fable*, pp. 152, 333; Charles Saumarez Smith, *The Rise of Design: Design and the Domestic Interior in Eighteenth-Century England* (London, 1993), pp. 57–8; Hannah Woolley, *The Gentlewomans Companion; Or, a Guide to the Female Sex* (London, 3rd edition, 1682) p. 90 for similar comment regarding women; Ann Bermingham, 'Introduction. The Consumption of Culture: Image, Object, Text', in Bermingham and Brewer (eds.), *The Consumption of Culture*, pp. 132–5 on reception and audience.

50 Mandeville, *Fable*, p. 176; Barbon, *Discourse*, p. 64.

greater degree of intimacy in domestic life and the development of restraint and sobriety in male dress and appearance.[51]

Within this segmented market, the court remained the '*source* and *foundation* of fashions', providing the largest concentration of wealthy consumers for stylish clothing and headwear, though its position was weakened by political controversy and crises, as well as economies in household expenditure.[52] The restored monarchy refurbished its public and ceremonial image under the influence of Louis XIV, encouraging the diffusion of French modes among courtiers and aristocrats. But it was tarnished by the libertine sexual conduct of the king and his close companions. The damage was overshadowed by political and religious disunity, and an enveloping crisis that led to the overthrow of his brother, James II, a convert to Catholicism, in 1688. James was replaced by his daughter and son-in-law, Mary and William of Orange, who ruled as joint sovereigns under the Settlement of 1689, which limited royal power and safeguarded the Protestant succession. The interplay between politics and personality, combined with the demands of war with France, exposed the decline of the court as a leader of fashion during the 1690s and beyond.[53]

The concern of Charles II to rebrand monarchy influenced its public image, though it threw into relief a disorderly court which lacked a formal, regulated dress code. By contrast with his predecessors, the king was usually portrayed in ceremonial or classical costume rather than contemporary dress.[54] Emphasizing convention and formality, royal portraits left little room for the artistic representation of stylish clothing and accessories, as demonstrated in the work of Van Dyck during the 1630s. Portraits of royal mistresses by Peter Lely also failed to conceal the seamy underside of court life. Their state of relaxed undress suggested sexual availability, hinting at a pattern of conduct that shocked some visitors to court. Within this febrile and competitive world, clothing and accessories retained their potency as symbols of wealth and status,

51 Breward, *Culture of Fashion*, pp. 100. 112–14; Kuchta, *The Suit*, pp. 122–30 argues for a 'renunciation' of fashion among elite males; Backhouse, *Fashion and Popular Print*, pp. 143–57, 185–7 notes the need for male fashion in 'proper social relations', but representations showed it was 'essential to civility and yet potentially ruinous to masculinity'.

52 Woolley, *The Gentlewomans Companion*, p. 90; Sharpe, *Rebranding Rule*, pp. 626–9; Brewer, *The Pleasures of the Imagination*, pp. 8–17.

53 Ashelford, *The Art of Dress*, pp. 106–9; Valerie Cumming, *Royal Dress: The Image and the Reality 1580 to the Present Day* (London, 1989), pp. 38–9; Philip Mansel, *Dressed to Rule: Royal and Court Costume from Louis XIV to Elizabeth II* (New Haven, 2005), pp. 11–12; Kuchta, *The Suit*, pp. 93, 121–3; Thomas, *Pursuit of Civility*, pp. 95–6. It was symbolized by the destruction of Whitehall Palace by fire in 1698, Sharpe, *Rebranding Rule*, p. 626.

54 Aileen Ribeiro with Cally Blackman, *A Portrait of Fashion: Six Centuries of Dress at the National Portrait Gallery* (London, 2015), p. 17.

or privilege and favour. Royal mistresses drew attention through their dress, including hats, some of which, as Pepys noted in 1663, were cocked, and adorned with brightly coloured plumes, anticipating the widespread adoption of a new style in headwear. But the studied informality of the king and his consort, Catherine of Braganza, also at times recalled the past. During a visit to court in September 1666 John Evelyn, a staunch royalist and diarist, met the queen 'in her cavalier riding-habit, hat and feather, and horseman's coat', as she was 'going to take the air', assuming a fashion that seemed to echo her predecessor, Henrietta Maria.[55]

Shortly after, Charles decided to adopt a simpler style of dress, made up of a long coat, over a waistcoat and breeches. It was welcomed by Evelyn as a renunciation of French fashion, but he subsequently noted that it was 'too good to hold, it being impossible for us in good earnest to leave the Monsieurs' vanities long'.[56] The new style was captured by Hendrick Danckerts, a Dutch artist who worked in England during the 1660s and 1670s, in a portrait of Charles dressed in an elegant suit, and a low-crowned, broad-brimmed beaver. For an accessible and informal monarch, such headwear was a valuable accessory. As one loyal courtier noted, 'in the galleries and park he would pull off his hat to the meanest', in a public display of civility and politeness.[57] Despite critics, under Charles II the court still served as a stage for fashionable display. Aware of its potential value, and keen to promote his new colony, in 1683 William Penn sent a gift of furs to Laurence Hyde, earl of Rochester, a well-connected courtier, with a request that 'Pennsilvania furnish the King, the Duke [of York] & thyself with Beavers & Otters for Hatts & Muffs'.[58]

Under the joint monarchy of William and Mary, royal concern to promote the cause of godly reform, combined with the personal taste of the king, encouraged greater restraint in clothing, which was reinforced by the death

55 E.S. de Beer (ed.), *The Diary of John Evelyn*, 6 vols. (Oxford, 1955), 3, p. 463; Ashelford, *The Art of Dress*, pp. 96–9; Latham and Matthews (eds) *The Diary of Samuel Pepys*, 4, p. 230.

56 de Beer (ed.), *Diary*, 3, pp. 464–5; Maria Hayward, 'Dressing Charles II: The King's Clothing Choices (1660–85)', *Apparence(s)* [Online], 6, 2015: http://journals.openedition.org/apparences/1320, pp. 7–8; Ashelford, *The Art of Dress*, pp. 31–3; Kuchta, *The Suit*, pp. 78–82, 89–90; Mansel, *Dressed to Rule*, pp. 12–6, 49–50. Though angry at the English response, apparently Louis XIV adopted the new style, Jennifer M. Jones, *Sexing* La Mode: *Gender, Fashion and Commercial Culture in Old Regime France* (Oxford, 2004), pp. 22–3.

57 N.H. Keeble, *The Restoration: England in the 1660s* (London, 2002), p. 61; Sharpe, *Rebranding Rule*, pp. 121, 192–3, who notes that Charles was the first monarch to 'pursue popularity by means of an image of ordinariness'; www.rct.uk/collection/406896/charles-ii-presented-with-a-pineapple; Reynolds, *In Fine Style*, pp. 96–101 on dress and comportment.

58 Dunn and Dunn (eds.), *Papers of Penn*, 2, pp. 351–2.

of the queen in 1694. Although William retained an interest in costly fabrics and furnishings, compared with his predecessors, personal expenditure on sumptuous dress was modest. Portraits of William from 1690 present him fashionably attired, wearing tall and wide-brimmed beaver hats, in some cases decorated with jewels.[59] Apart from the requirements of court ceremony, however, his clothing was increasingly marked by its sobriety. Royal wardrobe accounts included the purchase of ceremonial dress for leading members of the household. During 1690 and 1691 four beaver hats and gold bands were acquired, at a total cost of £26, for the Yeoman of the Robes. Both the Master and the Clerk of the Robes were furnished with a fine beaver at a charge of £5 each.[60] A decade later, during the year from May 1700 to May 1701, wardrobe accounts indicate the purchase of 28 Carolina beaver hats, in addition to 11 Carolina hats and four fine black beavers. The total charge of the latter amounted to £18, and suggests that they were intended for the king, but the Carolina hats, with an average price of £1 5s, were probably for members of the household.[61]

Court consumption was complemented by expenditure on dress by country aristocrats and gentry. As in the past, the relationship between court and country overlapped, though it was increasingly politicized. It was overlaid by the growth of semi-permanent residence by wealthy landowners in the newer, more fashionable districts of London. Consumption across the country was multi-layered, reflecting differences in income and region, socio-cultural attitudes and the development of non-conformity, as well as taste. Such conditions fostered varied patterns of expenditure on clothing and accessories. Landowners were alert to the real and symbolic value of personal appearance in expressing and strengthening social capital in a rural and provincial world. At the same time, for some, spending was calibrated to avoid the appearance of excess, favouring a simpler style for men, which in the longer term created the opportunity for the widespread adoption of the suit.[62] The range and variety of country consumption and expenditure is illustrated by the household accounts for two gentlemen from contrasting regions in the south east and north west.

The account book for James Master of Kent covers the period from 1647 to 1675. With an annual income of about £400 in 1650, which was free from the expense of a family until his marriage in 1666, Master was able to indulge his

59 Patricia Wardle, *For Our Royal Person: Master of the Robes Bills of King-Stadholder William III* (Apeldoorn, 2002), pp. 10, 19, 29–36, 47; Tony Claydon, *William III* (London, 2002), pp. 20, 44–5, 79–80 on moral reform at court and Sharpe, *Rebranding Rule*, pp. 343–50, 385–93, 469–80 on the decline of the court under William.

60 Wardle, *For Our Royal Person*, pp. 27, 48.

61 Ibid., pp. 47–8, 126, 132.

62 Kuchta, *The Suit*, pp. 71–85, 93–8.

taste in stylish headwear. His accounts record the regular acquisition of beavers and castors, as well as demi-castors, some of which were from overseas. They included the purchase of French castors in 1648 and 1649, and a demi-castor in 1650. The following year he acquired a French beaver and demi-castor. He bought French demi-castors in 1652 and 1654. Two were purchased in 1655 and 1657, and a castor was acquired in 1659 and 1661. Following the purchase of a demi-castor in 1663, the rest of Master's acquisitions demonstrated a preference for beavers, which were bought in 1666 and each year from 1666 to 1669, as well as in 1673 and 1675, suggesting the influence of life-cycle on taste and consumption. Over a period of 28 years he purchased 11 beavers and nine demi-castors. The former ranged in price from £2 2s to £3 10s, the latter from £1 16s to £2 6s 6d. Hats of this quality were among the more expensive accessories in Master's wardrobe, with the exception of wigs, for which he sometimes paid more than £4.[63]

The household accounts for Sir Daniel Fleming of Westmorland, covering the years from 1689 to 1701, also included regular disbursements on headwear. By contrast with Master, his spending was shaped by the demands of an extensive family, was less subject to the influence of London, and did not include costly beavers or demi-castors. A widower since the death of his wife in 1675, Fleming had a daughter, Alice, who took over responsibility for running the household, and ten sons, one of whom died in infancy. He was elected to parliament in 1685, but turned down the opportunity of re-election on the grounds that 'absence from home in London is very prejudicial to [my] large family of young children'.[64] His accounts illustrate the role of the family household as a unit of consumption, which included the regular purchase of headwear. But the most expensive, for which he paid 12s 6d, was less than half the price of a demi-castor bought by Master.[65] Of necessity Fleming's expenditure was structured and discriminating. It demonstrated a concern for family hierarchy, based on age and position. Hats purchased for Fleming and his elder son, Daniel, who helped in the management of the estate until his death in 1698, cost between 10s and 12s. Spending on headwear for the other sons was lower, ranging from 4s to 11s, but crept up with age. The four

63 Canon Scott Robertson (ed.), 'The Expense-Book of James Master, Esq. A.D. 1646 to 1676', in 4 parts, *Archaelogia Cantiana*, 15 (1883), pp. 166–216; 16 (1886), pp. 244–59; 17 (1887), pp. 323–52; 18 (1889), pp. 116–54.

64 www.historyofparliamentonline.org/volume/1660–1690/member/fleming-sir-david-1633–1701.

65 Blake Tyson (ed.), *The Estate and Household Accounts of Sir Daniel Fleming of Rydal Hall, Westmorland from 1688–1701* (Cumberland and Westmorland Antiquarian and Archaeological Society, Record Series, 13, 2001), p. 91.

younger sons received new hats each year, at prices of 2s 6d for the youngest to 4s for his siblings. As they grew older, it increased to 10s and 11s.[66]

Fleming's expenditure on headwear indicates the growing value of the market for the sons of country gentry. For some, this included acquisitions of fashionable and expensive wares. Sir Thomas Myddelton, a wealthy landowner of Chirk in north Wales, who with his second wife had seven sons and six daughters, purchased two demi-castors for boys, each costing £1 5s, in 1652. Fifteen years later, he spent £2 2s on the purchase of three beaver hats for boys.[67] By the 1670s, the accounts of a London haberdasher indicate that wealthy city consumers were also buying costly headwear for their sons.[68]

With such a scattered pattern of consumption across the country, it was the growth of urban centres which cultivated the market for fashionable hats during the later seventeenth century and beyond. London led the way, working as a generator for the expansion of expenditure and consumption. Despite plague and fire, the physical and social development of the capital widened the market, while increasing and improving the public arena for its display. Parks, theatres, shops, and the emergence of new spaces, such as squares, coffee houses and clubs, provided sociable experiences for city dwellers, courtiers and visitors. In conjunction with improvements to streets, which acquired clearly-defined pavements and, in some cases, lighting, a new cityscape fuelled the growth of demand for stylish dress.[69] The capital represented a diverse market, including semi-resident landowners and the wealthier ranks of middling groups. Collectively, merchants, businessmen, professionals and government officials represented a concentration of

66 Ibid., pp. 80, 86, 114, 126, 130, 134, 140, 143, 148, 169, 188, 207, 241, 243, 278, 304 for examples.

67 W.M. Myddelton (ed.), *Chirk Castle Acounts A.D. 1605–1666* (St Albans, 1908), pp. 56, 147; W.M. Myddelton (ed.), *Chirk Castle Accounts A.D. 1666–1753* (Manchester, 1931), p. 81.

68 Guildhall Library, London, MS. 24201, unfoliated.

69 E.A. Wrigley, 'A Simple Model of London's Importance in Changing English Society and Economy 1650–1750', *Past & Present*, 37 (1967), pp. 60–9; de Vries, *Industrious Revolution*, pp. 123, 169–70. The growth of consumption was accompanied by a 'cultural reconception of space' after the fire according to Cynthia Wall, *The Literary and Cultural Spaces of London* (Cambridge, 1998), pp. 4–28, 39 and Elizabeth McKellar, *The Birth of Modern London: The Development and Design of the City* (Manchester, 1999), pp. 193–4, 201–5; Miles Ogborn, *Spaces of Modernity: London's Geographies, 1680–1780* (London, 1998), pp. 76–9, 110–11, 115 for fashion on the street; Maurice Exwood and H.L. Lehmann (eds.), *The Journal of William Schellinks' Travels in England 1661–1663* (Camden Society, Fifth Series, 1, 1993), pp. 51–8, 84 on shops, parks and gardens; Christopher Breward, *Fashioning London: Clothing and the Modern Metropolis* (Oxford, 2004), pp. 29–30, 42–3; Heal and Holmes, *The Gentry in England and Wales*, pp. 140–1, 316 on the season.

experienced and discriminating consumers, with distinctive lifestyles, which was beginning to rival the court. During the 1660s and 1670s some members of this group spent nearly one-quarter of their disposable income on clothing. By the early eighteenth century, they accounted for between 20,000 and 25,000 households, the vanguard for an emerging middle class in provincial cities like York, Norwich and Bristol.[70] Such centres, including Dublin and Edinburgh, followed London in the elaboration and improvement of an urban fabric and facilities. Though not uniform, the attractions of sociability, entertainment and sport, as well as the availability of shops and markets, enabled them to grow as fashionable centres for well-off consumers keen to advertise status, civility, and appearance.[71]

Pepys' diary provides a revealing insight into the lifestyle of a busy official, keenly aware of the importance of self-presentation in a world of distracting entertainment and leisure that linked court and city. In March 1662, after spending a morning working in the office, he walked to the 'Exchange to see and be seen'.[72] Weeks later, after attending church, he accompanied his wife 'to Grayes Inne to observe fashions of the ladies'.[73] But city audiences were discerning and critical. During a subsequent visit to Whitehall, he noticed the king 'in a suit laced with gold and silver, which it was said was out of fashion'.[74] During a hectic period of theatre-going, dining and visiting, he confessed it was a 'hard matter to settle to business after so much leisure and pleasure'.[75] Determined to adopt a more frugal course, Pepys' efforts to control his expenditure were qualified by the acquisition of fine clothing and hats, which included the gift of a beaver, 'an old ... but a very good one', from Sir William Batten, an associate in the navy office, and a new one, for which

70 Peter Earle, *The Making of the English Middle Class: Business, Society and Family Life in London, 1660–1723* (London, 1989), pp. 80–1, 281–90; Berg, *Luxury and Pleasure*, pp. 209–18 and Peter Borsay, *The English Urban Renaissance: Culture and Society in the Provincial Town* (Oxford, 1989), pp. 6–7, 28–35 on regional centres; Trentmann, *Empire of Things*, pp. 93–4 on a 'new culture of appearance' and urban living; Phil Withington, 'Citizens, Community and Political Culture in Restoration England', in Alexandra Shepard and Phil Withington (eds.), *Communities in Early Modern England: Networks, Place, Rhetoric* (Manchester, 2000), pp. 135–55.

71 Borsay, *The English Urban Renaissance*, pp. 74–9, 117–27, 150–72, 227, 237–41; Joyce M. Ellis, *The Georgian Town 1680–1840* (Basingstoke, 2001), pp. 20–2, 71–3, 139 (for more cautious comment on London); Sybil M. Jack, *Towns in Tudor and Stuart Britain* (Basingstoke, 1996), pp. 106–17 for Dublin and Edinburgh.

72 Latham and Matthews (eds.), *The Diary of Pepys*, 3, p. 47; Ian W. Archer, 'Social Networks in Restoration London: The Evidence from Samuel Pepys's Diary', in Shepard and Withington (eds.), *Communities in Early Modern England*, pp. 79–84.

73 Latham and Matthews (eds.), *The Diary of Pepys*, 3, p. 77.

74 Ibid., p. 81.

75 Ibid., p. 78.

he paid £4 5s.[76] It was so expensive that he looked after it with great care, on one occasion borrowing a poor, ill-fitting hat to save it from unnecessary wear. On another visit to the Exchange with his wife, he was 'in a humour of laying out money, but not prodigally, but only in clothes'.[77] Over the course of one month, in October 1663 he spent £67 on clothes for himself and his wife, including a new hat, two periwigs, two new suits and a velvet cloak.[78]

London was of such a size to sustain more specialized markets, which included clergymen, some of whom enjoyed access to other sources of income. Jonathan Swift, cleric and author, wore plain clerical dress, though it was enhanced by a beaver, at least three of which he purchased during his career. They were regularly maintained and dressed. On his death, he left them to three friends in the church.[79] Mischievously Mandeville exploited the ensemble to attack the hypocrisy of the clergy, whose attempts to conceal their vanity and pride, behind plain apparel, were exposed by their love of fashionable hats and wigs. Thus, the wealthy parson 'scorns ever to be seen abroad with a worse Beaver than what a rich Banker would be proud of on his Wedding Day'.[80]

The use of fine and fashionable clothing informed a perception of the city as a beacon for new forms of civility, woven into the fabric of a commercial and wealthy society. Style was an attribute of people of quality, a term that acquired new meaning during the 1660s, foreshadowing the emergence of the *beau monde* as a social description in the 1690s.[81] Yet there were alternative scenarios on display throughout the city and its poorer suburbs, which compromised or subverted such ideals. Restoration comedies registered the growth of the town as a distinct space, but they also drew attention to its reputation for sexual danger and disguise, which was linked to wider anxiety at the re-structuring of urban spaces. Political and religious division were confused with sexual intrigue and libertinism.[82] St James' Park, renovated by the monarchy, attracted 'gentlemen of the highest fashion' during the day, but

[76] Ibid., pp. 64, 67.

[77] Ibid., 4, p. 343.

[78] Ibid., pp. 357–8. Pepys' salary in 1664 was £324 16s, Ashelford, *The Art of Dress*, p. 93. It would have been enhanced by gifts and perquisites.

[79] Paul V. Thompson and Dorothy Jay Thompson (eds.), *The Account Books of Jonathan Swift* (London, 1984), pp. lxxviii, 61, 66.

[80] Mandeville, *Fable*, p. 156.

[81] Keeble, *The Restoration*, pp. 145, 179–80; Hannah Greig, *The Beau Monde: Fashionable Society in Georgian London* (Oxford, 2013), pp. 243–58; Berg, *Luxury and Pleasure*, pp. 86–8.

[82] See for example John Crowne, *City Politiques*, ed. John Harold Wilson (London, 1967) and George Etherege, *The Man of the Mode*, ed. John Conaghan (Edinburgh, 1973).

under cover of darkness it was portrayed as a 'sin-sheltering grove' by the dissolute court poet John Wilmot, earl of Rochester.[83]

Within such contradictory and contrasting city spaces, headwear could be worn in a transgressive and idiosyncratic manner, providing rich material for newspapers and journals. In 1709 *The Tatler* reported a scurrilous story about Thomas Coulson, a wealthy East India merchant and MP, who sat in state in a Drury House seraglio dressed as an eastern mogul, wearing a beaver adorned with one of the largest jewels in Europe.[84] The following year a correspondent for *The Spectator* described an encounter with a young man on horseback, with well-curled hair and a 'little Beaver Hat edg'd with Silver, ... made more sprightly by a Feather'.[85] On closer inspection the rider was wearing a petticoat, provoking doubts that 'a very handsome Youth, may not be in Reality a very indifferent Woman'.[86]

Using such fragmentary and anecdotal material to estimate the volume of annual consumption is an impossible task. Modern estimates, based on figures provided by Gregory King during the 1690s, suggest that annual sales of headwear, including hats and caps, amounted to more than three million, with a total value of £387,000.[87] Beaver hats, selling at prices beyond the reach of a majority of the population, formed a small fraction of this total. Undoubtedly consumption revived after 1660, encouraging the expansion of manufacturing in London, which dominated the trade in quality headwear. It was strengthened by the emergence and expansion of overseas markets, estimates for which shed incidental light on the likely scale of domestic consumption. In 1663 exports of felt hats amounted to 30,070, of which 11,270 were beavers. By 1700 overseas shipments had increased to 68,000 hats, much of it occurring during the 1680s and 1690s.[88] If, as representatives for the London Feltmakers

[83] David M. Vieth (ed.), *The Complete Poems of John Wilmot, Earl of Rochester* (New Haven, 1962, repr. 2002), p. 41; Exwood and Lehmann (eds.), *Journal of Schellinks' Travels*, p. 84; Wall, *Literary and Cultural Spaces*, pp. 150–67; Jason Scott-Warren, *Early Modern English Literature* (Cambridge, 2005), pp. 220–2 comments on the 'status confusion and ritual shaming' in this work; Roy Porter, *London: A Social History* (London, 1994), pp. 93–106, 170–2 on the development of the town and commercialisation.

[84] Donald F. Bond (ed.), *The Tatler*, 3 vols. (Oxford, 1987), 1, pp. 329–30.

[85] Donald F. Bond (ed.), *The Spectator*, 5 vols. (Oxford, 1965), 1, p. 434.

[86] Ibid., p. 435; Ribeiro with Blackman, *A Portrait of Fashion*, p. 18; Brewer, *The Pleasures of the Imagination*, pp. 101–3 on the role of the press in promoting ideas of politeness.

[87] Margaret Spufford, 'The Cost of Apparel in Seventeenth-Century England, and the Accuracy of Gregory King', *Economic History Review*, 53 (2000), p. 679; N.B. Harte, 'The Economics of Clothing in the Late Seventeenth Century', *Textile History*, 22 (1991), pp. 277–96; Corner, 'The Tyranny of Fashion', p. 154.

[88] Ibid., pp. 154–5.

claimed in 1695, exports amounted to 40% of their business each year, and assuming that the proportion of beaver and other shipments remained the same, this would suggest that domestic sales were in the region of 48,000 to 50,000 annually by the end of the seventeenth century.[89] It is unlikely that the volume of provincial manufacturing and trade would significantly alter this crude estimate. While demonstrating sustained growth in domestic consumption after 1660, despite slow or stable population growth, sales were influenced by prices and the growing availability of an array of competing commodities, many of them new. For wealthy consumers, furnishing the house was assuming as much importance as fashioning the body.[90] As such, the emergence of overseas markets, though starting from a low base and often speculative in character, was significant. Their importance could only have increased with the rapid growth of fur imports after 1670, which domestic consumption struggled to absorb.

Craft and circulation

During the 1690s these challenges were exacerbated by the disarray of the Feltmakers' Company, as it faced a variety of internal and external threats. An angry dispute between masters and journeymen disrupted the company, with damaging, short-term consequences for the manufacture of headwear. According to its leading officers, at the end of the century their trade in London had ground to a halt. At the same time, production and consumption were affected by the circulation of goods within a half-hidden market in second-hand and stolen wares. Although there is scant evidence for its economic significance, criminal proceedings suggest that hat theft was growing, facilitated by the illicit re-distribution of stolen wares.

During the 1640s the Feltmakers' Company assumed control over beaver-making in London. It strengthened its authority over the trade in a piecemeal manner. In September 1649 the company joined with the Hatbandmakers to petition parliament against imported wares.[91] As a result, not only was the import of foreign goods prohibited, but also company officers were

[89] Although the proportion had undoubtedly shifted since 1663, the really significant change took place after 1700. In 1736 more than 700,000 hats were exported, (a peak), of which 65% were beaver and castor, Corner, 'Tyranny of Fashion', p. 155. These figures for domestic consumption should be viewed as very crude and imperfect pointers to the volume of activity.

[90] On new goods and furnishings see Berg, *Luxury and Pleasure*, pp. 49–50, 113–17, 205–6; Saumarez Smith, *The Rise of Design*, pp. 154–5, 186–7, 207–8 on domestic interiors.

[91] http://www.british-history.ac.uk/no-series/acts-ordinances-interregnum/ pp. 242–4.

authorized to conduct searches for them in the city and its liberties. The following year the company was admitted to the freedom of the city. By an act of the Court of Common Council, of 1658, all feltmakers in the capital were required to be a member of it. Corporate lobbying led to the imposition of a high tariff on imported felt hats from Spain, Portugal and the Netherlands at the restoration and the issue of a new charter in 1667.[92] It confirmed that of 1604, as well as legislation dealing with the manufacture and sale of headwear. Its main provisions concerned the regulation of apprenticeships and the employment of journeymen, and the right of the company to take action so that the trade 'might be better ordered and Governed'.[93] Under this authority, at various times during the 1670s its officers seized and destroyed illegal imports of headwear.[94]

Like other city companies and guilds, the Feltmakers was a hierarchical institution with its own officers, hall and seal. For administrative purposes it was in the hands of a master, elected annually, four wardens and 21 assistants, who were supported by two beadles and a clerk. As a recent creation, it was not among the wealthiest city companies. The destruction of the hall during the fire of 1666 forced it to hire the buildings of other corporations for meetings and events. Its membership was predominantly male, though it included a small number of women, the widows of feltmakers, who maintained an interest in the business. In 1679 Grace Dawby was accused of keeping three apprentices, against company rules, although the following year, on paying her quarterly fee, she took on another.[95] One of Joan Ryder's apprentices was discharged

92 The duty was initially 9s 6d, but increased thereafter. It was partly offset by a duty on exports of hats, Carlos and Lewis, *Commerce by a Frozen Sea*, pp. 18–19; Unwin, *Gilds and Companies of London*, p. 237; Corner, 'The Tyranny of Fashion', p. 154 which notes subsequent protection and the exclusion of French wares.

93 Regulation extended to within four miles of the city's boundary. J.H. Hawkins, *History of the Worshipful Company of the Art or Mistery of Feltmakers of London* (London, 1917), pp. 25–30 for the charter (quote at p. 27); Weinstein, *Company of Feltmakers*, p. 21.

94 Ibid., p. 34; the scale of this illegal trade is difficult to gauge. According to Samuel Fortrey, in a work that was first published in 1663 and re-published ten years later, imports of 'bever, demicaster and felt hats' from France amounted in value to £120,000 *per annum*. But the trade was severely disrupted by the prohibition on French manufactures. Samuel Fortrey, *England's Interest and Improvement* (London, 1673), in J.R. McCulloch (ed.), *Early English Tracts on Commerce* (London, 1856, repr. Cambridge, 1954), p. 232.

95 Guildhall Library, MS 1570/1, f.86; Unwin, *Industrial Organization*, pp. 247–52 includes extracts.

in May 1695, after she accused him of being 'very negligent & stubborn ... [and] calling her ill names'.[96]

The company's main purpose was to protect its privileges within the city. Corporate life was upheld by an annual cycle of meetings and feasts, which included the collection of fees and searches for illegal goods. Administration and regulation were the responsibility of officers, meeting quarterly each year as a general court. More serious matters were handled by a special court, usually convened about the same time. Committees of leading officers, including the master, were established to provide advice on various issues, particularly setting annual wage rates.[97]

Within this regulatory structure, one of the key aspects of the company's responsibilities was to ensure the enforcement of rules regarding training and employment, progressing through a clearly defined rite of passage. It began with an apprenticeship of seven years. Fees seem to have varied according to individual circumstances, but were not as expensive as for some of the wealthier livery companies. The number of apprentices employed by masters was limited, though the court allowed additional recruitment on the payment of a fine. Most recruits came from modest and widely scattered backgrounds. In May 1694, for example, Richard Owens, son of a husbandman of Leintwardine in Herefordshire, was bound to Nicholas Watts for seven years, 'to sell hats only'.[98] Not all completed their service. A small number were discharged for poor work and behaviour, or gave up their training. Roger Roberts was formally released in November 1677 after the court received information that he had migrated to Virginia. He was followed by two more in 1700, including Thomas Wynn, who left with the consent of his parents. Others found alternative employment. In 1693 the court was informed of an apprentice who went 'to sea in a Privateer & cannot be found'.[99]

Apprenticeships ran alongside the employment of boys for specific tasks in the preparation of felts, which may have served as a route into the trade for those unable to pay fees. By custom they could only be employed up to the age of 18. In February 1677 Godfrey Wheeler, aged about 12, hired himself to serve as a 'singeing boy', who maintained the hearths, for five years, while during 1696 the court fined one master £6 for employing a boy 'twelve weeks after he attained his age of 18 years'.[100] Their work was carefully defined and

96 Guildhall Library, MS 1570/2, f.93. As women were effectively excluded from the craft, there was no opportunity for using low-paid female labour as in the clothing trade, Lemire, *Dress, Culture and Commerce*, pp. 4, 43.

97 Guildhall Library, MS 1570/1, ff.8, 16v, 81v, 167; MS 1570/2, ff.100, 149.

98 Ibid., f.57.

99 Guildhall Library, MS 1570/1, f.38v; MS 1570/2, ff.23, 46, 48, 297.

100 Guildhall Library, MS 1570/1, f.14v; MS 1570/2, f.133; Corner, 'The Tyranny of Fashion', p. 162.

monitored, particularly by craftsmen concerned at the dilution of skills and the exploitation of cheap labour. Following a petition from the journeymen, in November 1680 the court limited their number to one for each master.[101]

The memoirs of Thomas Tryon, published posthumously in 1705, provide an insight into the recruitment and experience of apprentices, which may have been widely shared by provincial recruits, despite his subsequently atypical career. Tryon was the son of a tiler and plasterer of Bibury in Gloucestershire, whose large family meant that the children were put to work at a young age. He left school before he was able to read or write, to work at spinning and carding. At the age of 10 or 11, he persuaded his father to buy a small flock of sheep for him to manage. He gained a reputation as one of the best shepherds in the county. After seven or eight years he grew 'weary of Shepherdizing, and had an earnest desire to travel'.[102] His father sold the sheep, and with £3 saved from their management, Tryon went to London. He used his savings to bind himself to a 'castor-maker' near Fleet Street.[103] The work involved long hours, stretching from five or six in the morning to 10 or 11 at night. Nonetheless he pursued his self-education, with the help of some tuition, reading works on astrology, medicine, the natural sciences and the arts in his spare time. According to his recollection, the training did not involve 'tedious daily working', but instead he benefited from a custom by which apprentices had 'a certain Task alotted them'.[104] Tryon fulfilled his with ease, earning between five and seven shillings a week, with which he purchased books. On gaining his freedom, he married and migrated to Barbados, where he spent several years making beaver hats for wealthy colonial consumers, eager to keep up with metropolitan fashion. Following his return to London, he 'stuck as close to [his] working Trade, as ever before'.[105] He continued to read widely, gained some proficiency in music, and during the 1680s and 1690s he embarked on a literary career, writing on a wide range of subjects. From a young age, he followed a life of abstinence and self-denial, which encouraged a concern to promote vegetarianism and animal welfare. In his memoirs he admonished men to avoid 'Violence, Oppression, and Cruelty, either to their own Kind, or any inferior Creatures', while exhorting women

101 Guildhall Library, MS 1570/1, ff.130v, 142. During the 1690s a second apprentice was permitted on payment of a fine of £5, Corner, 'The Tyranny of Fashion', p. 162.

102 *Some Memoirs of the Life of Mr. Tho. Tryon, Late of London, Merchant* (London, 1705), pp. 5–13, 16. The memoirs were assembled presumably by a friend, based on a draft version, which she/he admitted was not what Tryon intended for publication (ibid., pp. 60–2).

103 Ibid., p. 17.

104 Ibid., pp. 19–20.

105 Ibid., pp. 41–3.

to use one fashion in dress, which was 'grave, decent, easie and convenient', and not made from the skins of animals.[106]

Apprentices who successfully completed their training, like Tryon, were admitted to the company as journeymen, on the attestation of their masters. For some this represented a pathway to further advance as a master workman. Although the time varied, promotion required a demonstration of competence and expertise, and came with a fee. In January 1677 the court recorded that Henry Fuller brought 'in his peices, and haveing beene a Journeyman Nine yeares,' paid his approbation money, on which he was admitted as a working master.[107] Yet many were either unwilling or unable to take up the opportunity for progression. As freemen of the company they formed a pool of skilled labour whose shared interests and common concerns set them apart from, and potentially in conflict with, masters. Indeed, the collection of fees, or quarterage, by officers, was an occasional flashpoint of tension. In July 1681 a group of journeymen refused to pay, forcing the court to take action against them.[108] Wages varied according to type of headwear, though they included provision for diet. By 1696, at a time when the company was seeking to impose reductions in pay, they ranged from nine pence for a hat with a market value of five shillings to three shillings for a beaver.[109]

Masters were at the pinnacle of the craft. Years of training and employment gave them an expertise that was respected, even if during the 1690s their authority was under challenge. They filled the leading offices in the company, which represented their interests in and beyond the city. It was a member of this select group who was chosen to make the beaver hats which were given as gifts to city officials, at the company's expense. As a body they tried to demonstrate their concern for the wider membership. In December 1676 the court cancelled a dinner, normally held on the quarter day, in order to set aside money for poor members at Christmas. The master and wardens were also responsible for managing and distributing the proceeds of bequests among needy workers and widows.[110]

[106] Ibid., pp. 55, 82, 125–6; Keith Thomas, *Man and the Natural World: Changing Attitudes in England 1500–1800* (London, 1983), pp. 170–1, 180, 291–2; Tryon also wrote against slavery, Philippe Rosenberg, 'Thomas Tryon and the Seventeenth-Century Dimensions of Antislavery', *WMQ*, 61, (2004), pp. 609–42.

[107] Guildhall Library, MS 1570/1, f.12v; Hawkins, *History of Feltmakers*, p. 68 on the practice of proof-pieces.

[108] Guildhall Library, MS 1570/1, f.152v. Increasingly many must have lacked the capital required to set up as a master, which ranged from £50 to £1,000 by the mid-eighteenth century, Corner, 'The Tyranny of Fashion', pp. 158–9.

[109] Guildhall Library, MS 1570/2, f.149.

[110] Guildhall Library, MS 1570/1, ff.8, 168v.

Most masters managed small or modest-sized workshops, located in Battersea, Bermondsey, Lambeth and particularly Southwark.[111] The account book of Thomas Fisher, from 1673 to 1677, a prominent figure in the company, who was elected master in 1679, illustrates the range and scale of such enterprises. His accounts show an interest in wholesale and personal transactions. The former was probably encouraged by growing demand for ready-made clothing, and made up a significant part of his business.[112] In October 1673 he sold a consignment of 70 castors and 20 beavers to John Newton. The castors were valued at between 10 and 12 shillings each, the beavers were worth about three times as much, at 35s. Sales varied in character. Single purchases, like the acquisition of a castor by John Sadler were common.[113] They were accompanied by multiple transactions by individual customers. From February to May 1675, for example, captain Bass spent £14 16s 6d on the purchase of two beavers and eight other hats, including one for his son, as well as a hat box. His total bill covered payment for renovating two hats, which were lined, stiffened and edged.[114] The location of Fisher's customers spanned the fashionable areas of the West End and city, such as Bloomsbury, Duke's Place and Whitechapel, and ranged into Essex to include Braintree, Chelmsford and Romford. In addition to the sale of new stock, Fisher engaged in the second-hand trade, occasionally buying old beavers or accepting them in part exchange for shop wares. He offered from six to 12 shillings for used beavers, a higher value than for some types of new castors.[115]

The difference in prices for headwear, due to the cost of raw materials and labour, structured Fisher's business. Prices for beavers ranged from £1 16s to £3 5s, while the cost of castors varied from 4s 9d to £1 2s. His accounts record the sale of 2,170 castors from 1673 to 1677, of which more than half were for men and nearly one third for boys. By contrast sales of beavers were much lower, ranging between 160 and 170.[116] This represented a fraction of his overall trade in terms of volume, but it was offset by their greater value. Undoubtedly Fisher organized his workshop, including the distribution of labour among apprentices and journeymen, and the purchase of fur and other raw materials, in response to this varied pattern of production.

111 In 1683 about 80% of members of the Feltmakers were based in Southwark, Corner, 'The Tyranny of Fashion', p. 158; Earle, *The Making of the English Middle Class*, pp. 24, 29, 344.

112 On the link between ready-made garments and the development of shops, see Shammas, *Pre-Industrial Consumer*, pp. 235–59.

113 Guildhall Library, London, MS 24201, unfoliated.

114 Ibid.

115 Ibid.

116 Ibid.

As a leading officer in the company, Fisher was acutely aware of the problems it faced in enforcing corporate rights and jurisdiction. Officers and the court dealt with intermittent infractions concerning the regulation of labour, the protection of the trade and the quality of wares. Much of this administrative work was petty business which could be handled on an *ad hoc* basis. During the 1680s and 1690s it was overtaken by more serious, loosely-linked issues concerning foreign goods and workers, wages, and piecework. The deterioration in relations between masters and journeymen weakened the company's internal cohesion and coordination, exacerbated by the opportunistic and contested use of corporate by-laws, and seriously disrupted the trade.

The company sought assistance in the city and parliament to deal with the problem of foreign goods and labour. In March 1677 it tried to mobilize support against a parliamentary bill allowing foreign Protestants to set up their trades in London. The threat to employment was revealed by a complaint to the court, the following year, that Richard Stiles hired overseas workers in preference to freemen of the company. At the same time the court used its authority to confiscate and destroy imported commodities, offering rewards to informers. In a more ambitious attempt to protect the industry, during the 1680s and 1690s company leaders lobbied parliament to encourage wearing hats, while opposing a proposal in 1695 for a tax on headwear.[117]

The problem of overseas workers intensified with the influx of large numbers of Huguenots from France, following the revocation of their liberties in 1685. They included a significant number of skilled hat-makers who settled in London and its suburbs. As a concession, in February 1692 the court authorized company members to employ foreign journeymen, but only in Battersea, Lambeth and Wandsworth, and for the manufacture of Carolina and Cordibark hats. It was withdrawn two years later, in response to complaints against the employment of unqualified workers by French masters. But the threat of further action was tempered by political support and sympathy for religious refugees.[118]

During the 1690s the issue of foreign workers included a growing number of country journeymen, who moved to London in search of work. In September

[117] Guildhall Library, London, MS 1570/1, ff.16v, 66v, 133v, 169; MS 1570/2, f.89.

[118] Ibid., ff.58, 93; Unwin, *Industrial Organization*, pp. 217–18. Cordibark hats were made of cheaper felt, the manufacture of which Huguenots brought with them from Caudebec in Normandy, Robin D. Gwynn, *The Huguenot Heritage: The History and Contribution of the Huguenots in Britain* (London, 1985), pp. 68, 122; Corner, 'The Tyranny of Fashion', pp. 156–7. Alison Matthews David, *Fashion Victims: The Dangers of Dress Past and Present* (London, 2015), pp. 47–8, 55–9, argues that Huguenot refugees probably introduced knowledge of using mercury, in a process known as carroting, to improve felting quality, with serious consequences for the health of hatters.

1695 John Stiles was summoned before the court to answer a charge that he employed such craftsmen. He successfully defended himself by claiming that they were only used to make coarse felts.[119] As a source of cheap labour, however, concern at the employment of country journeymen mounted. Many seem to have been employed by the French hatters. A group of company journeymen, led by George Buckridge, complained in 1696 that they left their employment to work in Southwark and other parts of the city, without the payment of a fine of £20 according to corporate ordinances. After a lengthy debate the court allowed them to continue working for another month, for their 'present releife'.[120] It recognized the potential value of such workers, as it tried to limit wage rates. Later in the year it considered 'whether it be prudentiall to call in the Countrey Journeymen to be employed', if new, lower rates were rejected by company members.[121]

In this way the issue of foreign workers was linked with a bitter dispute over pay. The publication of revised wage rates by the court in November 1696 also authorized the employment of foreign journeymen, if they were not accepted, on condition that they became members of the company. It provoked a swift and angry response. George Buckridge and a group of others rejected the new rates and demanded that the court's order be revoked. Shortly after, a number of apprentices rioted outside the house of the company's master.[122] The ensuing campaign of the journeymen flouted a corporate ordinance against the use of combinations to raise wages. In November 1697 the court complained of 'disorders and disorderly meetings' by the journeymen, who abruptly left the service of masters without cause or one month's notice.[123] But its attempt to resolve the dispute through compromise and coercion met with limited success, sowing disunity among masters as much as workers. On the one hand, journeymen who accepted lower pay faced the organized hostility of the apprentices. On the other, while some masters supported a collection to prosecute unlawful workers, there were others who offered higher wages. The company responded by authorizing the employment of foreign journeymen, on payment of an entry fine of £1, and fining recalcitrant masters who claimed it 'had no power to settle Rates or Wages'.[124]

With divisions among, and between, masters and journeymen, the dispute was put to arbitration by the members of parliament for Surrey. According to the terms of their award, rates of pay for the manufacture of some hats, including beavers, were raised, but others remained unchanged. Both sides

119 Guildhall Library, MS 1570/2, f.103.
120 Ibid., f.120.
121 Ibid., f.147.
122 Ibid., ff.149, 159, 167, 172–3.
123 Ibid., ff.181, 183–4; Unwin, *Industrial Organization*, p. 246.
124 Guildhall Library, MS 1570/2, ff.195, 207–8, 226–7, 233.

accepted the compromise, and copies of the revised rates were printed and distributed throughout the city.[125] But the dispute had taken a toll on the company, suggesting the power of workers' combinations to defend pay, through organization and action.

The disunity was aggravated by the problem of piecework, which in theory was prohibited under the company's ordinances. It was a complicated issue, covering working practice and the provision of raw materials. Piece-masters and -men were accused of using poor quality material supplied by skinners and unqualified cutters. Facing complaints during 1694 that the sale of 'very defective and unworkmanlike' hats was damaging trade, the court tried to enforce its ordinances.[126] Yet the problem persisted. In 1697 it received a petition from 69 masters, which complained of abuses and requested a ban on 'peecework and all other unlawfull works'.[127] Struggling to enforce its regulations, in 1700 the company took legal action against the piece-men. As in the past, some members defended the practice on the grounds that it covered 'divers old men who could not work a week together but only set two or three hats a week'.[128] Unconvinced, the court stood by the regulations, which it applied to all members regardless of age.

These interrelated problems, which reportedly brought the trade in London to a stop, coincided with an angry dispute between the Feltmakers and Hudson's Bay Company. Since its establishment in 1670, the latter acquired a dominant position in the transatlantic fur trade, furnishing the metropolitan fur market with much of its supply of beaver skins. But its sales policy and practices to cope with a saturated market, intensified by competition between traders and furriers who supplied feltmakers with their raw material, affected prices which were subject to short-term volatility and variability between different furs. In July 1681 James Claypoole, a London merchant who traded with Pennsylvania, noted that the price of beaver skins had fallen over the past three months by about 20%. Moreover, it was likely to 'fall much lower, for a vast quantity is expected from Hudson's Bay'.[129] Like the company, he resorted to exporting furs to Russia, though he lost on recent deals. By January 1682 he complained that the 'fur trade was not so encouraging as to pay £8 …

[125] Ibid., ff.229, 255, 262.

[126] Ibid., ff.74, 78, 82; Unwin, *Industrial Organization*, pp. 218–20; Weinstein, *Company of Feltmakers*, pp. 28–9, 33.

[127] Guildhall Library, MS 1570/2, ff.175–6, 278.

[128] Ibid., ff.82, 278. But the practice of sub-contracting work continued, despite the regulations, Corner, 'The Tyranny of Fashion', pp. 159–60.

[129] Marion Balderston (ed.), *James Claypoole's Letter Book: London and Philadelphia 1681–1684* (San Marino, 1967), pp. 47, 50 (for other furs 'exceeding dear'), 63.

per annum for a warehouse' to store them in.[130] Cumulatively these problems encouraged the concentration of the metropolitan wholesale trade into the hands of a small number of suppliers, provoking widespread resentment. When the company's charter came up for renewal in 1690, therefore, it was opposed by the Feltmakers, who claimed that its members were forced to pay excessive prices for poor quality skins. The company also complained about the private sale of large parcels of better furs to leading furriers, who re-exported them to markets in Northern Europe, as a means of cushioning the fall of prices in London.[131] Although the Hudson's Bay Company agreed to some concessions, they failed to satisfy city craftsmen. In 1693 the Feltmakers supported a parliamentary bill to prevent fraudulent sales by the trading company. Five years later, with the support of the Skinners, they revived their opposition to the renewal of its charter. Although the company defended itself by pointing to the falling price of furs in London, it failed to secure sufficient support in parliament to extend its charter, and the dispute rumbled on.[132]

Although little is known of the relationship between production and circulation, the disorganization of the industry during the 1690s favoured the growth of trade in second-hand and recycled headwear. Rarely recorded, the dispersal of used or stolen hats involved a myriad of petty transactions in improvised markets, which ran parallel with the sale of refurbished wares by master craftsmen like Thomas Fisher. Such an irregular business exploited an urban culture of fashion, dependent on public display, creating opportunities for the growth of hat theft by small, organized gangs operating on the streets of London during the later seventeenth and early eighteenth centuries. Though immeasurable in terms of its economic significance, the circulation of such headwear affected producers and consumers, representing a form of imitation or surrogate fashioning.[133]

Indirectly, notices in newspapers, on either side of the Atlantic, of runaway servants provide some insight into the recycling and theft of hats, not least because they were a distinctive mark of identification. An advertisement in *The London Gazette* of June 1674 offered a reward for information on a black servant, John Angola, who ran away from St Michael's Mount in Cornwall, dressed in a long coat, purple breeches and a 'very old white Beaver hat'.[134]

130 Ibid., pp. 90, 98.

131 Rich, 'Russia and the Colonial Fur Trade', pp. 319–27; Corner, 'The Tyranny of Fashion', pp. 155, 160–1; Wagner, *The English Chartered Trading Companies*, pp. 46–9. For similar problems in France see Pritchard, *In Search of Empire*, pp. 157–9.

132 Wagner, *The English Chartered Trading Companies*, pp. 170–1; Guildhall Library, MS 1570/2, f.205.

133 On the second-hand trade in clothing and the role of women in it, see Lemire, *Dress, Culture and Commerce*, pp. 101–13, 145.

134 *The London Gazette*, 18–22 June 1674, at www.thegazette.co.org.

Two years later another notice offered a reward of £5 for the arrest of a runaway servant who, accompanied by his wife, left with a parcel of stolen clothes and a large, black beaver hat.[135] Occasionally, runaways absconded with possessions of much greater value. In August 1686 a servant of Heneage Norton, merchant, fled with money, bills and a bond to the value of £460. He and an accomplice wore brown wigs, and took with them two new beaver hats and a pair of boots.[136] During the early eighteenth century *The American Weekly Mercury* carried similar notices, including one of August 1723 concerning 'a Madagascar Negro', named Jack, who ran off wearing an old beaver hat, a dark homespun jacket and a more fashionable close-bodied coat.[137] Another notice later in the year reported a runaway whose dress also included a 'large old Beaver Hat'.[138]

Legal proceedings at the Old Bailey furnish more evidence for the theft and re-distribution of headwear in London. In September 1675 the court heard a case involving a group of five robbers, operating around Islington, who seized purses and 'sometimes with sudden violence took ... Hats and Cloakes'.[139] Servants carrying goods through the streets were exposed to the cunning practices of small gangs. In November 1695 Thomas Whitehead was assaulted on the highway by two or three men. Two of the attackers grabbed a box off his head, which contained three beaver hats valued at £6. Another man, who apparently went to assist a boy accompanying Whitehead, snatched a beaver muff, worth £1 10s, from under his arm.[140] There were others who operated in a more rudimentary manner. In 1717 a man appeared in court accused of stealing 20 hats and wigs 'by throwing Ashes in Person's Eyes'.[141] The following year, the City Marshal reported the 'general Complaint of the Taverns, the Coffee-Houses, the Shopkeepers and others, that many of their Customers are afraid when it is dark, to come to their Houses and Shops, for fear that their Hats and Wigs should be snatch'd from off their Heads'.[142]

135 Ibid., 9–12 October 1676.

136 Ibid., 5–9 October 1686.

137 *The American Weekly Mercury*, 1–8 August 1723.

138 Ibid., 24–31 December 1723. Advertisements for runaways also included detailed descriptions of clothing, Kassia St Clair, *The Golden Thread: How Fabric Changed History* (London, 2018), pp. 159–60; Steele, *The English Atlantic*, pp. 259–60.

139 www.oldbaileyonline.org, version 7.2, March 2015, t16750909–4. For earlier complaints, of 1662, of the theft of hats, cloaks and even breeches in Cheapside, Cornhill and the back lanes see BL, Additional 10117, f.5.

140 www.oldbaileyonline.org, version 7.2, March 2015, t16960227–35.

141 Ibid., t17171016–20.

142 Charles Hitchin, *A True Discovery of the Conduct of the Receivers and Thief-Takers in and About the City of London* (London, 1718), p. 8; Gregory Durston, *Moll Flanders: An Analysis of an Eighteenth Century Criminal Biography* (Chichester, 1997), pp. 24, 141; Lemire, *Dress, Culture and Commerce*, pp. 131–4, 188–9.

If the capital was a favourable environment for street robbers, it was also a refuge for highwaymen who exploited its insecure edge-land in a varied and opportunistic manner. In 1681 *The London Gazette* reported the theft of a dark brown gelding by two highwaymen who also carried off a white beaver hat and wig, as well as pieces of silver and gold. Reportedly, they left behind an old white hat and a lean mare.[143] Such criminals acquired a reputation for their conduct and dress, which was celebrated in street literature. The hero of the ballad, *The Flying Highwayman*, for example, a 'flashy blade', spent his ill-gotten gold on 'flashy lasses' in bagnios, and went to his trial dressed in a fine beaver hat and overcoat.[144]

Shop thieves and burglars targeted expensive headwear and other accessories. In February 1679 a man was convicted 'for breaking open a Shop in *Fetter-lane*, … and stealing one Beaver, and several other Hats, to the value of Ten pound, some of which were taken upon him in *Middlesex*'.[145] Several years later John Belzer was tried for stealing three beavers from a haberdasher's shop on Holborn. He was taken by a Quaker, whose refusal to provide the court with sworn testimony led to his acquittal.[146] In August 1688 John Averye faced transportation to the colonies for the theft of two beaver hats, valued at £2, and a demi-castor, worth eight shillings, from a shop, and 'not much denying it'.[147] By comparison, in February 1694 William Gillet defended himself against a charge that he stole six black castor hats, claiming that he found them in the street, though he was found guilty after the prosecution successfully established they were taken from a shop.[148] At times the opportunities were too tempting to resist. In 1723 Stephen Dyer was accused of stealing a beaver hat and four castors, valued at £3 8s, while Thomas Howes 'was out of his Shop'.[149]

Burglary, usually during darkness, fed the market in stolen goods for headwear and clothing. In February 1688 James Jordan was accused of breaking into a house, with others, and stealing two beavers valued at £3, two castors worth £1, and 11 dozen other hats of a total value of £44. Jordan confessed to his role in the break-in, admitting that 'he had his share of the … goods'.[150] Such small-scale and opportunistic criminal activity was difficult to eradicate. In June 1717 Henry Sewel was found guilty of breaking into a

143 *The London Gazette*, 18–22 August 1681, at www.thegazette.co.org.

144 Gillian Spraggs, *Outlaws and Highwaymen: The Cult of the Robber in England from the Middle Ages to the Nineteenth Century* (London, 2001), pp. 182–3.

145 www.oldbaileyonline.org, version 7.2, March 2015, t16790226–13.

146 Ibid., t16820223–2.

147 Ibid., t16880831–1.

148 Ibid., t16940221–18.

149 Ibid., t17231204–39.

150 Ibid., t16880222–21.

house which he called, in canting language, a 'Bob Ken', because it was such a soft target.[151] Raising a window sash, he helped himself to three hats hanging on pegs.

Little evidence survives for the volume of trade in stolen hats, but their re-sale and re-distribution were shrouded in ambiguity, and accomplished by varied means of exchange. According to subsequent legal proceedings, in 1738 a night watchman admitted the theft of a hat, with a value of between 12s and 14s, which he sold to a woman who kept a public house in Grub Street for six shillings and six glasses of beer.[152] Thirty years later, ten beavers, stolen from a hat-maker's workshop, appeared for sale in a shop, where a craftsman recognized his 'own work upon them'.[153] From this perspective the theft of headwear was part of an alternative, half-hidden economy characterized by a permeable boundary between legal and illegal enterprise which extended the circulation of wares among less wealthy consumers.

Demonstrably, as this chapter argues, the disruption to the fur trade which alarmed colonial officials, such as the governor of New York, had a wider transatlantic dimension. In London these problems may have encouraged the reorganization of feltmaking, as indicated by the growth of large workshops, which were well-placed to take advantage of the rapid growth of overseas trade during the early eighteenth century.[154] Admittedly the volume of exports was initially small. In 1672 about 200 beavers and demi-castors, as well as 7,500 castors, were exported from London to markets including Spain, Portugal, the Canary Islands, and the Caribbean colonies of Barbados and Jamaica. According to a report of 1680, moreover, the English lost the profitable Spanish trade to their rivals in France.[155] The emergence of colonial markets, based on the widespread imitation of metropolitan style and fashion, was more promising. From the early 1660s to the mid-1680s exports of all headwear from London to the colonies increased from 7,400 to 41,500, much of which was made up of cheap castors and felts. Markets for beavers, particularly in North America, remained modest in size and speculative in character. In 1683 the Quaker merchant, James Claypoole, sent 18 beaver hats, bought in London at prices ranging from £2 10s to £3, which he was unable to sell in Philadelphia, to his brother, Edward, in Barbados. Three years later, just under

[151] Ibid., t17170606–10.

[152] Ibid., t17381011–2.

[153] Ibid., t17681019–36.

[154] Unwin, *Industrial Organization*, pp. 224–5; Corner, 'The Tyranny of Fashion', pp. 155, 158–61. The concentration of industry was undoubtedly affected by the recovery in the price of beaver skins, which doubled, in value between the 1720s and 1750s, Wagner, *The English Chartered Trading Companies*, pp. 107–8.

[155] TNA, E 190/54/1; *Britannia Languens, or a Discourse of Trade* (London, 1680), in McCulloch (ed.), *Early English Tracts on Commerce*, p. 410.

270 beaver hats were shipped to the American colonies, though most were destined for the Caribbean.[156] Yet the expansion of overseas markets was of little consolation to marginal suppliers of fur of variable quality, particularly in Chesapeake Bay, where colonial traders increasingly were unwilling to pursue a competitive business with insecure returns in London. In these circumstances the interaction between colonial and metropolitan contexts foreclosed the revival of serious interest in the trade either in Virginia or Maryland at the end of the seventeenth century.

[156] Of a total of 269, 220 were shipped to the West Indies. The total for castors was 17,200. Nuala Zahedieh, 'London and the Colonial Consumer in the Late Seventeenth Century', *Economic History Review*, 47 (1994), p. 256; Corner, 'Tyranny of Fashion', pp. 155–6; Lawson, *Fur*, pp. 118–24; Claypoole admitted that they cost him less as he purchased them in bulk, Balderston (ed.), *Claypoole's Letter Book*, pp. 224–5; Shammas, *Pre-Industrial Consumer*, p. 65; Rich, 'Russia and the Colonial Fur Trade', p. 328; Berg, *Luxury and Pleasure*, pp. 281–90 on colonial markets.

Conclusion

In *The Planter's Speech* of 1684 Thomas Tryon provided a voice for the complaints of mute animals against the oppression and violence they suffered at the hands of English colonists in North America.[1] With the recently-established Quaker settlement of Pennsylvania in his sights, he mocked the absurdity of 'those who fly from Violence in one place', to inflict it on the 'Innocent in those places where they take *shelter*'.[2] It seemed as if the settlers had declared war against the wildlife of their new habitations. With the advantage of muskets and snares, they were more efficient at killing animals than the natives, who hunted only for food and necessity. But even among the Indians, intensive hunting and destruction had become both 'an Occupation and a Trade'.[3] Through the acquisition of guns, they grew 'more expert in all kind of Violence', travelling 'night & day with all Pains and Cunning imaginable, to hunt … Creatures, not so much now for Food, as for the Skins, Feathers or Carkasses to sell'.[4] Contracting diseases 'never before heard amongst them', they 'put themselves to a World of needless Slavery and Toil'.[5] More than a century later Thomas Jefferson claimed, in his influential *Notes on the State of Virginia*, that the 'general destruction' of North American game by the Indians began with their trading relations with Europeans, 'for the purpose of purchasing matchcoats, hatchets, and fire locks, with their skins'.[6]

These insights have been echoed by modern scholarship on the fur trade. It is widely recognized that the beaver was the victim of an unparalleled and

[1] Thomas Tryon, *The Planter's Speech to his Neighbours & Country-Men of Pennsylvania, East & West-Jersey* (London, 1684), p. 41.

[2] Ibid., p. 44.

[3] Ibid., pp. 44, 51–2; Richter, *Facing East from Indian Country*, pp. 53–5 notes the environmental and cultural consequences; Axtell, *The Indians' New South*, p. 69 for change to 'hunting ethic'.

[4] Tryon, *The Planter's Speech*, p. 52.

[5] Ibid., p. 53. Eric R. Wolf, *Europe and the People Without History* (Berkeley, 1982), p. 194 describes the Indians as specialized labourers in a 'putting-out system'.

[6] Thomas Jefferson, *Notes on the State of Virginia*, ed. William Peden (Chapel Hill, 1955), p. 54. The *Notes* were written and revised during 1781 and 1782, and subsequently published in 1787.

devastating hunt. The consequences were evident along some parts of the eastern seaboard by the mid-seventeenth century, in the depletion or disappearance of local populations of fur-bearing animals. During this early period of interethnic commercial activity, exports of beaver skins from Canada to France may have reached a high point of about 30,000, while later annual shipments from New Netherland were even greater.[7] By comparison, the volume of trade from English colonies in the Chesapeake was much less, amounting to between 2,500 and 3,000 skins in some years, though exports were higher for New England. In the latter case, by the 1640s beavers were scarce in coastal regions, as they probably were in parts of the Bay area. The impact of such a decline in beaver populations on the wider environment was extensive, though little understood.[8]

From this perspective the fur trade contained a deep-seated contradiction. Without careful control and conservation, the supply of wildlife would be destroyed, irreparably so in some cases. There is little evidence that colonial traders within the Bay, or in other parts of North America, were aware of the problem. The peculiar character of the trade depended on native hunters and suppliers, who provided unpaid skilled labour, to hunt fur-bearing fauna, often in territory neither settled nor claimed by Europeans, in order to acquire a varied range of trade goods. Under these conditions native cultures of hunting were disrupted by the intrusive impact of the growing European demand for furs. But the creation of competing transatlantic markets was fostered by the Indian consumption of commodities such as cloth, metal wares, guns and alcohol.[9] In these circumstances, the intermeshing between supply and demand inexorably led to over-hunting, and a sustained onslaught on local and regional resources of beavers and other animals whose skins were highly valued. The damage was intensified by the introduction of metal traps, and improvements to hunting efficiency, as noted by Tryon and William Byrd II during the late seventeenth and early eighteenth centuries. Such pressures led to the commercialization and commodification of customary

7 John F. Richards, *The Unending Frontier: An Environmental History of the Early Modern World* (Berkeley, 2003), pp. 467, 477–81; Krech, *The Ecological Indian*, pp. 175–7. The volume of trade was often much lower.

8 Richards, *The Unending Frontier*, pp. 509–14; Richter, *Facing East from Indian Country*, pp. 47–53; Kulikoff, *Tobacco and Slaves*, p. 220 and Hinderaker, *Elusive Empires*, p. 30 for decline of game in the Bay and along the Susquehanna. Beavers can be hunted all year, as noted by Innis, *The Fur Trade in Canada*, pp. 3–4 and 17–18 for rapid extermination; Olive Patricia Dickason, *The Myth of the Savage and the Beginnings of French Colonialism in the Americas* (Edmonton, 1984), pp. 111–12; White, *The Middle Ground*, pp. 47–8, 488–93.

9 Ibid., pp. 43–9; Steele, *The English Atlantic*, p. 259; Ewen and Ewen, *Banister*, pp. 382, 385.

native hunting practices, fuelling fissures and rivalries within, and between, competing groups.[10]

Within this wider Atlantic context, the English made repeated attempts to develop the fur trade in the Bay. Lacking much experience of interethnic relations, their early commercial initiatives were sometimes experimental in character and rarely sustained. They met with varied success. Initially, interest in the fur trade was overshadowed by the need to acquire essential supplies of maize and other provisions from the Powhatans and groups along the Eastern Shore and the Potomac River. It was also delayed by Anglo-Powhatan conflict. During the 1620s and 1630s the trade gained greater definition, acquiring new direction and purpose, which focused the attention of competing colonial traders on the middle and upper reaches of the Bay. Commercial ambition and expansion, driven by the fashion for beaver hats among wealthy consumers in England, paved the way for the establishment of transatlantic joint stock ventures. The Kent Island partnership began with ambitious plans for the re-direction of the rich northern fur trade into the Bay. It depended on the willingness and ability of the Susquehannocks to act as middlemen. At the same time, the Maryland joint stock sought to establish commercial ties with the Piscataways along the Potomac, while hoping to draw down furs from the north by means of rival Indian intermediaries. Commercial competition thus inflamed colonial and native rivalries, as they cut across ethnic boundaries. The formation of competing interethnic commercial partnerships and associations exposed conflicts of interest within English colonial enterprise, while also revealing the limitations of metropolitan authority and regulation within the Bay.

The failure of these ambitious schemes was instructive. Structural weaknesses, including weak integration and capitalization, aggravated by the variable quality of English trading commodities, endangered the development of interethnic commerce. They were compounded with combustible colonial competition and native hostilities. Among the English, the problem was confused with divisive political and religious issues, entangled with territorial rivalry. It was impossible to insulate the fur trade from these pressures. Within the confines of the colonial Chesapeake, therefore, the experience of the 1630s demonstrated the damaging consequences of competition under a regime of weak, self-interested regulation.

The abandonment of transatlantic joint stock enterprise left the trade in the hands of independent colonial traders, who faced the difficulty of reconstructing and maintaining interethnic contacts on the margin of expanding agricultural economies. Against a background of local disunity and conflict,

[10] Hinderaker, *Elusive Empires*, pp. 67–73; Richter, *Facing East from Indian Country*, pp. 51–3, 177–9 for dependence; Beinart and Hughes, *Environment and Empire*, pp. 41, 43–5, 52 on technology.

complicated by the consequences of the civil war across the Atlantic, commercial activity made little progress during the 1640s and 1650s. English traders struggled to respond to competition from either the Swedes or Dutch, losing control over much of the supply of fur in the upper Bay and its wider hinterland. European rivalries within the strategically sensitive region between the Chesapeake and Delaware Bays provided native groups, particularly the Susquehannocks, with greater economic leverage. In these circumstances, commercial and diplomatic strategies led to the growing use of guns and alcohol as trading goods, provoking ripples of disruption and unsettlement across an ever-widening region of indirect contact and exchange. For the English, these rivalries were underpinned by claims to land and sovereignty. As the commercial threat from their European competitors faded, they asserted jurisdiction over the Delaware, paving the way for the introduction of new colonial settlement.

Thereafter attempts to revive the fur trade in Maryland foundered. If colonial competition damaged trading activity during the 1630s and 1640s, its subsequent recovery faltered in the face of renewed conflict between Indian groups. The resurgence of Iroquoian raiding from the north during the second half of the seventeenth century undermined the key commercial role and position of the Susquehannocks. In a striking reversal of fortune, they were forced to seek sanctuary in the colony. Exposed to the animosity of mistrustful and suspicious settlers, and facing a combined force of colonial militia, they fled, fragmenting into smaller groups. Their displacement left much of the lower Susquehanna Valley open to a new wave of colonists, whose leaders were soon embroiled in a bitter dispute with Maryland over territorial boundaries. While providing no protection against the spread of settlement, interethnic commerce also acted as a carrier for disease and cultural disruption, though it was rarely acknowledged as such. According to a report of 1699 by Hugh Jones, a clergyman, the number of native 'fighting men' who still lived within the bounds of the colony had fallen to fewer than 500.[11] Most were located in two or three settlements on the Eastern Shore. Some crossed the Bay during the winter to hunt deer for the settlers, though they declined to embrace their 'way of living or worshipp'.[12] Echoing other colonial commentators, Jones claimed that the decline of the Indian population was due to endemic conflict among rival groups, rather than with the colonists.

11 Michael G. Kammen, 'Maryland in 1699: A Letter from the Reverend Hugh Jones', *Journal of Southern History*, 29 (1963), p. 372.

12 Ibid., p. 372. During 1681 a party of Eastern Shore Indians crossed the Bay in search of work. While their leader, known to the English as Robin Hood, worked on making canoes, the others went hunting for game, Browne (ed.), *Proceedings of the Council of Maryland 1671–81*, pp. 413–17.

Yet he noted that smallpox had 'swept away a great many, so that now they are dwindled almost to nothing'.[13]

Despite divergent commercial experiences, it was a similar situation in Virginia. The decline of the native population in the colony, combined with the growing scarcity of local supplies, meant that the revival of the trade during the 1670s and 1680s drew on inland sources of furs and skins. The trading shallop gave way to the overland caravan. Using native guides and pathways, and relying on horses for transportation, frontier traders opened commercial access to new or little-known Indian groups. It was a competitive and difficult business, though it led to the acquisition of an increasingly diverse range of peltry. As in the past, competition among colonists was overlaid by native rivalries. During the 1670s the Occaneechees tried to establish themselves as middlemen between colonial traders and interior Indian groups, but they became the focus for widespread resentment. Subject to an unprovoked attack during Bacon's uprising in 1676, their subsequent decline, as explained by William Byrd II, was due to 'their perpetual Wars against all other Indians'.[14]

The experience of the Occaneechees resembled that of the Susquehannocks. Struggling to adapt to unfavourable conditions, they re-located, joining other native groups, including the Saponis, for their self-defence. At the invitation of the lieutenant governor, Alexander Spotswood, they settled near Fort Christanna, in the south west of the colony. Established in 1714, the fort was partly intended to serve as a trading outpost, under the jurisdiction of the short-lived Virginia Indian Company, which was awarded monopolistic rights over interethnic commerce, to the resentment of other colonial traders. As well as providing security for scattered, dislocated groups who faced the enmity of Indians from the north and south, it was hoped that their congregation at the fort would provide protection 'against the Incursion of all Foreign Indians'.[15]

The initiative met with limited success. During 1716 John Fontaine, a Huguenot refugee seeking land for his family, visited the fort with Spotswood, who, he noted, received an annual tribute in skins from the Saponis, 'to renew and confirm the peace and show their submission'.[16] About 200 Indian men, women and children inhabited the nearby town, where they 'live as lazily and miserable as any people in the world'.[17] Despite the apparent protection of the fort, they remained the victims of Seneca raiding. Their leaders complained

[13] Ibid., p. 372.

[14] W.K. Boyd (ed.), *Byrd's Histories of the Dividing Line Betwixt Virginia and North Carolina* (Raleigh, 1929), p. 310.

[15] Ibid., p. 310; Edward Porter Alexander (ed.), *The Journal of John Fontaine: An Irish Huguenot Son in Spain and Virginia* (Williamsburg, 1972), pp. 155–6; Webb, *Marlborough's America*, pp. 332–3, 343–8, 362.

[16] Alexander (ed.), *Journal of John Fontaine*, p. 93.

[17] Ibid., pp. 91, 97.

to Spotswood that during one recent incident, 15 men were killed without cause. Although the governor refused to provide the Saponis with assistance, he authorized their leaders to seek revenge for the deaths. He also provided compensation, in response to complaints that they were cheated by colonial traders. During his brief visit, Fontaine recorded the arrival of a trading party of 10 Meherrins with beaver, bear and deer skins to exchange. They 'delivered up their arms to the white men of the fort, and left their skins and furs there also'.[18] But because of their enmity with the Saponis, they refused to stay in the Indian town, seeking shelter in the woods until the trading was completed. Subsequently the situation at the fort grew worse. According to Byrd, the Saponis would have served as useful defenders of the colony, 'if the White People in the Neighbourhood had not debauch't their Morals, and ruin'd their Health with Rum, which was the Cause of many disorders'.[19] Travelling through the region during 1728, as a member of the commission to establish the boundary between Virginia and North Carolina, he accused George Hicks, an Indian trader and commander of 12 rangers at the fort, of being one of the main culprits. Alcohol, he observed, 'kills more of them than the Northern Indians do'.[20]

The growth of the overland trade during the late seventeenth and early eighteenth centuries, which led to a recovery in fur exports from the colony, contributed to the expansion and consolidation of the frontier. But the expeditions of explorers and traders did little to dislodge a widely held belief that the advancing borderland of colonial settlement was a necessary barrier between civil and uncivil worlds. At the same time, however, it provided an ambiguous zone of interaction between natives and settlers, as well as serving as a crossing point to inland trading partners. During the 1720s Byrd noted that traders from Virginia travelled more than 250 miles beyond the Roanoke River to trade with the Catawbas. Some expeditions were made up of 100 horses, each laden with packs weighing between 150 and 200 pounds. Conducted by 15 or 16 men, 'these Indian Caravans' were capable of covering 20 miles a day, depending on the availability of forage.[21] Though the trade was in decline, with the number of ventures falling by as much as half, according to Byrd,

18 Ibid., p. 98. The use of 'white men' in this context is revealing.

19 Boyd (ed.), *Byrd's Histories of the Dividing Line*, p. 310. Like refugee centres farther north, such outposts and forts were vulnerable to the spread of disease, White, *The Middle Ground*, pp. 40–2.

20 Boyd (ed.), *Byrd's Histories of the Dividing Line*, p. 311; Mancall, *Deadly Medicine*, pp. 153, 179 notes that alcohol became part of the fur trade during the eighteenth century, though it eroded interethnic relations.

21 Boyd (ed.), *Byrd's Histories of the Dividing Line*, p. 298; Hinderaker and Mancall, *At the Edge of Empire*, pp. 163–4 for changes to the fur trade. Such large expeditions were in decline by the 1720s, Briceland, *Westward from Virginia*, p. 177.

it was the means by which distant Indian consumers gained access to new or scarce commodities. In this way, the extension of English influence and interests served as the advance guard for speculators, settlers and farmers, primarily interested in the search for land to cultivate tobacco. In the face of widespread unsettlement and division, increasingly Indian groups were propelled into a strategy of resistance by relocation.[22]

Suspended between two worlds, the development of the fur trade during the seventeenth century required skill and expertise, as well as interested partners. It called for some degree of mutual understanding, not least because the participants were often concerned with the wider benefits of commerce. Yet it failed to promote either close intimacy or empathy. Conditions in the Bay were thus unsuited to the cultivation of a 'middle ground' which French and Indian groups established around the Great Lakes region after 1650.[23] Within a different environment, such a space provided opportunities for the negotiation of misunderstanding and difference. Despite French dependency, commerce was part of a wider alliance network which served as a channel for mediation. In the face of hostility from colonial officials and clergy, it included intercultural marriage and informal unions.[24] By contrast, English experience, the product of a distinct pattern of maritime expansion and colonial settlement, was marked by deep ambiguity regarding relationships with indigenous peoples. It was manifest in the erratic growth and character of the fur trade. Operating across an insecure and ill-defined commercial region, interethnic commerce was increasingly influenced by the centrifugal force of expanding colonial settlements. At the same time, the instability and structural weakneses of a new transatlantic enterprise were compounded with intense competition. Trade and rivalry were inseparably entangled.

The impact of these conditions on an extensive, but poorly coordinated, commodity chain was reflected in irregular and often modest levels of exports of beaver from the Bay. As this study demonstrates, this pattern was punctuated by twin peaks of rapid growth during the 1630s and 1670s, though the latter

[22] Kulikoff, *Tobacco and Slaves*, pp. 52–4, 92–3 for land; Hinderaker, *Elusive Empires*, pp. 67–71, 111, 120–1; Richter, *Facing East from Indian Country*, p. 59; Merrell, *The Indians' New World*, pp. 38–9, 43 59–61 for impact on native groups; Howard Lamar and Leonard Thompson (eds.), *The Frontier in History: North America and Southern Africa Compared* (New Haven, 1981), pp. 28, 39; Ralph Davis, *The Rise of the Atlantic Economies* (London, 1973), p. 271 for the fur trader as pioneer.

[23] White, *The Middle Ground*, pp. 50–93; Michael A. McDonnell, *Masters of Empire: Great Lakes Indians and the Making of America* (New York, 2015), pp. 91–4, 103–6 on kinship and trade.

[24] White, *The Middle Ground*, pp. x–xi, 25–6, 33–4, 50–60, 69–74, 96–7; McDonnell, *Masters of Empire*, pp. 104–6, 241, 253–7, also argues that French relations with the Indians were not as good as previously thought.

may have persisted, despite disruption, into the 1690s. Estimating the profitability of such enterprise is problematic, particularly given different attitudes towards profit and wealth accumulation between colonial and native traders.[25] Ambitious transatlantic joint stock ventures may have led to an increase in the volume of trade during the 1630s, but they failed to secure profit for their investors. Independent traders, active during the later period, were probably more advantageously situated to secure better returns, but even adventurers like William Byrd struggled to cover operating costs. The establishment of forts and outposts along the outer limits of colonial settlement reduced such charges, but at the risk of provoking problems concerning the assembly of disparate groups of demoralized Indian refugees and exposing long-standing concern at the regulation of trade. This environment failed to sustain wider interest in a difficult and demanding business, particularly within colonial economies focused on agriculture and husbandry. Revealingly, schemes to promote economic diversification rarely included the fur trade.[26] Indeed the priorities and requirements of settler colonialism pointed in another direction. In these circumstances, Indian traders such as Claiborne, Cornwallis, Byrd and Bacon, just as easily assumed the mantle of Indian fighters.

Nonetheless, a myriad of exchanges, many of them small-scale and unrecorded, cumulatively contributed to a radical re-configuration of the Bay during the seventeenth century. While the creation of an expansive tobacco culture has generally been identified as a key driver of change, this study argues that it worked in tandem with the wider impact of cross-cultural commerce. At critical times, their combination exerted inexorable pressure on the native inhabitants of the region. This hybrid colonial enterprise envisaged the exploitation or exclusion of neighbouring Indians, in favour of seeking trading partners beyond the area of settlement. By these means native agency was imperceptibly and increasingly secured, to serve the interests of colonists. As a result, the interaction between trade and plantation qualified the wider characteristics of the North American fur trade, particularly its human geography and spatial organization, which enabled the survival of Indians in the far north.[27] Within the Bay, however, it led to the marginalization and disappearance of Indian groups, part of a complex of changes which were socio-economic and geopolitical in character. As a commercial venture, it thus contained the seeds of its own decline.

But the decline of the fur trade in the Chesapeake needs to be set within a transatlantic dimension, reflecting the changing relationship between colonial supply and metropolitan demand, which ultimately rested on the market for

25 For Indian views see, White, *The Middle Ground*, pp. 99–103, 335; Richter, *Facing East from Indian Country*, pp. 44–7, 51–4.

26 Russo and Russo, *Planting an Empire*, pp. 7, 30–1, 41–2, 151–5.

27 See especially, Hornsby, *British Atlantic, American Frontier*, pp. 5–6, 63–7.

headwear. The appeal of the beaver hat was based on the vagaries of fashion and taste, as much as utility. Yet its quality and malleability gave it distinct advantages over other types of hats, enabling its long-term survival as a desirable accessory. Among wealthy aristocratic and courtly consumers, it faced little competition, though individual wardrobes included a variety of cheaper caps and hats. Styles changed, as reflected in the width of brims and the height of crowns. But the cultural value of the fur hat, within a hierarchical and divided society, persisted, outliving the growing use of periwigs during the later seventeenth century. Other types of headwear came in and out of fashion, including the Carolina, which provoked the concern of the governor of New York in 1700. Their emergence undoubtedly affected the market for beavers, especially in the short-term, but they were less of a threat than the availability of cheaper imitations. The versatility of felt made from beaver wool provided for varied use, even among consumers with sharply contrasting preferences in style. Most notably, while courtiers and royalists adopted the wide-brimmed, low-crowned beaver, adorned with jewels and feathers during the 1630s and 1640s, their critics and opponents wore plainly decorated, taller headwear made from the same material.

The distinctive quality of the beaver hat was affirmed by its market value. Prices varied, reflecting differences in craftsmanship and the appearance of the fur. Yet fine headwear maintained its value across the period. During the 1630s hats acquired for Charles I cost between £4 and £5. In 1651 the earl of Bath paid £4 10s for a 'very good beaver'.[28] Forty years later the price of headwear purchased for William III was £5. Even among wealthy consumers this represented a substantial investment in personal wardrobes and appearances. Expensive headwear also required careful maintenance. During the early eighteenth century, for example, Jonathan Swift had his three beaver hats regularly dressed at a charge that ranged from under one shilling to 2s 6d.[29]

In these circumstances, consumption was limited to an elite, but relatively open, domestic market. It was segmented in character, reflecting distinct communities of consumers at court, in the city and country. There were inter-connections and a degree of overlap between these specialized markets, which facilitated the diffusion of fashion and new styles. Their relative importance shifted over the course of the seventeenth century, broadly at the expense of the court and country in favour of an expanding, multi-layered urban network. Underpinned by the unrivalled expansion of London, it was supported and diversified by the growth of provincial centres. They included social and recreational towns and spas, such as Bath, where the congregation of wealthy,

28 Gray (ed.), *Devon Household Accounts*, 2, p. 158; for other prices, Strong, 'Charles I's Clothes', pp. 81–2 and Wardle, *For Our Royal Person*, pp. 27, 47–8.

29 Thompson and Thompson (eds.), *The Account Books of Swift*, p. lxxviii.

landed and urban consumers created a venue for the more aesthetic performance of dress and manners. These contrasting socio-cultural environments were marked by varied patterns of demand and consumption. Rooted in differences affecting wealth and income, they were reinforced by diffuse variables, including geographical location, individual life-cycle, age and gender, as well as consumer preference and experience.

Economic and commercial expansion encouraged the growth of domestic and overseas markets. Although modest in scale, increasing domestic consumption reflected wider access to the market for a range of consumer goods, including clothing and fashionable accessories. While reliant on the continuing purchasing power of well-established landed and mercantile elites, it included newer, upwardly mobile urban groups keen to express their civility and taste through consumer behaviour and public appearance. Fuelled by social emulation and competition, headwear retained its essential symbolic value, encoded in the ritualization of gesture and deportment. Increasingly, moreover, domestic consumption was augmented by overseas sales. Initially of marginal significance, the export of small parcels of beaver hats can be detected as early as the 1630s. The volume of trade grew progressively during the second half of the seventeenth century, albeit from a small base, though it met strong competition from the French.

Nonetheless the growth of demand for beaver hats was outstripped by the increase in the supply of fur from North America, following the establishment of the Hudson's Bay Company in 1670. With a saturated metropolitan fur market, the price of beaver skins began to fall. The company responded with various measures to stabilize prices, including the re-export of fur to Russia and Northern Europe. These commercial problems were aggravated by the disorganization and disarray of the Feltmakers' Company, which seriously disrupted manufacturing and production during the 1680s and 1690s. At the same time, the decision of company leaders to pay higher wage rates to craftsmen may have narrowed the opportunity for a significant reduction in the market price of headwear.

Yet the beaver hat, reinvented as the tricorne, retained its long-standing appeal. Falling prices, partly the result of productivity gains linked to the emergence of larger workshops in London during the early eighteenth century, extended the market, with the assistance of improvements in the standard of living for many middling groups. Growth was facilitated by the expansion of provincial shops and shopping. Individually crafted or ready-to-wear, fashionable or otherwise, headwear continued to be a vital part of day-to-day and ceremonial wear, and an essential accessory for social performance. Richard 'Beau' Nash, one of a new type of fashion-leaders, earned renown at Bath for his dress, which included a white beaver hat. Well-off consumers, such as George Lucy, a landowner from Warwickshire, were able to buy fine headwear during visits to the spa.[30] As an eye-catching and focal point of appearance, it continued to provoke comment that was freighted with implications regarding personal taste or character, while serving varied functions. One of Horace Walpole's correspondents reported an incident at the Sheldonian Theatre, in Oxford, during 1756, when a window beam fell onto the head of Parson Fletcher, who was 'brute enough' to be wearing a 'vast beaver … which preserved his brains'.[31] At the same time fur hats were worn by the royal family at court ceremonial and public displays of state power. In 1742 Walpole reported the presence at a military review of George II and his sons, 'Messieurs d'Allemagne', who 'roll their red eyes, stroke up their great beavers, and look fierce'.[32] Indeed, the adoption of various types of beaver headwear as regulation head-dress by the British army during the eighteenth century opened new markets, reflecting its value as a marker for rank and deference.[33]

The wider appeal of fur hats supported the growth of overseas markets after 1700. Exports of headwear from London in 1736 were 700,000 in number, two-thirds of which were made up of beavers or castors.[34] With their higher price, the beavers accounted for about 80% of the total value of the trade. Thereafter the volume of exports fluctuated during the 1740s and 1750s. But commercial volatility was followed by striking, though uneven, growth during the closing decades of the eighteenth century. Markets ranged across Southern and Northern Europe. For example, from 1729 to 1735 annual exports of beaver and castor hats to Sweden and Russia grew from 24 dozen to 264 dozen. Exports to Portugal from 1767 to 1771, while lower than the volume of trade during the late seventeenth century, ranged from 523 to 886 dozen. By this time trade to the East Indies and China was growing, reaching a peak of nearly 7,000 dozen in 1782.[35] English colonial markets in North America and the Caribbean, benefiting from the protection of the Hat Act of 1732, increasingly supplemented domestic consumption. The prohibition on intercolonial trade in American headwear enabled English hat-makers to consolidate and expand

30 Wilcox, *The Mode in Hats*, pp. 114, 141; Borsay, *The English Urban Renaissance*, pp. 28–35.

31 Wilmarth S. Lewis (ed.), *The Yale Edition of Horace Walpole's Correspondence*, 48 vols. (New Haven, 1937–83), 9, pp. 193–4.

32 Ibid., 17, p. 410.

33 A.V.B. Norman, 'Regulation Head-Dresses of the British Army, 1812', *Journal of the Society for Army Historical Research*, 49 (1971), pp. 38–41; Ewing, *Fur in Dress*, pp. 83–4. Lemire, *Dress, Culture and Commerce*, pp. 38–41 notes the importance of the armed services for the clothing trade in general.

34 Corner, 'Tyranny of Fashion', p. 155.

35 TNA, T64/273, nos. 20 (East Indies and China), 45 (Sweden and Russia), 50 (Portugal).

their commercial interests in the colonies. In 1748 about 10,000 beavers and castors were shipped to Jamaica. Within seven years the total had risen to nearly 15,000. By 1770 nearly two-thirds of total exports of beaver hats were destined for the colonies.[36]

With the passage of time, and as the mode in headwear changed, the beaver lost much of its fashionable and symbolic function. Yet it lived on in fiction as a visual cue to character. The eponymous heroine of Charlotte Bronte's novel, *Jane Eyre*, published in 1847, wore a black beaver bonnet, as befitted her modest dress and sensibility. In contrast, the hypocrisy of the headmaster, Brocklehurst, whose concern to teach his pupils 'to clothe themselves with shame-facedness and sobriety, not with braided hair and costly apparel', was exposed by the entry of his two daughters, dressed in velvet, silk and furs, including fashionable grey beaver hats, with ostrich plumes.[37] By this time the Bay had long ceased to be a supplier of beaver skins for the British market. Yet the self-destructive character of an enterprise exemplified by deep-seated tension between consumption and conservation lay unresolved. Shortly after the publication of *Jane Eyre*, in 1854, 500,000 skins were put up for auction in London by the Hudson's Bay Company. Despite a growing awareness of the implications of resource depletion, the hunt for wildlife to meet the demands of European markets, so angrily denounced by Thomas Tryon, proceeded unabated.[38]

36 Ibid., no. 35 (Jamaica); Kenneth Morgan, *Bristol and the Atlantic Trade in the Eighteenth Century* (Cambridge, 1993), p. 89; Wagner, *The English Chartered Trading Companies*, p. 185 for the Hat Act; T.H. Breen, '"Baubles of Britain": The American and Consumer Revolutions of the Eighteenth Century', *Past and Present*, 119 (1988), pp. 85–7 on the influence of London fashions in the colonies.

37 Charlotte Bronte, *Jane Eyre* (New York, 1997), pp. 91–2, 168–9; John Harvey, *Men in Black* (London, 1995), p. 199.

38 Beinart and Hughes, *Environment and Empire*, pp. 47, 54–5 note that changes to fashion saved the beaver; David Arnold, *The Problem of Nature: Environment, Culture and European Expansion* (Oxford, 1996), pp. 123–4; Krech, *The Ecological Indian*, pp. 177–8, 188–94 which also considers attempts at regulation.

APPENDIX

Table 1: Imports of furs and skins into London from 1670 to 1680.

	1671/72	1675/76	1676/77	1677/78	1679/80
Beaver	2,503	2,858	1,118	1,260	1,445
Deer	1,261	7,911	2,996	4,037	4,220
Raccoon	94	1,731	870	597	575
Muskrat	18	1,366	394	705	226
Fox	20	881	243	575	676
Otter	359	757	162	394	306
Cat	209	670	133	253	305
Wolf	41	515	191	189	126
Mink	0	409	165	422	60
Bear	3	176	51	102	177
Fisher	0	203	98	0	0
Elk	11	11	10	9	10
Buffalo	0	29	0	0	0
Moose	0	1	0	6	0
Marten	0	0	0	10	0

Sources: TNA, E 190/56/1 (1671/72); 190/64/1 (1675/76); 190/68/1 (1676/77); 190/75/1 (1677/78); 190/90/1 (1679/80)

Table 2: Imports of furs and skins into Bristol from 1670 to 1678.

	1670/71	1673/74	1674/75	1677/78
Beaver	34	12	94	0
Deer	90	88	0	33
Raccoon	170	0	18	30
Muskrat	160	0	0	0
Fox	15	0	12	12
Otter	0	0	2	4
Cat	0	0	12	0
Wolf	0	0	0	1
Bear	0	0	0	1

Sources: TNA, E190/1137/3 (1670/71); 190/1138/2 (1673/74); 190/1138/3 (1674/75); 190/1139/2 (1677/78)

SELECT BIBLIOGRAPHY OF WORKS CONSULTED

Manuscript Sources

The National Archives, Kew

C 24/621, 629, 690 (Chancery proceedings)
CO 1/1, 6, 8–9, 36, 39, 5/728, 1371, 1376 (Colonial office, miscellaneaous papers)
E 134.11 Chas.I/Mich.42 (Exchequer depositions)
E 190/16/2; 190/22/9; 190/25/9; 190/29/4; 190/31/3; 190/35/1,5; 190/36/1,5,7; 190/38/1,5,7; 190/43/5; 190/44/1; 190/50/1; 190/54/1; 190/56/1; 190/64/1; 190/68/1; 190/75/1; 190/90/1; 190/425/1; 190/426/1; 190/427/6; 190/427/8; 190/947/8; 190/1032/13; 190/1033/15; 190/1137/3; 1138/2,3; 190/1139/2 ; 190/1448/8 (Port books)
HCA 1/33, 34, 37, 38, 40, 44, 45, 48 (High Court of Admiralty, oyer and terminer records)
HCA 13/52, 57–58, 60, 243 (High Court of Admiralty, examinations)
HCA 14/9 (High Court of Admiralty, exemplifications)
HCA 15/1 (High Court of Admiralty, instance and prize courts)
HCA 24/96, 99, 100, 102, 105, 106, 108 (High Court of Admiralty, libels)
LR 5/66 (Royal bills and accounts)
PC 2/41–8, 50 (Privy Council registers)
SP 16 (State Papers, Charles I)
T 64/273 (Customs papers)

The British Library, London

Additional MSS 12505, 12496, 14285, 22085, 25302
Cotton MS Nero B III
Cotton MSS Otho E VIII, IX
Egerton MSS 921, 2395
Lansdowne MSS 26, 33, 142, 162
Sloane MSS 3662, 4432
Stowe MS 184

The Enoch Pratt Library, Baltimore

Young Collection, Document 7 (A Relation of a Voyage by Cyprian Thorowgood)

The Guildhall Library, London

MSS 1570/1 and 1570/2
MS 15842/1
MS 15857
MS 24201

Lambeth Palace Library, London

MS 688

Printed Sources

A Relation of Maryland (Ann Arbor, 1966)

Abbott, W.C. (ed.), *The Writings and Speeches of Oliver Cromwell*, 4 vols. (Cambridge, Mass., 1937–47)

Adams, C.F. (ed.), *The New English Canaan of Thomas Morton* (The Prince Society, 14, 1883)

Alexander, E.P. (ed.), *The Journal of John Fontaine: An Irish Huguenot Son in Spain and Virginia 1710–1719* (Williamsburg, 1972)

Ames, S.M. (ed.), *County Court Records of Accomack-Northampton, Virginia 1632–1640* (Washington, 1954)

——, *County Court Records of Accomack-Northampton, Virginia 1640–1645* (Charlottesville, 1973)

Andrews, C.M. (ed.), *Narratives of the Insurrection 1675–1690* (New York, 1915)

Appleby, J.C. (ed.), *A Calendar of Material Relating to Ireland from the High Court of Admiralty Examinations 1536–1641* (Irish Manuscripts Commission, Dublin, 1992)

Arnold, J. (ed.), *'Lost from Her Majesties Back': Items of Clothing and Jewels Lost or Given Away by Queen Elizabeth I Between 1561 and 1585, Entered in One of the Day Books Kept for the Records of the Wardrobe of Robes* (The Costume Society, Extra Series, 7, 1980)

——, *Queen Elizabeth's Wardrobe Unlock'd* (Leeds, 1988)

Baines, B. J. (ed.), *Three Pamphlets on the Jacobean Antifeminist Controversy* (Delmar, 1978)

Balderston, M. (ed.), *James Claypoole's Letter Book: London and Philadelphia 1681–1684* (San Marino, 1967)

Barbon, N., *A Discourse of Trade* (London, 1690)

Barbour, P.L. (ed.), *The Complete Works of Captain John Smith (1580–1631)*, 3 vols. (Chapel Hill, 1986)

——, *The Jamestown Voyages Under the First Charter 1606–1609*, 2 vols. (Hakluyt Society, Second Series, 136 & 137, 1969)

Beer, E.S. de (ed.), *The Diary of John Evelyn*, 6 vols. (Oxford, 1955)

Berkeley, W., *A Discourse and View of Virginia* (London, 1663)

Bettey, J.H. (ed.), *Calendar of the Correspondence of the Smyth Family of Ashton Court 1548–1642* (Bristol Record Society, 35, 1982)

Beverley, R., *The History and Present State of Virginia*, ed. L.B. Wright (Chapel Hill, 1947)

Biggar, H.P. (ed.), *The Works of Samuel Champlain*, 6 vols. (Champlain Society, 1922–36)

Billings, W.M. (ed.), 'Some Acts not in Hening's *Statutes*: The Acts of Assembly, April 1652, November 1652, and July 1653', *Virginia Magazine of History and Biography*, 83 (1975), pp. 22–76

——, *The Papers of Sir William Berkeley, 1605–1677* (Richmond, 2007)

Birch, T. (ed.), *A Collection of the State Papers of John Thurloe*, 7 vols. (London, 1742)

Birch, T. (ed.), *The Court and Times of Charles the First*, 2 vols. (London, 1848)

Bond, D.F. (ed.), *The Spectator*, 5 vols. (Oxford, 1965)

——, *The Tatler*, 3 vols. (Oxford, 1987)

Boyd, W.K. (ed.), *William Byrd's Histories of the Dividing Line Betwixt Virginia and North Carolina* (Raleigh, 1929)

Bradford, W., *History of Plymouth Plantation 1620–1647*, 2 vols. (New York, 1912)

Brown, A. (ed.), *The Genesis of the United States*, 2 vols. (Boston, 1891)

Browne, W.H. (ed.), *Proceedings and Acts of the General Assembly of Maryland, January 1637/8-September 1664* (Maryland Historical Society, 1, 1883)

——, *Proceedings and Acts of the General Assembly of Maryland April 1666-June 1676* (Maryland Historical Society, 2, 1884)

——, *Proceedings of the Council of Maryland 1636–1667* (Maryland Historical Society, 3, 1885)

——, *Judicial and Testamentary Business of the Provincial Court 1637–1650* (Maryland Historical Society, Court Series, 4, 1887)

——, *Proceedings of the Council of Maryland 1667–1687/8* (Maryland Historical Society, 5, 1887)

——, *Proceedings and Acts of the General Assembly of Maryland October 1678-November 1683* (Maryland Historical Society, 7, 1889)

——, *Judicial and Testamentary Business of the Provincial Court 1649/50–1657* (Maryland Historical Society, Court Series, 10, 1891)

——, *Proceedings and Acts of the General Assembly of Maryland April 1684-June 1692* (Maryland Historical Society, 13, 1894)

——, *Proceedings of the Council of Maryland 1671–1681* (Maryland Historical Society, 15, 1896)

Bruce, J., et al. (eds.), *Calendar of State Papers, Domestic Series, of the Reign of Charles I, 1625–1649*, 21 vols. (London, 1858–93)

Bry, Theodor de, *Thomas Hariot's Virginia* (Ann Arbor, 1966)

Bullock, W., *Virginia Impartially Examined* (London, 1649)

The Calvert Papers, 3 vols. (Maryland Historical Society, Fund-Publication, 28, 1889)

Carr, C.T. (ed.), *Select Charters of Trading Companies A.D. 1530–1707* (Selden Society, 28, 1913)

Cary, W., *The Present State of England* (London, 1626)

Cell, G. (ed.), *Newfoundland Discovered: English Attempts at Colonisation 1610–1630* (Hakluyt Society, Second Series, 160, 1982)

'Claiborne vs. Cloberry et als. in the High Court of Admiralty', *Maryland*

Historical Magazine, 26, (1931), pp. 381–404; 27 (1932), pp. 17–28, 99–114, 191–214, 337–52; 28, (1933), pp. 26–43, 172–95, 257–65, 345–6

Colby, F. T. (ed.), *The Visitation of the County of Devon in the Year 1620* (Harleian Society, 1872)

Collections of the Massachusetts Historical Society (Fourth Series, 9, 1871)

Copland, P., *Virginia's God Be Thanked* (London, 1622)

Crowne, J., *City Politiques*, ed. John Harold Wilson (London, 1967)

Cumming, W.P. (ed.), *The Discoveries of John Lederer* (Charlottesville, 1958)

Dahlgren, S., and H. Norman (eds.), *The Rise and Fall of New Sweden: Governor Risingh's Journal 1654–1655 in its Historical Context* (Uppsala, 1960)

Dankers, J., and P. Sluyter, *Journal of a Voyage to New York in 1679–80*, ed. Henry C. Murphy (Brooklyn, 1867, repr. 1966)

Dasent, J.R. (ed.), *Acts of the Privy Council of England 1542–1631*, 46 vols. (London, 1890–1964)

Dekker, T., *The Gull's Horn-Book: Or, Fashion to Please All Sorts of Gulls*, ed. E.D. Pendry (London, 1967)

Donck, A. van der, *A Description of the New Netherlands*, ed. T.F. O'Donnell (Syracuse, 1968)

Dunn, R.S., and M.M. Dunn (eds.), *The Papers of William Penn*, 5 vols. (Philadelphia, 1981–7)

Etherege, G., *The Man of the Mode*, ed. John Conaghan (Edinburgh, 1973)

Exwood, M., and H.L. Lehmann (eds.), *The Journal of William Schellinks' Travels in England 1661–1663* (Camden Society, Fifth Series, 1, 1993)

Fernow, B. (ed.), *Documents Relating to the History of the Dutch and Swedish Settlements on the Delaware River* (New York, 1877)

Flaherty, D.H. (ed.), *For the Colony in Virginea Britannia: Lawes Divine, Morall and Martiall, etc.* (Charlottesville, 1969)

Force, P. (ed.), *Tracts and Other Papers, Relating Principally to the Origin, Settlement, and Progress of the Colonies in North America, from the Discovery of the Country to the Year 1776*, 4 vols. (Washington, 1836–47)

Fox, G., Journal of: https://docsouth.unc.edu/csr/index.html/document/csr01–0085

Gamble D.P., and P.E.H. Hair (eds.), *The Discovery of River Gambra by Richard Jobson 1623* (Hakluyt Society, Third Series, 1999)

Gehring, C.T. (ed.), *New Netherland Documents Series: Laws & Writs of Appeal 1647–1653* (Syracuse, 1991)

——, *New Netherland Document Series: Correspondence 1647–1653* (Syracuse, 2000)

——, *New Netherland Document Series: Correspondence, 1654–1658* (Syracuse, 2003)

Gerald of Wales, *The Journey Through Wales and the Description of Wales*, translated by Lewis Thorpe (Harmondsworth, 1978)

Gray, T. (ed.), *Devon Household Accounts, 1627–59*, 2 vols. (Devon and Cornwall Record Society, 38 & 39, 1995–96)

Green, M.A.E. et al. (eds.), *Calendar of State Papers, Domestic Series, of the Reign of James I, 1603–1625,* 4 vols. (London, 1856–9)

——, *Calendar of State Papers, Domestic Series, 1649–1660*, 13 vols. (London, 1875–86)

——, *Calendar of State Papers, Domestic Series, of the Reign of Charles II, 1660–1685*, 28 vols. (London, 1860–93)

Hakluyt, R., *The Principall Navigations, Voiages & Discoveries of the English Nation* (London, 1589)

——, *Discourse of Western Planting*, eds. D. B. and A. M. Quinn (Hakluyt Society, Extra Series, 45, 1993)

Hall, C.C. (ed.), *Narratives of Early Maryland 1633–1684* (New York, 1925)

Hamor, R., *A True Discourse of the Present State of Virginia* (London, 1615, repr. Richmond, 1957)

Harlow, V.T. (ed.), *Colonising Expeditions to the West Indies and Guiana, 1623–1667* (Hakluyt Society, Second Series, 56, 1925)

Harrison, W., *The Description of England*, ed. G. Edelen (Ithaca, 1968)

Hartwell, H., J. Blair and E. Chilton, *The Present State of Virginia and the College*, ed. Hunter Dickinson Farish (Williamsburg, 1940)

Hening, W.W. (ed.), *The Statutes at Large: Being a Collection of all the Laws of Virginia from the First Session of the Legislature, in the Year 1619*, vols. 1 and 2 (New York, 1823)

Hiden, M.W. (ed.), 'Accompts of the Tristram and Jane', *Virginia Magazine of History and Biography*, 62 (1954), pp. 424–47

Hinds, A.B. (ed.), *Calendar of State Papers Relating to English Affairs in the Archives of Venice, Volume 21, 1628–1629* (London, 1916)

Hitchin, C., *A True Discovery of the Conduct of the Receivers and Thief-Takers in and About the City of London* (London, 1718)

Hosmer, J.K. (ed.), *Winthrop's Journal 'History of New England' 1630–1649*, 2 vols. (New York, 1908)

Hotten, J.C. (ed.), *The Original Lists of Persons of Quality who went from Great Britain to the American Plantations* (London, 1874)

Hughes, P.L., and J.F. Larkin (eds.), *Tudor Royal Proclamations*, 3 vols. (New Haven, 1964–69)

Jeayes, I.H. (ed.), *Letters of Philip Gawdy of West Harling, Norfolk, and of London to Various Members of His Family 1579–1616* (Publications of the Roxburghe Club, 1906)

Jefferson, T., *Notes on the State of Virginia*, ed. William Peden (Chapel Hill, 1955)

Jensen, M. (ed.), *English Historical Documents Volume IX: American Colonial Documents to 1776* (Oxford, 1964)

Jester, A.L. (ed.), *Adventurers of Purse and Person: Virginia 1607–1625* (Richmond, 1964)

Johnson, A. (ed.), *Geographia Americae with an Account of the Delaware Indians Based on Surveys and Notes Made in 1654–1656* (Philadelphia, 1925)

Jonson, B., *Cynthia's Revels or, the Fountain of Self-love*, ed. Alexander Corbin Judson (New York, 1912)

——, *Every Man in His Humour*, ed. Martin Seymour-Smith (London, 1966)

——, *The Magnetic Lady*, ed. Peter Happe (Manchester, 2000)

Kammen, M. (ed.), 'Maryland in 1699: A Letter from the Reverend Hugh Jones', *Journal of Southern History*, 29 (1963), pp. 362–72

——, 'Virginia at the Close of the Seventeenth Century: An Appraisal by James

Blair and John Locke', *Virginia Magazine of History and Biography,* 74 (1966), pp. 141–69

Kingsbury, S.M. (ed.), *The Records of the Virginia Company of London*, 4 vols. (Washington, 1906–35)

Klene, J. (ed.), *The Southwell-Sibthorpe Commonplace Book Folger MS. V.b.198* (Renaissance English Text Society, Seventh Series, 20, 1995)

Krugler, J.D. (ed.), *To Live Like Princes: A Short Treatise Sett Downe in a Letter Written by R.W. to His Worthy Friend C.J.R. Concerning the New Plantation Now Erecting Under the Right Ho[nora]ble the Lord Baltimore* (Baltimore, 1976)

Laer, A.J.F. van (ed.), *Documents Relating to New Netherland 1624–1626* (San Marino, 1924)

Laing, D. (ed.), *Royal Letters, Charters, and Tracts Relating to the Colonization of New Scotland* (Edinburgh, 1867)

Larkin, J.F. (ed.), *Stuart Royal Proclamations*, 2 vols. (Oxford, 1983)

Latham, R., and W. Matthews (eds.), *The Diary of Samuel Pepys,* 11 vols. (London, 1970–83)

Lawson, J., *A New Voyage to Carolina*, ed. Hugh Talmage Lefler (Chapel Hill, 1967)

Lemon, R., et al. (eds.), *Calendar of State Papers Domestic, 1547–1603 & Addenda*, 7 vols. (London, 1856–71)

Lescarbot, M., *Novia Francia: A Description of Acadia, 1606*, translated by P. Erondelle, 1609 (London, 1928)

'Letter from John Rolfe to Sir Thos. Dale', *Virginia Magazine of History and Biography,* 22 (1914), pp. 150–7

Lewis, W.S. (ed.), *The Yale Edition of Horace Walpole's Correspondence*, 48 vols. (New Haven, 1937–83)

Loades, D. (ed.), *The Papers of George Wyatt Esquire of Boxley Abbey in the County of Kent* (Camden Society, Fourth Series, 5, 1968)

Macray, W.D. (ed.), *The History of the Rebellion and Civil Wars in England Begun in the Year 1641, By Edward, Earl of Clarendon*, 6 vols. (Oxford, 1888)

Mandeville, B., *The Fable of the Bees*, ed. P. Harth (London, 1970)

Matthews, W. (ed.), *The Diary of Dudley Ryder 1715–1716* (London, 1939)

McCulloch, J.R. (ed.), *Early English Tracts on Commerce* (London, 1856, repr. Cambridge, 1954)

McGrath, P. (ed.), *Merchants and Merchandise in Seventeenth-Century Bristol* (Bristol Record Society, 19, 1955)

McIlwaine, H.R. (ed.), *Journals of the House of Burgesses of Virginia 1659/60–1693* (Richmond, 1914)

——, *Journals of the House of Burgesses of Virginia 1619–1658/59* (Richmond, 1915)

——, *Minutes of the Council and General Court of Colonial Virginia 1622–32, 1670–76* (Richmond, 1924)

Merritt, E. (ed.), *Proceedings of the Provincial Court of Maryland 1670/71–1675* (Maryland Historical Society, Court Series, 65, 1952)

Middleton, T., *A Mad World, My Masters and Other Plays*, ed. Michael Taylor (Oxford, 1995)

Middleton, T., and T. Dekker, *The Roaring Girl*, ed. Paul A. Mulholland (Manchester, 1987)

Morton, T., *The New English Canaan* (Amsterdam, 1637, repr. New York, 1967)

Myddelton, W.M. (ed.), *Chirk Castle Accounts A.D. 1605–1666* (St Albans, 1908)

——, *Chirk Castle Accounts A.D. 1666–1753* (Manchester, 1931)

Myers, A.C. (ed.), *Narratives of Early Pennsylvania, West New Jersey and Delaware 1630–1707* (New York, 1912)

Neill, E.D. (ed.), *The Founders of Maryland as Portrayed in Manuscripts, Provincial Records and Early Documents* (Albany, 1876)

Neville, J.D., (compiler), *Bacon's Rebellion: Abstracts of Materials in the Colonial Records Project* (Jamestown, 1976)

Nugent, N.M. (ed.), *Cavaliers and Pioneers: Abstracts of Virginia Land Patents and Grants: Volume I 1623–1666* (Richmond, 1934)

O'Callaghan, E.B., and B. Fernow (eds.), *Documents Relative to the Colonial History of the State of New York*, 15 vols. (Albany, 1853–87)

Ogle, Rev. O. et al. (eds.), *Calendar of Clarendon State Paper,* 5 vols. (Oxford, 1872–1970)

Peacham, H., *The Complete Gentleman*, ed. V. B. Heltzel (Ithaca, 1962)

Penn, W., *No Cross, No Crown: A Discourse, Shewing the Nature and Discipline of the Holy Cross of Christ* (London, 1682)

Pleasants, J.H. (ed.), *Proceedings of the Provincial Court of Maryland 1663–1666* (Maryland Historical Society, Court Series, 49, 1932)

——, *Proceedings of the Court of Chancery of Maryland 1669–1679* (Maryland Historical Society, Court Series, 51, 1934)

——, *Proceedings of the County Courts of Kent (1648–1676), Talbot (1662–1674), and Somerset (1665–1668) Counties* (Maryland Historical Society, Court Series, 54, 1937)

——, *Proceedings of the Provincial Court of Maryland 1666–1670* (Maryland Historical Society, Court Series, 57, 1940)

Powell, W.S. (ed.), *Ye Countie of Albermarle in Carolina: A Collection of Documents 1664–1675* (Raleigh, 1958)

Pulsifier, D. (ed.), *Records of the Colony of New Plymouth in New England: Acts of the Commissioners of the United Colonies of New England: Volume 1 1643–1651* (Boston, 1859)

Purchas, S., *Hakluytus Posthumus, or Purchas his Pilgrimes*, 20 vols. (Glasgow, 1905–7)

Quinn, D.B. (ed.), *The Roanoke Voyages 1584–1590*, 2 vols. (Hakluyt Society, Second Series, 104 & 105, 1955)

——, *New American World: A Documentary History of North America to 1612*, 5 vols. (London, 1979)

Ransome, D.R. (ed.), 'The Parliamentary Papers of Nicholas Ferrar 1624', in *Camden Miscellany*, (Camden Society, 33, 1996)

Raymond, J. (ed.), *Making the News: An Anthology of the Newsbooks of Revolutionary England 1641–1660* (Moreton-in-Marsh, 1993)

Robertson, Canon S., 'The Expense-Book of James Master, Esq. A.D. 1646 to 1676', in 4 parts, *Archaelogia Cantiana,* 15 (1883), pp. 161–216; 16 (1886), pp. 244–59; 17 (1887), pp. 323–52; 18 (1889), pp. 116–54

Rogers, Rev. C. (ed.), *The Earl of Stirling's Register of Royal Letters Relative to the Affairs of Scotland and Nova Scotia from 1615–1635*, 2 vols. (Edinburgh, 1885)

Rublack, U., and M.Hayward (eds.), *The First Book of Fashion: The Book of Clothes of Matthäus & Vert Konrad Schwarz of Augsburg* (London, 2015)

Sainsbury, W.N. (ed.), *Calendar of State Papers, Colonial Series 1547–1660* (London, 1860)

Sainsbury, W.N., et al. (eds.), *Calendar of State Papers, Colonial Series, America and West Indies, 1661–1730*, 37 vols. (London, 1880–1937)

Salley, A.S. (ed.), *Narratives of Early Carolina 1650–1708* (New York, 1911)

Schreeven, W.J. Van, and G.H. Reese (eds.), *Proceedings of the General Assembly of Virginia July 30-August 4, 1619* (Jamestown, 1969)

Scouloudi, I. (ed.), *Returns of Strangers in the Metropolis 1593, 1627, 1635, 1639* (Huguenot Society of London, Quarto Series, 57, 1985)

Scull, G.D. (ed.), *The Evelyns in America: Compiled from Family Papers and other Sources, 1608–1805* (Oxford, privately printed, 1881)

Secord, A.W. (ed.), *Defoe's Review. Reproduced from the Original Editions, with an Introduction and Bibliographical Notes*, 22 vols. (Facsimile Text Society, New York, 1938)

The Shaftesbury Papers: South Carolina Historical Society (Stroud, 2000)

Steckley, G.F. (ed.), *The Letters of John Paige, London, Merchant, 1648–1658* (London Record Society, 21, 1984)

Steiner, B.C. (ed.), *Proceedings of the Provincial Court of Maryland, 1658–1662* (Maryland Historical Society, 41, 1922)

Stith, W., *The History of the First Discovery and Settlement of Virginia* (Williamsburg, 1747, repr. Spartanburg, 1965)

Stock, L.F. (ed.), *Proceedings and Debates of the British Parliaments Respecting North America: Volume 1, 1542–1688* (Washington, 1924)

Strachey, W., *The Historie of Travell into Virginia Britania*, eds. Louis B. Wright and Virginia Freund (Hakluyt Society, Second Series, 103, 1953)

Strange News from Virginia; Being a Full and True Account of the Life and Death of Nathanael Bacon Esquire (London, 1677)

Stubbes, P., *The Anatomie of Abuses* (London, 1583)

Taylor, E.G.R. (ed.), *The Original Writings and Correspondence of the Two Richard Hakluyts*, 2 vols. (Hakluyt Society, Second Series, 76 & 77, 1935)

Thompson, P.V., and D.J. Thompson (eds.), *The Account Books of Jonathan Swift* (London, 1984)

Tinling, M. (ed.), *The Correspondence of the Three William Byrds of Westover, Virginia 1684–1776*, 2 vols. (Charlottesville, 1977)

[Tryon, T.], *Some Memoirs of the Life of Mr. Tho. Tryon, Late of London, Merchant* (London, 1705)

Tryon, T., *The Planter's Speech to his Neighbours & Country-Men of Pennsylvania, East & West-Jersey* (London, 1684)

Tyler, L.G. (ed.), *Narratives of Early Virginia, 1606–1625* (New York, 1907)

Tyson, B. (ed.), *The Estate and Household Accounts of Sir Daniel Fleming of Rydal Hall, Westmorland from 1688–1701* (Cumberland and Westmorland Antiquarian and Archaeological Society, Record Series, 13, 2001)

Walwyn, W., *The Power of Love* (London, 1643)
Wardle, P., *For Our Royal Person: Master of the Robes Bills of King-Stadholder William III* (Apeldoorn, 2002)
Waterhouse, E., *A Declaration of the State of the Colonie and Affaires in Virginia* (London, 1622)
Whitaker, A., *Good Newes from Virginia* (London, 1613)
Williams, E., *Virgo Triumphans: Or Virginia Richly and Truly Valued* (London, 1651)
——, *Virginia: More Especially the South Part thereof, Richly and Truly Valued* (London, 1650)
Winthrop Papers, 5 vols. (Massachusetts Historical Society, 1929–57)
Woolley, H., *The Gentlewomans Companion; Or, a Guide to the Female Sex* (London, 3rd edition, 1682)

Secondary works

Adams, S., *The Best and Worst Country in the World: Perspectives on the Early Virginia Landscape* (Charlottesville, 2001)
Alpert, J.L., 'The Origin of Slavery in the United States – The Maryland Precedent', in B.A. Glasrud and A.M. Smith (eds.), *Race Relations in British North America, 1607–1783* (Chicago, 1982), pp. 117–43
Altman, I., and J. Horn (eds.), *"To Make America": European Emigration in the Early Modern Period* (Chapel Hill, 1994)
Alvord, C.W., and L. Bidgood, *The First Explorations of the Trans-Allegheny Region by the Virginians 1650–1674* (Cleveland, 1912)
Ames, S.M., *Studies in the Eastern Shore in the Seventeenth Century* (Richmond, 1940)
Amphlett, H., *Hats: A History of Fashion in Headwear* (London, 1974)
Amussen, S.D., and D.E. Underdown, *Gender, Culture and Politics in England, 1560–1640: Turning the World Upside Down* (London, 2017)
Anderson, V.D., *Creatures of Empire: How Domestic Animals Transformed Early America* (New York, 2004)
Andrews, C.M., *The Colonial Period of American History*, 4 vols. (New Haven, 1934–38)
Andrews, K.R., *Trade, Plunder and Settlement: Maritime Enterprise and the Genesis of the British Empire, 1480–1630* (Cambridge, 1984)
——, *Ships, Money and Politics: Seafaring and Naval Enterprise in the Reign of Charles I* (Cambridge, 1991)
Andrews, M.P., *History of Maryland: Province and State* (New York, 1929)
Appelbaum, R., and J.W. Sweet (eds.), *Envisioning an English Empire: Jamestown and the Making of the North Atlantic World* (Philadelphia, 2005)
Archer, G.W., *The Dismemberment of Maryland: An Historical and Critical Essay* (Baltimore, 1890)
Archer, I., *The History of the Haberdashers' Company* (Chichester, 1991)
Arnold, R., *Fashion* (Oxford, 2009)
Ashelford, J., *A Visual History of Costume: The Sixteenth Century* (London, 1983)
——, *Dress in the Age of Elizabeth I* (London, 1988)

——, *The Art of Dress: Clothes Through History 1500–1914* (London, 1996)

Ashton, R., *The City and the Court 1603–1643* (Cambridge, 1979)

Auslander, L., *Cultural Revolutions: Everyday Life and Politics in Britain, North America, and France* (Berkeley, 2009)

Axtell, J., *The Invasion Within: The Contest of Cultures in Colonial North America* (New York, 1985)

——, *After Columbus: Essays in the Ethnohistory of Colonial North America* (New York, 1988)

——, *The Indians' New South: Cultural Change in the Colonial Southeast* (Baton Rouge, 1997)

——, 'Babel of Tongues: Communicating with the Indians in Eastern North America', in E.G. Gray and N. Fiering (eds.), *The Language Encounter in the Americas, 1492–1800* (New York, 2000), pp. 15–60

Bachman, Van Cleaf, *Peltries or Plantations: The Economic Policies of the Dutch West India Company in New Netherland 1623–1639* (Baltimore, 1969)

Backhouse, C., *Fashion and Popular Print in Early Modern England: Depicting Dress in Black-Letter Ballads* (London, 2017)

Bailey, A.G., *The Conflict of European and Eastern Algonkian Cultures 1504–1700* (Toronto, 2nd edition, 1969)

Bailyn, B., *The New England Merchants in the Seventeenth Century* (Cambridge, Mass., 1955)

——, *The Peopling of British North America: The Barbarous Years, the Conflict of Civilizations, 1600–1675* (New York, 2012)

Banks, K.J., *Chasing Empire Across the Sea: Communications and the State in the French Atlantic, 1713–1763* (Montreal, 2003)

Barbour, P.L., *The Three Worlds of Captain John Smith* (London, 1964)

——, *Pocahontas and Her World* (London, 1969)

Beier, A.L., and R. Finlay (eds.), *London 1500–1700: The Making of the Metropolis* (London, 1986)

Beinart, W., and L. Hughes, *Environment and Empire* (Oxford, 2007)

Berg, M., *Luxury and Pleasure in Eighteenth-Century Britain* (Oxford, 2005)

Berkhofer, R.F., Jr., *The White Man's Indian: Images of the American Indian from Columbus to the Present* (New York, 1979)

Bermingham, A., and J. Brewer (eds.), *The Consumption of Culture 1660–1800: Image, Object, Text* (London, 1995)

Bernard, L.L., 'Some New Light on the Early Years of the Baltimore Plantation', *Maryland Historical Magazine*, 44 (1949), pp. 93–100

Berry, H.F., 'The Records of the Feltmakers' Company of Dublin, 1687–1841: Their Loss and Recovery', *The Journal of the Royal Society of Antiquaries of Ireland*, Sixth Series, 1, (1911), pp. 26–45

Biggar, H.P., *The Early Trading Companies of New France* (New York, 1901)

Billings, W.M., J.E. Selby and T.W. Tate, *Colonial Virginia: A History* (White Plains, 1986)

Billings, W.M., *Sir William Berkeley and the Forging of Colonial Virginia* (Baton Rouge, 2004)

Blake, J.W., 'The Farm of the Guinea Trade, 1631', in H.A. Cronne (ed.), *Essays in British and Irish History in Honour of James Eadie Todd* (London, 1949), pp. 85–106

Bliss, R.M., *Revolution and Empire: English Politics and the American Colonies in the Seventeenth Century* (Manchester, 1990)

Blom, P., *Nature's Mutiny: How the Little Ice Age Transformed the West and Shaped the Present* (London, 2019)

Bogen, D.S., 'Mathias de Sousa: Maryland's First Colonist of African Descent', *Maryland Historical Magazine*, 96 (2001), pp. 68–85

Bolus, M. (ed.), *People and Pelts: Selected Papers of the Second North American Fur Trade Conference* (Winnipeg, 1972)

Bond, E.L., 'Source of Knowledge, Source of Power: The Supernatural World of English Virginia, 1607–1624', *Virginia Magazine of History and Biography*, 108 (2000), pp. 105–38

Borsay, P., *The English Urban Renaissance: Culture and Society in the Provincial Town* (Oxford, 1989)

Boucher, P., *Les Nouvelles Frances: France in America, 1500–1815* (Providence, 1989)

Bowen, H.V., E. Mancke and J.G. Reid (eds.), *Britain's Oceanic Empire: Atlantic and Indian Ocean Worlds, c. 1550–1850* (Cambridge, 2012)

Bradburn, D., 'The Visible Fist: The Chesapeake Tobacco Trade in War and the Purpose of Empire, 1690–1715', *William and Mary Quarterly*, 68 (2011), pp. 361–86

Bradburn, D., and J.C. Coombs (eds.), *Early Modern Virginia: Reconsidering the Old Dominion* (Charlottesville, 2011)

Braddick, M., *God's Fury, England's Fire: A New History of the English Civil Wars* (London, 2008)

Brandâo, J.A., *"Your Fyre Shall Burn No More": Iroquois Policy towards New France and its Native Allies to 1701* (Lincoln, 1997)

Braund, K.E.H., *Deerskins & Duffels: Creek Indian Trade with Anglo-America, 1685–1815* (Lincoln, 1993)

Breen, T.H., *Puritans and Adventurers: Change and Persistence in Early America* (New York, 1980)

——, '"Baubles of Britain": The American and Consumer Revolutions of the Eighteenth Century', *Past and Present,* 119 (1988), pp. 73–104

Brenner, R., *Merchants and Revolution: Commercial Change, Political Conflict, and London's Overseas Traders, 1550–1653* (Cambridge, 1993)

Breward, C., *The Culture of Fashion: A New History of Fashionable Dress* (Manchester, 1995)

Brewer, J., *The Pleasures of the Imagination: English Culture in the Eighteenth Century* (New York, 1997)

Briceland, A.V., *Westward from Virginia: The Exploration of the Virginia-Carolina Frontier 1650–1710* (Charlottesville, 1987)

Bridenbaugh, C., 'The Old and New Societies of the Delaware Valley in the Seventeenth Century', *Pennsylvania Magazine of History and Biography*, 100 (1976), pp. 143–72

——, *Jamestown 1544–1699* (New York, 1980)

Brooke, I., *English Costume in the Seventeenth Century* (London, 1934)

Brown, C., and H. Vlieghe (eds.), *Van Dyck 1599–1641* (London, 1999)

Brown, M.L., *Firearms in Colonial America: The Impact on History and Technology 1492–1792* (Washington, 1989)

Brown, P.M., 'Early Indian Trade in the Development of South Carolina: Politics, Economics, and Social Mobility During the Proprietary Period, 1670–1719', *South Carolina Historical Magazine*, 76 (1975), pp. 118–28

Bucholz, R.O., 'Going to Court in 1700: A Visitor's Guide', *The Court Historian*, 5, (2000), pp. 181–215

Bunker, N., *Making Haste from Babylon. The Mayflower Pilgrims and Their World: A New History* (London, 2010)

Burke, P., B. Harrison and P. Slack (eds.), *Civil Histories: Essays Presented to Sir Keith Thomas* (Oxford, 2000)

Bushkovitch, P., *The Merchants of Moscow 1580–1650* (Cambridge, 1980)

Butler, J., *Awash in a Sea of Faith: Christianizing the American People* (Cambridge, Mass., 1990)

Butler, L.S., 'The Early Settlement of Carolina: Virginia's Southern Frontier', *Virginia Magazine of History and Biography*, 79 (1971), pp. 20–8

Byrd, M., *London Transformed: Images of the City in the Eighteenth Century* (New Haven, 1978)

Byrde, P., *The Male Image: Men's Fashion in Britain 1300–1970* (London, 1979)

Calloway, C.G., *Crown and Calumet: British-Indian Relations, 1783–1815* (Norman, 1987)

——, *New Worlds for All: Indians, Europeans, and the Remaking of Early America* (Baltimore, 1997)

Canny, N. (ed.), *The Oxford History of the British Empire. Volume I: The Origins of Empire* (Oxford, 1998)

Carlos, A.M., and F.D. Lewis, 'Indians, Beaver, and the Bay: The Economics of Depletion in the Lands of the Hudson's Bay Company, 1700–1763', *Journal of Economic History*, 53 (1993), pp. 465–94

——, *Commerce by a Frozen Sea: Native Americans and the European Fur Trade* (Philadelphia, 2010)

Carr, L.G., 'Sources of Political Stability and Upheaval in Seventeenth-Century Maryland', *Maryland Historical Magazine*, 79 (1984), pp. 44–70

Carr, L.G., P.D. Morgan and J.B. Russo (eds.), *Colonial Chesapeake Society* (Chapel Hill, 1988)

Carr, L.G., R.R. Menard and L.S. Walsh, *Robert Cole's World: Agriculture and Society in Early Maryland* (Chapel Hill, 1991)

Carocci, M., and S. Pratt (eds.), *Native American Adoption, Captivity, and Slavery in Changing Contexts* (Basingstoke, 2012)

Cell, G.T., *English Enterprise in Newfoundland 1577–1660* (Toronto, 1969)

Chaplin, J.E., *Subject Matter: Technology, the Body, and Science on the Anglo-American Frontier, 1500–1676* (Cambridge, Mass., 2001)

Clay, C.G.A., *Economic Expansion and Social Change: England 1500–1700*, 2 vols. (Cambridge, 1984)

Clemens, P.G.E., *The Atlantic Economy and Colonial Maryland's Eastern Shore: From Tobacco to Grain* (Ithaca, 1980)

Coclanis, P.A. (ed.), *The Atlantic Economy during the Seventeenth and Eighteenth Centuries* (Columbia, 2005)

Coleman, J.T., *Vicious: Wolves and Men in America* (New Haven, 2004)

Comer, D.C., *Ritual Ground: Bent's Old Fort, World Formation, and the Annexation of the Southeast* (Berkeley, 1996)

Cook, M.G., 'Sir Thomas Wyatt, Governor: Documents, 1624–1626', *William and Mary Quarterly*, 8 (1928), pp. 157–67

Corfield, P. J. 'Dress for Deference and Dissent: Hats and the Decline of Hat Honour', *Costume*, 23 (1989), pp. 64–79

Corner, D., 'The Tyranny of Fashion: The Case of the Felt-Hatting Trade in the Late Seventeenth and Eighteenth Centuries', *Textile History*, 22 (1991), pp. 153–78

Corns, T. (ed.), *The Royal Image: Representations of Charles I* (Cambridge, 1999)

Crane, V.W., *The Southern Frontier, 1670–1732* (Durham, 1928)

Craven, W.F., *The Southern Colonies in the Seventeenth Century, 1607–1689* (Baton Rouge, 1949)

——, *Dissolution of the Virginia Company: The Failure of a Colonial Experiment* (Williamsburg, 1957)

——, *The Colonies in Transition 1660–1713* (New York, 1968)

——, *White, Red, and Black: The Seventeenth-Century Virginian* (New York, 1977)

Crean, J.F., 'Hats and the Fur Trade', *Canadian Journal of Economics and Political Science*, 28 (1962), pp. 373–86

Crow, S.D., '"Your Majesty's Good Subjects": A Reconsideration of Royalism in Virginia, 1642', *Virginia Magazine of History and Biography*, 87 (1979), pp. 158–73

Cruickshanks, E. (ed.), *The Stuart Courts* (Stroud, 2000)

Cumming, V., *Handbook of English Costume 1500–1900* (London, 1981)

——, *Royal Dress: The Image and the Reality 1580 to the Present Day* (London, 1989)

Curtin, P.D., *Cross-Cultural Trade in World History* (Cambridge, 1984)

David, A.M., *Fashion Victims: The Dangers of Dress Past and Present* (London, 2015)

Davis, R., *The Rise of the English Shipping Industry in the Seventeenth and Eighteenth Centuries* (Newton Abbot, 1962)

——, 'English Foreign Trade, 1660–1700' in W.E. Minchinton (ed.), *The Growth of English Overseas Trade in the Sevententh and Eighteenth Centuries* (London, 1969)

——, *English Overseas Trade 1500–1700* (London, 1973)

——, *The Rise of the Atlantic Economies* (London, 1973)

Davis, R.B., *George Sandys, Poet Adventurer: A Study in Anglo-American Culture in the Seventeenth Century* (London, 1955)

DeJong, G.F., *The Dutch in America, 1609–1974* (Boston, 1975)

Delâge, D., *Bitter Feast: Amerindians and Europeans in Northeastern North America, 1600–1664* (Vancouver, 1993)

Dennis, M., *Cultivating a Landscape of Peace: Iroquois-European Encounters in Seventeenth-Century America* (Ithaca, 1993)

Dickason, O.P., *The Myth of the Savage and the Beginnings of French Colonialism in the Americas* (Edmonton, 1984)
Dolin, E.J., *Fur, Fortune, and Empire: The Epic History of the Fur Trade in America* (New York, 2010)
Dongen A. van et al. (eds.), *'One Man's Trash is Another Man's Treasure': The Metamorphosis of the European Utensil in the New World* (Rotterdam, 1996)
Duckworth, H., *The Early History of Feltmaking in London 1250–1604*, www.feltmakers.co.uk/our-history
DuPlessis, R.S., *The Material Atlantic: Clothing, Commerce, and Colonization in the Atlantic World, 1650–1800* (Cambridge, 2016)
Earle, P., *The Making of the English Middle Class: Business, Society and Family Life in London, 1660–1723* (London, 1989)
Elliott, J.H., *Empires of the Atlantic World: Britain and Spain in America 1492–1830* (New Haven, 2006)
Ellis, J.M., *The Georgian Town 1680–1840* (Basingstoke, 2001)
Entwistle, J., *The Fashioned Body: Fashion, Dress and Modern Social Theory* (Cambridge, 2nd edition, 2015)
Ewan, J. and N., *John Banister and His Natural History of Virginia 1678–1692* (Urbana, 1970)
Ewing, E., *Fur in Dress* (London, 1981)
Fausz, J.F., 'Fighting "Fire" with Firearms: The Anglo-Powhatan Arms Race in Early Virginia', *American Indian Culture and Research Journal*, 3 (1979), pp. 33–50
——, 'Profits, Pelts, and Power: English Culture in the Early Chesapeake', *Maryland Historian*, 14 (1983), pp. 15–30
——, 'Present at the "Creation": The Chesapeake World that Greeted the Maryland Colonists', *Maryland Historical Magazine*, 79 (1984), pp. 29–47
——, 'The Invasion of Virginia: Indians, Colonialism, and the Conquest of Cant', *Virginia Magazine of History and Biography*, 95 (1987), pp. 135–56
——, 'Middlemen in Peace and War: Virginia's Earliest Indian Interpreters', *Virginia Magazine of History and Biography*, 95 (1987), pp. 41–64
——, '"An Abundance of Blood Shed on Both Sides": England's First Indian War', *Virginia Magazine of History and Biography*, 98 (1990), pp. 3–56
Feest, C.F., 'Powhatan: A Study in Political Organization', *Wiener Völkerkundliche Mitteilungen*, 13 (1966), pp. 69–83
Fischer, D.H., *Albion's Seed: Four British Folkways in America* (New York, 1989)
——, *Champlain's Dream* (New York, 2008)
Fisher, F.J. (ed.), *Essays in the Economic and Social History of Tudor and Stuart England* (Cambridge, 1961)
——, *London and the English Economy, 1500–1700*, eds. P.J. Corfield and N.B. Harte (London, 1990)
Fitzhugh, W.W. (ed.), *Cultures in Contact: The Impact of European Contacts on Native American Cultural Institutions A.D. 1000–1800* (Washington, 1985)
Flavin, S., *Consumption and Culture in Sixteenth-Century Ireland: Saffron, Stockings and Silk* (Woodbridge, 2014)
Franklin, W.N., 'Virginia and the Cherokee Indian Trade, 1673–1752', *East Tennessee Historical Society*, 4 (1932), pp. 22–8

Gallay, A., *The Indian Slave Trade: The Rise of the English Empire in the American South, 1670–1717* (New Haven, 2002)
Gaskill, M., *Between Two Worlds: How the English Became Americans* (Oxford, 2014)
Gereffi, G., and M. Korzeniewicz (eds.), *Commodity Chains and Global Capitalism* (Westport, 1994)
Glasrud, B.A., and A.M. Smith (eds.), *Race Relations in British North America, 1607–1783* (Chicago, 1982)
Gleach, F.W., *Powhatan's World and Colonial Virginia: A Conflict of Cultures* (Lincoln, 1997)
Gradie, C.M., 'Spanish Jesuits in Virginia: The Mission that Failed', *Virginia Magazine of History and Biography*, 96 (1988), pp. 131–56
Grassby, R., *The Business Community of Seventeenth-Century England* (Cambridge, 1995)
Gray, E.G., and N. Fiering (eds.), *The Language Encounter in the Americas, 1492–1800* (New York, 2000)
Greene, J.P., and J.R. Pole (eds.), *Colonial British America: Essays in the New History of the Early Modern Era* (London, 1984)
Greene, J.P., *Pursuits of Happiness: The Social Development of Early Modern British Colonies and the Formation of American Culture* (Chapel Hill, 1988)
Greig, H., *The Beau Monde: Fashionable Society in Georgian London* (Oxford, 2013)
——, 'Faction and Fashion: The Politics of Court Dress in Eighteenth-Century England', *Apparence(s)* [Online], 6, 2015: http://journals.openedition.org/apparences/1311
Gwynn, R.D., *The Huguenot Heritage: The History and Contribution of the Huguenots in Britain* (London, 1985)
Hale, N.C., *Virginia Venturer: A Historical Biography of William Claiborne 1600–1677* (Richmond, 1951)
——, *Pelts and Palisades: The Story of Fur and the Rivalry for Pelts in Early America* (Richmond, 1959)
Hall, D.D., *Cultures of Print: Essays in the History of the Book* (Amherst, 1996)
Hall, P., *Cities in Civilisation: Culture, Innovation, and Urban Order* (London, 1998)
Harper, L.A., *The English Navigation Laws: A Seventeenth Century Experiment in Social Engineering* (New York, 1939)
Harris, T., *Restoration: Charles II and his Kingdoms, 1660–1685* (London, 2005)
Hart, S., 'The Dutch and North America in the First Half of the Seventeenth Century. Some Aspects', *Medelingen van de Nederlandse Vereniging voor Zeegeschiedenis*, 20 (1970), pp. 5–17
Harte, N.B., 'State Control of Dress and Social Change in Pre-Industrial England', in D.C. Coleman and A.H. John (eds.), *Trade, Government and Economy in Pre-Industrial England* (London, 1976), pp. 132–65
——, 'The Economics of Clothing in the Late Seventeenth Century', *Textile History*, 22 (1991), pp. 277–96
Hartsook, E., and G. Skordas, *Land Office and Prerogative Court Records of Colonial Maryland* (Annapolis, 1946)

Hatch, D.B., 'Venison Trade and Interaction between English Colonists and Native Americans in Virginia's Potomac River Valley', *Northeast Historical Archaeology,* 41 (2012), pp. 18–48

Hatfield, A.L., *Atlantic Virginia: Intercolonial Relations in the Seventeenth Century* (Philadelphia, 2004)

Havran, M.J., *The Catholics in Caroline England* (Stanford, 1963)

Hawkins, J.H., *History of the Worshipful Company of the Art or Mistery of Feltmakers of London* (London, 1917)

Hayward, M., 'Dressing Charles II: The King's Clothing Choices (1660–85)', *Apparence(s)* [Online], 6, 2015: http://journals.openedition.org/apparences/1320

Heal, F., and C. Holmes, *The Gentry in England and Wales, 1500–1700* (London, 1994)

Hillier, S.E., 'The Trade of the Virginia Colony: 1606 to 1660' (University of Liverpool Ph.D. thesis, 1971)

Hinderaker, E., *Elusive Empires: Constructing Colonialism in the Ohio Valley, 1673–1800* (Cambridge, 1997)

—— and P.C. Mancall, *At the Edge of Empire: The Backcountry in British North America* (Baltimore, 2003)

Hoffecker, C.E., R. Waldron, L.E. Williams and B.E. Benson (eds.), *New Sweden in America* (Newark, 1995)

Hoffman, R., *Princes of Ireland, Planters of Maryland: A Carroll Saga, 1500–1782* (Chapel Hill, 2000)

Hoffman, R., M. Sobel and F.J. Teute (eds.), *Through a Glass Darkly: Reflections on Personal Identity in Early America* (Chapel Hill, 1997)

Horn, J., *Adapting to a New World: English Society in the Seventeenth-Century Chesapeake* (Chapel Hill, 1994)

——, *A Land as God Made It: Jamestown and the Birth of America* (New York, 2005)

Hornsby, S.J., *British Atlantic, American Frontier: Spaces of Power in Early Modern British America* (Hanover, 2005)

Householder, M., *Inventing Americans in the Age of Discovery: Narratives of Encounter* (Farnham, 2011)

Hudson, C., and C.C. Tesser (eds.), *The Forgotten Centuries: Indians and Europeans in the American South, 1521–1704* (Athens, 1994)

Hughes, C., *Hats* (London, 2017)

Hume, I.N., *The Virginia Adventure: Roanoke to James Towne, An Archaeological and Historical Odyssey* (Charlottesville, 1994)

Hunt, A., *Governance of the Consuming Passions: A History of Sumptuary Law* (London, 1996)

Hunt, G.T., *The Wars of the Iroquois: A Study in Intertribal Relations* (Madison, 1940)

Ingle, E., *Captain Richard Ingle, the Maryland 'Pirate and Rebel' 1642–1653* (Baltimore, 1884)

Innis, H.A., *The Fur Trade in Canada: An Introduction to Canadian Economic History* (New Haven, 1930)

Isaac, E., 'Kent Island, Part 1: The Period of Settlement', *Maryland Historical Magazine,* 52 (1957), pp. 93–119

Isaac, R., *The Transformation of Virginia 1740–1790* (Chapel Hill, 1982)
Israel, J., *Dutch Primacy in World Trade, 1585–1740* (Oxford, 1989)
Jack, S.M., *Towns in Tudor and Stuart Britain* (Basingstoke, 1996)
Jennings, F., 'Glory, Death, and Transfiguration: The Susquehannock Indians in the Seventeenth Century', *Proceedings of the American Philosophical Society*, 112 (1968), pp. 15–53
——, *The Invasion of America: Indians, Colonialism, and the Cant of Conquest* (Chapel Hill, 1975)
——, *The Ambiguous Iroquois Empire: The Covenant Chain Confederation of Indian Tribes with English Colonies from its Beginnings to the Lancaster Treaty of 1744* (New York, 1984)
——, *The Founders of America* (New York, 1993)
Jensen, A.L., *The Maritime Commerce of Colonial Philadelphia* (Madison, 1963)
Johnson, A., *The Swedish Settlements on the Delaware 1638–1664*, 2 vols. (Philadelphia, 1911)
Johnson, R.C., 'Virginia in 1632', *Virginia Magazine of History and Biography*, 65 (1957), pp. 458–66
Jones, A.R., and P. Stallybrass, *Renaissance Clothing and the Materials of Memory* (Cambridge, 2001)
Jones, R., and C. Dyer (eds.), *Farmers, Consumers, Innovators: The World of Joan Thirsk* (Hatfield, 2016)
Jordan, D.W., *Foundations of Representative Government in Maryland 1632–1715* (New York, 1987)
Kammen, M., *Colonial New York* (Oxford, 1975)
Keeble, N.H., *The Restoration: England in the 1660s* (London, 2002)
Kelso, W.M., *Jamestown: The Buried Truth* (Charlottesville, 2006)
Kent, B.C., *Susquehanna's Indians* (Harrisburg, 1989)
Koot, C.J., *Empire at the Periphery: British Colonists, Anglo-Dutch Trade, and the Development of the British Atlantic, 1621–1713* (New York, 2011)
Kraft, H.C., *The Lenape: Archeaology, History and Ethnography* (Newark, 1986)
Krech, S., III, *The Ecological Indian: Myth and History* (New York, 1999)
Kruer, M., 'Bloody Minds and Peoples Undone: Emotion, Family, and Political Order in the Susquehannock-Virginia War', *The William and Mary Quarterly*, 74, (2017), pp. 401–36
Krugler, J.D., '"With Promise of Liberty in Religion": The Catholic Lords Baltimore and Toleration in Seventeenth-Century Maryland, 1634–1692', *Maryland Historical Magazine*, 79 (1984), pp. 21–43
——, *English and Catholic: The Lords Baltimore in the Seventeenth Century* (Baltimore, 2004)
Kuchta, D., *The Three-Piece Suit and Modern Masculinity: England, 1550–1850* (Berkeley, 2002)
Kulikoff, A., *Tobacco and Slaves: The Development of Southern Cultures in the Chesapeake, 1680–1800* (Chapel Hill, 1986)
Kupperman, K.O., 'Apathy and Death in Early Jamestown', *Journal of American History*, 66 (1979), pp. 24–40
——, *Settling with the Indians: The Meeting of English and Indian Cultures in America, 1580–1640* (Totowa, 1980)

——, *Providence Island, 1630–1641: The Other Puritan Colony* (Cambridge, 1993)
——, *Indians and English: Facing Off in Early America* (Ithaca, 2000)
——, *Roanoke: The Abandoned Colony* (Lanham, 2nd edition, 2007)
——, *The Jamestown Project* (Cambridge, Mass., 2007)
Land, A., 'Economic Base and Social Structure: The Northern Chesapeake in the Eighteenth Century', *Journal of Economic History*, 25 (1965), pp. 639–54
——, *Colonial Maryland: A History* (Millwood, 1981)
Landsman, N.C., *Crossroads of Empire: The Middle Colonies in British North America* (Baltimore, 2010)
Latané, J.H., *The Early Relations Between Maryland and Virginia* (Baltimore, 1895)
Laver, J., *Costume and Fashion: A Concise History* (London, 5th edition, 2012)
Lawson, M.G., *Fur: A Study in English Mercantilism 1700–1775* (Toronto, 1943)
——, 'Fur Traders *vs.* Feltmakers', *The Beaver*, 28 (1948), pp. 34–7
Lemire, B., 'Consumerism in Preindustrial and Early Industrial England: The Trade in Secondhand Clothes', *Journal of British Studies,* 27 (1988), pp. 1–24
——, 'The Theft of Clothes and Popular Consumerism in Early Modern England', *Journal of Social History*, 24 (1990), pp. 255–76
——, *Dress, Culture and Commerce: The English Clothing Trade Before the Factory* (London, 1997)
Lenman, B., *England's Colonial Wars 1550–1688: Empire and National Identity* (Harlow, 2001)
Lewis, C.M., and A.J. Loomie, *The Spanish Jesuit Mission in Virginia, 1570–1572* (Chapel Hill, 1953)
Lindley, K., 'The Lay Catholics of England in the Reign of Charles I', *Journal of Ecclesiastical History*, 22 (1971), pp. 199–221
——, *Popular Politics and Religion in Civil War London* (Aldershot, 1997)
Linthicum, M.C., *Costume in the Drama of Shakespeare and His Contemporaries* (Oxford, 1936)
Loades, D., *England's Maritime Empire: Seapower, Commerce and Policy, 1490–1690* (Harlow, 2000)
Lynn, E., *Tudor Fashion* (New Haven, 2017)
Mackenthun, G., *Metaphors of Dispossession: American Beginnings and the Translation of Empire, 1492–1637* (Norman, 1997)
Main, G.L., *Tobacco Colony: Life in Early Maryland, 1650–1720* (Princeton, 1982)
Mallios, S., *The Deadly Politics of Giving: Exchange and Violence at Ajacan, Roanoke, and Jamestown* (Tuscaloosa, 2006)
Mancall, P.C., *Deadly Medicine: Indians and Alcohol in Early America* (Ithaca, 1995)
—— (ed.), *The Atlantic World and Virginia, 1550–1624* (Chapel Hill, 2007)
Mancke, E., and C. Shammas (eds.), *The Creation of the British Atlantic World* (Baltimore, 2005)
Mansel, P., *Dressed to Rule: Royal and Court Costume from Louis XIV to Elizabeth II* (New Haven, 2005)
Martin, C., *Keepers of the Game: Indian-Animal Relationships and the Fur Trade* (Berkeley, 1978)

Martin, J., *Treasure of the Land of Darkness: The Fur Trade and its Significance for Medieval Russia* (Cambridge, 1986)
Marye, W.B., 'The Wicomiss Indians of Maryland', *American Antiquity*, 4 (1938), pp. 146–52
Matson, C., *Merchants and Empire: Trading in Colonial New York* (Baltimore, 1998)
McCartney, M.W., 'Seventeenth Century Apartheid: The Suppression and Containment of Indians in Tidewater Virginia', *Journal of Middle Atlantic Archaeology*, 1 (1985), pp. 51–80
McCusker, J.J., and R.R. Menard, *The Economy of British America, 1607–1789* (Chapel Hill, 1985)
McCusker, J.J., and K. Morgan (eds.), *The Early Modern Atlantic Economy* (Cambridge, 2000)
McDowell, C., *Hats: Status, Style and Glamour* (London, 1992)
McFarlane, A., *The British in the Americas 1480–1815* (London, 1994)
McGrail, T.H., *Sir William Alexander, First Earl of Stirling: A Biographical Study* (Edinburgh, 1940)
Mcintyre, R.A., 'John Pynchon and the New England Fur Trade, 1652–1676', https://www.colonialsociety.org/node/814#rch04
McKellar, E., *The Birth of Modern London: The Development and Design of the City* (Manchester, 1999)
McKendrick, N., J. Brewer and J.H. Plumb, *The Birth of a Consumer Society: The Commercialization of Eighteenth-Century England* (London, 1983)
McPherson, E.G., 'Nathaniel Batts, Landholder on Pasquotank River, 1660', *North Carolina Historical Review*, 43 (1966), pp. 66–81
Meinig, D.W., *The Shaping of America, Volume I: Atlantic America, 1492–1800* (New Haven, 1986)
Menard, R.R., 'Maryland's "Time of Troubles": Sources of Political Disorder in Early St Mary's', *Maryland Historical Magazine*, 76 (1981), pp. 124–40
——, *Economy and Society in Early Colonial Maryland* (New York, 1985)
Merrell, J.H., 'Cultural Continuity among the Piscataway Indians of Colonial Maryland', *William and Mary Quarterly*, 36 (1979), pp. 548–70
——, *The Indians' New World: Catawbas and their Neighbors from European Contact Through the Era of Removal* (Chapel Hill, 1989)
——, *Into the American Woods: Negotiators on the Pennsylvania Frontier* (New York, 1999),
Merritt, J.T., *At the Crossroads: Indians and Empires on a Mid-Atlantic Frontier, 1700–1763* (Chapel Hill, 2003)
Merwick, D., *Possessing Albany, 1630–1710: The Dutch and English Experiences* (Cambridge, 1990)
Meyers, D., and M. Perreault (eds.), *Colonial Chesapeake: New Perspectives* (Lanham, 2006)
Miller, C.L., and G.R. Hamell, 'A New Perspective on Indian-White Contact: Cultural Symbols and Colonial Trade', *Journal of American History*, 73 (1986), pp. 311–28
Miller, S., *Invested with Meaning: The Raleigh Circle in the New World* (Philadelphia, 1998)

Moloney, F.X., *The Fur Trade in New England 1620–1676* (Cambridge, Mass., 1931)
Morgan, E.S., *American Slavery, American Freedom: The Ordeal of Colonial Virginia* (New York, 1975)
Morgan, K., *Bristol and the Atlantic Trade in the Eighteenth Century* (Cambridge, 1993)
Morrill, J., *The Nature of the English Revolution* (London, 1993)
Morrison, A.J., 'The Virginia Indian Trade to 1673', *William and Mary Quarterly*, 1 (1921), pp. 217–36
Morriss, M.S., *Colonial Trade of Maryland 1689–1715* (Baltimore, 1914)
Morse, J.M., *American Beginnings: Highlights and Sidelights of the Birth of the New World* (Washington, 1952)
Morton, R.L., *Colonial Virginia*, 2 vols. (Chapel Hill, 1960)
Munroe, J.A., *Colonial Delaware: A History* (Millwood, 1978)
Murphy, A.R., *William Penn: A Life* (Oxford, 2013)
Nash, G.B., 'The Free Society of Traders and the Early Politics of Pennsylvania', *Pennsylvania Magazine of History and Biography*, 89 (1965), pp. 147–73
Neill, E.D., *Virginia Carolum: The Colony under the Rule of Charles the First and Second A.D. 1625-A.D. 1685* (Albany, 1886)
Norton, M.B., 'Gender and Defamation in Seventeenth-Century Maryland', *William and Mary Quarterly*, 44 (1987), pp. 3–39
Norton, T.E., *The Fur Trade in Colonial New York 1686–1776* (Madison, 1974)
Oberg, M.L., *Dominion and Civility: English Imperialism and Native America, 1585–1685* (Ithaca, 1999)
——, *The Head in Edward Nugent's Hand: Roanoke's Forgotten Indians* (Philadelphia, 2008)
Ogborn, M., *Spaces of Modernity: London's Geographies, 1680–1780* (London, 1998)
Olson, A.G., *Anglo-American Politics 1660–1715: The Relationship between Parties in England and Colonial America* (Oxford, 1973)
Pagan, J.R., 'Growth of the Tobacco Trade between London and Virginia, 1614–40', *Guildhall Studies in London History*, 3 (1979), pp. 248–62
——, 'Dutch Maritime and Commercial Activity in Mid-Seventeenth-Century Virginia', *Virginia Magazine of History and Biography*, 90 (1982), pp. 485–501
Palliser, D.M., *The Age of Elizabeth: England under the Later Tudors 1547–1603* (London, 2nd edition, 1992)
Papenfuse, E.C., A.F. Day, D.W. Jordan, G.A. Stiverson (eds.), *A Biographical Dictionary of the Maryland Legislature, 1635–1789*, 2 vols. (Baltimore, 1979–85)
Parker, G., *Global Crisis: War, Climate Change and Catastrophe in the Seventeenth Century* (New Haven, 2013)
Parker, J., *Van Meteren's Virginia 1607–1612* (Minneapolis, 1961)
Peck, L.L., *Consuming Splendor: Society and Culture in Seventeenth-Century England* (Cambridge, 2005)
Pendergast, J.F., *The Massawomeck: Raiders and Traders into the Chesapeake Bay in the Seventeenth Century* (Transactions of the American Philosophical Society, 81, 1991)

Perry, J.R., *The Formation of a Society on Virginia's Eastern Shore, 1615–1655* (Chapel Hill, 1990)

Pestana, C.G., *The English Atlantic in an Age of Revolution, 1640–1661* (Cambridge, Mass., 2004)

Phillips, P.C., *The Fur Trade*, 2 vols. (Norman, 1961)

Piponnier, F., and P. Mane, *Dress in the Middle Ages* (New Haven, 1997)

Poliquin, R., *Beaver* (London, 2015)

Porter, H.C., *The Inconstant Savage: England and the North American Indian 1500–1660* (London, 1979)

Porter, R., 'The Crispe Family and the African Trade in the Seventeenth Century', *Journal of African History*, 9 (1968), pp. 57–77

Potter, S., *Commoners, Tribute, and Chiefs: The Development of Algonquian Culture in the Potomac Valley* (Charlottesville, 1996)

Powell, W.S., 'Carolana and the Incomparable Roanoke: Explorations and Attempted Settlements, 1620–1663', *North Carolina Historical Review*, 51 (1974), pp. 1–21

——, *John Pory, 1572–1636* (Chapel Hill, 1977)

Preston, R.A., 'The Laconia Company of 1629: An English Attempt to Intercept the Fur Trade', *Canadian Historical Review*, 31 (1950), pp. 125–44

Price, J.M., *Perry of London: A Family and a Firm on the Seaborne Frontier, 1615–1753* (Cambridge, Mass., 1992)

Pritchard, J., *In Search of Empire: The French in the Americas, 1670–1730* (Cambridge, 2004)

Quimby, G.I., *Indian Culture and European Trade Goods* (Madison, 1966)

Quinn, D.B., *Ralegh and the British Empire* (London, 1947)

——, *Set Fair for Roanoke: Voyages and Colonies, 1584–1606* (Chapel Hill, 1985)

——, *England and the Discovery of America, 1481–1620* (London, 1994)

——, *Explorers and Colonies: America, 1500–1625* (London, 1990)

—— (ed.) *Early Maryland in a Wider World* (Detroit, 1982)

Quinn, D.B., and A.N. Ryan, *England's Sea Empire, 1550–1642* (London, 1983)

Quitt, M.H., 'Trade and Acculturation at Jamestown, 1607–1609: The Limits of Understanding', *William and Mary Quarterly*, 52 (1995), pp. 227–58

Rabb, T.K., *Jacobean Gentleman: Sir Edwin Sandys, 1561–1629* (Princeton, 1998)

Rainbolt, J.C., *From Prescription to Persuasion: Manipulation of Eighteenth Century Virginia Economy* (Port Washington, 1974)

Ramsey, W.L., *The Yamasee War: A Study of Culture, Economy, and Conflict in the Colonial South* (Lincoln, 2008)

Ransome, D.R., 'Pocahontas and the Mission to the Indians', *Virginia Magazine of History and Biography*, 99 (1991), pp. 81–94

Reid, J.G., *Acadia, Maine, and New Scotland: Marginal Colonies in the Seventeenth Century* (Toronto, 1981)

Reséndez, A., *The Other Slavery: The Uncovered Story of Indian Enslavement in America* (Boston, 2016)

Reynolds, A., *In Fine Style: The Art of Tudor and Stuart Fashion* (London, 2013)

Ribeiro, A., *Fashion and Fiction: Dress in Art and Literature in Stuart England* (New Haven, 2005)

Ribeiro, A. with C. Blackman, *A Portrait of Fashion: Six Centuries of Dress at the National Portrait Gallery* (London, 2015)
Riordan, T.B., *The Plundering Time: Maryland and the English Civil War 1645–1646* (Baltimore, 2004)
Rice, J.D., *Nature & History in the Potomac Country: From Hunter-Gatherers to the Age of Jefferson* (Baltimore, 2009)
——, *Tales from a Revolution: Bacon's Rebellion and the Transformation of Early America* (New York, 2012)
Rich, E.E., 'Russia and the Colonial Fur Trade', *Economic History Review,* 7 (1955), pp. 307–28
——, *Hudson's Bay Company 1670–1870,* 2 vols. (London, 1961)
——, *The Fur Trade and the Northwest to 1857* (Toronto, 1967)
Richards, J.F., *The Unending Frontier: An Environmental History of the Early Modern World* (Berkeley, 2003)
Richter, D.K., *The Ordeal of the Long-house: The Peoples of the Iroquois League in the Era of European Colonization* (Chapel Hill, 1992)
——, *Facing East from Indian Country: A Native History of Early America* (Cambridge, Mass., 2001)
——, *Before the Revolution: America's Ancient Pasts* (Cambridge, Mass., 2011)
——, *Trade, Land, Power: The Struggle for Eastern North America* (Philadelphia, 2013)
Richter, D.K., and J.H. Merrell (eds.), *Beyond the Covenant Chain: The Iroquois and their Neighbours in Indian North America, 1600–1800* (Syracuse, 1987)
Rink, O., *Holland on the Hudson: An Economic and Social History of Dutch New York* (Ithaca, 1986)
Rosenberg, P., 'Thomas Tryon and the Seventeenth-Century Dimensions of Antislavery', *William and Mary Quarterly*, 61, (2004), pp. 609–42
Rothschild, N.A., *Colonial Encounters in a Native American Landscape: The Spanish and Dutch in North America* (Washington, 2003)
Rountree, H.C., *The Powhatan Indians of Virginia: Their Traditional Culture* (Norman, 1989)
——, *Pocahontas's People: The Powhatan Indians of Virginia Through Four Centuries* (Norman, 1990)
—— (ed.), *Powhatan Foreign Relations 1500–1722* (Charlottesville, 1993)
Rountree, H.C., and E.R. Turner III, *Before and After Jamestown: Virginia's Powhatans and Their Predecessors* (Gainesville, 2002)
Rountree, H.C., and T.E. Davidson, *Eastern Shore Indians of Virginia and Maryland* (Charlottesville, 1997)
Rublack, U., *Dressing Up: Cultural Identity in Renaissance Europe* (Oxford, 2010)
Russo, J.B., and J.E. Russo, *Planting an Empire: The Early Chesapeake in British North America* (Baltimore, 2012)
Rutman, D.B. and A.H., *A Place in Time: Middlesex County, Virginia 1650–1750* (New York, 1984)
Scammell, G.V., *The World Encompassed: The First European Maritime Empires, c. 800–1650* (London, 1981)
——, *The First Imperial Age: European Overseas Expansion c. 1400–1715* (London, 1989)

Scharf, J.T., *History of Maryland from the Earliest Period to the Present Day*, 3 vols. (Baltimore, 1879)
Schubel, J.R., *The Living Chesapeake* (Baltimore, 1981)
Scott, D., *Leviathan: The Rise of Britain as a World Power* (London, 2013)
Scott, M., *Medieval Dress & Fashion* (London, 2009)
Scott, W.R., *The Constitution and Finance of English, Scottish and Irish Joint-Stock Companies to 1720*, 3 vols. (Cambridge, 1910–12)
Seed, P., *American Pentimento: The Invention of Indians and the Pursuit of Riches* (Minneapolis, 2001)
Semmes, R., *Captains and Mariners of Early Maryland* (Baltimore, 1937)
——, 'The *Ark* and the *Dove*: Transcripts from the Public Record Office, London', *Maryland Historical Magazine*, 33 (1938), pp. 13–22
Shammas, C., *The Pre-Industrial Consumer in England and America* (Oxford, 1990)
Sharpe, K., *The Personal Rule of Charles I* (New Haven, 1992)
——, *Remapping Early Modern England: The Culture of Seventeenth-Century Politics* (Cambridge, 2000)
——, *Rebranding Rule: The Restoration and Revolution Monarchy, 1660–1714* (New Haven, 2013)
Sheehan, B.W., *Savagism and Civility: Indians and Englishmen in Colonial Virginia* (Cambridge, 1980)
Shirley, J.W., 'George Percy at Jamestown, 1607–1612', *Virginia Magazine of History and Biography*, 57 (1949), pp. 227–43
Silver, T., *A New Face on the Countryside: Indians, Colonists, and Slaves in South Atlantic Forests, 1500–1800* (Cambridge, 1990)
Skelton, R.A., *Explorers' Maps* (London, 1958)
Skordas, G. (ed.), *The Early Settlers of Maryland* (Baltimore, 1968)
Sleigh-Johnson, N., 'Aspects of the Tailoring Trade in the City of London in the Late Sixteenth and Earlier Seventeenth Centuries', *Costume: The Journal of the Costume Society*, 37 (2003), pp. 24–32
Sloan, K., *European Visions: American Voices* (London, 2009)
Smith, J.M. (ed.), *Seventeenth-Century America: Essays in Colonial History* (New York, 1959)
Snow, D.R., *The Iroquois* (Cambridge, Mass., 1994)
Soderlund, J.R., *Lenape Country: Delaware Valley Society Before William Penn* (Philadelphia, 2015)
Sokolow, J.A., *The Great Encounter: Native Peoples and European Settlers in the Americas, 1492–1800* (New York, 2003)
Speck, F.G., 'The Functions of Wampum Among the Eastern Algonkian', *Memoirs of the American Anthropological Association*, 6, (1919), pp. 22–66
Spufford, M., 'The Cost of Apparel in Seventeenth-Century England, and the Accuracy of Gregory King', *Economic History Review*, 53 (2000), pp. 677–705
St Clair, K., *The Golden Thread: How Fabric Changed History* (London, 2018)
Stahle, D.W., M.K. Cleaveland, D.B. Blanton, M.D. Therrell, D.A. Gay, 'The Lost Colony and Jamestown Droughts', *Science*, 280 (1998), pp. 564–7
Steele, I.K., *The English Atlantic 1675–1740: An Exploration of Communication and Community* (New York, 1986)

——, *Warpaths: Invasions of North America* (New York, 1994)
Steiner, B., *Beginnings of Maryland 1631–1639* (Baltimore, 1903)
——, *Maryland during the English Civil Wars* (Baltimore, 1906)
——, *Maryland under the Commonwealth: A Chronicle of the Years 1649–1658* (Baltimore, 1911)
Stilgoe, J.R., *Common Landscape of America, 1580 to 1845* (New Haven, 1982)
Stone, G.W., 'Manorial Maryland', *Maryland Historical Magazine*, 82 (1987), pp. 3–36
Stone, L., *The Crisis of the Aristocracy 1558–1641* (Oxford, 1965)
Streeter, S.F., *Papers Relating to the Early History of Maryland* (Baltimore, 1876)
——, *The First Commander of Kent Island* (Baltimore, 1868)
Swanton, J.R., *Early History of the Creek Indians and Their Neighbors* (Washington, 1922)
Sweet, D.G., and G.B. Nash (eds.), *Struggle and Survival in Colonial America* (Berkeley, 1981)
Tarrant, N., *The Development of Costume* (London, 1994)
Tarter, B., 'Bacon's Rebellion, the Grievances of the People, and the Political Culture of Seventeenth-Century Virginia', *Virginia Magazine of History and Biography*, 119 (2011), pp. 2–41
Tate, T.W., and D.L. Ammerman (eds.), *The Chesapeake in the Seventeenth Century: Essays on Anglo-American Society* (Chapel Hill, 1979)
Taylor, A., *American Colonies: The Settlement of North America to 1800* (London, 2001)
Taylor, E.G.R., *Late Tudor and Early Stuart Geography 1583–1650* (London, 1934)
Thirsk, J., *Economic Policy and Projects: The Development of a Consumer Society in Early Modern England* (Oxford, 1978)
Thomas, K., *Man and the Natural World: Changing Attitudes in England 1500–1800* (London, 1983)
——, *In Pursuit of Civility: Manners and Civilization in Early Modern England* (New Haven, 2018)
Tilghman, O., *History of Talbot County, Maryland 1661–1861*, 2 vols. (Baltimore, 1915)
Trelease, A.W., *Indian Affairs in Colonial New York: The Seventeenth Century* (New Brunswick, 1972)
Trentmann, F., *Empire of Things: How We Became a World of Consumers, from the Fifteenth Century to the Twenty-first* (London, 2016)
Trigger, B.G., 'The Mohawk-Mohican War (1624–28): The Establishment of a Pattern', *Canadian Historical Review*, 52 (1971), pp. 276–86
——, *The Children of Aataentsic: A History of the Huron People to 1660*, 2 vols. (Montreal, 1976)
—— (ed.), *Handbook of North American Indians, Volume 15: Northeast* (Washington, 1978)
——, *Natives and Newcomers: Canada's "Heroic Age" Reconsidered* (Manchester, 1986)
—— and W. E. Washburn (eds.), *The Cambridge History of the Native Peoples of the Americas. Volume I: North America* (Cambridge, 1996)
Trudel, M., *The Beginnings of New France 1524–1663* (Toronto, 1973)

Turner, F., 'Money and Exchange Rates in 1632', www.1632.org/1632-tech/faqs/money-exchange-rates-1632/
Unwin, G., *The Guilds and Companies of London* (London, 3rd edition, 1938)
——, *Industrial Organization in the Sixteenth and Seventeenth Centuries* (London, 2nd edition, 1963)
Van Zandt, C.J., *Brothers among Nations: The Pursuit of Intercultural Alliances in Early America 1580–1660* (Oxford, 2008)
Vaughan, A.T., *American Genesis: Captain John Smith and the Founding of Virginia* (Boston, 1975)
——, *Roots of American Racism: Essays on the Colonial Experience* (New York, 1995)
Veale, E.M., *The English Fur Trade in the Later Middle Ages* (Oxford, 1966)
Vero, J., *'A Concern in Trade': Hatting and the Bracebridges of Atherstone, 1612–1872* (Warwick, 1995)
Vincent, S., *Dressing the Elite: Clothes in Early Modern England* (Oxford, 2003)
Vries, J. de, *The Industrious Revolution: Consumer Behavior and the Household Economy, 1650 to the Present* (New York, 2008)
Wagner, M., *The English Chartered Trading Companies, 1688–1763: Guns, Money and Lawyers* (New York, 2018)
Wall, C., *The Literary and Cultural Spaces of London* (Cambridge, 1998)
Wallace, A.F.C., *Jefferson and the Indians: The Tragic Fate of the First Americans* (Cambridge, Mass., 1999)
Walsh, L.S., *Motives of Honor, Pleasure, and Profit: Plantation Management in the Colonial Chesapeake, 1607–1763* (Chapel Hill, 2010)
Walter, D., *Colonial Violence: European Empires and the Use of Force*, trans. P. Lewis (London, 2017)
Warkentin, G., and C. Podruchy (eds.), *Decentring the Renaissance: Canada and Europe in Multidisciplinary Perspective, 1500–1700* (Toronto, 2001)
Washburn, W.E., *The Governor and the Rebel: A History of Bacon's Rebellion in Virginia* (Chapel Hill, 1957)
——, *Virginia under Charles I and Cromwell, 1625–1660* (Williamsburg, 1957)
Weatherill, L., *Consumer Behaviour and Material Culture in Britain 1660–1760* (London, 2nd edition, 1996)
Webb, S.S., *1676: The End of American Independence* (New York, 1984)
——, *Marlborough's America* (New Haven, 2013)
Weinstein, R., *The History of the Worshipful Company of Feltmakers 1604–2004* (Chichester, 2004)
Wertenbaker, T.J., *Patrician and Plebeian in Virginia* (New York, 1910)
Weslager, C.A., and A.R. Dunlap, *Dutch Explorers, Traders and Settlers in the Delaware Valley 1609–1664* (Philadelphia, 1961)
Weslager, C.A., *The English on the Delaware: 1610–1682* (New Brunswick, 1967)
——, *The Delaware Indians: A History* (New Brunswick, 1972)
White, R., *The Middle Ground: Indians, Empires and Republics in the Great Lakes Region, 1650–1815* (Cambridge, 1991)
White, S., *A Cold Welcome: The Little Ice Age and Europe's Encounter with North America* (Cambridge, Mass., 2017)
Whitelaw, R.T., *Virginia's Eastern Shore: A History of Northampton and Accomack Counties*, 2 vols. (Richmond, 1951)

Wilcox, R. Turner, *The Mode in Hats and Headdress* (New York, 1952)
Williams, N., 'England's Tobacco Trade in the Reign of Charles I', *Virginia Magazine of History and Biography*, 65 (1957), pp. 403–49
Williams, P., *The Later Tudors: England 1547–1603* (Oxford, 1995)
Willan, T.S., *The Early History of the Russia Company 1553–1603* (Manchester, 1956)
——, *Studies in Elizabethan Foreign Trade* (Manchester, 1959)
Wilson, C., *Profit and Power: A Study of England and the Dutch Wars* (London, 1957)
——, *England's Apprenticeship 1603–1763* (London, 2nd edition, 1984)
Witthoft, J., and W.F. Kinsey (eds.), *Susquehannock Miscellany* (Harrisburg, 1959)
Wolf, E.R., *Europe and the People Without History* (Berkeley, 1982)
Wood, B., *The Origins of American Slavery: Freedom and Bondage in the English Colonies* (New York, 1997)
Wood, P.H., G.A. Waselkov and M.T. Hatley (eds.), *Powhatan's Mantle: Indians in the Colonial Southeast* (Lincoln, 1989)
Woodward, D.M., *Men at Work: Labourers and Building Craftsmen in the Towns of Northern England, 1450–1750* (Cambridge, 1995)
Wright, I.A., 'Spanish Policy towards Virginia, 1606–1620', *American Historical Review*, 25 (1920), pp. 448–79
Wright, L.B., *Middle Class Culture in Elizabethan England* (London, 1935)
Wrightson, K., *Earthly Necessities: Economic Lives in Early Modern Britain* (New Haven, 2000)
Wrigley, E.A., 'A Simple Model of London's Importance in Changing English Society and Economy 1650–1750', *Past and Present*, 37 (1967), pp. 44–70
Wroth, L.C., *Tobacco or Codfish: Lord Baltimore Makes his Choice* (New York, 1954)
Zahedieh, N., 'London and the Colonial Consumer in the Late Seventeenth Century', *Economic History Review*, 47 (1994), pp. 239–61
——, *The Capital and the Colonies: London and the Atlantic Economy, 1600–1700* (Cambridge, 2010)
Zeller, N.A.M. (ed.), *A Beautiful and Fruitful Place: Selected Rensselaerswicjk Seminar Papers* (Albany, 1991)

Web sites

http://www.british-history.ac.uk/no-series/acts-ordinances-interregnum/
http://collections.vam.ac.uk/item/O98558/hat-unknown/?print+1
https://docsouth.unc.edu/csr/index.html/document/csr01-0085
www.feltmakers.co.uk/our-history
www.file:////l:/1666%20Hatmaking%20process%20-%20Welcome.html
www.historyofparliamentonline.org/volume/1660-1690/
www.oldbaileyonline.org
www.oxforddnb.com
www.thegazette.co.org

INDEX

Printed and bound by CPI Group (UK) Ltd, Croydon, CR0 4YY

15/09/2026

14962416-0006